Presidents Above Party

RALPH KETCHAM

Presidents Above Party

The First American Presidency, 1789–1829

Published for the
Institute of Early American History and Culture
Williamsburg, Virginia
by The University of North Carolina Press
Chapel Hill

The Institute of
Early American History and Culture
is sponsored jointly by
The College of William and Mary
and The Colonial Williamsburg Foundation.

© 1984 The University of North Carolina Press

Manufactured in the United States of America

94 93 92 91 90   7 6 5 4 3

Library of Congress Cataloging-in-Publication Data

Ketcham, Ralph Louis, 1927–
Presidents above party.

(Institute bicentennial studies on the Constitution
and Early American law and government)
Includes bibliographical references and index.
1. Presidents—United States—History.   2. Executive
power—United States—History.   3. Political science—
United States—History.   4. United States—Politics and
government—1789–1815.   5. United States—Politics and
government—1815–1861.   I. Institute of Early American
History and Culture (Williamsburg, Va.)   II. Title.
III. Series.

JK511.K47   1984   353.03′1′09   83-12517

ISBN 0-8078-1582-9
ISBN 0-8078-4179-X (pbk.)

FOR
Paul Knights
Marvin Wachman
Philip M. Williams
William T. Hutchinson
Joseph Tussman
Martin Diamond
and, especially,
Stuart Gerry Brown

Preface

Perhaps the most commonplace theme in eighteenth-century political discourse was the condemnation of faction or party. Lord Halifax's "Maxim" in 1693 was that "parties in a State generally, like Freebooters, hang out False Colours: the pretence is the Publick Good; the real business is, to catch Prizes; like the Tartars, where-ever they succeed, instead of improving their Victory, they presently fall upon the Baggage." A century later, Madison's definition of faction was any group, minority or majority, "who are united and actuated by some common impulse of passion, or of interest, adverse . . . to the permanent and aggregate interests of the community." Similarly, Washington warned in his Farewell Address (1796) against the peril of "party spirit" in free governments: where it prevailed, "the alternate domination of one faction over the other . . . has perpetuated the most horrid enormities, [and] is itself a frightful despotism."

The contrary idea, that factional dispute, party advocacy, and accommodation of diverse interests might be useful, even indispensable, in a free government, was stated only occasionally and never gained wide acceptance. In consequence, the establishment of American government following the Declaration of Independence, and especially the fashioning of a novel executive office in 1787 and afterward, took place in the presence of assumptions about leadership and party radically different from those accepted as axiomatic in the era of Jackson and Peel, Lincoln and Gladstone, Franklin Roosevelt and Winston Churchill, or Lyndon Johnson and Harold Wilson.

Yet, the hostility of the early presidents to party and their earnest intention to be nonpartisan executives have seemed perverse, naive, and even disingenuous in a scholarly context in which it is generally assumed that discord and party are both inevitable and valuable. Joseph Charles, for example, in *The Origins of the American Party System* (1956), noted that Washington tried to prevent the growth of parties and saw no place for them in American government. "Had he been successful in this," Charles added, "it is most doubtful that representative government in this country would have outlived him for long." That is, Charles assumed that representative government could not survive *without* political parties, a view exactly the opposite of Washington's. Or, note Richard Hofstadter's more direct

statement at the beginning of *The Idea of a Party System, 1780–1840*
(1969): "I do believe that the full development of the liberal democratic
state in the West required that political criticism and opposition be incar-
nated in one or more opposition parties, free . . . to form permanent . . .
recognized oppositional structures." That is, political parties were the very
incarnation, the flesh and blood, the body, of the otherwise presumably
unreal, ephemeral spirit and principle of self-government. In the eighteenth century, of course, commentary on political parties would as unselfconsciously have used images and metaphors of exactly opposite connotation: political parties were considered to be poisonous, corroding,
cancerous, and parasitic. But with assumptions like Charles's it is not surprising that he sees only gain in the growth in the 1790s of what he argues
was the first flowering of a sustained party system in the United States.
Nor is it surprising that Hofstadter sees "the gradual acceptance of parties
and of the system of a recognized partisan opposition" as "a net gain in the
sophistication of political thought and practice over the antiparty thought
. . . of the eighteenth century and earlier."

More recently James MacGregor Burns (*Leadership*, 1978) has emphasized the difference between a "negative liberty," important in the seventeenth and eighteenth centuries when the need in religion, politics, and
economics was for *freedom from* "the authority of establishments," and a
"positive liberty," crucial since the industrial revolution, when the people
need to "expand their liberties through the use of governmental power,
. . . to gain education, nutrition, health, employment." The eighteenth-
century drafters of the American Constitution provided admirable *defenses
against* arbitrary power, but they failed to envision a positive use of power
to improve human life. "The American Presidency," according to Burns,
"was not designed to be the center of leadership." Rather, the framers
hoped and assumed "that the President would be 'above' political conflict,
. . . [a] high-minded chief magistrate somewhat removed from the turbulence of factional strife" and, apparently, removed also from the important political concerns of the nation. Burns thinks it fortunate that circumstances soon corrected this "vain hope" and that the office moved toward
more political engagement. Good leadership, he adds, is "dissensual" and,
far from seeking to be consensual or above party, should seek "to expand
the field of combat, to reach out for more followers, to search for allies."
"The dynamo of political action," Burns assumes, is "meaningful conflict,
. . . [which] produces engaged leaders who in turn generate more conflict
among the people." In order for a president to become such a "key democ-
ratizer of leadership," he must, even while in office, be an active, avowed,
effective head of *party*. Washington, Jefferson, and J. Q. Adams, however,
would have been appalled at the assignment of such a role to the presidency.

Remembering that praise of party and of conflict are by now entirely conventional among both British and American students of politics only increases the difficulty of taking quite seriously the scorn Washington, Jefferson, and the Adamses felt for faction and party. And because their idea of executive leadership was linked closely to their view of party, the difficulty is transferred to our effort to understand and appreciate what they sought to be as presidents. But without such an understanding we are unlikely to grasp what the presidential office was in its first conception, and we may even be unnecessarily restricted in contemplating what it might be in the last quarter of the twentieth century. Suppose, for example, that it is not entirely correct to assume that active, systematic partisanship everywhere is "good for the health" of democratic government, or that "organizing conflict" is not always the best style for democratic leadership. Might it be useful, possibly, to look once more at the views of the founders and to consider whether an effort at greater nonpartisanship by the executive could improve the public life of the nation? Must the president function openly, unashamedly, and enthusiastically as "the leader of his party"? Should the common judgment that it is impractical for an effective president to be, even in the Oval Office, anything other than a zealous party leader, go unchallenged? Do we need to accept it as natural and proper, as happened in 1978, that wealthy people with obvious special interests would be invited to lunch at the White House and have the president's closest advisers freely admit that it was hoped the luncheon would encourage the guests to help fill party campaign coffers? (Everything was all right legally, it was explained, as long as no direct request for political contributions was made "on government property.") Or must we accept it as proper that, as happened in 1982, those who had contributed more than one thousand dollars to the president's campaign were, because of that support, "given access to the president's ear"? (In the opinion of White House aides this arrangement neither conferred privilege on wealth nor exerted undue influence on the president.) In any case, assumptions of the sort made by Charles, Hofstadter, and Burns, however useful or even urgent in improving current understanding of party and leadership, are best set aside during any search for the ideas and models of executive leadership that guided the first presidents. Not to do this is to infect the public philosophy of one era with the biases of another.

The search for the assumptions, preconceptions, and models of leadership the early presidents took into office with them can take many directions, of course. Some scholars have examined the institutional and constitutional precedents of the presidency in Great Britain and its colonies and have studied the political ideas influential in eighteenth-century America. Others have analyzed the growth of political parties, the early administrative history of the United States, and the career and public philosophy of each of the first six presidents. Indeed, the growth of the presidency into

what often has been called "the most powerful office in the world" has led
to careful and revealing study of its origins and early development. Yet the
chasm between the assumptions about party and leadership almost axiomatic in the twentieth century and the earnest, often-expressed views of
the early presidents suggests that another viewpoint might be useful: What
did the first six presidents intend to be in their unformed and unprecedented office? What admired models, what warning examples, what fears
and aspirations did they carry with them into the chief magistracy?

To answer these questions we must probe for the largely unstated values, preconceptions, sense of history, and hero models of the men who
first gave shape to the presidency. What views did these men have about
leadership, politics, and national purpose? Their view of public life, we
know, derived in part from the Classical and Christian precepts built into
their education and upbringing, from their experience with English and
colonial modes of government, and from seventeenth- and eighteenth-
century political thought. Most fundamentally, however, their conceptions
of executive leadership rested on the neoclassical age of English literature,
beginning with John Dryden and ending with Samuel Johnson, and particularly on the world view of the great writers of the era of Joseph Addison, Jonathan Swift, and Alexander Pope. It is perhaps not too much to
say that Washington, Jefferson, Madison, Monroe, and the Adamses hearkened all their lives to these Augustan giants, accepting not so much their
explicit politics as their evocation of the admired, civilized, moral life.
Since this view, moreover, was also self-consciously Classical and Christian, it complemented, on the whole, the other traditions important in
eighteenth-century America. To understand the preconceptions about executive office of the first six presidents, then, I have looked especially for the
implications and models they might have drawn from the cultural milieu of
seventeenth- and eighteenth-century Britain.

This focus does not so much reject Richard Pious's argument in *The
American Presidency* (1979)—that the "American elites" who adopted the
Constitution "preferred elective politics and capitalist enterprise rather
than monarchy and mercantilism"—as supplement and refine it. Enlarged
government by consent and the protection of free enterprise were indeed
important to the American revolutionaries and nation-builders, and within
fifty years these values would lead gradually to a "modern" political party
system. Especially before 1829, though, they were mingled with still-
potent assumptions and attitudes linked to monarchy and national co-
hesiveness. The result, perhaps seen most clearly in the Washington-
Hamilton government of the 1790s and in the "amalgamated" politics of
Monroe and J. Q. Adams, was a view of leadership by no means attuned to
the diversified, competitive, brokering public style dominant in Anglo-
America from Peel and Jackson onward. The first six American presidents,

that is, were caught—creatively in many respects—in a time of transition when the virtues of monarchy at its best were still widely accepted and the dynamics of two-party politics were still widely suspect. It has seemed important, to me, then, to look closely at the tensions in values and habits that accompanied the commercial and industrial revolutions of the seventeenth and eighteenth centuries.

As the study went ahead, two significant propositions took shape. First, the early presidents, through John Quincy Adams, despite many substantial differences in both ideology and political practice, shared an essentially nonpartisan conception of the presidency. One can find in the words and deeds of each of them important agreement on posture or style in office—and this shared attitude seemed to be particularly illuminated when viewed in the light of the history, literature, and ideology of the Augustan Age. Second, it became apparent that it was this general stance or aspiration that most importantly and precisely separated the first six presidents from their successors. In fact, it was the articulation by Martin Van Buren of a new style of partisan politics, and its incorporation into the presidency by the enormously popular Jackson, that transformed American public life and gave it the dynamic that has ever since characterized it. As a way of clarifying the "premodern" view of the early presidents, I have tried to explain this contrast with some thoroughness and long-range perspective. Then, because changing conceptions of the role of factions and parties and of what it meant to be virtuous in public life undergirded the altered ideas of presidential leadership, I have used the thought of Jefferson, Franklin, and Hamilton to explicate those changes. The result, explained in the final chapter, is a nonpartisan ideal of leadership that contrasts importantly with both "partisan" and "popular" conceptions of the presidency influential in the twentieth century. My chief concern throughout, however, has been to reveal and clarify the understanding of the presidency held by its pre-1829 incumbents.

Many people have been most helpful as I have worked on this study. John Murrin of Princeton University let me read and talked with me about his seminal paper on Anglo-American politics, 1688–1815. Stuart Gerry Brown and John Wilson of the University of Hawaii read and criticized parts of the manuscript. Friends at Syracuse University have been persistently kind and incisive in their criticism. The wisdom of longtime teacher-colleagues, Nelson Blake, Donald Meiklejohn, David Owen, Michael Sawyer, and T. V. Smith, has been drawn on throughout the whole study. Michael Mooney, Nicholas O'Donahue, Anthony Trimarchi, and Joseph Wagner took time from their graduate studies to read and improve parts of the first four chapters. Arthur Hoffman (English), Joseph Levine (history), Peter Marsh (history), Amanda Porterfield (religion), Roger Sharp (history), and Stephen S. Webb (history), in reading chapters in need of their expert commentary, have helped make up for gaps in my own knowledge and understanding. Marie Provine (political science) and William Stinchcombe (history), in going more than the second mile to read the whole manuscript, were able to make important suggestions about style, emphasis, and organization. Editors and readers at the Institute of Early American History and Culture have exceeded, it seems to me, even their usual high standards of incisive and painstaking criticism. Helene Fineman and Julia Ketcham, as they have often done before, have worked with great skill and patience to improve expression and readability. Wonder-working sisters, Nancy Dore and Jeanne Erwin, have contended cheerfully and efficiently with my almost impenetrable scrawl, and with reiterated pleas for changes, deletions, and additions, to produce a legible manuscript. My own greatest debts as a student, still accumulating and incurred now over three decades or more, are gratefully acknowledged in the dedication.

RALPH KETCHAM
Syracuse University
May 1983

Contents

Presidents Above Party

Introduction: The Unsettledness
of 1789

I n an 1821 letter from Thomas Jefferson to his grandson, we find this curious remark: "You ask my opinion of Lord Bolingbroke and Thomas Paine. . . . Both were honest men; both advocates for human liberty. . . . Bolingbroke . . . was called indeed a tory; but his writings prove him a stronger advocate for liberty than any of his countrymen, the whigs of the present day."[1] What could have made Jefferson see both men as friends of freedom, the one a radical revolutionary spokesman and the other a Tory, a defender of monarchy, and even for a time a conspirator to restore the Stuarts to the British throne? How is it that he could link the two as "advocates for human liberty" and could admire an Augustan nobleman above Whig parliamentarians? These paradoxes, in fact, reveal that Jefferson had a view of free government significantly different from that common today and suggest that early American political institutions, especially the presidency and political parties, took shape amid assumptions and aspirations not now easily given credence.

To take another example, John Adams, although an earnest and prideful man, nonetheless refused to campaign either to gain the presidency in 1796 or to retain it in 1800. Well aware of the bitter partisanship of the 1790s (which he had both heightened and taken part in), Adams generally failed to see his election as chief executive in relation to it. He regarded his elevation to the presidency as due his seniority and previous service to the nation, a service he could continue, he believed, only if he could insulate his office from partisanship. Moreover, his opponent in the close election of 1796 agreed with Adams's "right" to the office and had even decided privately to cede it to Adams had there been a tie in the electoral college. Writing to Adams in December 1796, Jefferson spoke of Adams's "just wishes" and worthy succession, took pride in his own "disinterestedness," and emphasized their common effort "working for our independance."[2] What was it about the office of the presidency that led these two men, retrospectively thought of as party leaders, as indeed they were in a sense, to scorn electioneering and to idealize the executive as above partisan strife? What outlook and attitudes did they share even at this moment when their political rivalry was at its height?

When John Quincy Adams became president in 1825, he persisted in

his father's antiparty outlook, by then widely regarded as even more eccentric, hypocritical, and ostrich-like than it had been in the 1790s. Although
the election of 1824 was among the most personally factious in American
history—Adams was both aware of and in part responsible for this development—its victor refused stubbornly to act as a party leader while in
office. Overwhelmingly defeated in 1828, he seems somehow to be in another age from that of his successor, whose administration was both highly
successful *and* highly partisan. Why is 1829 such a turning point in the
history of the presidency? What values and attitudes distinguished the
Adams and Jackson presidencies? In what way did the leader of the first
modern American political party embody a new conception of executive
office?

Like J. Q. Adams, James Madison and James Monroe earlier viewed
their tenures as successful in the degree to which they subdued or transcended partisanship. For Madison, the bitter, debilitating struggles of his
first six years in office, both within his own "party" and with the shrill and
sectional Federalists, were personally and philosophically vexatious and
troubling. Madison is rightly celebrated as a realist in his view of the nature of politics in a free society, but it seemed to him that if public purpose
and leadership in the new nation were to be derived not from a national
unity intent on the general good but merely from the interplay of factional
politics, then something vital had disappeared. Thus, when his ideal of
above-party leadership very nearly materialized in his last two years in
office, Madison felt triumphantly vindicated. Monroe's largely uncon-
tested succession in 1817 and reelection in 1820 also pointed toward an
executive office above faction and a leadership national in scope. Again,
though, one is puzzled by the paradox of the president insisting on his
antiparty views amid seething factional politics as intense as any in American history. Some say this posture was hypocrisy or a cover for ineffectual
leadership. How can we understand this least partisan of our presidencies?

Monroe's model for nonpartisanship was George Washington, whose
own model was the idea of a "patriot king"—an ancient conception of
leadership above party and without corruption, articulated for Washington's generation by Henry St. John, Lord Bolingbroke. In surrounding
himself with certain ceremonies of courtly dignity, in trying earnestly to
make Jefferson and Alexander Hamilton work together in his cabinet, and
in seriously attempting to preserve in himself both the image and the reality of the national patriot, Washington made manifest his conception of
executive power. Yet, from his day to the present, critics have scorned these
"trappings of royalty" as a betrayal of the ideas of the Revolution. Did
Washington not understand this, or was he, after all, not really a believer in
the ideas of liberty and self-government supposedly for which he had
fought for eight years? He was most disturbed by the factionalism of the

1790s, and he would find the irony bitter indeed that he has been considered, in his second term especially, himself the instrument of a party. In fact, Washington, like the other early presidents, faced the need to devise and exemplify an executive office compatible with republican principles when virtually all precedent and experience associated executive power with hereditary monarchy. Could there be such a thing as a *republican executive?*

Although American thinking about executive power rested ultimately on images of Biblical and Classical heroes, it had more immediate origins in the turbulence of the Puritan revolution, in the theory and practice of British government after the "settlement" of 1689, and particularly in the long period of oligarchy and constitutional monarchy that followed the Peace of Utrecht (1713) and the ascension of the house of Hanover (1714). According to the Whig history learned by the Adamses, Jefferson, and Madison, the "Glorious Revolution of 1688" had issued in a masterpiece of balanced government protecting liberty to a degree unrivaled anywhere in the world. The touchstone was the limitation placed on the exercise of political power and the subjugation of all temporal authority to some form of higher law. Besides a carefully devised frame of government (in the English model, containing a balance of king, Lords, and Commons), the key bulwarks of freedom were bills of rights defining the limits of government and the privileges of men and the right of government by consent through some representative process. All of this became revered gospel in the colonies. "American whigs" in 1776, Jefferson remarked in old age, were of "one opinion" on the "harmonizing sentiments" found in "the elementary books of public right, as Aristotle, Cicero, Locke, Sidney, etc."[3] This "opinion," elaborated in the eighteenth century by John Trenchard and Thomas Gordon, Montesquieu, Francis Hutcheson, James Burgh, and others, became the foundation of American republican ideology, erecting the barriers against tyranny needed in 1776 and marking out the first principles of government by consent. This "radical Whig ideology," however, says much more about restraining than about using executive power.

The *events* leading to the American Revolution seemed to corroborate this ideology. The colonial assemblies, blessed by distance from the mother country or benign neglect, again and again enlarged their powers and by 1763, whatever the theory of imperial rule, had achieved substantial government by consent. The exaltation of the legislature was further emphasized as the struggle with the mother country took the form of elected assemblies resisting tyrannical royal governors. The decentralized character of the War of Independence and the heavy emphasis on legislative bodies in the first state governments had the same effect. Certainly Whig principles, Revolutionary rhetoric, and colonial government all seemed headed in the same direction. Furthermore, American constitutional development was positioned nicely to take its place in later Whig history, which would see a steady Anglo-American progress toward modern democratic government: limitation of aristocracy, improvement of representative institutions, protection of individual liberties, enlargement of suffrage, fuller response to vox populi, the rise of parties, and so on.

Thus the ideology and experience of the Revolutionary leaders made them at first both suspicious of and inattentive to what might replace the authority of their departed royal governors. Nor were the theorists they favored very helpful, for the main concern of these writers had also been to justify the restraint of kingly power. In a way, both in the history of Great Britain and in the conceptions of the Whig writers, executive power was simply "what was left" of the traditional monarchy after proper restraints and *legislative* prerogatives had been authorized. The revised coronation oath of 1689 simply required assent to the question "Will you promise to govern the people of this your kingdom . . . according to the statutes in parliament agreed upon and the laws and customs of the same?" In Britain this arrangement worked well because the power left to the monarch was considerable and well entrenched; he was still to govern his people. In the colonies after 1776, however, with George III and his commission holders literally toppling everywhere and without the awesome sentinels of royal power that abounded all over the British Isles, executive authority contracted severely—and precious little theory or experience, consistent with Revolutionary ideology, was available to fill the vacuum. Madison summed up the basic difference: "In Europe, charters of liberty have been granted by power. America has set the example . . . of charters of power granted by liberty."[4]

As the states and the nation debated, drafted, and implemented constitutions between 1776 and 1789, then, the nature and justification of executive power emerged as the least settled and the most puzzling of the problems of government. There were, of course, some guidelines. Executive tyranny, of either the royal variety exercised by a Philip II or a Louis XIV, or the republican version attempted by Oliver Cromwell, was as abhorred in America as it was in Britain. Also, by 1787 following many tryouts, simple legislative dominance had been generally condemned as unworkable, as Jefferson and Madison found, for example, in Virginia under its Constitution of 1776. Other cardinal principles—natural rights, the rule of law, and a balance of powers, as set forth by Locke and by Montesquieu—proscribed not only a Hobbesian Leviathan or a Machiavellian Prince but also a Rousseauistic general will or a unitary assembly of the sort advocated by Paine, the marquis de Condorcet, and others.

As attention turned increasingly to creating effective government, and as the opprobrium cast over executive power by the Revolution faded, however, the nation-builders discovered they were still heir to ancient conceptions of authority and leadership. They retained some of their pre-Independence conviction that England in the eighteenth century had been governed by "a successful aristocracy" whose authority was justified "by the quality of its rule. . . . The ancient assumption . . . that superiority should be unitary, that leadership in politics should fall to the leaders of society— . . . leaders in status, in wealth, and in the skills associated with a superior style of life" was still axiomatic to many Americans.[5]

Hallowed authorities also emphasized the importance of leadership. Locke had declared that where legislative and executive powers were properly divided, "the good of society requires that several things should be left to the discretion of him that has the executive power. For the legislators not being able to foresee and provide by laws for all that may be useful to the community, the executor of the laws, having the power in his hands, has by the common law of Nature a right to make use of it for the good of the society." This discretionary power Locke termed *prerogative*, which was *"the power of doing public good without a rule"* (that is, without specific law; Locke's emphasis). Conversely, executive action contrary to the public good was not legitimately part of prerogative. Failure to hold monarchs to this distinction had been a great source of tyranny, Locke noted, but it was equally true in English history "that prerogative was always largest in the hands of our wisest and best princes" because the people saw that such rulers "acted conformable to the foundation and end of all laws, the public good." Such "God-like princes . . . partaking of His wisdom and goodness, . . . indeed, had some title to arbitrary power." Locke warned, however, that the danger that subsequent hereditary rulers, unblessed with such virtue, would claim similar power validated the principle that the people had to judge princes as well as legislators by whether they acted in accord with the public good—that is, conformed to natural law.[6] Although Locke had written in defense of limited monarchy, a conception of government repudiated by the American Revolution, and although the notion of prerogative was generally unwelcome to Americans in 1787, the ideas remained in force that governments should seek "wisdom and goodness" and that the executive was somehow the special protector of those virtues. Executive power in the United States would have to be fashioned within important limits, but it also carried, in the prevailing but not always consistent implications of the theories of Locke, Montesquieu, and Sir William Blackstone, "a broadly discretionary, residual power which is available when other governmental powers fail."[7]

Both the virtues and dangers of executive power were thus on the minds of the delegates to the Federal Convention when on June 1, 1787, they "proceeded to Resolution 7 [of the Virginia Plan] that a national Executive be instituted, to be chosen by the National Legislature . . . to possess the executive powers of Congress." To start debate, James Wilson "moved that the Executive consist of a single person." James Madison recorded, for the only time in the Convention, that a "considerable pause ensu[ed]." As members were well aware that perhaps the most difficult question before the Convention had been reached, the chairman, George Washington, was probably puzzled at the silence; but seeing no one preparing to speak, he properly asked "if he should put the question." Benjamin Franklin rescued his colleagues from their discomfort by observing that because the composition of the executive was "a point of great importance," he wished "gentlemen would deliver their sentiments on it before the question was put." Thus prodded, John Rutledge of South Carolina asked the delegates to be candid and bold and spoke for Wilson's motion as likely best to secure responsibility and administrative efficiency. Roger Sherman of Connecticut, an upholder of legislative supremacy, thought the number composing the executive ought to be left to the legislature to change "as experience might dictate." In quick succession Wilson argued for a single executive "as giving most energy, dispatch, and responsibility to the office," Elbridge Gerry of Massachusetts for "the policy of annexing a Council to the Executive," and Edmund Randolph of Virginia for throwing aside the British model and recognizing a single executive "as the foetus of Monarchy." After one more brief attempt by Wilson to defend his motion, it "was postponed by common consent, the Committee [of the whole] seeming unprepared for any decision on it."[8]

As this inconclusive beginning made clear, the Convention faced not only a wide array of options on the formal structure of executive power but also profound differences about its principles and purposes. As it continued its work, almost every conceivable solution to the structure, election, and powers of the executive received serious consideration. Proposals for a plural executive, for election of the president by Congress or by the state legislatures, and for an absolute veto were all entertained. Even life tenure for the executive was suggested, to say nothing of the widely credited rumor that the younger brother of George III would be invited to become king of America. Only the widespread willingness to entrust one man, General Washington, with executive power (itself an unrepublican sentiment, of course) allowed the delegates to fashion and then the people to accept such an untested presidential office.

When Washington took his oath of office in April 1789, then, far from everything being settled, virtually nothing was. Not only were a multitude of details of organization, procedure, and etiquette yet to be decided; the underlying question of what executive power in a republic was to be had scarcely been asked seriously. As Emmet Hughes has put it, the constitutional phrase "the executive power shall be vested in a President of the United States" may be the most "cryptic in substance . . . in all the annals of politics. . . . Beyond decreeing a single executive, the words specified nothing. Unlike the first sentence of Article I on the Congress, there . . . appeared no precise or limiting reference to 'Powers *herein granted*.' Instead, there was very little plainly given, very little clearly withheld. As a summation of all the labyrinthine debates of the Convention, this did not define: it deferred. With a truly 'peculiar' restraint—or spectacular shrewdness—the Founding Fathers thus left the Presidency, their most special creation, to be shaped by the live touch of history."[9] In fact, study of the views of Gouverneur Morris, who was responsible for the phrasing of the statement of powers for the three departments, suggests strongly that he intended the executive branch to have the widest latitude in its powers and that he accepted the common eighteenth-century emphasis on the need for executive leadership. That his Convention colleagues may have shared this intention and emphasis (however unarticulated) is evident in their approval of his language about executive power generally and in the relatively few specifications about it elsewhere in the document.[10] But it is precisely this unsettledness and this implicit openness that lurk behind the puzzles and paradoxes in the administrations of the first six presidents—each holder of the office had to work out in his own mind what sort of executive he intended to be, what his leadership role was, and what obligation he had to guide the nation and the people he had sworn to serve. He was not a king, yet he was more than a representative or legislator. What was he? To answer this question each of the early presidents and his advisers relied most immediately on the theory, practice, idealization, and criticism of executive authority in seventeenth- and eighteenth-century Britain.

❧ I ❧

Ideas of Leadership in
Anglo-America, 1600–1789

Morality, Commerce, and Leadership in Seventeenth-Century England

A merican thinking and feeling about executive power was bound, by the fateful beheading of Charles I in 1649, to the conviction that rulers must abide by a higher law. The execution of the king remained a symbol of the limitations applicable to any government, especially in New England, where the last of the regicides had found refuge. Yet, Englishmen living in America unavoidably shared some of the uneasiness and revulsion at the act that in only eleven years had been followed by the restoration of another Stuart monarch. A great deal, after all, had been changed, and lost, on January 30, 1649, on the block at Whitehall in London. Held as a prisoner and condemned to die "as a tyrant, traitor, murderer, and public enemy," Charles had asked, "What hope of [peace] is there, so long as power reigns without rule or law, changing the whole frame of government under which this Kingdom hath flourished for many hundred years?" "The Commons of England," Charles warned his judges, "will not thank you for this change; for they will remember how happy they have been of late years under the reigns of Queen Elizabeth, the King my father, and myself, until the beginning of these unhappy troubles."[1]

As the earl of Clarendon himself put it in a history (and implicitly a political philosophy) widely read in the colonies, "In that very hour when [Charles I] was thus wickedly murdered in the sight of the sun, he had as great a share in the hearts and affections of his subjects in general, was as much beloved, esteemed, and longed for by the people . . . of the three nations [England, Scotland, and Ireland], as any of his predecessors had ever been." In introducing *The History of the Rebellion and Civil Wars in England*, Clarendon evoked all the ancient beneficences of the traditions symbolized by the monarch: "The rebellion was a record of how a poor people, under pretence of zeal to religion, law, liberty and parliaments (words of precious esteem in their just signification) are furiously hurried into actions introducing atheism, and dissolving all the elements of the Christian religion, cancelling all obligations, and destroying all founda-

tions of law and liberty, and rendering not only the privileges, but the very
being, of parliaments desperate and impossible."[2] This idealization of
monarchy, this sense of a national unity and destiny linked in the person of
the king to the moral nature of the universe ("divine right"), and this contempt for disruption and sacrilege was bone deep in English consciousness
and remained powerful long after 1649. Although few of Clarendon's
North American readers agreed with his politics, it is also clear that conceptions of and hopes for moral leadership, authority, and national unity
did not perish with Charles I.

Puritan Ideas of Leadership

Indeed, among the very Puritans who beheaded Charles I the ideal of the
good ruler cloaked in magisterial authority remained essential to their
vision of a godly commonwealth. Long before the English Civil War, William Perkins and other Puritans had insisted on qualities of leadership admired for centuries. In fact, the intense, often anguished, writers about authority in government during the reign of James I, Anglicans as well as
Puritans, agreed generally on five essential, if conventional, traits of the
good ruler: wealth, piety, moderation, wisdom, and justice.[3] The list applied to local as well as national rulers and assumed that in a well-ordered
community authority could be exercised legitimately only by those possessing the necessary qualities. This assumption was as explicit in the defense of the divine right of kings as it was in the most fervent protests by
Christopher Goodman and other Puritan "prophets" against misrule.
Kings ruled by divine right, according to James I, because they were
"GODS Lieutenants upon earth, and sit upon GODS throne"; that is, they
were part and parcel of divine providence and thus embodied the qualities
hallowed by God's laws.[4] The vivid character sketches in Clarendon's *History*, furthermore, conveyed the notion that the study of public affairs was
at root a study of the vice or virtue of the politician. Clarendon's readers
would absorb from the *History* the belief that the good society was one
having a highly developed sense of morality, where the actions of individuals mattered and where moral issues could be discussed intelligently.[5]
Clarendon and the Puritans, like Plutarch, mingled ethics and politics in
making moral judgments of rulers. Puritan dissenters disagreed with
James's view only in their rejection of the principle that the qualities
thought essential in rulers were *inherently* possessed by the wearer of a hereditary crown—or a bishop consecrated in Rome—or a member of the

House of Lords or the House of Commons—or anyone holding a position of authority.

The Puritans also accepted the traditional sense of hierarchy in society that held that some were fit to rule and some to be ruled and that every Christian had a "calling" defining his particular niche in the divine plan. On the other hand, all privileges and responsibilities of place and rank in society were to be guided by higher law, that of Christian duty. Thus, William Perkins insisted, "Every man must joyne the practise of his personall calling, with the practice of the generall calling of Christianity. . . . As for example. A Magistrate must not onely in generall be a Christian, as every man is, but he must be a Christian Magistrate, in executing the office of a Magistrate in bearing the sword. . . . A Schoolemaster must not onely be a Christian in the assembly, when hee heareth the word, and receiveth the Sacraments, but he must also shew himselfe to bee a Christian in the office of his teaching. . . . The particular calling and practise of the duties thereof, severed from the foresaid generall calling, is nothing else but a practise of injustice and profanenes."[6]

Puritan conceptions of the good ruler, then, following centuries of Christian teaching, arose from the Apostle Paul's evocation of the Christian church and community: "Now there are diversities of gifts, but the same Spirit. And there are differences of administrations, but the same Lord. And there are diversities of operations, but it is the same God which worketh all in all. . . . For as the body is one, and hath many members, and all the members of that one body, being many, are one body; so also *is* Christ. . . . And whether one member suffer, all the members suffer with it; or one member be honoured, all the members rejoice with it. Now ye are the body of Christ, and members in particular." And further in the familiar Epistle to the Romans: "Let every soul be subject unto the higher powers. For there is no power but of God. . . . Whosoever therefore resisteth the power, resisteth the ordinance of God. . . . For rulers are not a terror to good works, but to the evil."[7] Men were to find their places and their fulfillment in the divine plan, whether they were rulers or ruled, in order that the Christian community, the Kingdom of God, might come on earth.

Additionally, a Christian magistrate had to have a flexible authority that would free him from the rigidity of the letter of the law and allow him to temper justice with mercy. "The godly Magistrate," wrote Perkins, would "by the force of his authoritie" moderate the harsh "extremities" of the law and instead "put in practice that equitie which becommeth Christians."[8] Perkins's readers could also have recognized in his call for equity and flexibility an echo of Tacitus: "Rome was never so corrupt as when its laws were so abundant." In this view, the disinterestedness, virtue, and wisdom of a ruler, not a rigid, detailed law code, however promulgated, had to be the main bulwark of good and free government. Perkins's position, then, like many Puritan arguments, could be enlisted on the side of executive authority and even prerogative, when seen apart from the many specific quarrels the Puritans had with royal officials.

But discretion and responsibility, another Puritan admonished in 1628, also "requireth [officeholders] to bee *men of activitie*." Nothing was more sinful and irresponsible, wrote Richard Carpenter in 1623, than "*luke-warme neuter-passive* Magistrates, . . . scarecrow Constables, and meale-mouthed under officers in Towne and Country, who resembling Ostritches, which have great feathers, but no flight . . . suffer many heinous and hidious enormities of whoredom, blasphemy, drunkennesse, prophaning of the Sabbath." The good society, the godly nation, depended on a vigorous executive who would faithfully and strenuously exert himself on behalf of God's law. Not surprisingly, such God-centered political writers condemned the "carnall wisdome" of Machiavelli, who had the "abominable conceit to distinguish religion from policy and government." Under such a conception, ambitious rulers "will not sticke to lie, dissemble, breake their words, forsweare, machiavellize, practice any policy or counterpolicy to honesty, reason, religion."[9] Massachusetts governor John Winthrop made the same point in 1642 when he scorned an argument by some church elders that it was better for the community when the magistrates were "divided in factions, etc." rather than "united in Love and affection," presumably because faction weakened the power monopoly of the tightly knit rulers of the colony. "If this passed for good doctrine," Winthrop responded, "then let us no longer professe the Gospell of Jesus Christ, but take up the rules of Matchiavell, and the Jesuits, for Christ sayeth Love is the bond of perfection, and a kingdom or house divided cannot stand."[10] It was scandalous, that is, for rulers merely to manipulate and manage cleverly, rather than to pursue actively the public good written in the law of God.

In the New World, removed as the Puritans saw it from some of the sinful ways of an increasingly corrupt English society, a magistrate should be held to even higher standards of personal morality than was customary and be expected more fully to insist that the community conform to the precepts of the Kingdom of God. John Winthrop defined this saintly obligation on his way to Massachusetts, aboard the *Arbella*, in a sermon that deliberately cast the speaker in the role of Moses: the active leader of a chosen people in quest of the promised land. "A speciall overruleing providence, and a more then an ordinary approbation of the Churches of Christ," Winthrop announced, sent the Puritans to the New World, where under God's ordinance they would have to establish "a due forme of Government both civill and ecclesiasticall." Because "the end is to improve our lives to doe more service to the Lord," Winthrop insisted that "the care of the publique must oversway all private respects" and that "perticuler estates cannott subsist in the ruine of the publique."[11] Winthrop thus echoed the sense of destiny and of united purpose John Foxe had heralded for England in the *Book of Martyrs* (1570): "No man liveth in that commonwealth where nothing is amiss. But yet because God hath so placed us Englishmen here in one commonwealth, also in one Church, as in one ship together, let us not mangle or divide the ship, which being divided perisheth, but every man serve in his order with diligence, wherein he is called."[12] With such overarching purposes and such heavy responsibilities, superhuman qualities seemed necessary in the magistrate—a burden that Winthrop's diary attests he was aware of almost every day.

Winthrop had been a magistrate in East Anglia before his removal to Massachusetts and may have heard there a sermon by Samuel Ward (whose brother, Nathaniel, was an early arrival in New England) warning against "strait-buttoned, carpet, and effeminate gentry [and] constables that are but cyphers in their places." Such officials sinned in not accepting the responsibility that governing was a "wise and serious business" requiring that, as another minister put it, magistrates have "*Moses* his spirit, *Phineas* his zeale."[13] Winthrop therefore did not conceive of his role in Massachusetts as that of deferring to popular will or to other elders or to persons in high places back in England; rather, it was incumbent on him to pursue actively the Kingdom of God on earth. Although Winthrop gradually, if grudgingly, allowed elected deputies a stronger voice in the government, he remained convinced that his fundamental obligation was to rule wisely according to God's law.

In 1645, after being accused and then acquitted of acting arbitrarily, Winthrop reminded the General Court that though the magistrates were chosen "from among yourselves, men subject to like passions as you are," nonetheless there was a covenant between rulers and ruled "that we shall govern you and judge your causes by the rules of God's laws and our own, according to our best skill." "We shall be willing (by God's assistance) to hearken to good advice from any of you," he said, but if the people of Massachusetts were "to enjoy such civil and lawful liberties, such as Christ allows you, then will you quietly and cheerfully submit unto that authority which is set over you . . . for your good." Liberty justly understood was not the right of a man "to do what he lists . . . to [do] evil as well as to [do] good," but rather it was "a liberty to do that only which is good, just, and honest . . . [which] is maintained and exercised in a way of subjection to authority; it is of the same kind of liberty wherewith Christ hath made us free"; that is, accepting the bond of his law.[14] Puritan political thinking, then, emphasized the role of the magistrate, and its thrust was "to set up some kind of a disciplined holy commonwealth [which] . . . fashioned all aspects of human existence around [a] desire to live a godly life." The Puritan leaders in many ways were "looking backward," it is clear, to the "corporate ideal of the medieval period, not ahead to the individualism of the Enlightenment."[15] In insisting that good government and a just society depended crucially on a wise and vigorous magistracy, Winthrop differed very little from Anglican orthodoxy—or even from the pretensions of the hated Stuart monarchs themselves.

John Winthrop, Nehemias Americanus

In his sketch of Winthrop, *Nehemias Americanus*, Cotton Mather summed up the leadership qualities many Puritans continued to admire. Winthrop, Nehemiah-like, had led his people back to the promised land and was in other ways comparable to the Old Testament hero revered for his personal goodness and justice as well as for his practical skill and diligence as a leader. Nehemiah's career had been one of incessant activity: he had rebuilt the walls of Jerusalem, defended the city from its enemies, served as governor without pay, reestablished order and ritual in the life of the Jews, and reformed the laws. Mather thus saw Winthrop as one who joined "the common good of the nation and the interests of religion," that is, one who governed politically according to the precepts of a higher law.

Mather also praised Winthrop for having prevented the "over-driving [of] . . . the whole government into something too democratical" and for instituting a high-and-mighty magistracy. "The magistrates, as far as might be, should aforehand ripen their consultations, to produce that unanimity in their public votes which might make them liker to the voice of God." The model of good government was not to exalt the will of the people for its own sake, or even to encourage open debate on matters of public policy, but rather to seek a unanimous conformity to right precepts, to the voice of God.

Winthrop, in Mather's mind, also invited comparison to other leaders familiar to eighteenth-century readers: to Moses, who delivered his people from bondage and gave them the law; to Daniel, whose "courage made him dare to do right"; to Joseph, to whom his people turned in time of need; to Abraham, who "saw that Hagar and Ishmael must be sent away" (as Winthrop did with unfit persons); to Jacob, who blessed his children; and to David, who "served his generation by the will of God." Mather also dwelt on the moral qualities of Winthrop's governorship by comparing him to various non-Biblical figures, especially Plutarch's pair of ancient lawgivers, Lycurgus and Numa Pompilius. He quoted Plato on the trials that a virtuous ruler would have to endure from vicious critics and likened Winthrop to Cato, for having many times been acquitted of unjust charges, and to Plutarch's Cleomenes, for having discouraged immoral customs and bad habits among the people. Mather further found Winthrop "not much unlike . . . the family of the Medici," who also had to suffer factions and seditious threats against the commonwealth. He even compared the Massachusetts governor to two of the first Christian emperors of Rome: Theodosius, for "the meekness of [his] wisdom," and Valentinian, for, in addition to his worldly victories, "his overcoming of himself" in achieving a calm and untroubled surrender to God at his death.[16]

Perhaps most revealing, however, Mather liked to suggest that Winthrop was an American Aeneas who led a saving remnant to a new land. "More clearly than any other pagan hero," a modern scholar has noted, "pious Aeneas, the Good Magistrate destined by Jove/Jehova to harrow hell, to rebuild the walls of Latium and change the course of civilization, enacts the design of exodus and restoration that unveils the prophetic sense of New England's Nehemiah."[17] Winthrop thus embodied the legendary qualities of leaders celebrated in many epic traditions: those of Virgil, Plutarch, the Christian emperors, the *Lives of the Saints*, and the heroes of the *Book of Martyrs*, as well as the judges, kings, and prophets (to say nothing of the example of Jesus) of the Bible itself. Mather's paragon was to be saintly, courageous, and active, without manipulation or compromise. And among all the heroes there was not one distinguished for his choice by the people or his deference to their will. All led and ruled in the best interest of the people, but according to a concept of the public good embedded in the purpose of history itself, not the public good as defined by the people themselves from day to day or year to year.

Although the religious intensity, and therefore some of the sense of purpose and magisterial self-righteousness so evident in Winthrop and Mather, diminished as the Puritan colonies gradually became more secular, the model of vigorous community leadership retained a firm hold in the public consciousness. The clergy themselves, for example, did not lose the "theocentric communalism" that changed them from local "officers" into itinerant "professionals" until well into the nineteenth century. During the eighteenth century "public moneys paid the minister," and the polity took part in his selection. "The minister conducted what was referred to as 'public worship,' performing the rituals and delivering the Word that ordered the community as an organic whole." By the Jacksonian era, however, the church ceased to be part of the polity; by then "it was purely a voluntary association, supported by private donation, and an exclusive one, serving and superintending only those who wished to join it."[18] The theocentric community had been the foundation of Winthrop's active magistracy and of Mather's idealization of him; the decline of that idea of society entailed similarly traumatic alterations in conceptions of political leadership. Until that happened, though, the same patriarchal attitude dominant among Puritans also characterized such Anglicized Massachusetts governors as Joseph Dudley, William Shirley, and Thomas Hutchinson. Preachers of election sermons, too, even as they increasingly charged leaders with the duty of listening to the voice of the people, seldom failed to extol as well the traits of magistracy held up by Perkins and Winthrop and to emphasize the need for correct, vigorous action. Moreover, faction, partisanship, and corruption continued to be just as heinous to the Puritans as they had been to Clarendon. New Englanders thus heard appeals from all sides for policy above party—for laws and acts, that is, that attuned the nation to a higher Providence under the guidance not of a "neuter-passive Magistrate" but of a purposeful, active one.

John Dryden: "Kings are the public pillars of the State"

The English and American Puritans who insisted on conceptions of active, moral leadership found an eloquent though partial ally in the Restoration poet laureate, John Dryden. By extolling the same traditions of legitimacy, authority, and the public weal on behalf of Charles II and James II that Clarendon had evoked so movingly in defending their father and that Winthrop had upheld in Massachusetts, Dryden proved again how deep those ideals were in English political consciousness. His praise first of Oliver Cromwell and then of Charles II, his comfortable life as a pensioner of the crown, and his conversion to Catholicism shortly after the accession of James II marked him in the eyes of many as a sycophant and trimmer. Yet, he did warn consistently of the evils of instability, chaos, and civil war (a plausible sentiment in an England giving birth to the philosophies of Thomas Hobbes and Robert Filmer), and of the dangers of a doctrine that

> Maintains the multitude can never err,
> And sets the people in the papal chair.[19]

Dryden defended the Restoration monarchs, for example, because he believed that only obedience to their legitimate rule would preserve ancient customs and authority and—even more critical—prevent a "Whig control over the destinies of England" that would speed the coming of a commercial age.[20]

He did this most thoroughly in 1681 in a long poem, *Absalom and Achitophel*, condemning the campaign of the first earl of Shaftesbury and the Whigs to exclude the Catholic duke of York from the English throne.

Drawing on Bible heroes, Dryden cast Charles II as King David defending the realm (and God's will) against the son-usurper Absalom (the duke of Monmouth) and his scheming counselor and political henchman, Achitophel (Shaftesbury). Thus the poem was another statement of a political philosophy condemning factions, ridiculing ambition and sophistry, extolling ancient morality, and calling for wise, courageous leadership to thwart pandering politicians. After damning sketches of Shaftesbury and other Whigs who sought to compel Charles to exclude his Catholic brother from the throne (and make parliamentary fiat sovereign), Dryden stated his own principles:

> For who can be secure of private right,
> If sovereign sway may be dissolv'd by might?
> Nor is the people's judgment always true:
> The most may err as grossly as the few;
> And faultless kings run down, by common cry,
> For vice, oppression, and for tyranny.
>
> . . . .
>
> But government itself at length must fall
> To nature's state, where all have right to all.
>
> . . . .
>
> To change foundations, cast the frame anew,
> Is work for rebels, who base ends pursue,
> At once divine and human laws control,
> And mend the parts by ruin of the whole.

Scorning the Whigs, who had whipped the nation into a fury over the Popish Plot, as "a numerous faction, with pretended frights," Dryden lamented

> That Absalom, ambitious of the crown,
> Was made the lure to draw the people down;
> That false Achitophel's pernicious hate
> Had turn'd the Plot to ruin Church and State.

Instead, the poet asked the nation to remember that

> Kings are the public pillars of the State,
> Born to sustain and prop the nation's weight.[21]

Although Dryden here and elsewhere candidly espoused a Tory philosophy and was himself blatantly partisan, the skill of his writing, as well as his popular translations of Virgil and Plutarch, gave his thought a lasting influence far transcending party. Abigail Adams, for example, mightily impressed by George Washington when she first met him in 1775, wrote her husband that "those lines of Dryden instantly occurd to me:

> Mark his Majestick fabrick! he's a temple
> Sacred by birth, and built by hands divine
> His Souls the Deity that lodges there.
> Nor is the pile unworthy of the God."[22]

Dr. Johnson would observe, in a famous remark, that Dryden's literary craftsmanship found the English language brick and left it marble. His admirers, perhaps especially colonials anxious to retain polish and elegance, might also absorb some of his conviction that a patriot leader could contribute more to the common good than could parliamentary demagogues pandering to popular emotions—or even more than well-intended politicians who might "mend the parts" while they unwittingly "ruin the whole."

The Growth of the Commercial Ethic

Although the exile of James II, the Acts of Settlement, and the elevation of the house of Hanover restrained the king's prerogative and ratified Whig principles of constitutional government in England, the older ideals of regal authority and Christian magistracy remained vigorous in both the Old and the New World. If one asks, then, what was "settled" in 1714 with the ascension of George I, the answer must be as ambiguous as it was in the United States at Washington's inauguration seventy-five years later. George I, parochial, ignorant of his English domain, and unable even to speak its language, was an ideal "monarch" in many respects for the Whig magnates who had placed him on the throne. While he carefully protected his Hanoverian interests and was far from a mere tool of his Whig ministers, the new king also was limited in his power by statute and in general had to defer to advisers deriving power from their control of Parliament. Because he thus reigned as perhaps the first truly constitutional monarch in history, to the Whigs of his day and ever since he holds an honored place in the growth of responsible government in Great Britain. His reign brought Stuart tyranny to an end, validated the rising commercial and bourgeois culture, and enabled party government under a "prime minister" to take root. The Hanoverian kings and their great prime minister, Robert Walpole, were self-proclaimed champions of the Protestant cause, defenders of the "English liberties" secured in the Glorious Revolution of 1688, and guardians of the prosperity afforded by the growth of commerce. These hallmarks of Whig-Georgian rule were cherished no place more than in the North American colonies, a bias Dryden had noticed in scorning the lust for gaining riches in the colonies:

> Since faction ebbs, and rogues grow out of fashion,
> Their penny scribes take care t' inform the nation,
> How well men thrive in this or that plantation.

And referring to those who had already gone to America, he observed:

> The factious natives never could agree;
> But aiming, as they call'd it, to be free,
> Those playhouse Whigs set up for property.[23]

The constitutional and geopolitical decisions marking "the growth of political stability" between 1675 and 1725[24] were widely applauded by Englishmen on both sides of the Atlantic, yet there was also a deep foreboding that much was being lost. A spectrum of opinion, extending from Anglicans still devoted to Stuart legitimacy to earnest, self-denying Puritans, was appalled at the morality of the new age shamelessly annunciated by Daniel Defoe:

> Antiquity and birth are needless here,
> 'Tis impudence and money makes a peer.
> For fame of families is all a cheat,
> It's personal virtue only makes us great.[25]

In fact, inexorable in retrospect as the drive toward the new culture of trade and commerce might appear, a powerful countercurrent longed for the England of the landed gentry, the pious yeoman, the village church, Tudor patriotism, and even Stuart regal authority. To many people of all classes, this earlier England was the real, the valued, the hallowed England where the traditional ways that gave life flavor and meaning could be preserved and cherished. In short, although constitutional questions appeared to be "settled" and the new commerce validated, both Augustan and Georgian Britain were filled with a moral and cultural uneasiness.

This anxiety is traceable most fundamentally to the revised notions of human motivation and its relation to the state that were implicit in the burgeoning free-market economy in England in the century following the defeat of the Spanish Armada. The free market and its ethic can be viewed as "one of the few true social novelties in history, changing the relation not only of person to person and of people to government, but also of human beings to nature."[26] Englishmen struggled to conceptualize what was happening to their values and their country as they glimpsed the staggering wealth available from expanded trade at home and abroad. In mid-seventeenth century, one of the earliest economic theorists, Thomas Mun, in a dawning sense of awe and of liberation from immemorial restraints, noted that although "Princes oppress, Lawyers extort, [and] Usurers bite," wealth would come from the free flow of trade, "and this must come to pass by a Necessity beyond all resistance."[27]

Fifty years before Bernard Mandeville published his famous and dis-
turbing *Fable of the Bees*, a Leicestershire clergyman generalized: "If merchants do buy an advantageous commodity, hath not the commonwealth
an advantage thereby as well as themselves? If men by good husbandry
. . . do better their land, is not the commonwealth enriched thereby? So
whatever benefit we make to ourselves, tends to the public good."[28] That
is, abundance would come only when the usual arbiters of "the public
good" were rendered impotent, when autonomous, self-seeking individuals exercised their full energies, and when "decisions" were made in the
marketplace.

In this model, men were encouraged to be industrious in their own self-
interest and nations were, in the understanding fully articulated by Adam
Smith in the year of the American Declaration of Independence, to grow
in wealth not by regulating trade but rather by simply leaving it alone. An
economic theorist noted that "men are most industrious, where they are
most free, and secure to injoy the Effects of their Labours" (1690); and
another, that "no People ever yet grew rich by Policies [government]; but
it is Peace, Industry, and Freedom that brings Trade and Wealth, and
nothing else" (1691). When a third theorist, revising natural law itself,
said that in the "naturall course of trade, each commodity will find its
price" and that "the supreme power can do many things, but it cannot alter
the Laws of Nature of which the most original is, that every man should
preserve himself" (1693),[29] the ethic of the age of Walpole took shape.

Slowly yet perceptibly, the norms of society were shifting from a fixed
amalgam of divine and natural law, ancient traditions, and a pervasive hier-
archical authority toward a flux of infinitely complex, autonomous, more
materialistic, and self-interested relationships. Models for both individuals
and governments, within this revised "natural order" of things, would
change radically. Governments, instead of having, as James I and John
Winthrop insisted, an obligation to fix the nation in the divine plan, had
only to allow, indeed encourage, the release of economic energies, whereas
individuals had not to subordinate themselves to some external will but
rather to pursue their own self-aggrandizement. For individuals, acquisi-
tiveness became not a vice but a virtue, and for governments, laissez-faire
became not irresponsibility but statesmanship. A wealthy merchant, Dudley North, explained the connections candidly in 1691: "The main spur to
Trade, or rather to Industry and Ingenuity, is the exorbitant Appetites of
Men, which they will take pains to gratifie, and so be disposed to work."
This fact of human nature was fortunate in North's view because "did Men
content themselves with bare Necessaries, we should have a poor World."
Even "the meaner sort seeing their fellows become rich, and great, are
spurr'd up to imitate [the] Industry" of the wealthy merchants. "A Trades-
man sees his Neighbour keep a Coach, presently all his Endeavours is at

work to do the like, and many times is beggered by it; however the extraordinary Application he made, to support his Vanity, was beneficial to the Publick." This was so, North argued, because "there can be no trade unprofitable to the Publick; for if any prove so, men leave it off; and wherever the Traders thrive, the Publick, of which they are a part, thrives also."[30] Slowly, an understanding of human nature emphasizing striving and self-aggrandizement was linked to an economics of growing wealth and unfettered trade to form a new, commercial, public philosophy.

The contrast with Classical and medieval society, where the individual found his identity as a part of the whole, was stark. An Elizabethan writer, for example, had written, as though stating an unchallenged axiom, that an ambitious man who sought his own self-interest forgot God's command that he was a "member of the huge and mighty body of humane society, and appointed him his distinct charge, not to be exercised to his own particular, but to the relief and common maintenance of the universal body."[31] A century later a Puritan clergyman applied the point specifically to individuals: "Man's fall was his turning from God to himself; and his regeneration consisteth in the turning of him from himself to God. . . . [Hence,] self-denial and the love of God are all [one]. . . . It is self that the Scripture principally speaks against. . . . The very names of Self and Own, should sound in the watchful Christian's ears as very terrible, wakening words, that are next to the names of sin and satan."[32] John Dryden voiced a similar sense of the moral dangers of self-seeking and wealth when he asked Englishmen to consider the state of their capital city:

> London, thou great *emporium* of our isle,
> O thou too bounteous, thou too fruitful Nile!
> How shall I praise or curse to thy desert;
> Or separate thy sound from thy corrupted part!
> I call'd thee Nile; the parallel will stand:
> Thy tides of wealth o'erflow the fatten'd land;
> Yet monsters from thy large increase we find,
> Engender'd on the slime thou leav'st behind.

Dryden then described the merchants crowding into London:

> In gospel-phrase their chapmen they betray;
> Their shops are dens, the buyer is their prey.
> The knack of trades is living on the spoil;
> They boast, ev'n when each other they beguile.
> Customs to steal is such a trivial thing,
> That 't is their charter to defraud their king.
> All hands unite of every jarring sect;
> They cheat the country first, and then infect.[33]

Although Dryden's scorn was in one sense a timeless wail against greed, his words were also a particular condemnation of powerfully swelling currents of English life at the close of the seventeenth century.

An economic theorist, Charles Davenant, writing in 1701, extended this moral contempt for the new ethic to the political implications of the new economics, to the Bank of England, to speculation in stock, and to the huge public debt, which was not only condoned but also celebrated. He pictured those enriched by their handling of the new modes of finance as an "army of men with their pockets full of bank bills, East India stock, malt and lottery tickets, exchequer bills, bankstock," and so on. They "have run the nation head and ears in debt by . . . funds and new devices." More ominous, though, was the "dependence . . . this way of raising money has occasioned." The men thus made wealthy would "stick" to the government leaders who would make laws that supported the new mechanisms of commerce, creating a corrupt alliance tying national policy to the special interests of the great merchants.[34] Worst of all, "while public debts enriched the monied class, they impoverished the country gentlemen who had to pay the bill. Eventually . . . the landed men would be unable to compete in [bought] parliamentary elections, and the monied creatures of the court would hold the places necessary to deliver total power" to the financial party.[35] "Trade," Davenant concluded, is "without a doubt . . . a pernicious thing; it brings in that Wealth which introduces Luxury; it gives a rise to Fraud and Avarice, and extinguishes Virtue and Simplicity of Manners; it depraves a People, and makes way for that Corruption which never fails to end in Slavery." Then, as Samuel Adams would do a century later, Davenant thought of Lycurgus, whose "most perfect Model of Government" had banished luxury, and hoped England might no more encourage trade and all its entailed corruptions than Sparta had done.[36]

In fact, the new economic theorists were pointing, only half-consciously, toward a radical deemphasis of the role of government and toward a much-weakened conception of disinterested patriotism and indeed of the very idea of a body politic. Thomas Paine drew the logical conclusions in *The Rights of Man* (1792): "A great part of the order which reigns among mankind is not the effects of government. It has its origins in the principles of society and the natural constitution of man. . . . The landholder, the farmer, the manufacturer, the merchant, the tradesman, and every occupation, prospers by the aid which each receives from the other, and from the whole. . . . Every man wishes to pursue his occupation, and enjoy the fruits of his labours, and the produce of his property in peace and safety, with the least possible expense. When these things are accomplished, all the objects for which government ought to be established are answered."[37] Although Paine had a more optimistic faith in "ungoverned," autonomous men than the English philosophers of commerce did, he also gave mature expression to their preoccupation with the benefits of individual human enterprise and to their departure from ancient notions of authority and a moral community.

Paine also revealed, in speaking of "the order which reigns among mankind," that even writers who emphasized individual autonomy and, in general, welcomed the commercial ethic long continued at the same time to work within concepts of providential purpose and design. Both Defoe and Adam Smith, for example, saw trade and economic growth in providential terms; indeed, Smith's "invisible hand" deliberately invoked divine imagery and simply included free trade within the meaning of "natural law." Probably "no British writer before Bentham . . . frankly renounced teleology, and . . . no important writers except Mandeville and David Hume— and perhaps also Thomas Hobbes . . . could plausibly be interpreted on the basis of their actual writings as not honestly accepting it."[38] However much thought and practice in the seventeenth and eighteenth centuries might seem in retrospect to have been moving inexorably toward the mundane, calculating views of Jeremy Bentham and David Ricardo, the habit of thinking in terms of overarching divine purpose and design remained strong.

Political thought in the seventeenth century also moved rapidly to cope with the new speculations about human nature. Hobbes, the Puritan Levellers, James Harrington, and Locke, whatever the differences among them, all tended to see each man not "as a moral whole, nor as part of a larger social whole, but as an owner of himself. . . . Society became a lot of free individuals related to each other as proprietors of their own capacities and of what they acquired by their exercise. Society consisted of relations of exchange between proprietors. Political society became a calculated device for the protection of this property and for the maintenance of an orderly relation of exchange."[39] Although the Levellers, Harrington, and Locke, like many of their contemporaries, continued to adhere more or less to the traditional assumptions about moral order and civic responsibility, they nonetheless were part of the "liberal ideology" that increasingly dominated English political thought from its early articulation by Hobbes to its mature expression by J. S. Mill.

The emergence of full-fledged bourgeois individualism in the eighteenth century, in sum, rested on new understandings of human nature and of the relation of the individual to society that upset ancient human perceptions. In struggling to legitimize self-love, as the economists seemed determined to do (and as Hobbes and Locke in different ways attempted to do), it was necessary to confront and overthrow both medieval and Reformation aspirations for mankind. Biblical injunctions were hostile to the validation of selfishness, and even ancient philosophy, though in some schools more bending and moderate in its moral teachings, could offer little support for an ideology that placed individual aggrandizement at the center of social well-being. Philosophers in the eighteenth century, then, faced with ideologies that gave "self-love . . . such license" had in desperation or ingenuity somehow at least to balance or counteract the new "socially sanctioned selfishness" with tenets more congenial to traditional morality.[40] In this context, the question of what virtue was and whether it could be somehow subsumed in an enlarged category of enlightened self-interest became a central concern during the colonial and Revolutionary periods of American history.

On matters of government the new *questions* addressed by Hobbes and Locke (even more than the *answers*) overturned Classical ideas of polis and community. Although the moral blind alleys of "modernity" (which in some analyses includes all post-Greco-Roman thought) would come under the most comprehensive scrutiny only in the nineteenth and twentieth centuries as all the consequences emerged,[41] it was apparent at once to many thoughtful people that there were profound and deeply troubling implications for politics in the new views of human nature. What became of the hallowed ideals of Greek love of one's city (as in Plato's *Crito*), for example, or of Roman citizenship (as in Cicero's *Orations*), if the state was thought of as a mere aggregation of individual interests, whether aggressive or benign? From Homer onward, proud, unquestioned emphasis had been placed on the importance of community, of social cohesion, and of service to the commonweal, but by mid-eighteenth century, genuine novelty seemed in view. Public philosophers in the seventeenth and eighteenth centuries were well aware of the wide divergences, and many argued powerfully on behalf of the older concepts, but again, as in ethics, fundamental challenges were abroad on questions of public purpose, legitimacy of rule, and leadership.

In the era between the chief magistracies of John Winthrop and of George Washington, then, for better or for worse a Pandora's box had been opened, and a great moral debate had begun: could self-interest, "possessive individualism," actually become a mark of virtue in individuals; could growth in wealth be the standard of national progress; could government be viewed largely as an arena of competing special interests; and could leadership be a matter of brokerage rather than of alignment with divine guidance? Even the serious asking of these questions amounted to a moral revolution that would have been as unwelcome to Clarendon as to Cotton Mather. For those responsible for establishing executive power in a new republic born amid that intellectual revolution, as well as amid the more immediate one resulting in national independence, particular questions of how to design the office and then act in it would in some degree be connected to weighty matters of ethics and political purpose.

❦ 2 ❦

Ancients and Moderns
in the Age of Pope
and Swift

In the sophisticated world of Augustan letters eloquent voices arose
readily to do battle with the new commercial ethic. The towering
figures of Jonathan Swift and Alexander Pope, and other brilliant
writers, including John Gay, Lord Bolingbroke, John Arbuthnot,
and William Pulteney, assaulted what they saw as a "commercialization
of values." Together they fashioned a compelling world view deeply at
odds with the ethical and political ideas implicit in the thought of the
seventeenth-century economists.[1] The verbal power of the Augustan critics, their indignation at what they saw happening around them, and their
vivid evocation of a neoclassical culture dominated English letters for
nearly a century. Across the Atlantic, furthermore, the leaders declaring a
new nation "independent" in 1776 were by no means cut off from this
phenomenon. Indeed, Augustan neoclassicism was a shaping force on
American thought, polity, and culture until the political age of Andrew
Jackson and the intellectual age of Ralph Waldo Emerson.

The "influence" of the moral and literary tradition of Pope, Swift, and
other Augustan writers in English America during the eighteenth century
is not difficult to discern, except insofar as it is so pervasive that one may
run the danger of simply taking it for granted. For example, in addition to
the heavy importation of English editions of the works of Pope and Swift
by colonial booksellers, there were at least 160 American imprints of
Pope's *Essay on Man* between 1747 and 1850, with the heaviest concentration coming during the years 1785–1830. Throughout the period 1700–
1813, Daniel Defoe, Pope, Joseph Addison, Bolingbroke, and Henry
Fielding appeared regularly on the lists and catalogs of American booksellers and libraries.[2] Nearly all the American colleges in the colonial and
the early national periods listed Pope and Swift along with Addison as the
modern writers most to be read and imitated, and popular textbooks in
rhetoric and ethics included example after example from them. Couplets
from the *Essay on Man* appeared as introductions or conclusions to countless colonial literary efforts, and its insistence that to be happy one had to

be virtuous was at the heart of eighteenth-century conventional wisdom. A South Carolina newspaper, for example, eulogized Pope on his death in 1744 as one

> Who dar'd defend the righteous Laws of God,
> And boldly in the bright Paths of Virtue trod.

More than half a century later a Baltimore printer announced his "intention of publishing . . . a series of ethical and descriptive Poems, taken from the most eminent Authors, . . . Pope, Swift, Goldsmith, Hayley, Darwin, etc., . . . [in] little volumes [whose] cheapness and portability may induce the rising generation 'their merits to scan, and their morals to love.'" The printer hoped for his readers that "by apt quotations, they may learn to think."[3]

Although the strictly satirical writings of both Pope and Swift were sometimes condemned as "gross and disgusting," more often, especially before the ascendancy of the sentimental tastes of the nineteenth century, the *Dunciad* and other critiques were heralded because they could "scourge the base follies of a guilty age." "A satirist of true genius," wrote an American journalist in 1759, "warmed by a generous indignation against vice, . . . merits the applause of every friend of virtue [and] may be considered as a sort of supplement to the legislative authority of his country." A Massachusetts newspaper poet similarly emphasized the public, even political importance of such writing:

> Let satire's wrath reclaim a harden'd race,
> Chill with contempt, improve by just disgrace,
> With public vengeance public vices meet,
> And awe the guilty in their dark retreat.[4]

Although all the major neoclassical writers, from John Dryden to Samuel Johnson, were admired for both style and content regardless of political coloration, in many ways Pope and Swift loomed largest. Hence, when Americans found on the title page of the *Essay on Man* that it was dedicated to Bolingbroke and read in the widely printed letters of Pope and Swift (especially those written in the 1720s) of the close personal, literary, and ideological connections among these eminent, admired writers, their pronouncements on the basic moral and political issues of the day took on oracular power and achieved axiomatic standing. The literary models and the moral guides were the Augustan sages.

Franklin, Madison, Jefferson, and the Adamses alike, along with their Americanness and their devotion to the Revolution, listened all their lives to these "courtly muses." It was highly significant, then, when it turned out that between 1722 and 1742 "almost every literary figure in England contributed to the mass of writing about Sir Robert [Walpole] and that almost all of their contributions were hostile." Swift, Pope, Gay, Fielding, James Thomson, and a host of lesser figures "exercised their talents to attack the person and the policies of the prime minister."[5] This remarkable unanimity among the best writers in scorning a new politics that embodied a new style of leadership had a special importance for those in America who would need to fashion their own conception of executive power.

Mandeville, Defoe, and "Modernity"

The real crisis for Pope, Swift, and their circle was the "corruption" they saw everywhere in the rule of Walpole. But for these critics *corruption* meant much more than the giving or taking of bribes or the taint of other forms of dishonest exchange or exercises of power by public officials. The term *corruption* carried the full Classical connotation of displacement of the public good by private interest. In this context, the phrase *private citizen* becomes a contradiction: to be a citizen in the Aristotelian sense means precisely and completely to transcend the private, selfish viewpoint. When self-interest entered politics, either in the actions of rulers or in the attitudes of those who took part in the mechanisms of consent, there corruption reigned. The distinction was essentially moral, defining the presence of virtue in public as well as in private life, and thus the extent to which one could admire the policy and conduct of one's country.

This conception of citizenship, derived by the English neoclassical writers from the Renaissance humanists, hearkened to the sternest Spartan ideals of disinterestedness. Not only was there a sharp distinction between a concern for the universal good (which made one a patriot) and a concern for "a multiplicity of particular goods" (which was corruption), but "the greater the number and diversity of particular goods available in a society, the greater the danger of corruption in which it stood." Only a "Spartan rejection of private satisfactions," this ideal held, could provide "the necessary guarantee of civic virtue." Conversely, the domination of politics by private, special interests would guarantee the triumph of the opposite of civic virtue—corruption—and that is, at bottom, what troubled Pope and Swift about Walpole. Rentiers and stockholders whose prosperity *depended* on the interest rates of government loans; officeholders (military and civilian) possessing sinecures or even occupations *dependent* on government payments; and cabinet officers *dependent* on special interests for support; all were tainted in the same way: they defined themselves factionally; that is, each lacked the independence, the disinterestedness, the moral accountability that was the essence of civic virtue. They were corrupt.[6]

Bolingbroke, well aware of the doctrines of the new economic thought, put the onus on the increasingly fashionable idea of individualism itself: "What expectation can be entertained of raising a disinterested public spirit among men who have no other principle than that of private interest, *who are individuals rather than fellow citizens*, who prey on one another, and are, in a state of civil society, much like to Hobbes's men in his supposed state of nature?" Such an emphasis on the individual, Bolingbroke insisted, destroyed "that public morality which distinguishes a good from a bad citizen."[7] James Wilson showed his acceptance of the same values and definitions when he told a Philadelphia audience in 1790 that for the good citizen, "whenever a competition unavoidably takes place between his interest and that of the publick, to the latter the former must be the devoted sacrifice. By the will and by the interest of the community, every private will and every private interest must be bound and overruled." In fact, Wilson emphasized, the citizen who is "governed by such affections, as sever him from the common good and publick interest, works, in reality, towards his own misery." In these remarks, Wilson was not merely stating that enlightened self-interest required public-spiritedness; he was endorsing the Classical idea that *only* one who took part *disinterestedly*, *independently*, and *freely* in public affairs could be regarded as living the good and complete life. Under this conception Wilson went on to argue that in a system of representative government only that citizen "whose circumstances do not render him necessarily dependent on the will of another, should possess a vote in electing" officials.[8] For Bolingbroke and Wilson, following ancient traditions of moral and political philosophy, to be responsible and free was not to live in a marketplace of selfish interests (a world of quid pro quos, dependence, bargains, and bondage), but rather to possess and to be motivated by a view of the public good; that is, to exercise the independent, disinterested, wise judgment properly associated with the words *citizen*, *magistrate*, and *patriot*.

The critics' most fundamental enmity, though, was not to the existence of self-interest in human affairs—which, after all, they recognized as pervasive and probably ineradicable—but to the positive defense of it in both moral and political philosophy, in thought as well as deed. For example, when early in the century Bernard Mandeville in *The Fable of the Bees* not only observed that "no calling was without deceit" but also actually proclaimed that this selfish chicanery could itself constitute public virtue, the traditional moralists were horrified. Mandeville put the new morality in epigrammatic verses:

> Thus every Part was full of vice,
> Yet the whole Mass a Paradise; . . .
> And Virtue, who from Politicks
> Had learn'd a Thousand Cunning Tricks,
> Was, by their happy Influence,
> Made Friends with Vice: And ever since,
> The worst of all the Multitude
> Did something for the Common Good.

Applying this morality to the power and prosperity Britain gained under the duke of Marlborough and Walpole, Mandeville fashioned a new public philosophy:

> T' enjoy the World's Conveniencies,
> Be fam'd in War, yet live in Ease,
> Without great Vices, is a vain
> EUTOPIA seated in the Brain.
> Fraud, Luxury and Pride must live,
> While we the Benefits receive.[9]

Mandeville combined the self-interest ethic of the rising world of commerce with a skeptical, sober, even cynical philosophy derived from Montaigne, the Jansenists, the duc de La Rochefoucauld, and especially Pierre Bayle, a group often referred to disapprovingly by English writers as "the French moralists." These French writers alleged that those who trumpeted a morality of benevolence and goodwill were dangerous deceivers sure to disappoint individuals and, if generally believed, to lead nations to ruin. A nation composed totally of believers in Christian benevolence, Bayle had written, "would be soon enslaved if an enemy undertook to conquer it, because they would be unable to furnish themselves with good soldiers, or enough money to pay the expenses of soldiers." "Maintain avarice and ambition in all their ardor," Bayle advised, to increase commerce and wealth, and remember "the maxim that a dishonest man is able to be a good citizen [because he] renders services that an honest man is incapable of rendering." Writing at about the same time (1690) in a work revealingly entitled *Political Arithmetick*, the leading English economist and theorist of mercantilism, Sir William Petty, explained how the coming commercial age required not only a new ethic but also a new language and even a new metaphysics. Petty found it necessary, he said, to express himself "in Terms of Number, Weight, or Measure; to use only Arguments of Sense, and to consider only such Causes, as have visible Foundations in Nature," rather than to use "only comparative and superlative Words, and intellectual Arguments," normally employed by philosophers.[10]

Accepting these "maxims" and this understanding of reality, Mandeville argued that "active, stirring, and laborious Men [who] . . . try Experiments, and give all their Attention to what they are about," who unashamedly devoted their energies to trade and wealth gathering, were the truly admirable citizens, whereas those who are "fond of Retirement, hate Business, and take delight in [philosophic] Speculation" were of little value. Mandeville further observed that to "render a Society of Men strong and powerful, you must touch their Passions. . . . Would you moreover render them an opulent, knowing and polite Nation, teach 'em Commerce with Foreign Countries, . . . encourage Trade; . . . this will bring Riches, and where they are, Arts and Sciences will soon follow, . . . Great Wealth and Foreign Treasure will ever scorn to come among Men, unless you'll admit their inseparable Companions, Avarice and Luxury." For a nation to become rich and civilized, Mandeville advised, it was necessary that its people have their "Desires enlarg'd," their "Appetites refin'd," and their "Vices increas'd."[11]

Unblushingly, then, Mandeville advocated that self-interest be accepted as the moral basis, even the cohesive force, of society, that a nation most value citizens single-minded in promoting commerce, and that the very councils of the nation be imbued with this spirit. Although the natural law theory admired by English and American Whigs was incompatible with Mandeville's unashamed defense of selfishness, it is also true that an emphasis, such as in Locke's writing, on the morally autonomous individual, and on the subordination of society and the state to that principle, could easily be construed by those preoccupied with economic individualism into an exaltation of government as management and into a conception of politics as merely an arena of contending amoral forces. Unselfconsciously accepting an amalgam of these strains of thought, a pro-Walpole newspaper worked out the implications for government: "Men are always corrupt, and must often be manag'd. . . . Corruption is good or bad in its Effects as good or bad Governors apply it." Walpole himself bespoke the same ethic when he noted, "I am no Saint, no Spartan, no Reformer."[12] It was not, of course, the novelty of such a posture in a ruler that scandalized the Augustan moralists; it was rather Walpole's *unabashed* self-acceptance of himself in that light.

Daniel Defoe fashioned the most candid and telling defense of the "virtue" of the new commercial age. "The wise, sober, modest tradesman," he declared, "when he is thriven and grown rich, is really a valuable man." With his "special experience and knowledge of business," such a man is better qualified to lead the nation than "men of ten times [his] learning and education," or those who "value themselves upon their pedigree" but actually are "boors, empty and swinish sots and fops."[13] In fact, "tradesmen," according to Defoe, are the "only gentry in England." Thus valuing these sorts of men and their endeavors, Defoe went on to point toward blunt realities in public policy: "This nation can no more support itself without trade than the Church can without religion. . . . Our interest is our trade; and our trade is, next to our liberty and religion, one of our most valuable liberties. If our neighbors pretend to slam the door against our commerce, we must open it; and that by force, if no other means will procure it."[14] "Trade is the Wealth of the World," Defoe wrote when Walpole was at the height of his power. "Trade makes the difference as to Rich and Poor, between one Nation and another; Trade nourishes Industry, Industry begets Trade; Trade dispenses the natural wealth of the world, and Trade raises new species of wealth, which nature knew nothing of; Trade has two daughters, whose fruitful progeny in Arts may be said to employ mankind; namely MANUFACTURE and NAVIGATION. See how they unite their powers to do good to the world, and to teach men how to live happy and comfortably."[15]

In Defoe's mind, and in the world of Augustan literature and science, the new ethic and the dazzling new bourgeois culture had implications in all areas of learning. In history, for example, Defoe and Bolingbroke came to opposite evaluations of two kings of England because the authors differed on the qualities needed in a good ruler and on basic questions of political philosophy. To Bolingbroke, Edward III (1327–1377), the victor at Crécy and the conqueror of most of France, was a "great prince" under whom "the constitution of our Parliaments, and the whole frame of our government became reduced into a better form." "A spirit of liberty breathes in the laws of this glorious king," Bolingbroke wrote. Hence, "few and short were the struggles between him and his people. . . . He not only observed the laws, but he made the sense of the nation, in some measure, a law to him." Defending the exertions required of the people by Edward III's campaigns, Bolingbroke argued that "for a few temporary contributions, [he] enriched his people to future generations."[16]

Defoe, on the other hand, noted that "these glorious things [Edward III's conquests] gutted England of its wealth, made the monarch powerful and his people poor." "In all his Parliaments," Defoe added, "we see not one act for the encouragement of trade, for enlarging commerce, for employment of the poor, for setting up manufactures." During Edward's campaigns "England lay neglected to the last degree; her sons knocking their heads against stone walls, and ranging the field of war in foreign countries, pursued their own poverty, and sought misery, for the glory of their monarch." Had not the people of England "been so exhausted by foreign wars, peel'd and pol'd by their tyrant Princes, . . . plunder'd and emptied by the foolish and ridiculous zeal, or rather fury, call'd *The Holy War*, they might have been infinitely richer than they were."[17]

In the case of Henry VII (1485–1509), Defoe's and Bolingbroke's evaluations are again opposed, but in the reverse way. Bolingbroke condemned the first Tudor monarch because he had been raised to the throne after the death of Richard III "in order to cut up the roots of faction; to restore public tranquillity; and to establish a legal government on the ruins of tyranny." Instead, "he planted faction anew" when (quoting the Huguenot historian Paul de Rapin) "he let slip no opportunity to humble the Yorkists; behaving towards them not as a just king, but like the head of a party." He let "his jealousy, his pride, and his insatiable, sordid avarice have their full swing" and was thus "the true cause of all the disturbances" and tyranny that followed his reign. Defoe, on the other hand, commended Henry VII for his "wisdom and sagacity." He saw that "England was much in the wrong" to let its wool be exported to the Continent for manufacture, and thus he labored diligently to find out how the work could be done in England. Henry VII had an "improving genius," and he sought with "the utmost Prudence and Caution . . . to encourage his people in working and manufacturing." "Thus it was," Defoe concluded, that the transformation of England into a great commercial nation began, which "arrived to its perfection" under Queen Elizabeth.[18]

It is perhaps no accident, either, that Defoe's evaluation of Henry VII concurred in many ways with Sir Francis Bacon's well-known *History of the Reign of King Henry the Seventh* (London, 1622). Bacon, the philosophical spokesman for the new world of science and material progress, had recommended that the Prince of Wales (later Charles I) take Henry VII as his model because the first of the Tudor monarchs had turned the attention of England away from the medieval world of the Plantagenets and the wasteful feuding of Lancastrians and Yorkists. Instead, Henry VII had worked for the prosperity of his kingdom, improved its commercial relations, and, by wise and careful management, left his heirs a full treasury and an efficient administration. (Bolingbroke quoted from Bacon and admitted that "husbandry, manufactures, general commerce, and increase of useful people were carefully attended to" by Henry VII, but Bolingbroke could not resist scorning these "benefits" as "drops of manna, which fell from the throne.")[19] Bacon and Defoe sided clearly with those who celebrated the new ethic of the age of commerce, a position that led them inevitably to contravene ancient conceptions of the purposes of government and the qualities of good leadership.

The deep tension in English society concerning the proper nature of leadership also revealed itself in a controversy revived in 1690 with the publication by Swift's patron, Sir William Temple, of an *Essay upon Ancient and Modern Learning*. In this work, Temple went beyond the existing seventeenth-century debate over the merit and methods of the science of William Harvey, Robert Boyle, and others to attack not so much the particular achievements of modern science and scholarship as what he took to be its intellectual pride. It was vain presumption, Temple asserted, for modern writers to suppose that their learning was unqualified "progress," that they were making great advances over the ancient authors in all fields. In rhetoric, in moral philosophy, and in aesthetic sensitivity, Temple argued, the ancient authors, especially Virgil, Cicero, Horace, and the other poets and essayists of Augustan Rome, whose Latin every schoolboy memorized, represented a pinnacle of human achievement. A good, wise, and learned person, therefore, should revere and imitate these authors, accepting them as matchless models, and discard the dangerous conceit that modern learning could in any basic way outshine them. Temple most profoundly scorned the "moderns" for neglecting the search for basic truth in order to produce inventions that, for example, merely allowed greater trade profits or served only to extend England's ability to exploit and despoil the ancient civilizations of the East.

By 1700 it was clear in the intellectual world of London that the quarrel between "Ancients" and "Moderns" was not just "paper warfare." Rather, their disputes were part of a fundamental moral and cultural tension. On one side stood a world of fixed values where sacred texts defined a metaphysics, an aesthetics, an ethic, and a public philosophy that gave the community (understood variously as "Christendom" or "Western Civilization") its purpose and sense of cohesion. On the other stood an open, changing world where scientific inquiry, individual self-interest, and material progress held out new and previously undreamed of vistas for mankind. When Swift joined the controversy with his *Battle of the Books* (1696), he mainly made fun of the whole squabble, but he heaped greatest scorn on the defenders of modernity. With Swift's entry into the fray, in any case, those on the Ancients side of the controversy began to deliver the more memorable and telling literary blows—most notably the broadside assaults mounted by Swift and the other "Scriblerians" (Pope and John Arbuthnot) in 1714, Swift's ridicule of "the Grand Academy of Lagado" in *Gulliver's Travels*, and Pope's scorn for pedants in the *Dunciad*. They also brought their critique of the Modernist trend in English culture in line with the lessons and lore of Greece and Rome that students had long imbibed as they learned the ancient languages, thus further amalgamating the values of the Classical and neoclassical eras.[20]

Indeed, the Ancients, deeply learned and attuned to European intellectual currents, saw themselves as continuers of the best traditions of Renaissance humanism and rejected the "Gothic" and "barbarous" medieval world no less than the modern world, with its excessive devotion to science, philosophical disputation, and philological precision. The Ancients hearkened especially to that part of Classical culture that saw the world whole, that viewed literature, history, and rhetoric as eloquent embodiments of timeless truths of inestimable value in public as well as private life. In championing Cicero and Lucian as rhetoricians, Livy and Tacitus as historians, and Horace and Virgil as poets, the Ancients allied themselves with wise precepts couched in matchless language and spoke from a perspective that had enduring appeal.[21] Furthermore, that Temple and Swift assumed as unreservedly as had Cicero and Horace that eloquent, graceful writing imparted implicitly to readers values useful both in personal life and in politics helped set standards for those concerned about the meaning and purpose of nationhood at a time when newness seemed to challenge everything.

For the transatlantic audience the effects were ambiguous. Like Franklin and Jefferson, New World intellectuals tended to be enthusiastic Baconians, devoted to modernity and all its associations with science, commercial growth, and the spread of liberty, but they also absorbed the powerfully stated case for the ancient values and world view. They were at least dimly aware, in the words of a recent student, that "modernity begins when men develop a sense of their own competence, when they begin to think that they can understand nature and society and can then control and change nature and society for their own purposes. Above all, modernization means the rejection of external restraints on men, the Promethean liberation of man from control by gods, fate, and destiny."[22] American political institutions, and ideas of leadership to go with them, took shape as the Western world opened itself to this "modernity," and the early presidents in general welcomed it, but they were also deeply uneasy about what might be lost if "gods, fate, and destiny" receded in human consciousness. The brilliant criticism of the Ancients, opposed as it was to a particular style of British politics, implanted itself forcefully in eighteenth-century thought. And because educated Americans continued to study Cicero and Horace, and to enjoy reading Swift and Pope long after "Modern" scholarship had been lost in the dusty back issues of the *Philosophical Transactions*, the perspective of the Ancients remained as a compelling counterpoint throughout the early national period of American history.

Walpole and Pope

Within the context of these deep differences over ethics, ancient authors, English history, and public philosophy, the political dominance of Sir Robert Walpole (1721–1742) became the focus of all that the foes of corruption and of the commercialization of values hated. Walpole not only achieved a brilliant mastery over English politics by manipulation of the king and his family and control of Parliament but also defended his method in principle. His willingness to compromise, his materialism, his mastery of the budget, and his control of offices, he asserted candidly, were all part and parcel of a mode of government and a sense of national destiny that ought to make Britons proud. His government was flexible, opportunistic, prosperous, and balanced—everything, Walpole's defenders asserted, that made Britain in the eighteenth century the freest and richest nation in the world.

These qualities were especially impressive to Voltaire, who lived in England from 1726 to 1728 and to Montesquieu, who came in 1732. "It was Walpole's England," John Morley has noted, "that inspired the *Philosophic Letters* and the *Spirit of Laws*. . . . [These] illustrious . . . [writers] felt the movement, the freedom, the full pulse and current of vitality" of Georgian Britain, however "uninteresting [the] surface."[23] Voltaire, banished from France for writing as he pleased, noted that in England "the feet of the peasant are not tortured by wooden shoes, he eats white bread, he is well clothed, and he is not afraid to increase the number of his cattle or to cover his house with tile, lest his taxes be raised. . . . A man is not exempt . . . from paying certain taxes because he is a nobleman or priest." Voltaire was as enthusiastic about the commercial dynamism of English society, especially as it contrasted with France's ancien régime: "Commerce, which has brought wealth to the citizenry of England, has helped to make them free, and freedom has developed commerce in its turn. By means of it the nation has grown great; it is commerce that little by little has strengthened the naval forces that make the English the masters of the seas. . . . Posterity may learn with some surprise that a little island with nothing of its own but a bit of lead, tin, fuller's earth, and coarse wool became, by means of its commerce, powerful enough" to control Europe. With heavy sarcasm Voltaire mused, "I don't know which is more useful to a state, a well-powdered lord who knows precisely what time the king gets up in the morning and what time he goes to bed, . . . or a great merchant who enriches his country, sends orders to Surat and to Cairo, and contributes to the well-being of the world."[24] To Voltaire, compared with France at least, England was not only rich and free but also just. It was not a declining, a demoralized, or a physically decadent culture that Walpole's critics disdained, then, but rather an assertively prosperous, practical, and expansive one. The choice before the political nation was between nothing less than visions of the national future.

Walpole and Pope, in fact, have been characterized as "mighty opposites." Walpole was "resilient, patient, stubborn, and shrewd, . . . an exceptionally skilled administrator and persuader who 'made the cumbersome machinery of eighteenth-century government work more efficiently than it was ever to work again,' and who held the nation together, by hook and sometimes by crook, for a crucial period of two decades while a change of

dynasty was effected and England grew strong in peace. This was a tre-
mendous feat of energy, strategy, and devotion."[25] Such praise for "the in-
ventor of the spoils system" may seem extravagant, but within his own
candidly expressed objectives, Walpole was a creative and, for his day, un-
oppressive leader. Pope, on the other hand, put the matter differently in an
"Epistle" addressed to Bolingbroke:

> And say, to which shall our applause belong,
> This new Court jargon, or the good old song?
> The modern language of corrupted Peers,
> Or what was spoke at CRESSY and POITIERS?
> Who counsels best? who whispers, "Be but great,
> With Praise or Infamy leave that to fate;
> Get Place and Wealth, if possible, with grace;
> If not, by any means get Wealth and Place."
>
> .   .   .   .
>
> Or he, who bids thee face with steady view
> Proud Fortune, and look shallow Greatness through:
> And, while he bids thee, sets th' Example too?[26]

As a eulogist of Pope expressed it, an idealist and a patriot would

> Point out the follies of the rich and great;
> Mark the Plebean soul disguis'd in state;
> Disclose the meanness of the Pension'd train;
> Thy theme will last while fools and knaves remain.[27]

This recurring vision of a moral, traditional, humanly decent culture struggling against corruption and debasement of all kinds was the aspiration
offered readers of Augustan literature on both sides of the Atlantic Ocean.
Its poignancy might be all the greater for those who saw themselves as
having a unique opportunity to decide the destiny of a new nation—and
to set the character of its leadership.

The giants of this critical tradition, Pope and Swift, sought and thrived
on controversy and had legions of detractors in the literary wars (indeed,
in Defoe and Richard Steele they had worthy foes), but in the end they
enthralled poets and essayists of the English-speaking world for the rest of
the century. By dint of their matchless style, their moral indignation, and
their force of intellect, they dictated literary canons, raised the issues, and
set the questions; others could respond and attempt to refute, but the
terms of discourse had been laid out. Furthermore, the ideas embedded in
their writings achieved a hold and a staying power that mere polemics, or
even profound theory and lively journalism, could not hope to equal. The
verbal skill of Swift and Pope gave them an unbeatable advantage in win-

ning the minds of their audiences. Could the reader of Swift's *A Modest Proposal*, for example, ever forget England's infamy in Ireland, or the reader of Pope's "Prologue to Addison's *Cato*" fail to sense the virtues of "what Plato thought, and Godlike Cato was"?

During the warfare in the reigns of King William and Queen Anne, and in the turmoil attending the Hanoverian succession, Pope and Swift established their literary preeminence. Swift particularly set a new standard of both political influence and literary journalism in his 1711 pamphlet, *The Conduct of the Allies* ("[Bolingbroke's] thoughts translated into Swift's words").[28] In condemning Marlborough and the long war against France, Swift made the *Examiner*, which he edited and largely wrote (1710–1711), into possibly the most scathingly effective magazine in English history. In these works he dismissed with an unescapable scorn the commercial concerns of the Whig magnates defended by Defoe: "These men come with the spirit of shop-keepers to frame rules for the administration of kingdoms; as if they thought the whole art of government consisted in the importation of nutmegs and the curing of herrings." Swift also made clear in the *Examiner* his contempt for morally neutral, laissez-faire government, and he "aligned the growth of professional politics with the dehumanized, calculating-machine, stock-price approach which . . . the triumph of the [commercial] party would bring with it."[29] As the nation went through the great crises of 1710–1715, Swift and others enlarged the opposition to "the commercial party" beyond merely partisan differences. The political debate reflected a cultural dispute that touched every part of English life, including qualities and style of leadership.

By 1721, when Walpole grasped power, Swift and Pope had each in a way "retired" from London, but they were still the siege guns whose force and range others sought in vain to match. As contempt for Walpole and his government mounted, each fired off a thundering salvo in the 1720s: Swift's *Gulliver's Travels* (1726) and Pope's *Dunciad* (1728). These works, coming with Bolingbroke's return to England in 1725 and Voltaire's sojourn there the next year, led to visits in country houses, coffeehouse conversations, exchange of manuscripts, and a shining moment in English letters. Although credit is due Walpole for not stifling this outburst while he had the power to do it, as Voltaire saw more keenly than his English hosts, its moral thrust was deeply damaging to the Whig oligarchs and challenged the very legitimacy of their rule. It was this critique that had such a massive impact on the Anglo-American mind in the eighteenth century.

In elaborate satire Swift and Pope heaped scorn and derision on petty and materialistic Lilliput (England), on the Reign of Dulness (the Hanoverian kings), and on their "Midas" lord chancellor, the "Great Dunce" (Walpole himself). When amid domestic strife and foreign humiliation, Walpole in the spring of 1738 chose to present at court and marry his again-pregnant mistress of many years, Molly Skerrett, Pope took advantage of the vulnerable moment and wrote indignantly and pointedly against "Vice enthroned" (the mistress become lady of the first minister):

> Her [i.e., Vice's] Birth, her Beauty, Crowds and Courts confess,
> Chaste Matrons praise her, and grave Bishops bless;
> In golden Chains the willing World she draws,
> And hers the Gospel is, and hers the Laws,
> Mounts the Tribunal, lifts her scarlet head,
> And sees pale Virtue carted in her stead.
> Lo! at the wheels of her Triumphal Car,
> Old England's Genius, rough with many a Scar,
> Dragged in the dust! his arms hang idly round,
> His Flag inverted trails along the ground!
> Our Youth, all liveried o'er with foreign Gold,
> Before her dance: behind her, crawl the Old!
> See thronging Millions to the Pagod run,
> And offer Country, Parent, Wife, or Son!
> Hear her black Trumpet through the Land proclaim,
> That NOT TO BE CORRUPTED IS THE SHAME.
> In Soldier, Churchman, Patriot, Man in Power,
> 'Tis Avarice all, Ambition is no more!
> See, all our Nobles begging to be Slaves!
> See, all our Fools aspiring to be Knaves!
> The Wit of Cheats, the Courage of a Whore,
> Are what ten thousand envy and adore:
> All, all look up, with reverential Awe,
> At Crimes that 'scape, or triumph o'er the Law:
> While Truth, Worth, Wisdom, daily they decry—
> "Nothing is Sacred now but Villainy."
> Yet may this Verse (if such a Verse remain)
> Show there was one who held it in disdain.[30]

Although Pope wrote these lines ten years after publication of the first version of the *Dunciad*, the same moral indignation, cultural criticism, and political assault infuses all of his poetry in this period. His claim in the *Dunciad* to political impartiality was utterly belied in his scorn of Walpole's literary defenders, in his praise of Swift and Gay, and in such obvious thrusts, a year after George II had succeeded George I, as: "Still Dunce the second reigns like Dunce the first." Pope's images of Walpole and the Georgian court as dull, corrupt, and vulgar sharpened and indeed immortalized the opposition attack on an administration candidly faithful to the new, commercial Britain. Pope's poetry portrayed how "the commercial and middle-class standards of the City invade the aristocratic province and corrupt the standards traditionally associated with the King and the nobility." England, to Pope, was "on the brink of cultural disaster"[31] caused by the insidious interplay of a morally bankrupt leadership, a selfish ethic spreading out from the nation's trading centers, and a loss of faith in ancient ideas of providence and community:

> O! would the Sons of Men once think their Eyes
> And Reason given them but to study *Flies*!
> See Nature in some partial narrow shape,
> And let the Author of the Whole escape:
> Learn but to trifle; or, who most observe,
> To wonder at their Maker, not to serve!
>
> .   .   .   .
>
> Or, at one bound o'erleaping all his laws,
> Make God Man's Image, Man the final Cause,
> Find Virtue local, all Relation scorn,
> See all in *Self*, and but for self be born:
> Of naught so certain as our *Reason* still,
> Of naught so doubtful as of *Soul* and *Will*.
> Oh hide the God still more! and make us see
> Such as Lucretius drew, a God like Thee:
> Wrapped up in Self, a God without a Thought,
> Regardless of our merit or default.[32]

Swift's Lilliputian England

In *Gulliver's Travels* Swift used deft characterizations and vivid incidents to etch indelibly the greed, corruption, and intrigue of the ruling circles of Britain. In the voyage to Lilliput—unmistakably the mean, small-minded England Swift meant to satirize—Gulliver found tiny, busy, ingenious people ruled by an apparently worthy and patriotic emperor, yet the court was dominated by a penny-pinching lord of the Treasury (Walpole), spitefully ambitious generals and admirals, and an intriguing empress. Furthermore, public life suffered from the rivalry of two parties, the "high heels" and "low heels" (court and country), and the nation was convulsed by an edict compelling that eggs be broken only at the small end. All "Big-Endians" (Roman Catholics) were persecuted severely and found refuge in a neighboring nation (France), where they conspired with Lilliput's enemies, leading to endless wars.

Having thus ridiculed party intrigue and religious intolerance, Swift had

Gulliver go next to Brobdingnag, where he was the midget among a huge and large-souled people. In this truly well-governed land, Gulliver, with proud (gullible) loyalty, described to the king the history, laws, and customs of his native England. One of the "wonderful" devices of the English, of which the Brobdingnagians were ignorant, for example, was gunpowder. "We often put this powder into large, hollow balls of iron," Gulliver explained, "and discharge them by an engine into some city we were besieging, which would rip up the pavements, tear the houses to pieces, burst and throw splinters on every side, dashing out the brains of all who came near." Thus the king could judge the "genius" of English inventions and practices. As Gulliver proceeded with idealized descriptions of the English constitution, the courts, the Church, and so on, the keen-minded monarch raised questions that revealed the seamy reality: that "bribes, partiality, and avarice" in fact governed appointments to office, that seats in the House of Commons were bought regularly, that lawyers were paid huge sums to plead "unjust, vexatious, or oppressive" cases, that Treasury figures showed revenues were double any useful, visible expenditures, that only "a quarrelsome people living among very bad neighbors" could be so often at war, and that the nobility was so addicted to gaming that "mean vicious people, by their dexterity in that art . . . keep [the] very nobles in dependence, as well as habituate them to vile companions."

The wise king concluded, after his sharp questioning of Gulliver, that English history for a century past "was only a heap of conspiracies, rebellions, murders, massacres, revolutions, banishments, the very worst effects that avarice, faction, hypocrisy, perfidiousness, cruelty, rage, madness, hatred, envy, lust, malice, or ambition could produce." There seemed to be among the English, the king observed, "some lines of an institution, which in its original might have been tolerable, but these [were] half-erased, and the rest blurred and blotted by corruptions." "It doth not appear from all you have said," the king told Gulliver, "how any one virtue is required towards the procurement of any one station among you; much less that men are ennobled on account of their virtue, that priests are advanced for their piety or learning, soldiers for their conduct or valour, judges for their integrity, senators for the love of their country, or counsellors for their wisdom." On the basis alone of Gulliver's account of what was unmistakably Walpole's England, the king voiced the conclusion that burned Swift's scathing condemnation into the minds of his readers: "The bulk of your natives must be the most pernicious race of little odious vermin that nature ever suffered to crawl upon the surface of the earth."[33]

Swift's king of Brobdingnag probably was not modeled on a particular ruler, though he possessed many of the qualities of leadership espoused by Swift's early patron Sir William Temple, and he resembled in some ways Charles XII of Sweden, whom Swift admired in 1718 for his "piety, liberality, self-control, courage, endurance, and frugality," virtues that Swift found lacking in George I, who had just ascended to the English throne. Swift was no friend of high-toned or absolute power, but he had a keen sense of the benefit a nation might receive from a good king, and he believed "in the determining effect a monarch's character might have on a nation's destiny."[34] The philosopher-king or good prince (Swift often evoked these ideals in his writings) was, like the king of Brobdingnag, "possessed of every quality which procures veneration, love, and esteem; of strong parts, great wisdom, and profound learning; endowed with admirable talents for government, and almost adored by his subjects," and he would rule with "common sense and reason, . . . justice and unity." With biting satire, Swift had Gulliver appear astonished that the king refused to build gunpowder factories in order to make himself the "absolute master of the lives, the liberties, and the fortunes of his people" and noted that this "defect" probably had "arisen from their ignorance; they not having hitherto reduced *politics* into a *science*, as the more acute wits of Europe have done." Swift accepted, in sum, ancient conceptions of government, hallowed by Livy, Cicero, and Plutarch, that placed simple virtues and paternalistic intentions at the center of good rule, and he made clear his scorn for "modern," excessively scientific ideas of leadership preoccupied with sheer power and "all *mystery, refinement*, and *intrigue*."[35]

In part 4 of *Gulliver's Travels*, full of more contempt for human depravity in general and English venality in particular, Swift often laced his diatribes with denunciations of the peculiar corruptions of the new commercial age. He scorned, for example, "gamesters, politicians, wits, . . . leaders or followers of party and faction, . . . encouragers to vice, by seducement or examples, . . . cheating shopkeepers or mechanicks, . . . [and] scoundrels raised from the dust upon the merit of their vices." Then, after a biting attack on Walpole, Swift went on to characterize the "nobility" that surrounded and depended on him: "Young *noblemen* are bred from their childhood in idleness and luxury; . . . as soon as years will permit, they consume their vigour and contract odious diseases among lewd females. . . . [Their] imperfections of . . . mind run parallel with those of . . . body, being a composition of spleen, dullness, ignorance, caprice, sensuality and pride." Although Swift professed that his descriptions "by no means affect the British nation," again and again they were all too familiar to his readers. They could not miss Swift's rage at English morality, commercial culture, and politics in the age of Walpole, nor could their minds escape his graphic images and language. Furthermore, Swift stated explicitly that his "sole intention was the PUBLIC GOOD," to make his countrymen ashamed of their vices, and to hold the depravity of Yahoo-like Europeans up against the "glorious virtue" of the Houyhnhnms and the "wise maxims in morality and government" of the Brobdingnagians.[36] If this public purpose was not apparent before, the brilliant, bitter satire and invective of Swift's last poems, savagely attacking Walpole and the England that sustained his rule, fixed *Gulliver's* author as the archenemy of the new style of political leadership.

Swift's satire had such force and impact not because the charges he made were in any way novel, but precisely because what he had to say so sharply and memorably was already common knowledge. His brilliant mingling of satire on the human condition in general with obvious jibes at contemporary affairs had the effect both of stimulating speculation about *Gulliver's* political thrusts (more and more scornful of Walpole, as commentary accumulated), and of giving his work lasting value.[37] Swift gave his readers a vocabulary, a series of dramatic incidents, a memorable cast of characters, and a string of epigrams that captured the mind of Anglo-America in the eighteenth century. After *Gulliver's Travels* Britons would read about party strife and picture "high heels" and "low heels," and pious accounts of English institutions could never again escape puncture by the Brobdingnagian monarch's searing critique of them.

By 1769, the popular historian and novelist Tobias Smollett could, in what was by then hallowed, conventional wisdom, satirize political parties: "The people of Japan had been long divided between two inveterate parties known by the names of Shit-tilk-ums-heit, and She-it-kums-hi-til, the first signifying *more fool than knave*; and the other *more knave than fool*. Each had predominated in its turn, by securing a majority in the assemblies of the people; . . . [employing] every art of corruption, calumny, insinuation, and priestcraft. . . . In short, both parties were equally abusive, rancorous, uncandid and illiberal."[38] Swift had made the same points in maxims accepted as gospel on both sides of the Atlantic: he characterized "party as the madness of many, for the gain of the few," and Parliament as "a knot of peddlars, pickpockets, highwaymen, and bullies." By commanding the field of English letters, Swift took command as well of the terms of political discourse and of social criticism that lasted into the era of the American Revolution.

The Eminence of Walpole's Critics

Another stunning satire of Walpole and the commercial world view linked to his ascendancy, with a major influence in America, was John Gay's *The Beggar's Opera*. The characters were so sharply drawn and their words so pointed and clever that audiences at its immensely popular first productions and at the frequent eighteenth-century revivals recognized at once Gay's intention. "Robin of Bagshot, alias Gorgon, alias Bluff Bob, alias

Carbuncle, alias Bob Booty," who "spends his life among women," was easily recognized as Walpole. Then, in the quarrel scene between the accountant-merchants Peachum and Lockit, Gay ridiculed Puritan hypocrisy (the quarrelers call each other "brother" as they cudgel and cheat) and expressed contempt for commercial values, just as Dryden had done in *Absalom and Achitophel*. The *Beggar's Opera* was performed at least fifty times in America between 1750 and 1800, including Williamsburg in 1768 and 1770, Marblehead and Boston in 1769–1770, Charleston, South Carolina, in 1774, and Charleston and Philadelphia during the 1790s. Americans could readily see in Gay's satire immediately relevant assaults on royal government and court politics, as well as commentary on the larger cultural and moral issues. Washington and Jefferson saw *The Beggar's Opera* in Williamsburg in 1768 and 1770, and Washington is said to have relished it as his favorite dramatic entertainment.[39]

Other satires, such as Arbuthnot's *The History of John Bull* and later some of the works of James Thomson and Henry Fielding, added further weight to the case against the England of Walpole and the Whig magnates. In defending Toryism, the landed gentry, and the established church, the critics were in part merely nostalgic upholders of hierarchy and traditional privilege, espousers, that is, of an Anglo-Saxon arcadia and a "Merry England" they knew was a myth. But they also evoked a vision of a culture whose standards of virtue, integrity, honor, and love of country did indeed make the ethic and world view of *The Compleat English Tradesman* and *The Fable of the Bees* seem Dunce-like and Lilliputian.

As the particular occasion for these literary works receded with the passage of time, a social vision and a public philosophy—of greater aesthetic and moral appeal than anything said in defense of Walpole, English trade, or political parties—was left enshrined. Lord Chesterfield hammered home the point in 1737: "Has there been an Essay, in Verse or Prose, has there been . . . an Advertisement, fit to be read, on the Side of [Walpole's] Administration?—But on the other Side, what Numbers of Dissertations, Essays, Treatises, Compositions of all Kinds, in Verse and Prose, have been written, with all that Strength of Reasoning, Quickness of Wit, and Elegance of Expression, which no former Period of Time can equal? Has not every body got by heart, Satires, Lampoons, Ballads, and Sarcasms against the Administration? And can any body recollect, or repeat one Line for it?"[40]

It was not mere chance, moreover, that the opposition to Walpole included writers of much greater talent than his defenders. Reflecting the tension between the "Ancients," who had argued that the Classical writers should be imitated for their literary and moral qualities, and the "Moderns," who had insisted that they should be examined in a more critical, scientific way, Walpole's defenders often asserted candidly that poets and satirists, however clever and elegant they might be, were of little use, indeed, would be a hindrance, in the practical world of government. "Tho' Poetry is a fine Amusement, and a Taste in it a great Accomplishment in Youth," one of Walpole's writers noted in 1731, "yet common Observation shews, that in Private Life 'tis so bewitching that wherever it gets firm Possession, it excludes from the Mind even a necessary Attention to Matters of more Moment: And shall a man be thought fittest to be trusted with the Concerns of the Publick for Talents, which, Experience shews us, render him incapable of managing his own?" The Walpolean defense accepted generally Defoe's assertion that public affairs had to be managed by practical men, men experienced in commerce and accounts, because such concerns were essential to the general welfare. Conversely, merely polite literature, skill "in making words clink" as one desperate administration writer put it in vilifying Pope's *Dunciad*, had no useful role in affairs of state. Swift capitalized on such admissions in 1730 in addressing a poem to Pope on the contrast between his virtue and learning and the vulgar administration:

> At Table you can *Horace* quote;
> they at a Pinch can bribe a Vote:
> You shew your Skill in *Grecian* Story,
> But, they can manage *Whig* and *Tory*.[41]

Then, when it appeared that most of the hack writers scorned in the *Dunciad* were patronized by Walpole and his friends, and the court sycophant Colley Cibber was made poet laureate in 1730, the linkage of the ruling circles to bad taste and prostituted pens became complete. Walpole's opposition not only possessed, therefore, the substance of the profound indictment of English society that Swift, Pope, and others fashioned in the 1720s and 1730s but also appeared as defenders of literary artistry itself. They gained the sympathy, that is, of those who agreed with what they wrote as well as of men and women who cherished the very idea of good writing and a sense of style. John Adams revealed the critical connections in his *Defence of the Constitutions of the Government of the United States of America* (1787) when he included long sections of Swift's *A Discourse of the Contests and Dissensions between the Nobles and Commons of Athens and Rome, with the Consequences they had upon both those States* (1701) among selections from political philosophers who extolled separation of powers in government. Admitting that Swift was "seldom quoted as a legislator," Adams nevertheless used the *Discourse* because "the history of every government . . . justified" its reasoning and "there are not to be found in any library so many accurate ideas of government, expressed with so much perspicuity, brevity, and precision." Benjamin Rush made the point in another way in 1778 when he wrote of his "great partiality to Swift, Hume, Bolingbroke, and Sir Wm. Temple as models of fine writing." He was not surprised, he added, that "Dr. Pope speaks of the 'majesty' . . . of simplicity in writing" as the most important quality of good composition.[42] Rush also made clear that Pope, Swift, and Bolingbroke in his mind were linked to an important tradition of political thought and admired writing reaching back to seventeenth-century historians and ahead to David Hume, who had an especially important influence on the American founders.

When such bright young men as Rush, Adams, Jefferson, and Madison read the acclaimed English literature, they also absorbed its moral and cultural idealism. They knew that the Augustan authors espoused a monarchism and a social conservatism increasingly out of place in the New World, but these transatlantic Britons nevertheless imbibed values and models that would always guide their public careers: respect for Classical rhythms of life, concern for literary artistry and style, love of the land, belief in a national purpose higher than material wealth, devotion to virtue and responsible citizenship, and a conception of government dedicated to the public good, not to the interest of a party. This chain of ideas, with its roots in Classical learning and Christian doctrine, but yet new and urgent, rested deeply and indelibly in the consciousness of the American nation-builders. Because the petty squabbles, political and literary, that thundered and whined in London echoed but faintly across the Atlantic, the ideas were particularly fresh and immediate to them. When ordering a large shipment of English books, Benjamin Franklin explained one reason for the popularity of their authors in America: "We know nothing of [the] personal Failings" of English writers, he wrote. "The Blemishes in their character never reach us, and therefore the bright and amiable part strikes us with its full Force. They have never offended us or any of our Friends, and we have no Competitions with them, and therefore we praise and admire them without Restraint."[43] Just as Americans could read and admire Swift largely untroubled by the internecine strife of London literary circles, they could also appreciate the ideas of an Addison or a Bolingbroke without too much discounting them because of their political prejudices.

Another part of Franklin's intellectual development also illustrates how eclectically the great Augustans impinged on transatlantic Britons. Franklin has often and properly been linked with Defoe as one of the supreme embodiments of the Puritan bourgeois ethic in Anglo-American culture, and he freely acknowledged his own debt to the London journalist. But Swift was also one of Franklin's literary heroes, and the Philadelphian's best satires, especially *The Rules by which a Great Empire May be Reduced to a Small One*, surely owe much to the author of *A Modest Proposal*. Furthermore, the great creations of Defoe and Swift, Robinson Crusoe and Lemuel Gulliver, are both good, solid Englishmen, alert, capable, simple, direct, and uncomplicated, suggesting that the basic virtues of English character could in some ways be assimilated to either the commercial or the tradi-tional world view. Franklin's own persona, created in his autobiography, is exactly the same sort of model Englishman, though in the New World there was no longer any need to create the fabulous surroundings Defoe and Swift found useful in old England. Franklin, then, had a firm, vig-orous sense of what an Englishman could be at his best, and he was con-fident that this sturdy goodness could be nourished and made use of in the new world of rising tradesmen and merchants in Philadelphia, as it had been in the Northamptonshire villages of his English ancestors. Yet, he was surely also aware of the chasm in culture and values between Defoe the London bankrupt and Swift the Dublin Dean.[44] Thus, the American, as he absorbed the dramatic delineations of English character, also responded to the great debates about the future of English culture and society, and Swift's "side" was fully as vivid and present to him as Defoe's.

The Opposition Whigs
and Bolingbroke

"Oppositionist" Crosscurrents, 1720–1742

ecause Alexander Pope and Jonathan Swift were, in the context of English political history, *Tory* writers there has been some tendency among historians to dismiss their influence in overwhelmingly Whig America, just as writers who later were close to the "American side" are often pictured as widely influential. In fact, however, the original polemical purposes of the Augustans faded in the course of time, and writers seen as highly partisan in their day, as well as those less political, all came to have prestige and influence simply as fine writers or wise preceptors. Far more important than distinctions, small or large, in the politics of the Augustan writers was their vivid evocation of a style, a sense of public life, and a world view that, at least in the long run and at long distances, would seem notable for its shared aspects.

In a deliberately eclectic fashion, Joseph Addison, admired and emulated in America as much as any English author, had particular skill, as Dr. Johnson put it, in voicing "just sentiments in elegant language." In his immensely popular play *Cato*, based on Plutarch's account of Cato the Younger (95–46 B.C.), who defended the ancient Roman virtues against the usurpations of the tyrant Caesar, Addison managed in many ways to transcend partisanship. He asked Pope to write a stirring, patriotic prologue that became as famous and often quoted as the play itself; a noted Whig wrote the epilogue. When *Cato* was first performed in London in 1713, Whigs cheered loudly, identifying Cato with their patriot hero the duke of Marlborough, whereas the Tories linked the English general to Caesar, the ruthless dictator, and applauded Cato as one of their own. The highlights of the play were Cato's declamations upholding love of country, fidelity to traditional virtues, and public-spiritedness. Corruption, intrigue, selfish ambition, and tyranny were condemned by implication and directly. Enthusiasm for the play and its sentiments spread to Britain's North American colonies, where it was reprinted at least seventeen times, performed before hundreds of audiences, and quoted or paraphrased on countless occasions. Even the famous Revolutionary epigrams of Patrick Henry and Nathan Hale in 1775 and 1776 were probably derived from the play.[1] In addition to these important Revolutionary uses, after 1789 Americans made Cato the model of the virtuous leader "bent on higher views . . . [seeking] to civilize the rude unpolished world . . . with wisdom, discipline, and lib'ral arts."[2] That Cato had been the leader of a community of Roman exiles in North Africa who sought to sustain the sterling qualities of the old republic when the "mother country" had become decadent and imperial made his life all the more apt as an example. As with Pope and Swift, then, when Americans read Addison they absorbed not only stylistic standards but also an esteemed world view and a public philosophy that scorned party and extolled active, moral leadership.

In another deliberate effort to transcend divisive issues, Addison wrote evenhandedly in his *Spectator* essays of the lives of the country gentleman Sir Roger de Coverley and the city merchant Sir Andrew Freeport. Like Pope and Swift, Addison admired Classical models of tradition, of authority, and of "good breeding," but he refused to see these values as incompatible with the new world of trade and commercial prosperity into which Britain, in his view, had entered irrevocably. Although Addison chides Sir Roger for his outmoded bigotry and country prejudices, the essayist nonetheless paints the squire as a generally admirable, even lovable gentleman—certainly not a personage to be scorned and discarded. Sir Andrew, on the other hand, though a man of good sense and enterprise who was helping to make England both prosperous and great, was warned, as Addison had expressed it in an earlier pamphlet (1708), that "minds that are altogether set on trade and profit, often contract a certain narrowness of temper, and at length become uncapable of great and generous resolutions."[3] Addison was keenly sensitive to the virtues of the old England revered by Pope and Swift and to the moral dangers that the new England of Daniel Defoe and Robert Walpole presented, but he would not look backward, and he saw no inevitable doom in the new economy and its attendant concerns and values. "The task before Addison . . . was to salvage the wholesome traditions of the past and blend them with a modernity purified of rawness and greed."[4]

Thus positioned between Defoe's enthusiasm for commercial values and the "projecting spirit" on one side and Swift's scorn for them on the other, Addison sought to teach his own ethic of moderation and sociability. He endeavored, he wrote in *Spectator*, Number 10, "to enliven morality with wit, and to temper wit with morality." This quality was one of those in Addison that so much impressed Benjamin Franklin as he molded his own prose style on the *Spectator* and that caused James Madison in old age to recommend Addison as the best author to encourage in young people "a lively sense of the duties, the virtues and the proprieties of life." (In the same letter Madison mentioned Swift as the best preceptor of good style.)[5] The American nation-builders, in sum, hoped that Addison's urbane, good-natured world outlook would flourish in the United States. But like all writers striving for synthesis and moderation, Addison ran the risk of being shallow and of being too bland to be helpful at critical junctures. If, for example, the new commercial ethic could not coexist with traditional values (as both Defoe and Swift asserted from opposite directions), then it simply obscured the issue to have, in Addison's symbolism, Sir Roger and Sir Andrew as congenial fellow members of the Spectator Club. Indeed, was the phrase *commercial ethic* itself a paradox, or even a contradiction?

Addison's writings and career amid the bitter polemics of his day foreshadow the dilemmas faced by American nation-builders. Was it possible to devise mechanisms of government based on moderation and accommodation and constructed with the unstated assumption that there are no unbridgeable conflicts of value and purpose? Or, were the world views that confronted each other in eighteenth-century moral discourse ultimately incompatible, with one side destined to win and the other to lose? More to the point politically, was the whole idea of national unity a menace or a chimera (especially in a free, commercial society), and was public life thus reduced to an arena of compromise and utility, as the Walpolean apologists often argued? The answers to such questions informed the definition of executive power in the Constitution of 1787 and gave shape to the exercise of it during the early presidencies.

Another group of English writers, retrospectively called "radical Whigs," urged on their readers a toleration and morality akin to Addison's, but they also developed a sharper critique of the political practices of Walpole's government, a critique that ran parallel in some respects to that articulated by Pope, Swift, and Bolingbroke. Devoted to the Glorious Revolution of 1688, the radical Whigs wanted to go on to more unqualified protection of English liberties, to further restraints on royal prerogative, and to a fuller representation of the interests of all the people in Parliament. They moved, in short, toward the purer ideas of liberty and of government by consent that found transatlantic expression in the Declaration of Independence and in the thought of such Revolutionary leaders as Thomas Jefferson, Samuel Adams, and Thomas Paine.

Interestingly, the ideas of the most eloquent of the early radical Whigs, John Trenchard, converged at critical points with those of Walpole's "Tory" critics. In his *History of Standing Armies in England* (1697) Trenchard warned that support of standing armies always led to a dangerous union of executive and legislative powers. Taking examples from the history of the Stuart kings, he contrasted the virtues of a citizen militia with the despotism of military rule. Swift mustered the same arguments in opposing Marlborough and his Whig supporters in the great polemical campaign of

1711 to 1713 against the seemingly endless War of the Spanish Succession, and again in 1721 when he wrote to Pope that "I always took Standing Armies to be only servants hired by the master of the family, for keeping his own children in slavery." In a pamphlet published in 1720 (the year the South Sea Bubble burst), *Considerations upon the State of Our Public Debts*, Trenchard complained of the excesses of the speculators and financiers, scorned the needless multiplication of offices and salaries, and yearned for "the noble spirit of our illustrious ancestors." After contrasting the virtue of a simpler England with the corruption of the new commercial Britain, Trenchard called for "a truly great man" who with a "generous and steady resolution [could] call up all our ancient virtue and restore so great a people to themselves"[6]—a longing implicit in Pope and Swift and developed fully in Bolingbroke's *Idea of a Patriot King*.

Trenchard's most important writings were *Cato's Letters* (4 volumes, 1724), written in collaboration with Thomas Gordon and first printed in the *London Journal*, 1720–1724. Outraged at the greed and scandal of the South Sea scheme, "Cato" warned that "publick Corruptions and Abuses have grown upon us: . . . Places and Employments, which ought not to be sold at all, are sold for treble Values . . . and as [public] Debts have been encreasing, and the People growing poor, Salaries have been augmented, and Pensions multiplied." Although "Cato" warily said he spoke of previous reigns in condemning corrupt rulers and was careful to make conventional obeisance to the present "most excellent King," his particular charges had obvious reference to contemporary events.[7] He thus blamed England's troubles in the first years of Walpole's dominance on "corruption" as it was understood in the Augustan Age: the ability of government (Walpole), through its patronage, manipulation of the public debt, and dispensing of offices in the armed forces, to eclipse the monarchy and to control Parliament in accordance with special interests. These charges were precisely those the Tory critics were laying against Walpole, a convergence underscored in 1731 when Bolingbroke's opposition paper, the *Craftsman*, approvingly quoted *Cato's Letters:* "Our principles of government seem to be generally the same. . . . The object of our complaint is the same. . . . Where ["Cato"] left off I began . . . against the mischievous consequences of venality and corruption." The opposition to Walpole in the *Craftsman* and in Parliament, in fact, took up the two key charges worked out by Trenchard and other radical Whigs at the end of the seventeenth century: that the maintenance of standing armies in peacetime threatened English liberties and that the influence "the Ministry" gained in Parliament through offices, pensions, and bribes upset the ancient balance of the constitution. These themes, moreover, both emphasized the "patriotism" of the opposition and furnished precisely the rhetoric American revolutionaries would need to denounce the armies of General Thomas Gage and the political machinations of Lord North. It was this convergence of ideologies, expressed in brilliant polemics, that "as much as any single influence . . . shaped the political awareness of eighteenth-century Americans. . . . [It formed] the assumptions and expectations, [and] furnished not merely the vocabulary but the grammar of thought, the apparatus by which the world was perceived."[8] If the radical Whigs provided good, English ammunition for the American Revolutionary leaders to use against their "Walpole," Lord North, they also were of special utility after Independence, when they supplied a treasure house of arguments and devices for frames of government keyed to restraints on power in general, and on executive power in particular.

Although there was much that "Cato" and Bolingbroke agreed on, there were also profound if temporarily submerged differences between them that would become significant in America as attention shifted from revolution to nation-building. The radical Whigs saw the restraining of government, the enlarging of personal liberties, the extension of consent, the restoration of "balance," and the liberation of Parliament from ministerial domination as the means of upsetting a corrupt, manipulative administration. In condemning the South Sea scheme, for example, "Cato" had concentrated on how "Monopolies and Exclusive Companies [were] pernicious to Trade" and how they "influence and hurt our Government." The danger Britain faced from "the Stock-Jobbers, Brokers, and those who cabal with them" arose not from the new wealth engendered by trade, which taken by itself benefited the nation, but from the *monopoly* given to the South Sea Company. This arrangement enabled the company not only to rig prices to its enrichment and to the detriment of the public but, even worse, to bribe officials and legislatures to continue its privileges and to rescue it from the fruits of its own greed and imprudence. Monopolies were thus exempted from the useful discipline of survival in the marketplace that kept independent traders industrious and vigilant. "All beneficial Trades are most successfully carried on by free and open Commerce," "Cato" concluded, as he laid bare the foundations of nascent English liberalism: "Monopolies are equally dangerous in Trade, in Politicks, and Religion: A free Trade, a free Government, and a free Liberty of Conscience, are the Rights and Blessings of Mankind."[9] Although "Cato" scorned corruption and parliamentary dependence on ministerial largess as much as the Tory critics did and as much honored fidelity to the public interest, his "solution" was more freedom and openness, and more dispersal of power, everywhere.

Bolingbroke, writing in 1733, was equally horrified at the South Sea scandal and at the manipulation of Parliament by money power, but he looked for succor to a traditional, broad-based "country spirit." The danger to Britain under Walpole, Bolingbroke insisted, was not that preroga-

tive would openly enslave the people, but that personal liberty, the independence of Parliament, the integrity of the crown, and the welfare of
the nation would all be undermined by a minister who gained unprecedented power by pandering to the needs of the stockjobbers. "If there was
merit . . . in opposing the asserters of prerogative formerly," Bolingbroke
avowed, then "there is great merit in opposing the asserters of corruption
now, and exposing the means by which this expedient may be improved to
the ruin of our constitution, and therefore of our liberty." He called for all
patriotic Tories, dissenters, and Whigs—that is, all those who believed in
ancient English liberties and opposed party and faction—to come together "to secure the independency of parliaments against the new influence of the crown [manipulated by Walpole], and against corruption." It
was necessary to thwart "one" who, lacking virtuous support, "gleaned up
. . . a faction, composed of the refuse of all parties." Bolingbroke's answer
to the danger of the corrupt influence of money power on government,
then, was not, as "Cato" argued, the removal of restraints and elimination
of privileges, but for good men to "lay aside . . . groundless distinctions,
. . . hold fast their integrity, and support with spirit and perseverance the
cause of their country."[10] The need, generally, was not for less restraint that
would disperse power, but rather for convergence, order, and harmony.

During the American Revolution the leaders on the whole accepted the
"radical Whig" ideology and program as basic to the government they
sought to establish. But its limitations, evident in America in the generation after 1776, were its neglect of the role of positive leadership and
legitimate authority and its failure to provide a system for the moral and
patriotic guidance of the nation/community—as John Winthrop and the
king of Brobdingnag would have recognized instantly. There was in some
radical Whig thought a supposition that somehow public morality and
even uncorrupted leadership would arise spontaneously from "the people,"
a faith that many American revolutionaries saw as dubious and uncertain.
In radical Whig political theory a vacuum of sorts existed in the space traditionally filled by an active, guiding executive. This lacuna led Walpole's
Tory critics toward the solution articulated in classic form in Bolingbroke's
Idea of a Patriot King, first circulated in England in 1738. Bolingbroke's
leadership proposals, moreover, made his writings especially pertinent to
the early molders and holders of executive office in America when it seemed
necessary for them to move beyond the problem of merely preventing tyranny. The "Country" party in Britain encompassing Whigs and Tories,
though united in its opposition to Walpole and the "Court" party, prescribed both "limited government" and "elevated government," a combination implicit in Jefferson's library arrangement where Bolingbroke's
Patriot King is followed immediately by *Cato's Letters*,[11] and acknowledged
again when he termed Paine and Bolingbroke "both advocates for human

liberty." The necessity of restraining or dispersing the powers of government, in short, was not the only theme sounded by Walpole's opponents; the opposition also had its own theory of more positive government.

The Idea of a Patriot King

Jefferson's linking of Bolingbroke with Paine seems paradoxical, and even contradictory, largely because of Bolingbroke's ambiguous political career. As a brilliant young Tory minister under Queen Anne, Henry St. John, later Viscount Bolingbroke, was himself high-handedly partisan both in opposing the Whig magnates and in quarreling with other Tories. He received both praise and condemnation for his negotiation of the Treaty of Utrecht (1713), but at the moment of his expected elevation to executive dominance, Queen Anne died (1714) and the Whigs regained power under George I. Fearing imprisonment or execution, Bolingbroke fled to France, where for a year or two he was a leading counselor to James Stuart, the Old Pretender—treason at that time. Soon, however, dismissed by James yet exiled from England, Bolingbroke repudiated Jacobitism, married a French noblewoman, took up residence near Orléans, and, often visiting with Voltaire, Madame du Deffand, and other luminaries, cultivated his always strong scholarly inclinations. Voltaire wrote that he "found in this illustrious Englishman all the learning of his country and all the politeness of ours. . . . This man who has all his life been plunged in pleasure and business has still been able to learn everything and to remember everything."[12]

In 1723 Walpole, securely in power, allowed Bolingbroke to return to England. Because he was still banned from Parliament, however, he was unable to resume his political career. Hence, until he died in 1751 Bolingbroke lived in apparent retirement, partly in England and partly in France, but in fact he wrote incessantly on politics and intrigued constantly with shifting alliances of Walpole's opponents. Because he had been tainted with treason, had been notoriously partisan as a minister of state, and had both acted the rake and written as an infidel, Bolingbroke could not escape assaults on his character that, especially in his lifetime, tended to discredit his political writings. One of Walpole's political hacks, for example, wrote that Bolingbroke's career was like that of "a Carted Whore, who had been whipt out of her native Town or Country; and upon Promise of Amendment of Life suffered to return," takes it on herself "to read Lectures upon Morality and Chastity; and in her scolding Fits to rave against the good Women of the Neighborhood as *saucy Creatures of Fortune*." Another noted with heavy sarcasm that Pope had dedicated his widely acclaimed *Essay on Man* to "that Pattern of exemplary Piety, Chastity, and Virtue, the Lord Viscount Bolingbroke." Indeed Swift himself had written in 1711, in the midst of Bolingbroke's public exertions and revelries, that "he was gone to his devotions, and to receive the sacrament; several rakes did the same; it was not for piety, but employments; according to act of parliament."[13] Nevertheless, Bolingbroke's brilliant, intrepid campaign against Walpole and the interests supporting him, and his implanting in opposition thought the conception of a patriot leader who would restore an ancient morality and way of life, had an important impact on eighteenth-century political thinking, especially as the scandals and animosities of Bolingbroke's career faded into history.

When Bolingbroke returned to England in 1723 he resumed his close relationship with Swift, Pope, John Gay, and the other writers who during Queen Anne's reign had entered the lists against the "Modernist" world view of Bernard Mandeville, Defoe, and Walpole. The circle developed a nourishing intimacy as it marshaled its wisdom, learning, and wit in a renewed campaign to turn England away from what it saw as a vulgar ethic and a pusillanimous public life. Swift wrote Pope that he looked "upon my Lord Bolingbroke and us two, as a peculiar Triumvirate . . . fittest to converse with one another." Pope replied that Bolingbroke was "pleas'd with your placing him in the Triumvirate between your self and me," and he later celebrated Bolingbroke's congeniality and good sense:

> There ST. JOHN mingles with my friendly bowl
> The Feast of Reason and the Flow of soul.

In fact, the three men were stimulating and encouraging one another to mount what they hoped would be crushing assaults on the age of Walpole. Bolingbroke wrote Swift from Pope's house in 1728 that "his *Dulness* [i.e., Pope's *Dunciad*] grows and flourishes. . . . It will indeed be a noble work: the many will stare at it, the few will smile, and all his Patrons from Bickerstaff to Gulliver will rejoice, to see themselves adorn'd in that immortal piece."[14]

Years later Benjamin Rush in America recognized the important cultural meaning of the work of this anti-Walpole circle when after complaining that "commerce . . . when pursued closely, sinks the man into a machine," he quoted Pope's couplet complimenting Bolingbroke. It exemplified, Rush thought, a style of life much superior to that of merchants, who "have little relish for the 'feast of reason and the flow of soul.'"[15] Rush and the other American founders sought to partake of "a feast of reason," but they wanted it flavored with a "flow of soul" rather than with the "thousand cunning tricks" Mandeville linked to "the Common Good." Pope's memorable words had wider meaning and influence, probably, than any learned tracts and treatises did and helped give Bolingbroke a prestige of immeasurable significance to Americans who read his political writings. The rhetorical and poetic perfection of Pope's couplet about Bolingbroke, which came so easily to Rush's mind as epitomizing much that he cherished, illustrates the enormous advantage Bolingbroke's circle possessed as a result of its members' sheer skill as writers.

Unable to forge an effective opposition in Parliament, Bolingbroke worked with his friends to develop an intellectual critique. He strengthened its political thrust in a newspaper, the *Craftsman*, which from 1727 to 1735 he edited and often largely wrote. Usually in sharp, wounding pieces excoriating the deeds of Walpole, his Parliament, and the Georgian court, but occasionally in longer, more sustained series of articles, Bolingbroke gave theoretical force to the opposition in a display of polemical journalism at times rivaling Swift's stunning performance in the *Examiner* twenty years earlier.[16] Bolingbroke's best theoretical efforts were twenty-four essays printed in the *Craftsman* in 1730–1731 and later published as *Remarks on the History of England* and another series printed in 1733–1734, published as *A Dissertation upon Parties*. Both were widely circulated in America and frequently advertised separately, or included in collections of his *Works* or *Political Tracts*. John Adams revealed the particular impact of the brilliant Tory journalism on young men interested in style as well as politics when he noted in 1765 that "no Books were more proper for . . . oratory, than the Examiner, Craftsman and such Controversial Writings of the best Hands."[17] The contrast with Walpole's "hacks," who, as we have seen, openly scorned attention to style, was unmistakable and had the effect, of course, of denigrating the content of their arguments in the eyes of aspiring writers.

In the *Remarks* Bolingbroke surveyed English history to 1640, emphasizing the difference between evil, faction-dominated reigns and monarchs who served the national interest through fidelity to the "ancient, balanced constitution" that preserved liberty. He depended on the Huguenot historian Paul de Rapin's *History of England* in tracing the ancient origins of English liberties and evoked the Classical expounder of cyclical and balance-of-power motifs in history, Polybius, to show why Britain under Walpole was headed for faction-ridden tyranny. Filled with maxims of good government and pointed warnings of the many ways liberty could be lost, *Remarks* seemed strikingly applicable to events of other times or places. An observer of George III's efforts to control the colonies in 1774–1775, or of Federalist measures of repression in 1798 (or of Richard Nixon in 1969–1974, for that matter), could scarcely miss the force of Bolingbroke's condemnation of Henry VII: "By making an ill use of his power, the king was the real author of all the disorders in the state, . . . and yet, the better to prevent such disorders . . . farther powers were intrusted to him. Because he had governed ill, it was put in his power to govern worse; and liberty was undermined, for fear it should be overthrown."[18] The *Remarks*, though, were finely tuned by Bolingbroke to his own partisan purposes. For example, when he blamed Henry VIII's slide into oppression on his evil "prime minister" Cardinal Wolsey, Walpole's alleged influence over George II was the immediate target, just as Americans in 1770–1776 would see Lord North as Wolsey—or as John Dryden's Achitophel.

A *Dissertation upon Parties* brought Bolingbroke's commentary on English history down to the 1730s. The theme was predictable to readers of the *Craftsman*: he pictured the tumultuous party strife of the years 1640–1714 as having given way to a new contest. On one side stood a "Country" allegiance (Bolingbroke's) that accepted the principles of 1688, revered ancient English liberties, and sought the welfare of the whole nation. But there was also a "Court" party (Walpole's) that by systematic corruption of Parliament and manipulation of the king had not only destroyed the liberty-preserving balance in the constitution but also had given over the government to a "party," the denizens of the new economic order, the speculators and stockjobbers whose wealth and greed controlled the nation. The sad, horrible facts in 1735, Bolingbroke concluded, were that the public debt as it had been manipulated by the Whig magnates since the 1690s was "the great source of corruption" and that "the power of money as the world is now constituted is real power."[19]

In these two works Bolingbroke presented his analysis, so to speak, of English politics in his day, identifying historical trends, the special interests exerting influence, their impact on society and the government, and the derangement of the constitution thus produced. His evocation of the dangers of faction, the need for "balance," and the harmful effects of "moneyed power" would appear in the American nation-building era to be strikingly pertinent, and these ideas readily became axioms of its political science. His assumption that "parties, even before they degenerate into absolute factions, are still numbers of men associated together for certain purposes and certain interests, which are not . . . those of the community . . . ,"[20] for example, was the same as Madison's in *The Federalist*, Number 10: "A faction [is] . . . a number of citizens, whether amounting to a majority or minority of the whole, who are united and actuated by some common impulse of passion, or of interest, adverse . . . to the permanent and aggregate interests of the community." Bolingbroke's analysis of the dangers of factious government was also essentially that of the radical Whigs, a circumstance nicely demonstrated not only by his frequent quotation of *Cato's Letters*, as we have noted, but also by the liberal use of *The Dissertation upon Parties* in the radical Whig treatise most immediately influential in America in the 1770s, James Burgh's *Political Disquisitions* (1774–1775).

Bolingbroke's greatest importance for American nation-building, how-ever, did not arise from his "oppositionist" thought. He is especially sig-nificant precisely because at the point of prescribing, so to speak, for the ills of party, he did *not* follow the radical Whigs in emphasizing structural changes to protect liberties, reform Parliament, and restrain the ministry. Nor did he depend, most radically, on the judgment and moral sense of "the people." Rather, Bolingbroke pointed straight at the character and re-sponsibility of the leader. As the *Craftsman* had asserted in 1728, when corruption is placed "on the Pinnacle of Power, in the very Heart of a first *Minister*, it will no longer be contained within any bounds; the Contagion will take and spread, and the whole Country become infected." Boling-broke increasingly hammered away at the theme that however useful par-ticular reforms might be, in the long run a nation could not escape from the truth that "the head of a state is responsible for the moral health of the body politic"[21]—an axiom fixed in the minds of readers who had also re-cently enjoyed *Gulliver's Travels*.

This emphasis on the need for virtuous leadership is central to Boling-broke's culminating work on politics, the *Idea of a Patriot King*, written in 1738 and addressed to Crown Prince Frederick, whom Bolingbroke hoped would soon succeed George II and humble Walpole. The tract was edited and circulated privately by Pope in 1740, first published in 1749, and often reprinted after that on both sides of the Atlantic. In delineating the character of his patriot king Bolingbroke began with the conventional wisdom of eighteenth-century Britain. Monarchy, he wrote, was the best form of government, and a limited, hereditary monarchy the best form of monarchy; that is, the structure devised in England in the 1640s and in 1689 was the ideal. He thus repudiated both the doctrine of the divine right of kings (especially as espoused by one of the worst English kings, James I) and the idea of an elected monarch. The former gave rise to ar-rogant pretensions and the latter to intrigue and faction. (Ironically, in a tract glorifying a *good* monarch, Bolingbroke anticipated both part of Paine's case against the kings of England and Antifederalist fears about vir-tually any device for choosing a republican executive.) Bolingbroke favored the hereditary principle as useful symbolically and less objectionable than other succession mechanisms, but he also insisted, in Puritan-Lockean fashion, that monarchs were limited by higher law. That is, they have au-thority (legitimate power) only insofar as they rule in the interests of the people, in defense of their liberties, in accord with the well-being of the nation, and in harmony with the grand design of the universe. Any other kind of monarchy is tyranny. "The good of the people is the ultimate and true end of government," Bolingbroke stated, and because the "greatest good of a people is their liberty" and the balanced constitution of England best protects liberty, "to defend and maintain the freedom of such constitutions will appear most sacred to a Patriot King." Bolingbroke even declared that "we may justly take arms against a prince whose right to govern we once acknowledged and who by subsequent acts has forfeited that right."[22] The *Idea of a Patriot King* as much upheld natural law and the right of revolution as did the Declaration of Independence itself.

Having set natural law ground rules for the patriot king, Bolingbroke next expounded his particular usefulness: he could restore and uphold a virtue and a patriotism unlikely to flourish under any other form of government. In coming to this conclusion Bolingbroke used as his exemplars of evil Walpole's regime and Machiavelli's political philosophy. Written after Bolingbroke had opposed Walpole for a lifetime and after Walpole had been in power nearly twenty years, the *Patriot King* was a culminating blow. Following on the details of the long opposition campaign in the *Craftsman*, Bolingbroke summarized his case: "The greatest iniquity of the Minister [Walpole], on whom the whole iniquity ought to [be] charged since he has been so long in possession of the whole power, is the constant endeavor he has employed to corrupt the morals of men." By this corruption Bolingbroke meant not so much bribes, dishonest bookkeeping, and so on (in fact, Walpole for his time was probably unusually efficient and personally honest), as Walpole's surrender to the commercial spirit and the factional approach to government recently condemned in *A Dissertation upon Parties*. The most serious *public* corruption was against "the minds of men, which this Minister has narrowed to personal regards alone"—"see all in self," in Pope's condemnation. Beyond simply acting factiously (and therefore corruptly), Bolingbroke scolded, "the Minister preaches corruption aloud and constantly, like an impudent missionary of vice."[23] Walpole's crime was not only that he ruled Britain by pandering to special interests and by manipulating the king and his patronage but also that he candidly and cynically defended this system as the "best" form of government, that is, that it most enhanced British wealth and trade and offered most opportunity to the enterprising men of the kingdom. The issue was between Walpole's celebration of the ethic of commerce and selfishness and the maintenance of a hallowed morality and public-spiritedness under a patriot leader, between a Lilliputian and a Brobdingnagian nation.

As Bolingbroke had chosen to write in the conventional pose of offering advice to a prince, he used Machiavelli's *Prince* both as a model form and as the work offering the most evil counsel to rulers. Indeed, Bolingbroke so closely followed the outline of Machiavelli and others who wrote "manuals for rulers" that Pope was able in 1740 to add chapter headings similar to those Machiavelli had used in *The Prince*.[24] Bolingbroke asked the same questions—"what are the duties of kings, how should he conduct himself with regard to parties, how should he judge the ability of ministers" and so on—but gave opposite answers because Machiavelli "requires no more than the appearance of [virtue]." "I would have the virtue [of the ruler] real," Bolingbroke asserted. In a distinction of central importance, Bolingbroke accused Machiavelli of counseling rulers not to be wise, but only to cultivate its counterfeit—cunning. All the maxims he offered to princes for "the amplification of their power, the extent of their dominion, and the subjection of their people," therefore, were to Bolingbroke wrongheaded because they were "without the consideration of any duty owing to God or man, or any regard to the morality or immorality of actions."[25]

Bolingbroke wrote in the ancient tradition of offering principled advice to rulers, exemplified in the Middle Ages by Thomas Aquinas's *De regimine principum* and in the Renaissance by Erasmus's *The Education of a Christian Prince*.[26] In condemning Machiavelli's amorality and in extolling the "civic humanism" of Erasmus, Bolingbroke was making a broadside cultural assault on the egotistical, opportunistic, commercial values of Defoe, Mandeville, and Walpole. The trouble, Bolingbroke complained, was that "men are apt to make themselves the measure of all being, [and] make themselves the final cause of all creation, [and believe] that the world was made for man, the earth for him to inhabit, and all the luminous bodies in the immense expanse around us for him to gaze at."[27] Such narrow self-centeredness, elaborated into a public philosophy by Walpole and his minions, Bolingbroke intoned, echoing Pope's ringing couplets, was destroying everything that was valuable in English life.

The remedy Bolingbroke proposed, however, was not to fetter the executive but rather to improve him, to make him a patriot king. A people taught to admire selfishness, a rising class wallowing in a "rapacious luxury," and a government resting on cynical manipulation, he felt, were on an almost irreversible downward spiral. Certainly the interested parties who controlled wealth and power could not be expected to reform themselves. More ominously, the people, from their own resources and institutions, could not restore themselves to virtue. They were too much at the mercy of their rulers, the greed of powerful factions, and the spreading of moral decay to be able to accomplish their own salvation. Even structural changes would be ineffectual: "To preserve liberty by new laws and new schemes of government whilst the corruption of a people continues and grows is absolutely impossible." To Bolingbroke, change had to begin where the poison now centered: at the top. A patriot king could, "without violence to his people, renew the spirit of liberty in their minds" by banishing "corruption [as] . . . an expedient of government." Under such a monarch the people "will not only cease to do evil but learn to do well, for, by rendering public virtue and real capacity the sole means of acquiring any degree of power or profit in the state, he will set the passions of their hearts on the side of liberty and good government." Furthermore, by presenting to his people an example of genuinely virtuous character and disinterested rule, a patriot king could be "the most powerful of all reformers, . . . a sort of standing miracle." The final triumph would be that "a new people will seem to arise with a new king."[28]

Having outlined so central a role for the ruler, Bolingbroke was at pains to expound on this patriot king's education, character, conduct, and policies. In a section with special meaning to Britons on both sides of the Atlantic while the future George III was coming of age during the 1750s, Bolingbroke emphasized that monarchs-to-be must have their education carefully supervised so that they become habituated to "great principles and . . . great virtues." Consistent with his view that the character of the ruler will have a marked effect on his people, Bolingbroke emphasized that only courtiers and tutors themselves good and patriotic should surround youthful princes. Ready at hand was the opposite example of Louis XIV, who as a child-king under the tutelage of the Machiavellian Cardinal Mazarin had learned the haughtiness, imperiousness, and deviousness that marked his bloody and tyrannical reign.[29] Jefferson, who spent a lifetime fretting over and planning for the education of "the aristocracy of talent and virtue," who should rule in a republic, would have agreed. Like Plato, Erasmus, and John Winthrop, neither Bolingbroke nor the Sage of Monticello ever doubted that the character of those who rule is of cardinal importance. And though Bolingbroke endorsed such conventional traits of good character as generosity and kindliness, he made clear that he had most in mind the need for the ruler to be patriotic, or uncorrupted, as defined by the Renaissance civic humanists; that is, to transcend party, faction, and self-interest so that he could attend to the public welfare, a need not at all diminished—indeed, in Jefferson's view, enlarged—in a shift from a monarchy to a republic.

Bolingbroke attended particularly to the rearing of the future ruler because his personal behavior and his manner of living had to set a proper moral example for his people. "A little merit in a prince is seen and felt by numbers: it is multiplied. . . . A little failing . . . is multiplied in the same manner." History had proven repeatedly that "the virtues of the king [could be] lost in the vices of the man." Mark Antony had destroyed his public usefulness by "his effeminate progress up the Nile," and Louis XV, "a mere rake," by his example was single-handedly destroying first the moral tone and then, inexorably, the dignity and greatness of a nation. It was no wonder, Bolingbroke noted, that a people, whether Romans, or Frenchmen, or Britons, who first accepted libertines as governors would soon accept tyrants. There simply was no escaping the maxim that "the character of a great and good king [must] be founded in that of a great and good man."[30]

As he began his reign, the first need of the patriot king was "to purge his court." The "crowds of spies, parasites, and sycophants [who] surround the throne under the patronage of [corrupt] ministers" had to be chased away, and even "a sort of men too low to be much regarded and too high to be quite neglected, the lumber of every administration, the furniture of every court" who knew only mean-spirited government, also had to be removed. Then, after the patriot king had selected worthy, more virtuous advisers, he would be able to "govern like the common father of his people," as in a patriarchal family where "the head and all the members are united by one common interest and animated by one common spirit." Instead of putting himself at the head of one party in order to govern his people, a patriot king "will put himself at the head of his people in order to govern or, more properly, to subdue all parties." A king who ruled in allegiance with a party (as George I and George II had done in giving power to Walpole) might "share the spoils of a ruined nation . . . [but] such a king is a tyrant, and such a government is a conspiracy."[31] As monarchs who had shunned such complicity and been patriot rulers Bolingbroke cited Henry IV of France and Elizabeth I of England—the heroes of Voltaire's epic the *Henriade*, which he rewrote in England from 1726 to 1728 and for which Bolingbroke was both a counselor and chief subscriber, taking twenty copies at one guinea each.[32]

Benjamin Franklin showed a similar admiration when he compared the hopes for government under the Constitution of 1787 with the aspirations of the French monarch. He wrote a friend in Paris at the close of the Federal Convention, "I do not see why you might not in Europe carry the Project of good Henry the 4th into Execution, by forming a Federal Union and One Grand Republick of all its different States and Kingdoms, by means of a like Convention, for we had many Interests to reconcile." In fact, idealizations of patriot rulers, and literary conventions ascribing to them all sorts of moral and public salvation, were commonplace as the Western world struggled with the reconceptions of leadership entailed by the rise of the commercial ethic. In Molière's *Tartuffe*, for example, just as religious hypocrisy and commercial "morality" seemed to have triumphed, a deus ex machina, in the form of an officer of the king (Louis XIV), exposed the villain and articulated the functions of the patriot leader:

> Sir, all is well, rest easy, and be grateful.
> We serve a Prince to whom all sham is hateful,
> A Prince who sees into our inmost hearts,
> And can't be fooled by any trickster's arts.
> His royal soul, though generous and human,
> Views all things with discernment and acumen;
> His sovereign reason is not lightly swayed,
> All his judgments are discreetly weighed.[33]

In imaging for English readers ideas of patriot kings, Bolingbroke knew that however much Britain might be moving toward limited, parliamentary government, strong sentiment still favored the ancient conceptions of active leadership that earlier had been so captivating to John Winthrop and Cotton Mather.

In scorning government "by the management of parties and factions in the state," Bolingbroke again reserved his greatest contempt for those who had the gall to extol such conduct by converting "a factious habit and a factious notion . . . into a notion of policy and honor." The ultimate corruption was to "contend that it is not enough to be vicious by practice and habit but that it is necessary to be so by principle. They make themselves missionaries of faction as well as of corruption: they recommend both. They deride all such as imagine it possible, or fit, to retain truth, integrity, and a disinterested regard to the public in public life and pronounce every man a fool who is not ready to act like a knave." To assume "that popular divisions must be cultivated because popular union cannot be procured," Bolingbroke asserted, was like saying that "poison must be poured into a wound because it cannot be healed." His point was not that self-interest and faction could be eliminated from human affairs, "especially in free countries, where the passions of men are less restrained by authority," nor was he "wild enough to suppose that a Patriot King can change human nature." Rather, he supposed enough reason in men so that a virtuous ruler might "defeat the designs and break the spirit of faction, instead of partaking in one and assuming the other."[34]

A deep attachment to precisely this hope, that a good leader will resist the unwelcome intrusions of party, characterized the first six American presidents. They supposed, like Bolingbroke, that a chief executive might display "a disinterested regard to the public in public life," that he would not "partake" in the spirit of party, and, most pointedly, that he had a duty not to "poison" politics by exalting partisanship in the nation's leaders.

The legitimate power of a good ruler, Bolingbroke observed, rested on his popularity with the people, his pursuit of their well-being, and the defense of their liberties. With such leadership, "things so seldom allied as empire and liberty are intimately mixed." Thus, he concluded, under a patriot king "concord will appear, brooding peace and prosperity on the happy land, joy sitting in every face, content in every heart, a people unoppressed, undisturbed, unalarmed, busy to improve their private property and the public stock."[35]

Legacy for Leadership in America

A generation before the Declaration of Independence, then, to the critical diagnosis Whig opposition leaders had already made of Walpole's party, government, and public philosophy, Bolingbroke had added a prescription that gave a crucial, positive role to executive leadership. That his tract was short, cogent, and eloquent, furthermore, gave it heightened appeal and impact. Even its immediate political purpose, to urge that a particular patriot prince supplant a particular corrupt regime, would enhance its meaning should it again appear to Englishmen (or ex-Englishmen anywhere) that greed, corruption, partisanship, and tyranny threatened public liberty and national self-respect. Just as the principles and programs of the "radical Whig" part of Walpole's opposition were of special use to the rebels of 1776 (and in some degree remained a vital part of American political ideology), a later generation preoccupied with nation-building might find special meaning in the *Idea of a Patriot King*.

It was not the merit or influence of Bolingbroke's tract standing by itself, however, that made it useful and important. He managed to draw together the moral force of an impressive array of traditions, still in varying degrees alive and well. Many of his readers on both sides of the Atlantic, for example, would have appreciated his Classical assumptions that the public good was vastly more than the sum of private goods and that a leader had a solemn obligation to act positively and disinterestedly to achieve the greater good—propositions highlighted by contrast with the increasingly candid celebration of enlightened self-interest as a sufficient public philosophy. Bolingbroke could also evoke in his readers a strong, lingering affection for the tradition of the Christian prince, insofar as he emphasized the benefit to all the people of political power exercised by a virtuous, nonpartisan ruler. That this sort of leadership had also been extolled for a century or more by Puritan ideologues who deemphasized hereditary aspects meant, additionally, that even Bolingbroke's readers inclined to discount his monarchical sympathies could agree with his view of the *characteristics* of the good ruler. And this concurrence would be of increased significance in a part of the British Empire where Puritan sentiment was especially strong and at a time when hostility to a particular king would cast the very idea of a hereditary monarch into disrepute.

The most immediate, influential crystallization of the emphasis on virtuous, positive, patriotic leadership, though, came from Bolingbroke's own circle of literary friends. That Bolingbroke was close personally as well as intellectually to the acknowledged masters of the literary style admired and emulated in America until well into the nineteenth century had the useful effect again and again of putting him in impressive company. Bolingbroke's conception of patriot leadership became part and parcel of the moral and cultural critique that, as we shall see, found wide response throughout Anglo-American society. It is not so much that the *Idea of a Patriot King* had substantial direct influence (although such was likely the case), but rather that the essay drew together and expressed eloquently ideas that were widely popular when Bolingbroke wrote and that remained ready at hand for a century. The idea of a patriot king, finally, resting on a political critique compatible with the radical Whig ideology of the American Revolution, was more pertinent and directly useful than that ideology was when the time came to fashion an executive office in the new nation. Swift had already epitomized, and idealized, this tradition-laden and deeply attractive public philosophy in a sentence in 1711: "A wise and good Prince, at the Head of an able Ministry, and of a Senate freely chosen, all united to pursue the true Interest of their Country, is a Power, against which, the little inferior Politicks of any Faction, will be able to make no long Resistance." "*Vox Populi*," Swift asserted, would be "indisputably declarative on the same Side."[36]

❦ 4 ❦

Executive Power in
the Era of the
American Revolution

William Pitt and George III: Ambiguous Models

Although political events in the half-century following the writing of the *Idea of a Patriot King* (1738) compelled attention primarily to the need to restrain executive power, a sense of the uses of strong, nonpartisan leadership did not disappear. The vogue of Jonathan Swift and Alexander Pope, together with the wide popularity of Lord Bolingbroke's works, provided eloquent support for such a sense. Moreover, the career of the elder William Pitt and then the high hopes for the young George III kept real the notion of the virtuous national leader. Pitt had begun his career in Parliament in the 1730s as one of the relentless critics of Robert Walpole, chastising him for his corruption and especially for his degrading, pusillanimous foreign policy. Pitt, yearning for English grandeur and power, was among the "Boy Patriots" who gathered at Bolingbroke's estate and looked to him as an elder statesman. Loathed by George II and denied office by Walpole and his successors for ten years, Pitt finally forced himself on the ministry in 1746 as paymaster general of the forces. To the astonishment of cynical politicians, but to cheers from the public, Pitt pointedly refused to profit from the perquisites of this potentially lucrative office. Earning a reputation as an honest patriot, he served brilliantly during the War of the Austrian Succession but remained often at odds with George II and his ministers. He found himself again an outcast during the disastrous beginning (1754) of the "Great War for the Empire."

As the nation fretted at its factious, self-indulgent ministers and feared invasion by France, Pennsylvania agent Benjamin Franklin arrived in London. Puzzled at the disarray, Franklin saw Pitt as the nation's (and America's) salvation and exulted at his accession to power in 1758. Pitt's "universal Character of Integrity," Franklin wrote, "is what gave him his present Power, rather than the Favour of the King which he had not, or Party Interest." In addition to his honesty, Pitt was also a man of great abilities, and "when Ability and Integrity meet in the same Person, his Power of doing Good must be greater," Franklin noted admiringly. A contemporary observed that in Parliament, "where the public good is so much talked of, and private Interest only pursued, [Pitt] set out with acting the Patriot, and performed that part so ably that he was adopted by the Publick [as] their Chief, or rather their only unsuspected Champion. . . . He managed [the war effort] with such ability, that while he served the King . . . he still preserved all his credit and popularity with the Publick."[1] In a way unique in the oligarchical politics of eighteenth-century Britain, Pitt managed for a time to espouse a patriot ideology that was both antiparty and anticorruption and to act the part of the leader whose autonomy and personal virtue let him place the national good above desire for power or profit.

In uncanny ways, that is, Pitt echoed, for colonials especially, themes that ran through and across Anglo-American politics for a century or two but which had received their most articulate formulation by Bolingbroke and the anti-Walpole writers of the 1720s and 1730s. An authority on Anglo-American politics of the period from 1660 to 1775 has noted, for example, that there was in Pitt's speeches of the decade 1765–1775 "a reiteration of the ideas in the *Craftsman* which makes him clearly the last British link in the tradition of agrarian populism stretching from the country gentlemen of the 1630s through Shaftesbury, the Tory writers of Queen Anne's time, and Bolingbroke, to Jefferson."[2] The point is not that clear connections and alliances are evident—the first earl of Shaftesbury, Tory publicists, and Bolingbroke in opposition make a mixed bag—but rather that someone like Thomas Jefferson, though heir to a "radical Whig" tradition that sometimes sounded like "agrarian populism," also hearkened to voices that transformed conventional antiparty, anticorruption sentiments into the belief that patriot leadership, of the sort provided by Pitt for a few glorious years, could be the salvation of the nation.

To those familiar with the inner workings of British politics, Pitt's standing as a patriot leader collapsed when he too seemed to become, like all the rest, intent only on personal rewards. In 1761, Horace Walpole wrote that he had at first admired Pitt for having "fallen in love with my father's enemies, because they served my country" and that he had "adored Mr. Pitt, as if I was just come from school and reading Livy's lies of Brutus and Camillus, and Fabius." But when Pitt accepted first a sinecure and then a title from a monarch he scorned, he became a common politician. "Alack! alack! Mr. Pitt loves an estate as well as my Lord Bath," Walpole exclaimed.[3] To Americans, though, Pitt remained a shining example of virtue, talent, and patriotism in a leader: he showed what could happen when national interests and executive authority triumphed over corruption, competition for offices, factious squabbles, and a waste of blood and treasure. That Pitt's policies, both in power and in opposition, favored worldwide imperial interests, as opposed to narrower, European strategies, further encouraged colonial Britons to picture him as a wide-visioned, enlightened leader.

With the accession of George III in 1760, amid the triumphs organized by Pitt, Britons in America shared the elation of having at long last an English rather than a German king and looked forward to his reigning as a monarch of all his people on both sides of the Atlantic. Franklin, proudly present at George III's coronation, saw the young king as a great and good prince. Two years later he wrote of his confidence that "Faction will dissolve and be dissipated like a Morning Fog before the rising Sun" as the "Virtue, and . . . sincere Intentions" of George III "to make his People happy, will give him Firmness and Steadiness in his Measures," and his reign becomes "happy and truly glorious." Franklin revealed his preoccupation with the *qualities* of the monarch's leadership, rather than with any mechanisms of consent or popular control, moreover, when he held up as a standard Frederick the Great, who had just established the happiness of his realm by vanquishing his foreign and domestic enemies and organizing a government of "excellent Oeconomy." Thinking of the good the two kings might accomplish, Franklin recalled the old saying, which he said was "certainly" true, that "Ad Exemplum Regis, etc." (The whole community is regulated by the example of the King).[4] Or, in a fuller version, "The manners of the world are formed after the example of the King; nor can edicts influence the human understanding, so much as the life of the ruler."

John Adams noted in his diary, on reading George III's first speech to Parliament, that the new king promised to "patronize Religion, Virtue, the british Name and Constitution, in Church and state, the subjects Rights, Liberty, Commerce, military Merit.—These are sentiments worthy of a King—a Patriot King," obviously having in mind Bolingbroke's tract, which Adams had recently read admiringly. Paradoxically, both Pitt and George III, who soon became antagonists, helped to sustain for transatlantic Britons the ideal and the peculiar contribution of the patriot leader. Perhaps self-servingly, George III adopted Pitt's antiparty stance, declaring that as "monarch of the *British Islands*, not King of a despicable party," he intended to "put an end to those unhappy distinctions of party called Whigs and Torys" by inviting into government men of talent and patriotism.[5] Having idolized Pitt as hero and savior, and willing to give the young king the benefit of every doubt, Americans as diverse as Franklin and Adams, fifteen years before the Declaration of Independence, had deep impressions of the uses and prospects of the patriot leader. Conversely, it was the corrupt oligarchs, the scheming merchants, and the practitioners of party politics whom the Americans saw as their foes—just as Swift and Bolingbroke had taught. That Pitt and George III would play conventional party politics to the hilt between 1760 and 1776 was taken as evidence of a natural backsliding, or perhaps the inevitable fruit of a corrupt British society, not as a sign that the ideal itself was flawed or fanciful.

American Antimonarchism and the Spirit of 1776

In fact, the long struggle between Britain and its American dominions that followed the patriotic triumphs of 1758–1760 served in the colonies to underscore the central role of virtuous leadership. Even amid the disaffection of the Stamp Act crisis, though some protests turned against George III, Americans generally proclaimed, as the Connecticut Sons of Liberty wrote, that they were "actuated by the Just Principles of true Loyalty to his Majesty King George." "French Agents," "Jacobitical Schemes," evil counselors, corrupt ministers, and "Parliamentary Error" were blamed, but the monarch was not; at worst, he was "misled." Public resolutions and private correspondence during 1765–1766 show that "loyalty to the King was the most significant bond linking the intercolonial Sons of Liberty."[6] Indeed, invoking a hallowed conception in English history (and following John Dryden's near-allegorical *Absalom and Achitophel*), colonial Britons were inclined to see the repeal of the Stamp Act in 1766 as evidence that a patriot king (George III) had joined with a patriot minister (Pitt) to rescue American liberty from the corrupt intentions of evil counselors and partisan parliamentarians.

As ministerial venality and a corrupt Parliament were alternately blamed for the alleged oppression and misrule of the colonies, hope after hope and appeal after appeal crossed the Atlantic that either a rejuvenated ministry or the king himself might set things right—good leadership alone could rescue the nation from the toils of faction and intrigue. The controversies of 1767–1773 produced no American indictments of George III, and even the more severe crisis provoked by the Coercive Acts of 1774 only gradually eroded American loyalty to the monarchy. Americans were aware that Edmund Burke and others in Britain were beginning to fashion a positive idea of party activity as beneficial rather than destructive to the state, but this did not displace the ancient conviction that in the long run salvation rested not in party strife but in rising above party.[7]

Jefferson's "Summary View" of 1774, though unyielding in its defense of American rights, still hoped George III might act the part of the patriot king and save the nation. Jefferson asked the king to reflect "that he is no more than the chief officer of the people, appointed by the laws, and circumscribed with definite powers, to assist in working the great machine of government." The throne was, Jefferson warned his sovereign, "surrounded by . . . counsellors [who] . . . are parties. . . . No longer persevere in sacrificing the rights of one part of the empire to the inordinate desires of another: but deal out to all equal and impartial right." Echoing another theme he had read in Bolingbroke, Jefferson advised George III that "the whole art of government consists in the art of being honest."[8]

Although Jefferson implied a disrespect still regarded as treason in Britain, he was also rehearsing a version of English history and a role above party for the sovereign set forth in *A Dissertation upon Parties* and in *Idea of a Patriot King*. James Wilson spoke similarly in January 1775: "The British liberties . . . and the means and the right of defending them, are not the grants of princes" because those rights inhered in a constitution that, Wilson insisted, quoting Bolingbroke, "binds the king as much as the meanest subject." "Are we enemies to the power of the crown?" Wilson asked. "No, sir: we are its best friends," because the colonies sought to open the eyes of the king to the machinations of his ministers and to the usurpations of Parliament. The colonies, Wilson asserted, would observe "the true form of loyalty—in obeying our sovereign according to law." In 1774–1775 Franklin, John Adams, and Alexander Hamilton, in addition to Jefferson and Wilson, all wrote tracts appealing to a patriot king (as they desperately hoped George III would be) to right the wrongs of a party-ridden Parliament or of corrupt ministers. Indeed, Lord North himself was provoked to complain of the "language of Toryism" in the petitions from the colonies. Even after fighting had begun in April 1775, Americans often referred to the soldiers they fought as "the Ministerial Army" or "the Parliament Troops." George Washington, on the eve of the Battle of Bunker Hill, wrote of the redcoats as "the Ministerial Troops (for we do not, nor can we yet prevail upon ourselves to call them the King's Troops)." After the battle, however, a Cambridge, Massachusetts, toast by the Sons of Liberty expressed the changing allegiance: "A patriot King, or none, over the British Colonies."[9]

Virtually until the moment of Thomas Paine's assault in 1776 on "the Royal Brute of Great Britain" descended from "a French Bastard" who had conquered England with "an armed Banditti," the colonists clung to the possibility of benign executive power exerted on their behalf—an authority that by transcending faction and corruption would act in the national interest. As the withering force and great influence of *Common Sense* attested, however, when the turn against the king occurred, it came with the fury of a lover scorned. Abigail Adams wrote her husband after seeing the king's arms removed from the statehouse in Boston in 1776 (while she was tutoring her son, the future sixth president, in Classical and Renaissance history) that "we have in G[e]orge a match for a Borgia or a Catiline, a Wretch Callous to every Humane feeling."[10]

The Colonial Governorship

In a way often overlooked because of the contempt heaped on the last royal governors in the colonies and their consequent place as devils in American history, English rule in North America had always contained within itself a tension between a "military, imperial, and executive" emphasis in governing the colonies and a contrary "civilian, localist, and legislative" outlook. The former emphasis, championed particularly by the duke of York (later James II) and his household but continuing to be influential right down to 1776, was "classic, avowedly Roman, [and] imperial"; that is, it sought to consolidate the empire under proconsular governors who served the crown as both protectors and symbols of national glory. The latter emphasis, on the other hand, espoused by Anthony Ashley Cooper (later the first earl of Shaftesbury) from 1660 onward, undergirded by Locke, and sustained by Robert Walpole, accepted the new England of "acquisitive capitalism, individual liberty, provincial autonomy and . . . oligarchy"[11]—the very difference, so rich in moral overtones, that Dryden had laid bare in *Absalom and Achitophel*, where Shaftesbury had been cast as "hell's dire agent." Thus, from the earliest years of the American colonies English imperial policy was divided along lines approximating the cultural chasm between Pope-Swift-Bolingbroke on one side and Mandeville-Defoe-Walpole on the other.

The actual experience of rule in British North America under colonial governors had left similarly ambiguous impressions about the uses of executive power. Although few later magistrates were able to sustain the active, authoritarian leadership exercised by John Winthrop, the office of the governor remained strong in the New England colonies, whether the incumbent was elected or was appointed by the crown. In the proprietary colonies, noble, principled intentions and the sweeping powers of the Penns and the Calverts enshrined a kind of patriot king ideal in their founding legends. The place of William Penn in Pennsylvania history, for example, evoked, perhaps even more than in Winthrop's case, the qualities of Moses and Nehemiah as the great and good leader of all the people in the pursuit of a grand design or divine purpose. This mode of leadership, together with the strongly nationalistic, even imperial and proconsular, style of many of the governors sent out by the crown, implanted in the colonies a tradition and experience of government that placed wide power and high responsibility in the hands of the leader. Although it was difficult in the crude surroundings of the New World to duplicate anything like the ceremonies, palaces, and paraphernalia usually associated with an exalted ruler, efforts by Francis Berkeley and William Gooch in Virginia, Robert Hunter in New York, and William Shirley in Massachusetts, for example, reveal that a strong tradition of conspicuous leadership came to the colonies from England. That much of this tradition amounted simply to harsh "garrison government" (nearly 90 percent of all governors-general of English overseas provinces between 1660 and 1727 had at one time been army officers[12]) had an important bearing eventually on American reservations about executive power, but at early stages, when colonial need for protection and for connection with Britain was paramount, the military emphasis could blend easily with more elevated notions of purpose and destiny. The army officers themselves, often imbued with a strong sense of loyalty to the crown, were for the most part firmly for prerogative and an imperial sense of "the public good" as opposed to provincial, commercial, or oligarchic interests. These officers also participated fully in all the place seeking, nepotism, and corruption that characterized the English imperial service, but they nonetheless conferred on their dominions an experience and tradition of active, vigorous leadership.

Increasingly in the eighteenth century, however, first as Walpole and his colleagues exerted influence on colonial administration and then as the colonies themselves grew stronger, executive power in America more and more confronted demands for commercial opportunity, legislative influence, and local autonomy. The "quest for power" by provincial legislatures, in particular, present in a way from the foundation of the colonies, became steadily more insistent following the Glorious Revolution until by mid-century the legislators could often "battle on equal terms with the governors and councils and challenge even the powers in London if necessary." Indeed, some colonies by 1763 "saw the virtual eclipse of the colonial executive." When after that date "one imperial measure after another threatened to deprive the lower houses [of colonial legislatures] of powers they had in many cases enjoyed for a long time," the response was direct challenge and, in a dozen years, armed rebellion.[13] As the issues became more sharply drawn, especially the crucial one of whether local assemblies or a distant Parliament had the right to tax, cogent theories of legislative dominance evolved on both sides of the Atlantic. Furthermore, when in the mid-1770s the colonists turned their fury on the king and his ministers as well as on Parliament, the effect in North America was to emphasize yet more categorically the powers of legislative bodies over *any* executive.

As a result, the colonial period in American history left a mixed legacy of executive leadership. The last generation or two before the Revolution acquired important experience in, and a sophisticated theory of, enlarged legislative power. Furthermore, since the Revolutionary triumph was linked closely to that growth, one of its cardinal tenets came to be the elevation of legislative over executive power. The often foolish or partisan or self-seeking or tyrannical behavior (or at least so it seemed to many colonials) of the last royal governors simply put the finishing touches on what by 1776 had become a systematic denigration of the idea of executive leadership in the public interest. At the same time, however, even as Revolutionary assemblies insulted and banished royal governors and as many state constitutions subordinated executive to legislative power, sentiments and symbols of a different emphasis remained. When in 1776, to mention one case, Patrick Henry became the first elected governor of Virginia, he moved into the elegant "palace" recently vacated by Lord Dunmore, and he presided in a council chamber in the state capitol formerly used by his royally appointed predecessors.[14] Thomas Jefferson, living in the same "palace" and presiding in the same chamber, soon came to believe the office he filled was far too weak and ineffective to provide proper leadership for the commonwealth. The cloud that descended over executive power during the last years of colonial rule, that is, did not entirely obscure the practices and tradition of active leadership that had often been both dominant and admired in the more than 150 years since the founding of the first colonies.

Nonetheless, it cannot be denied that the crushing defeat of the "imperial and executive" emphasis in British rule of the thirteen colonies in the 1776–1783 war blighted not only militarism and royal prerogative but also traditional ideals of national leadership and administrative excellence. The commercial, legislative, autonomous, and provincial forces that became "the . . . authors of the American Revolution" embedded their ideology and vision of the future in the institutions and public life of the new nation.[15] In 1776 and the following years, as the Revolutionary leaders consolidated their own power by proscribing "Tories" and acted to embody in the new governments Whig axioms of local autonomy and legislative supremacy, it sometimes appeared that there was no longer a place in the newly independent nation for *any* part of the discredited "military, imperial, and executive" viewpoint. Jefferson's recollection in 1821 that "before the Revolution we were all good English Whigs, cordial in their free principles, and in their jealousies of their executive Magistrate," referred not generally to "before the Revolution" but precisely to the revolution in loyalty that, as John Adams often noted, was accomplished between 1761 and 1776 and that made possible a "declaration of independence" from king and country.[16]

Virtue and Leadership in New Constitutions

The years 1776–1787, when the nation was created, were an era of enthusiastic republican theorizing.[17] As the malfeasance of the last royal governors seemed to desecrate the very notions of dutiful obedience, executive leadership, and national purpose, radical Whigs celebrated the growth of both individual freedom and scope for enterprise. But, excluding Tom Paine, who had declared in *Common Sense* that government itself was "but a necessary evil, . . . the badge of lost innocence," and a few others, the idea of a merely free and open society governed lightly by a simple legislative assembly still frightened many American Revolutionists. The sharp decline in symbolic veneration of the "Rebel-Saints," John Hampden and Algernon Sydney, in America after 1776, for example, measured the shift in attention from restraint on government to its positive uses. John Adams even proclaimed Paine a "Star of Disaster," and an earnestly republican clergyman in the western part of Adams's home state declared his new nation still subject to the Classical relation between citizens and the state: "Men become virtuous or vicious, good commonwealthsmen or the contrary, generous, noble, and courageous, or base, mean-spirited, and cowardly, according to the impression that they have received from the government that they are under."[18] Samuel Adams and Washington, Jefferson and Hamilton—and Erasmus and Bolingbroke—would have agreed. A huge gap, however, faced republicans if they accepted this connection: traditionally the moral nurture of the people, the cultivation of virtue in government, and leadership in common purposes had come from a legitimate monarchy and such allied institutions as an established church, the nobility, and national patronage of art and learning. Pure republicanism, on the other hand, rejected these devices, at least in their usual forms. Where, then, would the "correct impressions" vital to good government and virtuous nationhood come from in a republic?

The century-old English tension between "Court" and "Country" (a division that had long supplied rhetoric for transatlantic orators and pamphleteers) sheds light on this dilemma and affords another way of understanding the context in which the American presidency took shape. In the twenty turbulent years after 1763, the compulsions of Revolutionary resistance to English government had driven both words and deeds in America "well beyond [even] the country wing of the old Court-Country spectrum." Thomas Paine ridiculed not only king, Lords, and Commons but also the whole venerable idea of mixed government. Pennsylvania established an omnipotent unicameral legislature, and even those states that retained bicameralism restricted executive power far beyond anything contemplated by English Whigs. Liberty gained everywhere: the social structure loosened, churches were disestablished, western representation in state legislatures became more equitable, and military arrogance declined. These developments, along with the demise of the customary colonial officers, the growth of extralegal local committees, and the enlargement and democratization of legislatures placed the new states on the radical fringe

of eighteenth-century notions of polity. Leadership and authority atro-
phied as the people of the former colonies set aside ancient concepts of
deference to superiors before they discovered "compelling reasons for
obeying their equals, even when they happened to be organized as a
legislature."[19]

Hence, not only did the antimonarchical thrust of declaring independence partially discredit the patriot king solution of the Bolingbroke seg-
ment of the "Country" opposition, but also Revolutionary dependence on
local committees and popular legislatures tended to place Americans outside the English political spectrum altogether—and provoked contempla-
tion, at least, of astoundingly radical solutions. Immemorial practice and
an enormous weight of political theory accepted that the character and
quality of a people depended on the good influence of their government
and also taught that this required attention to the virtue of the rulers, assumed to be a prince or some sort of aristocracy. The converse also had
become a hoary orthodoxy: that the people generally—the demos, in Aristotelian terms—were a turbulent mob, too much the slave of passion and
ignorance to possess the "talent and virtue" needed to provide or even discern the good government that could in turn make a people "generous,
noble, and courageous." But with monarchy and titled aristocracy discredited, and even the very ideas of national leadership and legitimate authority "from above" called into question, the only resort left for investing
government with virtue was to find it, or train and bring it forth, in the
mass of the people. It was to this challenging possibility that the most
hopeful, and in a way the most consistent, of the American nation-builders
turned.

If one searches Antifederalists' arguments against various clauses of the
Constitution of 1787 to discern what they were *for*, one finds an intriguing, even compelling and noble, aspiration to work out this thoroughly
republican mode of achieving virtuous government. Their arguments for a
small rather than an "extended" republic, for instance, rested on three
propositions: First, only in a small republic could there be willing, largely
voluntary, compliance with laws and acceptance of government. Second,
only such a republic could retain meaningful bonds between the people
and their elected officials. Third, most fundamentally, only a small republic
could properly nourish and encourage the kind of citizenship required if
the practice of self-government was to result in *good* government.[20] The
ideal of the Antifederalists, that is, was somehow to achieve a polity where
moral qualities such as willing assent, heartfelt representation, and virtue
in the citizens would create a truly republican public life.

At the close of the Federal Convention, George Mason complained that
because the House of Representatives provided for "not the substance, but
the shadow only of representation, [it could] never . . . inspire confidence

in the people." One New York Antifederalist declared that only a government that has the trust and confidence of the people could be supported without standing armies or swarms of officials. Another insisted that only if those who governed came from "the substantial yeomanry of the country," whose callings made them "more temperate, of better morals, and less ambition, than the great," would the new nation be spared what a Massachusetts Antifederalist called degeneration "to a compleat Aristocracy . . . which in its vortex swallows up every other Government upon the Continent . . . [and would] be nothing less than a hasty stride to Universal Empire."[21] Other Antifederalists complained in conventional "Country" rhetoric of the virtue-corroding tendency of Federalist preferences for commercial growth, a grand federal capital, standing armies, and increased national revenues. Some even echoed the Country argument for churches and schools "*adequate* to the *divine, patriotick purpose* of training up the children and youth at large, in that solid learning, and in those pious and moral principles, which are the *support*, the *life* and SOUL of republican government and liberty."[22] The ideal, in sum, to many Antifederalists was a polity where virtuous, hardworking, honest men and women, living simply in small communities, enjoying ancient ties to family and neighbors, and devoted to the common welfare, possessed such churches, schools, trade associations, and institutions of local government as they needed to sustain their common values and way of life. Only with such a foundation would the people be able to fulfill the demanding responsibilities of republican citizenship.[23]

Samuel Adams, earnestly moral and purely republican, confronted the problem of creating a government that would nourish virtue. Friends in admiration and foes in derision alike saw Adams as of "Spartan character" or as an American "Cato," meaning that he stood for a simple, frugal, uncorruptible sense of republican virtue and patriotism, scornful of the tendencies toward greedy commercialism, imperial grandeur, and dissipation he saw in eighteenth-century Anglo-America. "Luxury and extravagance," he wrote in 1778 as Boston relaxed a bit after the British evacuation, "are in my opinion totally destructive to those virtues which are necessary to the Preservation of the Liberty and Happiness of the People." Twelve years later, amid the debates over the new Constitution, Adams rejected dependence on sophisticated devices for "separation of powers" and called instead for "divines and philosophers, statesmen and patriots, to . . . educate everyone, including *little boys and girls* in universal philanthropy, . . . in the art of self-government, . . . and in the study and practice of the exalted virtues of the Christian system." It was necessary, he insisted, to "cultivate the natural genius, elevate the soul, excite laudable emulation to excel in knowledge, piety, and benevolence; and finally it will reward its patrons and benefactors by shedding its benign influence on the public mind."[24]

Adams believed as intensely as Plato or Erasmus or Bolingbroke that good
government depended on virtue in those who ruled, but his radical departure was in supposing that virtue could be found and nourished in the people, thus allowing republican government by the people to measure up to
the standards expected of a philosopher-king, or a Christian prince, or a
patriot leader.

Adams accepted the ancient equation between good government and
virtuous rulers, but at the same time he cherished the hope that the people
at large, who ruled in a republic, could possess virtue. To this end he determinedly (his enemies charged dogmatically) urged state support of science
and the arts, of religion, and of all levels of education—how else but
through institutions designed to nourish and guide all the people could
they achieve what had previously been thought vital in kings and magistrates? He therefore approved enthusiastically the clauses in the Massachusetts Constitution of 1780 providing for state support of churches and
of Harvard College. It was the responsibility of government, the constitution avowed, "to cherish the interests of literature and the sciences, and all
seminaries of them; . . . [and] public schools and grammar schools in the
towns; to encourage private societies and public institutions, rewards and
immunities, for the promotion of agriculture, arts, sciences, commerce,
trades, manufactures, and a natural history of the country; to countenance
and inculcate the principles of humanity and general benevolence, public
and private charity, industry and frugality, honesty and punctuality in their
dealings; sincerity, good humor, and all social affections, and generous
sentiments, among the people."[25] In fact, the concern and admonition expressed in the 1780 Massachusetts constitution, so strange and even dog-
matic sounding to political sensibilities chary of publicly promoted virtue, could have come almost phrase by phrase from a handbook for the
education of a benevolent prince—but in a republican commonwealth *all*
the citizen-rulers had to be so "inculcated." The constitution drafters revealed their continuing deference to traditional conceptions of leadership,
though, where they declared that the governor, popularly elected, was
"emphatically the Representative of the whole People." John Adams, the
chief draftsman, saw this direct connection with the people as allowing the
executive, "which ought to be the reservoir of wisdom" in the constitution
on behalf of the people and the common good, to resist the influence of
wealth, luxury, intrigue, corruption, and faction that would otherwise be
dominant in the affairs of the commonwealth.[26]

The more radically republican constitution of Pennsylvania, after stipu-
lating that the laws be made by a legislature closely accountable to the
people, also undertook to ensure that the people had the virtue to execute
properly their public trust. "Every freeman," the constitution stated, "to
preserve his independence . . . ought to have some profession, calling,

trade or farm, whereby he may honestly subsist." In addition to the usual protection of rights that would prevent arbitrary interference with this honest pursuit of calling, the constitution welcomed "foreigners of good character" as citizens, provided that schools be supported in each county, and required that one or more universities should encourage and promote "all useful learning." Furthermore, in a sweeping injunction the government was instructed that "laws for the encouragement of virtue, and prevention of vice and immorality, shall be made and constantly kept in force."[27] The logic was the same as that endorsed in Massachusetts: if the people were to rule and government was to be good, then the people would have to be made wise and virtuous.

Most of the Revolutionary leaders, however, could not accept this nicely consistent vision; it placed too much hope, John Adams said, "in the universal, or at least more general, prevalence of knowledge and benevolence." James Madison wrote in *The Federalist* that though trust in the virtue of the people had to be "the primary control of [republican] government," human weakness made "auxiliary precautions" such as separation of powers also necessary.[28] Although thus committed basically to "the republican principle"—some form of nonmonarchical government by consent—many "good republicans" also remained in a dilemma for which there was no pat resolution, and which, as experience with government after 1776 seemed increasingly to demonstrate, would thus require "mixtures" or "composites," or "alloys." No doubt all just government must have at least a "popular branch," and doubtless, too, some "refinements" and checks and balances, but beyond these general principles, much seemed unsettled. The dilemma was especially marked in American attitudes toward executive power, as William Cobbett noticed in 1794 in assessing the Federal Constitution: "The many of all countries stand in need of a monarch, at once to keep them in obedience to itself, and to protect them from the tyranny and rapacity of the aspiring, rich and avaricious few. The people of America wanted such a protector [in 1788], but the delusion of the times would not have permitted him to be called a *monarch*."[29]

Federalists and Antifederalists alike, then, remained committed to the ancient propositions that good government required virtue in the ruler(s) and that positive, perhaps even energetic, action to give public effect to that virtue was a crucial responsibility of those who ruled, whether monarchs, elected officials, or citizens. Even Antifederalist emphasis on state and local government did not so much seek to diminish the importance of government as to place its powers in the most virtuous and efficacious hands. Oppositely, Federalist attention to the usefulness of countervailing factions in an extended republic and to the benefits of commercial expansion was aimed generally not at the intrinsic merits of these things but rather at their auxiliary utility in protecting and in leaving scope for many of the same "republican virtues" extolled by the Antifederalists, which both sides agreed defined the goals of the American Revolution. The problem for each side was to discern the extent and assignment of the powers of government that would most faithfully and practically allow the pursuit of republican principles.[30]

Antifederalists faced the difficulty especially in thinking about executive power, of which, with their generally Whiggish preconceptions and the hard "lessons" of the last years of British rule, they were deeply skeptical. Echoing Edmund Randolph's assertion in the Federal Convention that a unitary executive was "the feotus of monarchy" and George Mason's insistence that the executive be required to act only with the consent of a council, many Antifederalists exhibited what by 1787 had become a conventional hostility to a strong executive. There were objections to the veto, appointment, and commander in chief powers conferred on the president in the proposed constitution, as well as warnings about his becoming arbitrary and overbearing because of the loose definition of executive powers in Article II—a point many critics made by referring to the office as that of "president general." Was there ever a commission so *brief*, so *general*, as this of our president, asked a Massachusetts Antifederalist? If the president could prevail in his own interpretation of how, under his oath, he would faithfully execute the laws, "would he not be to all intents and purposes absolute?"[31]

Nevertheless, there was surprisingly little concentration by the Antifederalists on executive powers as such. More ominous to many was the joining of the Senate and the president in the treaty-making and appointing powers, suspect theoretically because it violated "separation of powers," but feared especially because it seemed to permit cabals, intrigue, and "an aristocratic junto." Mason predicted to the Virginia Ratifying Convention that there would be a "marriage" between the president and the Senate that would overawe the other branches.[32] Indeed, Antifederalists tended more to fear the Senate than the president in such a combination, and some even felt the president was too weak to be able properly to uphold the public interest. "The Federal Farmer" in New York, worried about the "aristocratic" power of the Senate, thought the nation would need a "first man" who could be "a visible point serving as a common centre in the government" and thus be "superior in the opinion of the people" to regional leaders and other forces that might otherwise too much divide the nation's councils.[33] A "first man" as an antidote, though in some ways a less attractive resort than pure, simple virtue and power in the people, was both a familiar tradition and a logically admissible counterweight to divisive tendencies implicit in the prevailing emphasis on local governments, regional power, and legislative dominance.

When contrasted with this Antifederalist willingness to countenance almost anything to thwart factional and divisive tendencies, the Federalists, despite their championship of stronger executive power, appear in some ways the more open to the diversities that accompanied politics in a free society. Indeed it seems at times that the authors and defenders of the 1787 Constitution thought the clever intricacy of its provisions would itself issue in good government, regardless, apparently, of the virtue, patriotism, or good intent of either leaders or the people (though they would have been appalled at the explicit statement of such a claim). In a way analogous to Adam Smith's argument that "the wealth of the nation" would flourish if individuals in it pursued private gain, the federal system seemed to offer a chance for a generally free and prosperous society without anyone being motivated overtly by either virtue or patriotism. Within such a system, if it really worked, it was neither likely nor necessary that positive leadership would have much of a role. With government reduced to a balancing of factions, and with the presumption that the executive would be no more attentive to virtue than would the people governed, ideas such as leadership in national purposes or the cultivation of virtue by the government could pass into disuse. Such an understanding of the new "system," perhaps implicit in the Constitution proposed in 1787 and increasingly congenial to interpreters in the nineteenth and twentieth centuries, validated the linkage between the assumed selfish nature of man, the conception of society as a summation of "special interests," the acceptance of "parties" as necessary and even useful in politics, and the notion that a leader was simply a more or less effective manager of the parts. Yet this view, consistent with the ethics of Bernard Mandeville and the practice of Sir Robert Walpole, perhaps, would have been repudiated by "Publius" as well as by the opponents of the new Constitution had it been set forth explicitly in 1788; indeed, in the eighteenth century public argument on behalf of such a political dynamic was rare and decidedly eccentric. Those who defended the Constitution of 1787 moved in potential projection and even some in practice toward a more "modern" politics, but they retained, fundamentally, the traditional assumptions about an objective public good, the need for virtue in government, and the key role of leaders in sustaining those qualities.

However fascinated the nation-builders were in some ways by a "new politics," that is, they were also unwilling that government have as its purpose only to balance interests and prevent tyranny. Nor could they accept a political philosophy resting on what John Adams saw as an assumption of "universal benevolence" by his cousin Samuel, not only because most Federalists were skeptical of the alleged goodness of human nature but also because they were by and large still intrigued with what might be accomplished by a patriot leader. Everything they had been taught about good government from Plato to Burke, and everything they had learned of history from ancient Sparta to the "benevolent despots" of eighteenth-century Europe, endorsed the axioms that the greatest blessing any society could have was virtuous rule, that such rule depended on concern for the public good rather than selfish interests, and that a patriot leader was the best protector of public virtue.

Indeed, the book perhaps most directly influential on James Madison as he wrote his *Federalist* essays (especially Number 10), David Hume's *Essays, Moral, Political, and Literary* (1742),[34] reveals the tension between the ancient reliance on the virtue of the monarch for good government and a newer, more "scientific" view of politics where, as Hume put it, "the force of laws and of particular forms of government" might have more importance than "the humors and tempers of men." Hume's discussion of the origins and "first principles" of government and his account of political parties in England (often using quotes from Bolingbroke) argue that it is possible to construct government so that liberty and the public good receive substantial protection even when the administration is in the hands of greedy, foolish, or otherwise flawed men. And it was this possibility that intrigued the drafters of the Federal Constitution and in particular inspired Madison as he worked out his famous theory about protection of liberty in an extended republic. Yet, in the very essay on the possibility "that politics may be reduced to a science," Hume had acknowledged that historical instances could be cited "almost without number" where the conduct of the sovereign made a crucial difference. He used as his prime example France under Henry III (r. 1574–1589) and under Henry IV (r. 1589–1610). "Oppression, levity, artifice on the part of the rulers, faction, sedition, treachery, rebellion, disloyalty on the part of the subjects—these compose the character of the former era," wrote Hume, whereas under the succeeding "patriot and heroic prince . . . the government, the people, everything seemed to be totally changed."[35] Although Hume, like many of his American admirers, was, in philosophy and temperament, hardly an "Ancient," he nonetheless worked within the assumptions and public-spiritedness of the neoclassical age. Madison and others impressed by his insight, cleverness, wit, and profundity would thus absorb both an intention to "reduce politics to a science" where possible and yet retain a strong disposition to see the character of the ruler as vitally important.

All of Locke's emphasis on the "Convenience" of government, all of the English "Cato"'s trumpeting of the many uses of freedom, all of the clever political science of Montesquieu and Hume, and all of Paine's denigration of the state, then, tending as they did to diminish the role of leadership, still could not erase the images of Lycurgus, Nehemiah, Trajan, Charlemagne, Elizabeth, and Henry of Navarre, nor could the corruption and tyranny of Lord Dunmore, Lord North, and even George III do more than renew a sense of the dangers of bad rulers. James Wilson told his colleagues at the Convention of 1787, echoing what Lord North had called the "Toryism" of the American Revolution, that "the people of America did not oppose the British King, but the Parliament: [the] . . . opposition was not against an unity, but a corrupt multitude."[36] As a new executive office was fashioned in 1787 and inaugurated in 1789, the need, in sum, was somehow to retain the character and benefits of a patriotic leadership within a republican framework. We can understand the self-conceptions and the conduct in office of the first six presidents only if we see how earnestly they accepted this necessity. And as attention again focused on executive leadership, explications such as that in Bolingbroke's *Idea of a Patriot King* set forth the *increment* that had to be added to what Jefferson thought of as the "harmonizing sentiments of American Whigs" in 1776. By 1789, both the problem and the ideological emphasis had changed. The task now, rather than dissolving authority and gaining independence, was that of establishing government, and the ideological emphasis had evolved from enthusiastic republican theorizing to more sober concern for the obligations of the body politic.

❧ II ❧

The American Presidency, 1789–1837

❦ 5 ❦

The Federalist Presidents

George Washington

George Washington had little taste for political theory, and we do not know that he ever read or made mention of *Idea of a Patriot King* or any other treatise on leadership. He had an early admiration for the heroic patriot of Joseph Addison's *Cato*, though, and as a young man he probably read Plutarch's *Lives*.[1] Furthermore, his exposure to the literature of Robert Walpole's critics, his intimate association with such scholars as Thomas Jefferson, James Madison, George Mason, and John Adams, and his deep self-consciousness of his unique role leave little doubt that he knew very well the themes and argument implicit in the debates over the foundations of national polity that agitated his more intellectual colleagues. Indeed, he so completely embodied the patriot king model that had Lord Bolingbroke been able to observe his conduct as general and president he surely would have listed Washington along with Elizabeth and Henry of Navarre as an ideal leader. With minor exceptions, historians ever since have portrayed Washington as attempting, at least, to live up to his own self-conception: the patriot leader above faction, working for national unity, and seeking to reign as well as to rule.

The critically important symbolic acts of Washington's Revolutionary War leadership both expressed his own patriotism and dramatized for the public a sense in him of disinterested commitment to the general welfare: his nomination as commander in chief by a New Englander, his insistence on sharing twelve months of the year with the vicissitudes of his army, his refusal of a salary, and the surrender of his sword to the Continental Congress at the end of the war. Firm Whiggish convictions in the new nation about the dangers of military dictatorship probably would have defeated a coup d'etat even by a general as "un-Cromwellian" as Washington, but his deliberate deference to the civilian authorities also revived the plausibility of the idea of a virtuous national leader. In fact, for more than twenty years Washington played that role very nearly to perfection and thus helped Americans get over the derelictions of George III and the Revolutionary bias against executive authority. Washington's performance from Valley

Forge onward seemed to demonstrate that patriot leadership, shorn of its hereditary aspects, not only could exist in but also was vital to the survival and well-being of a republic.

In the years between 1783 and 1789, Washington sought to blend his sense of the need for leadership and "energy" in government with a sober faith in the ability of the people to rule themselves. In 1783 he blamed most of the difficulties of fighting the Revolution on a "want of energy in the Federal Constitution" (meaning the Articles of Confederation), and he warned that "unless the principles of the federal government were properly supported and the powers of the union increased, the honour, dignity, and justice of the nation would be lost forever." He often declared that government must act in accord with the interests of the people, but this view did not mean immediate response to popular will. It was appropriate that state legislatures listen carefully to public opinion, he thought, but members of a national congress had to attend to long-range needs, and thus shun sectional and partial interests. The executive had to be even more above party, keeping his eye on the virtue, honor, and justice of the nation—objectives so important, Washington noted, that "even respectable characters" contemplated monarchy "without horror" if it would rescue the nation from an otherwise inevitable factional strife and anarchy.[2] He also made clear, however, that he repudiated monarchy and that he was glad he was peculiarly disqualified from sustaining its hereditary principle in the United States: "Divine Providence hath not seen fit that my blood should be transmitted or that my name perpetuated by . . . immediate offspring. I have no child . . . no family to build in greatness upon my country's ruins."[3]

It is clear that as Washington assumed the presidency he wanted somehow to provide the executive leadership so often deemphasized in radical Whig, Revolutionary, Antifederalist, and even some Federalist rhetoric. At Mount Vernon, he had busts of Alexander the Great, Charles XII of Sweden, Julius Caesar, Frederick of Prussia, the duke of Marlborough, and Prince Eugene—marks of his military interests but also evidence of his fascination with patriotic leadership. It is not surprising that in 1789 he sought to encourage positive action toward the public good by asking Congress, in an eventually discarded (for tactical reasons) inaugural address, "to take measures for promoting the general welfare. . . . To use your best endeavors to improve the education and manners of a people; to accelerate the progress of arts and Sciences; to patronize works of genius; to confer rewards for inventions of utility; and to cherish institutions favourable to humanity."[4] Among the institutions most to be nourished in Washington's view (and in that of each of the first six presidents) was a national university, where, he told the nation in his last annual message, "a portion of our youth from every quarter" of the nation could assimilate common "principles, opinions, and manners." Such an encouragement to a "homogeneous" citizenry, Washington argued, would vitally improve the bonds of "permanent union." Furthermore, "a primary object of such a national institution should be the education of our youth in the science of *government*." "In a republic," Washington asked, "what species of knowledge can be equally important and what duty more pressing on its legislature than to patronize a plan for communicating it to those who are to be the future guardians of the liberties of the country?"[5] Thus the first president accepted the ancient connection between the well-being of a nation and the proper education in "principles, opinions, and manners" of its rulers—in a republic, no longer just the leader or prince on whom Erasmus, Bolingbroke, and others had focused attention but also all those who held public office and, ultimately, all participants in the process of self-government.

Washington did not view such a national university or the rest of his ambitious program as either dictatorial or imperial. He warned against standing armies or even much of a navy and cautioned that the country "shou'd not, in imitation of some nations which have been celebrated for a false kind of patriotism, wish to aggrandize our own Republic at the expence of the freedom and happiness of the rest of mankind." For Washington, national patriotism had positive, public-spirited connotations that in the eighteenth-century ideal would lead not to conquest and tyranny but to a time when, in Benjamin Franklin's vision on the eve of the French Revolution, "not only the love of Liberty, but a thorough Knowledge of the Rights of Man may pervade all the Nations of the Earth." Washington wrote similarly to the marquis de Lafayette as he began his presidency: he thought he could "see a *path*, as clear and as direct as a ray of light, which leads to the attainment of . . . permanent felicity to the Commonwealth." "Nothing but harmony, honesty, industry and frugality are necessary to make us a great and happy people," the first president concluded.[6]

Washington's attention, as he took office, to pomp and etiquette, which in retrospect has often seemed ridiculous and misguided in a republic, was in fact another manifestation of his deliberate intention to *lead* the nation not only in a formal, political sense but also in "tone-setting," moral ways. He saw nothing unrepublican about ceremonies, paraphernalia, and even a certain aloofness if such would nourish public respect for the head of the nation and therefore for the nation as a whole—a linkage assumed in monarchies familiar to Washington. Even Madison and others who denied the need for "superb and august titles . . . or splendid tinsel or gorgeous robe" sought not to diminish presidential dignity but rather to find rational and republican ways to enhance and express it.[7] Thus during the first months of government under the new Constitution a remarkable harmony prevailed, and an impressive array of constructive, generally nonpartisan acts issued from Congress and from the president's office. The positive aspiration was the same as Jonathan Swift's: to have "a wise and good Prince" heading an "able Ministry" united with a "Senate freely chosen" in pursuit of "the true Interest of their Country." As was the negative one: to thwart "the little inferior Politicks of any Faction." This compelling model guided all the early presidents who knew Washington, served in office under him, and shared his conception of executive leadership—that is, all presidents through John Quincy Adams.

Washington's determination to be the patriot leader was frustrated in practice, however, by unyielding partisanship around him. In 1792–1793 Alexander Hamilton and Jefferson refused to leave the president any "middle ground" between them,[8] and in 1795–1796 he felt forced to move toward a more Federalist position when it seemed his Republican colleagues had deserted or betrayed him. He had no choice, he thought, but to support the advisers who best coped with the problems facing the nation. Nothing more troubled and upset him, though, than the barrage of charges in the last two years of his presidency that he had himself become the creature of a party and thus was no longer the patriot leader of the whole nation.

The accusations of hypocrisy and Washington's keen sense of the encumbrance imposed on his office by partisanship, which even he could not fully evade, caused him to speak out sharply in his Farewell Address against the growth of "party spirit" in the nation. This condemnation subsumed in a way the better-known warning against entangling alliances, which to Washington were simply international factionalism. Beginning with stress on the inseparable benefits of liberty and union, and the shared, common elements of the national experience, the first president discounted sectional differences. "With slight shades of difference," he told the American people, "you have the same religion, manners, habits, and political principles." He urged the public to support "consistent and wholesome plans, digested by common counsels and modified by mutual interests," rather than those who sought "to make the public administration the mirror of the ill-concerted and incongruous projects of faction." This "most solemn" admonition, moreover, was not merely against the dangers of particular factions, but against "the baneful effects of the spirit of party generally" as well. That spirit, he admitted, was "inseparable from our nature" and might, especially in monarchies, furnish "useful checks upon the administration of the government, and serve to keep alive the spirit of liberty, . . . [but] in governments purely elective, it is a spirit not to be encouraged. From their natural tendency it is certain there will always be enough of that spirit for every salutary purpose; and there being constant danger of excess, the effort ought to be by force of public opinion to mitigate and assuage it. A fire not to be quenched, it demands a uniform vigilance to prevent its bursting into a flame, lest, instead of warming, it should consume." When such vigilance was lacking, Washington warned, "the alternate domination of one faction over another . . . has perpetrated the most horrid enormities, [and] is itself a frightful despotism."[9]

The greatest evil of faction and party was not its effect on public policy (though that was bad enough), but rather its narrowing and degradation of political motives, long regarded as the essence of corruption. Parties riveted public attention on partialities and self-interest, and the effect was nothing less than enslavement of the nation to sin and vice. Liberty, for Washington as for John Winthrop, was not doing what one pleased, if that meant satisfying selfish (factional) interests; rather, it was a positive act of rising above such enthrallment to understand and seek the public good. As Washington made quite clear, and as each of the first six presidents would have agreed, the gravest danger republican government faced was its tendency to gratify self-interest to the point of being "consumed" by it. History was filled, these men thought, with evidence of "the most horrid enormities" caused by such a spirit "burst into flames." The last years of the Roman republic, English government under Walpole or Lord North, state government in Massachusetts and Rhode Island during the 1780s, and the party strife of the 1790s were among the monitory examples. That Washington took part in the intrigue of his advisers to manipulate and release the Farewell Address for party purposes is evidence, of course, that partisanship was as "inseparable" from his nature as it was from that of any mortal. But he would never have considered celebrating it; rather, a good politician would "mitigate," "assuage," and guard against it as much as possible. The calculated language of the Farewell Address, its wide acclaim, and Washington's self-conscious conveyance of it as a "Political Testament" to the nation reveal that the posture of patriot leadership was admired and cherished even amid the party warfare of the 1790s.[10]

John Adams

John Adams shared the ideal of disinterested leadership entirely, though his temperament, reputation, and circumstances made it even less achievable during his administration than it had been for his predecessor. In his inaugural address Adams proclaimed his lack of sectional bias, his desire to love "virtuous men of all parties and denominations," and his "wish to patronize every rational effort to encourage schools, colleges, universities, academies, and every institution for propagating knowledge, virtue, and religion among all classes of the people . . . as the only means of preserving our Constitution from its natural enemies, the spirit of sophistry, the spirit of party, the spirit of intrigue, the profligacy of corruption, and the pestilence of foreign influence, which is the angel of destruction to elective governments." Two weeks later he wrote his wife of the "scene of ambition" he faced, horrid "beyond all my former suspicions or imaginations." At the next election he feared that "England will set up Jay or Hamilton, and France, Jefferson, and all the corruption of Poland will be introduced; unless the American spirit should rise and say, we will have neither John Bull nor Louis Baboon." His task, he wrote, was clear: to find "checks and balances" that would be "antidotes" to these "jealousies and rivalries,"[11] to proceed, that is, according to his lifelong political philosophy.

Adams had honed his view of the contradiction between partisanship and patriotism through study of Bolingbroke's *Remarks on the History of England, A Dissertation upon Parties,* and *The Spirit of Patriotism.* In the 1750s he read and commented on them "pretty industriously" and bought his own separate editions before the American Revolution. As early as 1761 a friend in Boston told him, "You have Ld. Bolinbroke by heart," and Adams wrote late in life that he had read Bolingbroke "through . . . more than five times." He pronounced Bolingbroke's letter explaining how the limited, balanced nature of the British constitution preserved English liberty "a jewel; . . . nothing so profound, correct, and perfect on the subject of government" existed in any language, he insisted. He also approved Bolingbroke's judgment that "absolute monarchy is tyranny, but absolute democracy is tyranny and anarchy both." Within the balanced forms, however, the danger was, as Adams paraphrased Bolingbroke, that "the spirit of faction will take advantage of the spirit of liberty." Adams shared Bolingbroke's hopes, though, that the spirit of liberty might prevail, giving "vigor" to a good constitution and laws. "Let one great, brave, disinterested, active man arise, and he will be received, followed, and almost adored." It was important only that "the public may be grown wise enough to judge" between genuine liberty and its bastard offspring, faction. Adams's sarcastic comment in the margin of *Remarks on the History of England* next to Bolingbroke's sketch of the patriot leader—"like Bonaparte, or Hamilton, or Burr"—indicates precisely, of course, the sorts of leadership *not* regarded as genuinely patriotic.[12]

In two ways, however, Adams departed from Bolingbroke to mold his own definition of patriotism. First, Adams insisted that Bolingbroke's skeptical deism caused him to omit "the most essential foundation of the duty of patriotism," which in fact made a mockery of his "whole idea of a patriot king." Such value-laden leadership was to Adams inseparably linked with "a belief in a future state of rewards and punishments" and other aspects of Christian morality, without which widespread virtue was unattainable. In 1767, writing in the newspapers to oppose some high-handed acts of Massachusetts governor Francis Bernard, Adams had cited Bolingbroke's *Remarks on the History of England* and commended his unrivaled understanding of the British constitution but had felt it necessary to apologize for "whatever may be justly said of his religion, and his morals." Secondly, Adams challenged Bolingbroke's fretting that there were not enough "men of superior genius." Perhaps as a consequence of his belief that Christian morality is the necessary foundation of virtue and thus of patriotism, Adams asked: "Is . . . the spirit of patriotism . . . peculiar to them or . . . [is it] their duty any more than of the common people? A laborer may have this spirit as well as a prince or noble, a soldier as well as a general, a sailor as well as an admiral."[13] A widespread morality, undergirded by Christianity, was a possible way, in Adams's view, to overcome faction in a government resting on consent.

Many of Adams's supposed unrepublican opinions are best understood in the light of his consistent view that human society needed every buttress it could find for firm moral leadership. His defense of "the aristocracy of birth and wealth," for example, was offered not to oppose Jefferson's "aristocracy of talent and virtue," as his critics have charged, but rather to add to it. Adams sought to strengthen the Jeffersonian foundations of good government—talent and virtue—with such support as could be derived from "good breeding," religious training, pride in family, opportunities for travel and education, and so on. He thought of these things as advantageous to the prospects for republican government, not as detrimental to it.

Even Adams's campaign in 1789 for a majestic title for the president, called "superlatively ridiculous" by Jefferson, was in fact part of a design to subordinate rapacious oligarchies. "You are apprehensive of Monarchy; I, of Aristocracy," Adams had written Jefferson in 1787 when both were in Europe. As vice-president, presiding over the Senate, Adams supported elegant titles for the executive officers named in the Constitution in order to humble "aristocratical pride." "The common people, if they understand their own cause and interest, will take effectual care to mortify that pride, by making the executive magistrate a balance against it which can only be done by distinguishing him clearly and decidedly, far above all others."[14]

Adams had developed this argument during the 1780s as part of his rejection of the view of Anne Robert Turgot, the marquis de Condorcet, and other French reformers that national programs of fundamental change depended on centralizing all power in one legislative assembly. Adams agreed instead with Jean Louis De Lolme's *The Constitution of England* that executive office had to be insulated from both popular and aristocratic interference, and be buttressed with pomp and ceremony, in order to protect virtue and public liberty from tumult and party.[15] Indeed, the argument of Adams's *Defence of the Constitutions of Government of the United States of America* (3 volumes; London, 1787) was an elaboration on De Lolme's

view that the balanced constitution of king, Lords, and Commons in Great
Britain was far more likely to result in free and good government than
were the unitary schemes of the French radical reformers. Adams's long
study of history and his debate with the "prophets of progress" left him
keenly aware of the passions and ignorance of the many (represented by
popular assemblies) and of the machinations and greed of the few (aristoc-
racies and oligarchies), but somewhat less fearful of the power of a monarch. And because it often seemed to Adams that such a ruler was the lesser
of the evils to which all governments are subject, he thought it necessary
that the "principal personage" (a term Adams used to evoke kingly connotations to an audience with antimonarchical sentiments) of a republic
have a dignified title, home, carriage, and so on, and be armed with an
absolute veto of legislation in order to defend his office and the public
good from the shortsightedness and rapacity of the other branches. "The
great desideratum in a government," Adams wrote in the *Defence*, "is a distinct executive power, of sufficient strength and weight to compel both
these parties [gentlemen and simplemen], in turn, to submit to the laws."[16]
Titles of deference and authority for the chief executive, far from being
unrepublican, then, were for Adams bulwarks against faction and sus-
tainers of the public good against a host of divisive elements. The titles he
suggested, in fact, came from republican Holland and in his mind were not
associated with monarchy or absolutism. Adams was also echoing the idea
of the Tudor monarchs that the people and the crown must unite to resist
aristocratic privilege and provincialism, an equation validated by the factious, centrifugal tendencies of the new republic, or so it seemed to its
scholarly vice-president.

   In Adams's own view of his presidency he had held a steady course,
above party and intent on the national interest, alternately enduring and
fighting off first Hamiltonian and then Jeffersonian partisans. His continuance of Washington's cabinet, encouragement of a militant patriotism in
response to the XYZ affair, and dispatch of the successful peace mission to
France were to Adams required by national, as opposed to party, interest.
He could not discharge capable officials because they were not his close
friends, he could not supinely endure foreign insults, and he could not refuse an honorable peace in order to ensure a party victory at the polls.
Adams, furthermore, agreed with a defense of the Alien and Sedition Acts
offered by a minority of the Virginia legislature: "Government is instituted
. . . for the general happiness and safety; the people therefore are interested in its preservation, and have a right to adopt measures for its security.
. . . But government cannot be thus secured, if, by falsehood and mali-
cious slander, it is deprived of the confidence and affection of the people.
. . . The calumnies of the factious and discontented may not poison the
minds of the majority of the citizens, yet they will infect a very con-

siderable number, and prompt them to deeds destructive of the public peace, and dangerous to the general safety. This the people have a right to prevent."[17]

Yet, to many, including Jefferson, who generally tried very hard during Adams's presidency to maintain the bonds that had made the two men such firm friends since 1775, the measures of 1798 blotted out freedoms for which the American Revolution had been fought. The president who signed the Alien and Sedition Acts had also signed the Declaration of Independence. How could that be? Circumstances, of course, might explain such an apparent incongruity; in 1776 Adams had been an "outsider" resisting a tyrant in power, whereas in 1798 he was himself in power resisting outsiders. Or one might reason that Adams's political views had changed; experience and the jaundice of advancing years had tempered his Revolutionary idealism and left him willing to restrain "seditious" activity.

To John Adams's mind, however, there was neither inconsistency nor declension in his actions. He provided the critical clue to his outlook in a letter written in 1799 when at the height of the crisis over new taxes, diplomatic intrigue, and especially war preparations, he told James McHenry that "all the declamations, as well as demonstrations, of Trenchard and Gordon, Bolingbroke, Barnard and Walpole, Hume, Burgh, and Burke, rush upon my memory and frighten me out of my wits."[18] This rather odd mixture of authorities had in common that each on occasion had warned against standing armies with the attendant debt and taxes that threatened prosperity and constitutional government, but the list also indicates the range and complexity of the problem Adams saw before him. As a good Whig, even a radical one, he was aware of the dangers of civil liberty posed by real or imagined "national emergencies" (thus the recollection of John Trenchard, Thomas Gordon, James Burgh, Sir John Barnard, and in a way, even Walpole himself), but he also believed that a national crisis required leadership above party and a sense of the enduring values of the nation, which provoked the listing of "the Tory historian" David Hume, the apologist of tradition Edmund Burke, and the advocate of the patriot king. In fact, Adams's incessant listing of statesmen and of knaves often revealed the heroic stature he admired and the scheming, partisan traits he scorned in leaders. To his young law clerk in 1774, for example, Adams "warmly recommended" Cicero, Demosthenes, the duc de Sully, Sir Robert Cecil, and the elder William Pitt" as model public servants, and he linked Tiberius, Iago, and Richard III as false and dangerous rulers.[19]

Like Washington, Adams accepted in dead earnest that the role of the leader, standing above party, was critical to the preservation of liberty, which meant in effect the guidance of policy in the public interest. Adams expressed the ideal of leadership he shared with his predecessor (and, substantially, with his first four successors) when in the margin of his copy of

Bolingbroke's *The Spirit of Patriotism* he reflected on the meaning of the word *patriotism*. It comprehended, Adams noted, "piety, or the love and fear of God; general benevolence to mankind; a particular attachment to our own country; a zeal to promote its happiness by reforming its morals, increasing its knowledge, promoting its agriculture, commerce and manufactures, improving its constitution, and securing its liberties: and all this without the prejudices of individuals or parties or factions, without fear, favor, or affection."[20]

In this view, liberty was not the absence of restraint or even the encouragement of diversity, but rather it was *acting* with the uncorruptibility, the disinterested virtue, and the attention to the common good implicit in the Athenian conception of citizenship. Applied to one in a position of power and leadership, liberty meant above all shunning partisanship, that is, avoiding the partial view or the alliance with faction that had defined corruption from the time of Cicero and Tacitus to that of the critics of Walpole whose words Adams had so taken to heart. Yet, this effort to quarantine the presidency from partisanship appears to many modern analysts as an "anachronism," a "vague, idealistic conception," "unsophisticated," and "eccentric."[21] Implicit in this criticism are the assumptions that a president must not only recognize but also engage with the inevitably partisan quality of politics in a free government and that he can be a "strong," "effective" executive only if he grasps the reins of his party to push for its programs—as Andrew Jackson and Franklin Roosevelt were to do. To seek to be "nonpartisan," or "independent," then, is, at the least, naive, probably ineffective, and possibly even irresponsible.

In this view, Adams's presidency might appear to be weak and ineffectual; at best quaint and perverse. He did not before his inauguration prepare a program that his partisans could push through Congress for his signature. He refused to dismiss cabinet members who disagreed with him (such a partisan act would be more harmful to the presidency, he felt, than enduring the strains of discordant counsel). To sustain nonpartisanship, he accepted both war-preparedness legislation and a de facto commander of the army (Alexander Hamilton) he knew might pose grave dangers to constitutional government. Finally, he dispatched a peace mission to France that helped so to fracture the Federalist party (one must resist saying Adams's party) that it lost the next presidential election. Such incongruities and paradoxes can be resolved only if we see the presidency as Adams saw it. He simply could not be partisan either in seeking or conducting office, or even in nourishing a party whose outlook he generally approved, because such were the certain paths to corruption and tyranny. Nor could he cut Gordian knots by becoming a dictator; he was too much the Whig of 1776 for that. Yet, neither could he abdicate leadership on matters of national importance.

In fact, throughout his presidency Adams served effectively according to his own exalted idea of what the office required of him. The critical transfers of power, which historically had almost always so compromised or destroyed nonhereditary rulers that the polity itself endured grievous wounds, first from the revered Washington and then to the (in Adams's opinion) tainted Jefferson, were accomplished safely. In defending the nation, within and without, from the passions and potential tyrannies engendered by the rise of Napoleon, Adams called forth a national strength and resolve probably vital to its independent survival. The acceptance and then the carefully measured enforcement of the Alien and Sedition Acts represented, in the president's view, only a temporary deviation from strict respect for civil liberties. Most important of all, Adams played the role of the patriot leader nearly to perfection in utterly ignoring party needs, in upholding the public interest against popular clamor, and in discerning a long-range wisdom when he insisted on the peace mission to France in 1799. Although quirks of personality and a certain impatience with some aspects of public life sometimes impeded his political effectiveness, by and large he served well under difficult circumstances.[22] Most of the depreciations of Adams's presidency rest either on a political philosophy that does not accept Adams's positive concept of the state and hence the heavy responsibility of officials to preserve and use it or on the assumption that the president *must* serve as a party leader. Adams's understanding of his role, however, was closer to that of George Washington, and even of John Winthrop and Elizabeth I, than to that of either Calvin Coolidge or Franklin Roosevelt—or that of John Kennedy or Ronald Reagan. Adams believed it was incumbent on him to exalt and dignify his office, so that he could arouse the nation in its own defense and guide it toward righteousness and prosperity. It followed from this belief that he had to shun party and stand forth against both popular excitement and vested interests. Reflecting all he had learned from Plutarch, Cicero, Bolingbroke, and a host of others, Adams believed a head of state and government had to lead virtuously and vigorously and to abhor faction and party. Otherwise he would be, quite simply, a bad and irresponsible executive.

❦ 6 ❦

The First Republican
Chief Magistrates

Thomas Jefferson

Jefferson's encounter with *Idea of a Patriot King* and its admonitions
for national leaders was at least as complex and revealing as Adams's.
Although the third president regarded himself as an ardent Whig,
Bolingbroke may possibly have been, as Gilbert Chinard judged
while editing Jefferson's commonplace book, the strongest and
most continuous single influence on Jefferson's intellectual development.
His early friend and mentor, Governor Francis Fauquier, was "known to
have been a follower of [the third earl of] Shaftesbury and Bolingbroke."
Although most of Jefferson's early reading of Bolingbroke concentrated on
his deism and attacks on Christian orthodoxy (the part of Bolingbroke
John Adams condemned), Jefferson also admired his style and his spirited
attacks on Walpolean politics. He owned early editions not only of Bolingbroke's *Philosophical Works* but also of all of his major historical and political writings and bound volumes of the *Craftsman*. Bolingbroke's writings,
Jefferson declared in 1821, were "the finest samples in the English language, of the eloquence proper for the Senate," matching at their best "the
lofty, rythmical, full-flowing eloquence of Cicero."[1] On the other side of
things, Jefferson had also read Bernard Mandeville and found his ridicule
of benevolence and his insistence that self-love was the only spring of human action as repellent as Machiavelli's political cynicism. Finally, Jefferson
read and generally accepted Francis Hutcheson's argument that man possessed an innate "moral sense" and that he had a naturally sociable disposition. Hutcheson, in fact, had taken direct aim not only at Mandeville but
also at Thomas Hobbes, the "French moralists," and others who saw selfishness as the essential bond of society. Man is "endowed with a sense of
right and wrong," Jefferson wrote his nephew in 1787, and his moral principles were formed "relative" to his destiny as a social and political being.[2]
Perhaps even more deeply than Adams, Jefferson was prepared to take to
heart the critique fashioned by Alexander Pope and Jonathan Swift of "the
commercialization of values" in early eighteenth-century Britain.

In 1771 Jefferson explained to a young friend that "every thing is useful which contributes to fix us in the principles and practice of virtue" and urged him particularly to read the best sentimentalist novels and other good writing that would "excite in any high degree this sympathetic emotion of virtue." His list of books suited for this purpose included Swift, Pope, Joseph Addison, John Gay, Voltaire in English, Samuel Richardson, and Henry Fielding. (He later recommended the works of Pope and of Swift to a young student as best to "form your style in your own language.") The emphasis on virtue, especially its emotional, "commonsense" quality present in all persons, and its necessary connection with a socially defined disposition toward benevolence, again revealed the basic influence on Jefferson of Hutcheson, Thomas Reid, Adam Smith, and other Scottish Enlightenment philosophers. Their thought, designed to defend Christian morality against not only the direct assaults of Mandeville and the economists but also against the contractual, "possessive individualism" of Hobbes and Locke, complemented the political and social critique of the English anti-Walpoleans.[3] Although Jefferson's admiration for Virgil, Seneca, Cicero, and the Roman moralists, for the Scottish "commonsense" philosophers, and for the anticommercial political economy of the Physiocrats cannot be doubted, the moral and cultural world view of the Augustan writers always remained the foundation of his thinking. One suspects Pope would have enjoyed Monticello, Swift have approved the Embargo, and Bolingbroke have admired the University of Virginia. Their view of the world and the good life furnished the purpose or goal, in fact, for the political career Jefferson always insisted was simply a part of a larger moral and cultural aspiration he had for the new nation.

Given this vision, it is clear that Jefferson, like John Adams, would have important, positive things for leaders to do. He came to feel that the weak governor's office he held for two years in Virginia (1779–1781) did not suit the needs of the commonwealth in war or in peace. Among his proposed reforms was to give the governor a five-year term, without eligibility for reelection, in order to protect him as much as possible from partisan pressures and intrigue. The governor under this plan was denied many powers associated with royal prerogative, but Jefferson also observed that "the application of the [extent of executive power] must be left to reason." In assessing the Federal Constitution of 1787, from Paris, Jefferson wanted the president eligible for only one term (though he favored a relatively long one of six years) to prevent him from being "an officer for life" with all the potential despotism that entailed. Such an office, he wrote to Adams in London, would make "every succession worthy of intrigue, of bribery, of force, and even of foreign interference." In reply, Adams wrote that he too was apprehensive of "foreign Interference, Intrigue, Influence," and all the corruptions attendant on elections, but his antidote, contrary to Jefferson's, was to have as few "successions" as possible by allowing and even encouraging the incumbent's reelection. More significant, however, than their difference over the point of reeligibility were Adams and Jefferson's common concern that temptations to corruption be diminished and the absence in this correspondence of serious concern about the extent of the powers conferred on the chief executive. Both men, in fact, saw the new Constitution, with its strengthened executive office, as an important advance in the evolution of American government. Adams declared it "conformable to such a system of government as I had ever most esteemed," and Jefferson thought it "unquestionably the wisest ever yet presented to men."[4]

Although some of the courtly trappings of Washington's presidency earned Jefferson's scorn, the first secretary of state actually worked hard to enhance the president's authority. Alexander Hamilton himself later noted that while they "were in the administration together, [Jefferson] was generally for a large construction of the Executive authority, . . . [and] he considered as improper the participation of the Senate in [it]." As differences between Jefferson and the Federalists grew during the 1790s, the Virginian most despised not the idea of an active, independent executive, but what he termed "Hamilton's financial system; . . . a machine for the corruption of the legislature, [designed] . . . to keep [it] in unison with the executive." The secretary of the Treasury allowed congressmen to become rich through his schemes, Jefferson charged, and "men thus enriched by the dexterity of a leader, would follow of course the chief who was leading them to fortune, and become the zealous instruments of all his enterprises."[5] Hamilton sought to govern, that is, in the way Robert Walpole had pioneered and Lord North had practiced, destroying the balance of powers and eventually strangling liberty.

A famous conversation reported by Jefferson captures the crucial distinction: John Adams had declared that the British system, balancing executive and legislative power, when purged "of its corruption, . . . would be the most perfect constitution ever devised by the wit of man." Hamilton retorted that the British system purged of corruption "would become an *impracticable* government"; it was most perfect "as it stands at present." Jefferson's equally famous letter to Philip Mazzei (1796) denounced "the monarchical . . . party" seeking to bring to the United States "the substance, [as well as] . . . the forms, of the British government" and castigated "men who were Samsons in the field and Solomons in the council, but who have had their heads shorn by the harlot England." This unmistakable thrust at Washington, for having allowed himself to be enlisted in the Hamiltonian party (and therefore corrupted), revealed the depth of Jefferson's disappointment, and implicitly, his nonpartisan conception of executive leadership. That the 1790s echoed for him the issues of the 1720s is also apparent in his plea that Americans "awake and snap the Lilliputian cords."[6] It was not dignity in office or even substantial executive power that Jefferson repudiated, but rather Hamilton's effort to govern by a systematic manipulation of various self-interests. To Jefferson, this kind of politics as much debased and corrupted the idea of republican government (in his view, congressional "approval" in no way cleansed the process, of course) as the similar manipulation by Sejanus, a Borgia prince, Cardinal Richelieu, or the duke of Newcastle corrupted their governments.

The ambiguity within the Jeffersonian party on positive leadership in a republic was revealingly displayed in 1794 in John Taylor of Caroline's *Enquiry into the Principles and Tendency of Certain Public Measures.*[7] Conventionally, it was addressed to the national leader, President Washington, hoping that he would see and oppose the corrupt, unrepublican effects of the national bank and Hamilton's other fiscal measures. Taylor chided Washington for having given his assent to the National Bank Act but charitably ascribed this action to his "republican principles" requiring acquiescence to the legislative will, rather than to the president's "approbation of [the] contents" of the bank law. He pleaded, therefore, that Washington would now see that Hamilton's influence in Congress, achieved, Taylor thought, by enlisting members' private interests in support of his schemes, indirectly but "deeply wounded" republican principles. He hoped that "the same laudable vigilance" that had once led Washington to act against "a direct attempt on the principles of representation" would now be used to thwart Hamilton's insidious measures. Taylor thus followed closely the tradition of petitioning the patriot leader to act in the national interest to root out "political immorality." He then lamented, however, that "a patriot magistracy hardly appears to gladden the historic page, once in a century." Because bad leaders so much outnumbered good ones, only a "blind fanaticism" would rely entirely on "the integrity of the magistracy" for the preservation of liberty and political virtue.

After what to Taylor had been a disappointing "presidential revolution" (the election of 1792), it was now necessary, he thought, to apply the pure republican principle of the vigilance of the people. "A frequent and firm national enquiry into the measures of government, will check political vice, and reward political virtue," Taylor intoned. He thus nodded in the direction of traditional dependence on patriot leadership, then doubted the efficacy of such dependence, and finally boldly appealed to public vigilance and legislative, representative power to thwart corrupt deeds. Throughout, however, the rhetoric, the abominated measures, and the appeal to virtuous principles mirrored Bolingbroke's *Craftsman*, and even reflected its discouragement that patriot leadership might not be able to overcome the moneyed interests. For all this, though, Taylor resembled

Samuel Adams more than Bolingbroke by calling for public intervention in a way that supposed the people, rather than the rulers, might possess the virtue to rescue the nation from "self-interest, chicanery, [and] peculation."

Taylor's other 1794 pamphlet, *A Definition on Parties* . . . ,[8] even more directly exemplifies the style and argument of *The Guardian*, the *Craftsman*, and "Junius" in branding the party of the secretary of the Treasury as a "paper money" faction whose corrupt influence over "king, lords, and commons" had subverted all balance, freedom, and virtue in government. Hamilton's incessant party-building had resulted, Taylor noted regretfully, in the growth of "two parties nearly poised as to numbers," which he thought "extremely perilous . . . [to] the public good." Despite his own intense partisanship, Taylor nonetheless drew back from a politics characterized by permanent party rivalry. Because "truth is a thing, not of divisibility into conflicting parts, but of unity," he observed in a profoundly unmodern stance, "both sides cannot be right. Every patriot deprecates a disunion."[9] Paradoxically, despite the growing party activity by both Federalists and Republicans, the theoretical consensus remained opposed to it. "Parties were incapable," in the words of a recent historian, "of realizing the truth; they were totally without regard to principle and they were against the national interest. They were, in addition, capable of corrupting the administration, enervating the principles of republican government, eroding the constitution and the spirit of the American Revolution, and ultimately of causing the dissolution of the republic itself."[10] The Jeffersonian Republicans continued to accept assumptions about the need for a patriotic national unity, and for virtue in the public councils, while they became more ambivalent on whether executive leadership—or the people—might best provide and protect those vital elements.

That ambivalence was heightened in another way by a decade of resistance to Hamilton's use of the executive department to consolidate the powers of the federal government. Hamilton's tactics forced Jefferson to go on record as opposing "loose construction" of the Constitution, institutions such as the national bank that centralized financial power, expansion of federal offices, high taxes, large armed forces, and interference with the prerogatives of the states. "I am not," Jefferson had written in 1799, "for transferring all the powers of the States to the General Government, and all those of that government to the executive branch."[11] Useful as such principles might be in opposing an administration in power, and however much they might recall the hallowed Whig axioms of the American Revolution, they were not likely to be useful to a president with a large agenda for change in mind.

Jefferson entered the presidency committed to what twenty years later he termed "the true principles of the revolution of 1800." This revolution, he said, was as "real" in the "principles of our government as that of 1776 was in its form," accomplished this time, however, not by the sword, but by "the rational and peaceable instrument of reform, the suffrage of the people."[12] Like John Adams, Jefferson believed the real American Revolution was ongoing, begun a generation before 1776 and needful of continuing into the future until habits, values, and attitudes had been republicanized. Jefferson wrote Pierre Samuel Du Pont de Nemours shortly after becoming president that though twelve years of government under "the contracted, English, half-lettered ideas of Hamilton [had] destroyed" the hope for "pure" republicanism in the near future, and that "some things may perhaps be left undone from motives of compromise for a time," he nonetheless intended such a thorough "reformation" as to return the nation to "sound principles." Jefferson further declared that when he took office he "found the country entirely in the enemy's hands," some of whom he would have to "dislodge" from their posts to achieve his "revolution." This done, and with the "artificial panic" (Jefferson's phrase for the party strife of the 1790s) over and factionalism reduced to "the noisy band of royalists inhabiting cities chiefly, and priests both of city and country," Jefferson was sure "the great body of well-meaning citizens" would "consolidate" and political feuding would disappear.[13] For all his reticence, then, Jefferson intended to give a firm if rather low-key direction to events. He was committed to a political and social philosophy for the nation that gave him, as the national leader, vitally important tasks, and he did not believe that that philosophy precluded positive acts by the federal government in the public interest.

At the moment he assumed power Jefferson wrote a close associate of his intention to woo the Federalist rank and file who "did not differ from us in principle, . . . and to urge a reunion on those principles. . . . They will in a little time cement and form one mass with us, and by these means harmony and union be restored to our country, which would be the greatest good we could effect." Outside this "amalgamation" or "orthodoxy" (favorite words in Jefferson's antiparty lexicon) would be only "desperadoes of the quondam faction"—hardly words compatible with acceptance of the notion of a "loyal opposition." He made the same harmonizing points when he told his inaugural audience that though he would "often go wrong through defect of judgment," it was also important to remember that many (partisans?), "whose positions will not command a view of the whole ground," would condemn the president. A year after he retired from the chief executive office Jefferson remained firm on the pre-eminent role of the president: "In a government like ours, it is the duty of the Chief Magistrate, in order to enable himself to *do all the good* which his station requires, . . . to *unite in himself* the confidence of the *whole people.* This alone, in any case where *the energy of the nation* is required, can produce a *union of the powers of the whole*, and point them in a *single direction*, as if all constituted but *one body and one mind*" (emphasis added). This would produce "the whole Constitutional vigor" of the Union and, because authority rested squarely on broad popular support, make American government "the strongest on earth."[14] In other words, instead of seeking to make the office of the president less powerful, Jefferson sought to make it *more popular*—the real essence of his disagreement with the Federalist presidents. Jefferson thus was not, in Isaiah Berlin's categories, a "fox" who led by manipulation toward pragmatic, short-term ends (à la Walpole), but rather a "hedgehog," who had a central vision and unifying values and who led actively toward that integrated world view.[15]

Noticing this active intention, politicians at the time and students of his presidency ever since have, either in condemnation or in praise, emphasized his "inconsistency" or "flexibility" in promptly jettisoning his nostrums about "legislative supremacy" and "strict construction" when he attained power. Such a view, however, highlighting the alleged "change" that occurred when Jefferson the opposition rhetorician became Jefferson the president, overlooks the complexity of his out-of-office attitude. In that position he had continued to accept *both* radical Whig scorn for imperial government *and* the ideal of the patriot king, and he sought earnestly to find a mode of republican leadership retaining the values of each.

Although much of Bolingbroke's best work on politics was written in opposition and in that way agrees substantially with the arguments of John Trenchard, Thomas Gordon, and the oppositionist radical Whigs,[16] other facets of the thought of Bolingbroke and his circle were also of crucial importance to Jefferson, and especially so when he had himself achieved executive power. Like Swift and Pope, Jefferson did not *merely oppose* in building his case against Hamiltonian Federalism, although the tactics of out-of-power politics created such an emphasis in the polemics of the 1790s. It is true that the desire to "win" in a diverse electorate led to the inclusion in Jefferson's "party" of elements that agreed on little more than getting the Federalists out of office. New York politician Aaron Burr, Baltimore merchant Samuel Smith, and Georgia hothead James Jackson are examples of the diversity in this coalition. But Jefferson himself, his most influential and thoughtful colleagues (James Madison and Albert Gallatin especially), and scores of journalists and political leaders all over the country had their own "vision" of what they wanted the nation to become, a "vision" that included an ethic, a political economy, and a social philosophy embedded in the moral values of the Augustan critics. The essence of this vision, inherited by the Augustans from antiquity and Renaissance humanism, was the belief that leaders had the responsibility of "making public [their] detachment from the lower motives: economic gain, physical comfort, personal survival at any cost." This political stance "constituted an affirmation of one's imaginative involvement with the well-being of the

State. It was thus a style designed for a ruling class,"[17] which, according to Jeffersonian republicanism, included the people themselves as well as officeholders.

Jefferson and his colleagues had their own idea of a national future, which they sought to substitute for Hamilton's candid "commercialization of values," his stress on industrialization and national wealth, and his acceptance of both the benefits and liabilities of Britain's domination of world trade. To accomplish this reversal of Hamiltonianism the Jeffersonians had not only to get the Federalists out of power but also to enact their own program. This included a process of "dismantling" to allow another life-style to flourish in the benign presence of liberty, and a positive program to encourage development in the proper direction, such as enlarging the nation's fertile land (an opportunity that arose in the case of the Louisiana Purchase) and substituting commercial coercion for war (the Embargo). Such moves, however, to Jefferson and Madison, still had to be undertaken within republican guidelines. In contemplating the danger at New Orleans in 1803, they worried about the constitutionality of a purchase of land and were cautious about any moves that might provoke hostilities, even though they were entirely enthusiastic about the acquisition itself. Hamilton, on the other hand, urged the administration instead of sending envoys to Paris to purchase part of Louisiana to "seize at once on the Floridas and New-Orleans, and then negociate." Likewise, in 1808 when Gallatin reported it would take "a little army" to uphold the Embargo on the Canadian border and "arbitrary powers . . . equally dangerous and odious" to prevent smuggling along the seacoast,[18] Jefferson and Madison decided to repeal the Embargo rather than be either oppressive or impotent to enforce the laws. Again, one can readily imagine Hamilton's likely different reaction in the face of such a dilemma. Indeed, the meaning of the "revolution of 1800" in some ways can best be understood by conjecturing how Hamilton might have differently conducted government had he been in power between 1801 and 1809.

Jefferson also urged, by constitutional amendment if necessary, internal improvements that would cement the union "by new and indissoluable ties" and a national university that would cultivate all the branches of learning that "contribute to the improvement of the country." But these political programs, relatively modest as Jefferson himself recognized and intended, were auxiliaries to the central purpose of his administration. More fundamentally, he had in mind "a great cultural revolution." To him, as to Benjamin Rush, independence from Britain was only "the first act of the great drama" of the American Revolution. Yet needed was "a revolution in our principles, opinions, and manners, so as to accommodate them to the forms of government we have adopted."[19] Jefferson sought to turn the nation from one path of development toward another. He had in mind profound moral and cultural redirections, which often provoked charges that he was "visionary" or "utopian"—or, as Hamilton said, of a "whimsical imagination"—but which nevertheless were a far-reaching agenda requiring active, yet scrupulously republican, leadership.

Though Samuel Adams and a few other Revolutionary leaders had supposed that such a profound change could somehow well up from the people, Jefferson did not rest his hopes on that entirely. For him, active leadership retained an important role, not only in the programs proposed in the national interest but also in the model, the style, the spirit of the executive office. It was *essential* to him, that is, not merely an act of carelessness, that he receive foreign emissaries in slippers or that "pell-mell" be the rule for guests coming to the president's table. It was important, too, for the president to be a scientist, a farmer, a man of reason, a patron of the arts, and so on, in order to indicate clearly what was honored in the country and would thus be cultivated there. Here as elsewhere Jefferson received positive guidance from the Augustan critics and from *Idea of a Patriot King*. Virtually everything that Bolingbroke had proposed the patriot king *do*, and which he argued could be done only by a national leader, Jefferson saw as part of his function as the chief executive in a republic. He had to govern according to natural law and within the constraints of the Constitution, of course, but he also had to set a moral example for the people, articulate national goals, and use the nation's influence in the world to extend freedom, virtue, and prosperity.

In fact, Jefferson's conduct as chief executive followed to a remarkable degree the five-step program Bolingbroke proposed for the patriot king.[20] First, "purge the court" of the partisans and corrupt placemen, and second, replace them with a new class of men Jefferson would himself characterize as "an aristocracy of talent and virtue." The third measure of the patriot king was "to espouse no party, but to govern like the common Father of his people," an ideal to which Jefferson aspired as he sought triumph *over* party, rather than *through* party. Fourth, the patriot king would encourage a balanced economy (including commerce) that would ensure the prosperity of the people, a conception not the least alien to one whose attention to practical improvements, profitable agriculture, and enlarged trade was as unceasing as Jefferson's. Finally, "the bearing of the patriot king constituted the fifth measure of his program." The leader, that is, had to be a moral guide for the people and in his bearing and manners a symbol of the best in the national heritage. One imagines, for example, that Pope would have found in Jefferson as he had in Bolingbroke "the feast of reason, and the flow of soul" necessary for leadership in its fullest sense. Thus, far from seeing Bolingbroke and his friends as merely "oppositionists" who diagnosed the evils of faction without offering an alternative, Jefferson found in the active idealism of the circle of Pope and Swift an admirable world view as well as some political precepts congenial to it.

Jefferson recognized the more practical dilemmas he faced as leader in a republic, however, when in 1806 he responded to a supporter who had pleaded for more visible guidance from the president: "If we recommend measures in a public message, it may be said that members [of Congress] are not sent here . . . to register the edicts of a sovereign. If we express opinions in conversation, we have then our . . . back-door counsellors. If we say nothing, 'we have no opinions, no plans, no cabinet.'" Jefferson solved the problem by what can be described only as a brilliant series of strategies. He began by remaining in close touch with members of Congress who generally agreed with him, providing thereby a kind of party leadership, but he was always careful to avoid imposing what would later be termed party discipline. In asking Barnabas Bidwell to guide administration measures on the floor of the House of Representatives, the president explained himself carefully: "I do not mean that any gentleman relinquishing his own judgment, should implicitly support all the measures of the administration, but that, where he does not disapprove of them he should not suffer them to go off in sleep, but bring them to the attention of the house and give them a fair chance. Where he disapproves, he will of course leave them to be brought forward by those who concur in the sentiment."[21] Jefferson justified the successful pressure to push John Randolph of Roanoke out of leadership positions in Congress on similar grounds: he had begun to oppose most administration measures and thus could not honestly or effectively be their advocate.

In addition to this general gathering of support, Jefferson and his cabinet colleagues funneled a steady stream of proposals, including drafts of legislation, to sympathetic members of Congress, again always asking them to exercise their own judgment. The president also often cautioned the legislators to shield his role in the measures "because you know with what bloody teeth and fangs the federalists will attack any sentiment or principle known to come from me." Jefferson's careful attention to legislation and his influence among members of Congress nonetheless became so well known that friends applauded and foes condemned his role as "*prime mover.*"[22] The result was that Jefferson both had greater impact on legislation and acted more effectively as a leader of his "partisans" than either of his predecessors (or than any of his first three successors, too), but he was a "party leader" only in the sense that he was extraordinarily skillful and persuasive in gathering and guiding willing followers.

If one adds to Jefferson's influence in Congress his attention to detail, his easy mastery of orderly and efficient methods of administration, and his plans to offer guidance to the state governors, the full dimensions of his leadership emerge. "Jefferson's review of the departmental business laid before him was never perfunctory," a recent student has observed. "Having instructed his department heads to submit policies to him for approval, he remained conversant with a wide range of problems and responded with informed opinions. Carefully reviewing their recommendations, he made alterations where he thought necessary, and although he often accepted their proposals without qualification, he never resorted to *pro forma* endorsements. The careful attention, the time, and the informed effort that Jefferson applied to . . . the business of government day after day, and year after year, is everywhere in evidence in the records of his administration." His assertion of leadership is evident in a letter he wrote to Governor Monroe of Virginia in 1801 in which he maintained that the national executive was "certainly preordinate" in commanding the militia and in the exercise of other powers granted to the general government. He also considered seriously a plan to send annual messages to all the state governors advising them of measures that, "from a view of the whole ground," were necessary for the public good but were within the powers reserved to the states. To one as intent on plan and harmony as Jefferson, even the useful decentralization of the federal system required guidance lest important public needs be neglected. In this way, Jefferson's genius enabled him at once to lead, to be unimperial, to be in close touch with the people, and to apply reason to national policy. He would not, he said, if he could help it, preside over "a government of chance and not of design,"[23] which is to say that he intended to bring to self-government the same positive guidance and pursuit of the "ideal" that had always characterized the admired eras of human history.

Jefferson's brilliant performance as a leader generally, and especially his effective guidance of like-minded congressmen, has often led to the mistaken conclusion that he represents a classic early instance of the supposed undeniable truth that a president must be an adroit, even manipulative, leader of his party in Congress if new programs are to be undertaken in the nation. Later presidents who did this, such as Theodore Roosevelt, Woodrow Wilson, and Franklin Roosevelt, are usually listed as among the "best" American presidents, and their mastery of Congress is generally seen as crucial to that stature. Such effectiveness, it is claimed, is closely tied to party leadership because it is often party means—distribution of patronage, endorsement for reelection, party accomplishment in the eyes of the public, and so on—that enable the president to garner support in Congress for his policies. Further, this understanding of the presidency often views the chief executive's role as party leader in the legislature as bringing informally to American government some of the benefits of party discipline and executive guidance characteristic of parliamentary systems. Indeed, the arrangement is sometimes seen as the only way the "checks" in a system of separation of powers can be overcome enough to make active government possible.

Yet, despite the assumed party division of Congress from 1801 to 1809 between Federalists, who opposed the president, and Republicans, who supported him, Jefferson never made party itself the key to his leadership, nor would he have been pleased to have been classed with Andrew Jackson, Franklin Roosevelt, Lyndon Johnson, and other avowed masters of partisan politics.[24] As the quotations above show, Jefferson did not distinguish in his thinking between those in Congress who were fellow party members and thus obliged for the sake of party success to vote with him as Republicans and those who for perfectly good and acceptable Federalist party reasons could be expected to vote against him. Jefferson did not consider it part of his role either to ensure the *organizational* strength of his party or to perpetuate a division in the country between an administration party and a "loyal opposition," although both of these goals are integral to the view that the president's power rests on his skill and authority as leader of his party. There is, in short, very little place in Jefferson's conception of executive leadership for the hallmarks of the post-1829 partisan presidency.

Jefferson's administrations suggest that it might not be necessary under all circumstances for a president to depend on control of, or influence through, a political party in order to be an effective executive. His posture and performance as president indicate that in important ways good leadership can depend on a muted partisanship and that it may not be necessary for the president to be an active party leader while in office in order for the Constitution to "work." Both in Congress and in the country at large Jefferson gathered support precisely because he appealed to Federalists, except for those "desperadoes of the quondam faction," to join him in pursuit of the public good and because he refused to placate dissident Republicans (such as John Randolph of Roanoke) in the interests of *party* unity. Like many great leaders in the past, monarchical and other, and even like many later presidents who enhanced their effectiveness by appeals that transcended party, Jefferson capitalized on the perennial attraction of harmony and cooperation, as opposed to the incessant "generation of conflict" often called for by partisan theories of leadership. Jefferson's presidency, and especially his skillful guidance of Congress, far from demonstrating that an effective president has to exert his will on Congress through the agency of party, proves on the contrary that legislative leadership can be achieved through persuasion, cultivation of supposed party opponents, and articulation of a program in the public interest that truly transcends party. On the model of Plutarch's heroes and the "good kings" of Dryden and Swift, Jefferson saw party and leadership as antithetical and conducted his relationship with Congress generally according to that precept.

Of the many evidences of this "patriot" style in Jefferson's words and deeds, an especially revealing one reverberates in the phrase "an empire of liberty," which Jefferson used so often to bring the idea of dominion within the moral framework of the Declaration of Independence. In sending George Rogers Clark to secure the Illinois country in 1778, in drafting the Northwest Ordinance in 1784, in purchasing Louisiana and in dispatching the Lewis and Clark expedition in 1803, in supporting the War of 1812, and in favoring the liberation of Spain's Latin American colonies in the 1820s, Jefferson had in view always the enlargement of the "empire of liberty." He had urged Clark in 1779 to respect the religion and customs of the people of the Illinois country so that there might be added "to the empire of liberty an extensive and fertile country, thereby converting dangerous enemies into valuable friends." He hoped that later the world would witness in the continental United States "such an extent of country under a free and moderate government as it has never yet seen," where "range after range" of new, equal, and self-governing states would cover the Mississippi Valley, and that in the whole American hemisphere European tyranny would be expelled and this vast area become filled with free nations.[25] Jefferson was not so naive as to believe that this dream could be realized without active leadership.

Although this idea of empire, associated with the extension of liberty rather than the spread of tyranny, might appear contradictory to readers of Lenin (as it did to those familiar with Roman history), in fact it had an ancient, honorable pedigree of which Jefferson himself was probably aware. In *Agricola*, Tacitus had noted the remarkable happiness of the reign of the Emperor Nerva, who "united things long incompatible, Empire and liberty" (*res olim dissociabiles miscuerit, principatum ac libertatem*). Then, Sir Francis Bacon in *Advancement of Learning* had quoted Tacitus (inaccurately, using the Latin "*imperium et libertatem*") as evidence of "the excellent temper" of Nerva's reign. Finally Bolingbroke, on the last page of *Idea of a Patriot King*, perhaps relying only on Bacon, asked what could be so lovely, so venerable as "a king, in the temper of whose government, like that of Nerva, things so seldom allied as empire and liberty are intimately mixed, co-exist together inseparably, and constitute one real essence?" (Tacitus's phrase finally received its modern connotation, of course, when "empire and liberty" was termed "the rightful aim of British policy" by Benjamin Disraeli, himself a fervent admirer of Bolingbroke.)[26] In so self-consciously using the phrase "empire and liberty," then, Jefferson indicated in yet another way that he saw a need for both the preservation of liberty and a provision for the various connotations of *principatum* and *imperium:* dominion, government, authority, empire, leadership. In fact, in his later linking of Thomas Paine and Bolingbroke as "both advocates of human liberty," he may have had in mind precisely the two "long incompatible" elements in need of reconciliation. That, indeed, is one way to put the thrust of Jefferson's presidency: somehow to republicanize the patriot king.

James Madison

The fourth president, James Madison, in general agreed with Jefferson's conception of executive authority. Madison's acceptance of Swift, Pope, and Addison as the preeminent guides in style and in outlook on life had been strengthened by his studies at the College of New Jersey (later Princeton), where these authors were often recommended by the faculty. President John Witherspoon, who was especially important in Madison's intellectual growth, relied also on the Scots, Lord Kames, Adam Ferguson, and Francis Hutcheson, to combat Mandeville, the third earl of Shaftesbury, Hume, and others, who, in Witherspoon's interpretation, were "infidel" writers. Witherspoon emphasized the "moral sense" and the affective sociability of mankind, as did Hutcheson and his other teachers in reaction to the self-centered individualism of the economic and social contract theorists. Although Witherspoon does not seem to have paid particular attention to the debates of the Augustan literary circles, at Madison's graduation the main address was "The Idea of a Patriot-King."[27] In general, Witherspoon was both deeply respectful of ancient pieties and assumptions (he taught politics straight from Aristotle, laced his lectures to Princeton seniors with anecdotes from Plutarch, and preached orthodox Calvinism in the college chapel) and fervently Whiggish in his insistence that all forms of authority conform to a higher law. The spirit of Princeton under Witherspoon is evident in the 1770 graduation exercises when one student argued in Latin that "Omnes Homines, Jure Naturae, liberi sunt" (all men, in the law of nature, are free) while others debated more particularly whether "subjects are bound and obligated by the law of nature, to resist their king if he treats them cruelly or ignores the law of the state, and to defend their liberty." Thus from his earliest study of philosophy, literature, and politics Madison had absorbed teachings both devoted to natural law and mindful of the uses of virtuous leadership.

As a member of the Governor's Council in Revolutionary Virginia, Madison came to believe (as did Governor Jefferson) that the executive in its first constitution was too weak. Both men also worked to strengthen the executive "departments" under the Articles of Confederation. In 1782 Madison supported Robert Morris's insistence that his subordinates in the Department of Finance be responsible to him, and not to Congress as a whole, and even defended Morris against charges of what would now be called "conflict of interest." Madison was well aware that Morris mingled private and public business and that he increased his personal fortune while in office, but to Madison the crucial fact was Morris's manifest public usefulness and his "honorable and patriotic" motives. Lacking proof of "misfeasance," Madison argued, "the same fidelity to the public interest which obliges those who are its appointed guardians to pursue with every vigor a perfidious or dishonest servant of the public requires [exposure of] imputations of malice against the good and faithful one."[28] Clearly, Madison took seriously the concept of the public interest, thought devotion to it was the critical mark of the good official, and saw a compelling need for active, honest executives.

Madison's sense of the importance of active government in the public interest was particularly heightened during the 1780s when he witnessed the poor performance of the state legislatures. His own experience in the Virginia legislature (1784–1786) as well as his observation of other states, especially Rhode Island, where a "paper money faction" defaulted flagrantly on state debts and brazenly injured out-of-state interests, led him to an ominous conclusion. The unwise and unjust laws passed by these bodies "brings . . . into question the fundamental principle of republican Government, that the majority who rule in such Governments, are the safest Guardians both of public Good and of private rights." Madison complained of the "multiplicity," the "mutability," and the "impotence" of state laws, calling them "nuisances," impractical, and even "vicious," but his deepest objection was to their poor *quality*: they lacked wisdom and virtue. The dilemma created by this discovery, that the basic principle of republican government (majority rule) could work against the even more fundamental need for just laws, was for Madison compounded by the realization that the source of this malfunction was to be found not only in the tendency toward imprudence and corruption in the representatives but also more fatally "among the people themselves." A host of private interests, real and imagined, divided the people of the states into conflicting groups, and these rival claims, Madison observed, generally overcame whatever virtuous motives might be expected to arise from "a prudent regard to their [the people's] own good as involved in the general and permanent good of the Community." Even "respect for character" and standards of morality derived from religious conviction were overrun by political interests. The states left to themselves, Madison concluded, seemed invariably to trample on both private rights and the public good, and this despite that the states more fully than any other governments in the world embodied the radical Whig principle of legislative supremacy.

To cope with this discouraging development, Madison hypothesized that in "an extended republic," on the continental scale of the United

States, "a greater variety of interests, of pursuits, of passions [would] check each other." In consequence, the general government would be less likely than the state governments to act unjustly and should therefore have "a negative" on the laws of the states, a power he advocated throughout the Federal Convention and, privately, even for some months afterward. "The great desideratum," he concluded, was "such a modification of the Sovereignty as will render it sufficiently neutral between the different interests and factions." But neutrality meant for Madison a point of view that was impartial, disinterested, a sovereignty above party such as that of "the prince . . . in absolute Monarchies." The characteristic vice of such a sovereign, that he would sacrifice the happiness of his people "to his ambition or his avarice," might be thwarted by the elimination of monarchy as such in a republic, but the need remained of guarding against the defects of republicanism itself.[29] Thus on the eve of the Federal Convention Madison had espoused a Bolingbrokean view of the inherent evil of factions, of their tendency to be dominant in legislative bodies, and of the possibility that some form of centralized executive power might help prevent these calamities.

At the Convention, however, Madison encountered powerful advocates of more Whiggish views of executive power. Roger Sherman of Connecticut, a ready defender of legislative power, "considered the Executive Magistracy as nothing more than an institution for carrying the will of the Legislature into effect." The legislature, Sherman insisted, "was the depository of the supreme will of the Society" and was therefore "the best judge of the business which ought to be done by the Executive department." Sherman sought definition of executive powers by the legislature, proposed various schemes for a plural executive and for its election by the legislature, and objected to an executive veto. He was insistent, that is, that the national government as much as possible reflect the principle of legislative supremacy as it existed in Connecticut's and in other Whiggish state constitutions. Madison, James Wilson, Gouverneur Morris, and others protested vigorously that such proposals strengthened rather than diminished the power of faction and of provincial interests in government. They admitted that any form of monarchy was out of the question in the United States, but they nonetheless sought somehow to retain the benefit of its ability to check legislative corruption and partisanship. Indeed, it can be argued that "the Presidency was designed in great measure to reproduce the monarchy of George III with the corruption . . . and . . . the hereditary feature . . . left out."[30] The debates in the Convention, as well as the final shape of the presidential office in the Constitution, show that by 1787 Sherman's Whiggish views were in decline as Madison and others sought ways to implant in republican government the benefits of energy and transcendence of party long associated with a patriot king.

Madison revealed his train of thought on June 4, when, defending executive veto, he noted the danger a republic faced from diversity of interests, demagoguery, and the power of a selfish majority. "In this view," Madison concluded, "a negative in the Ex[ecutive] is not only necessary for its own [protection], but for the safety of a minority. . . . The independent condition of the Ex[ecutive] who has the Eyes of all Nations on him will render him a just Judge." Madison even sought some way to combine the judiciary with the executive in the veto power, in order to increase the sense of wisdom and respectability in this vital restraint on the presumed-to-be-factious legislature. Two days later he noted the difficulty in a republic of finding a source of power that, like a "hereditary magistrate," would have a "personal interest agst. betraying the national interest." Remembering the host of philosophers and historians who had argued that a good king would have a personal stake in upholding the national interest, Madison sought earnestly, even desperately, to find a republican equivalent.[31]

When it appeared that the Convention might have the legislature elect the executive (as many delegates favored at some stage), Madison wondered out loud whether executive tenure "during good behavior" might be preferable to a president thus dependent on legislative intrigue. Although Madison later explained away this nod toward an unrepublican life tenure, he was willing to do almost anything to resist the fatal tendency in republics of throwing "all power into the Legislative vortex." Four days later, Madison urged that the executive be given the power to appoint federal judges because he would be "a national officer, acting for and equally sympathising with every part of the U. States."[32] Throughout the debates Madison consistently sought to establish an executive department that would be independent of the legislature, and insofar as that independence was secure, he was willing to grant wide powers to the executive. In his mind, faction, all too dominant in legislatures, posed the greatest threat to free government, and Bolingbroke's model of a king (executive) above party was always an appealing if incomplete antidote.

Madison also sought ways to combine power and virtue in the executive office as he tussled with the crucial question of how the president was to be selected. A good executive would have to be not only "separate" from the other branches but also protected as much as possible from corruption, which meant to Madison not only dishonesty and intrigue but also, more fundamentally, pursuit of private (partial) over public (common) interest. This danger of corruption more and more ruled out election by an "existing authority," that is, by the national or state legislatures, by state governors, by a judicial body, or whatever. Furthermore, the near-universal eighteenth-century assumption that direct popular election would be a circus in public and a bazaar in private made Madison skeptical of that process. He approved of the electoral college scheme, then, as "least objectionable" given the arguments against the other possibilities and as best calculated to prevent intrigue and faction from controlling the election. The need, he wrote Jefferson, was to "unite a proper energy in the Executive . . . with the essential characters of Republican Government,"[33] or, to put the matter in terms of the century-long English debate, to retain the manifest moral and positive qualities of the patriot king (that is, to lead with "proper energy") while also being faithful to the republican principles of consent and of constitutional restraint.

Even in defending the House of Representatives against charges that its members would always act factiously, as he would do most systematically in *The Federalist*, Number 57, Madison began with the need for *good* rulers. "The aim of every political constitution," he wrote, "is or ought to be first to obtain for rulers, men who possess most wisdom to discern, and most virtue to pursue the common good of society; and in the next place, to take the most effectual precautions for keeping them virtuous; whilst they continue to hold their public trust." In Madison's mind the starting point was to be sure that those who held political power possessed proper character. In a republic this essential need meant good character in the representatives who made the laws as well as in the other officers of government. It is apparent that Madison regarded even the basic republican idea of making representatives accountable to the people as a useful rule only insofar as it kept officeholders on the proper path and counteracted the tendency of hereditary and oligarchic executives to betray the public interest. To Madison, as to Jefferson, Adams, and Washington, possession of virtue by the ruler was the cardinal ingredient of good government. Indeed, the principle of consent itself could be justified only insofar as it sustained that *summum bonum*.

Gouverneur Morris emphasized a slightly different benefit to the polity from the virtuous ruler in noting that "the Executive Magistrate should be the guardian of the people, even of the lower classes, against Legislative tyranny, against the Great and the wealthy who in the course of things will necessarily compose the Legislative body." Pointing to what he said "History proves . . . to be the spirit of the opulent," Morris leveled more "Country" party charges at the legislature: "Wealth tends to corrupt the mind and to nourish its love of power, and to stimulate it to oppression." Morris asserted that if the executive is thus "to be the Guardian of the people let him be appointed by the people." In a country as large as the United States, Morris further argued, such a mode of election could resist influence "by those little combinations and those momentary lies which often decide popular elections within a narrow sphere."[34]

Both Morris and Madison, however, increasingly adopted James Wilson's solution to the problem of how vigorous, impartial executive power could be squared with the principle of government by consent. Starting with that principle generally, Wilson accepted as "the great desideratum in politics . . . a government [both] . . . efficient and free. . . . But, I think, it can be done only by forming a popular government. To render government efficient, power must be given liberally; to render it free as well as efficient, those powers must be drawn from the people, as directly and as immediately as possible." In Wilson's oft-used metaphor, a "pyramided government," resting on the broad base of the people, would be the strongest and most stable form. But Wilson moved beyond his more conventionally Whiggish colleagues to argue that the principle of consent could also be applied effectively to the executive. Then, "he who is to execute the laws will be as much the choice, as much the servant and, therefore, as much the friend of the people as he who is to make them." With the executive thus fully responsible, it was proper, in Wilson's view, to unify and enlarge his power to take advantage of the traditional benefits of "efficient" leadership. Such a single executive elected by the people and responsible to them would also "be impartial . . . [and] promote the interests of the whole." With this "chain of connection," Wilson argued, the reputation of the executive would be tied to the public interest, and the nation would be able to have its affairs conducted according to the "very quintessence of impartiality."[35] The plan was to link together popular election, a liberal grant of power, clear responsibility, and impartiality in order to make republican government good government.

Madison worked in yet another way toward the goal of uniting republican principles with strong executive leadership in his now-famous theory of the extended republic, first stated publicly in the tenth *Federalist* essay. Madison argued that protection against tyranny and the effects of "the factious spirit" would be found in the many particular and divided interests that a large republic would inevitably contain. The self-interested parties would cancel out one another, be neutralized and reduced to no effect, allowing "the interest of the entire Society" to gain sway. Madison did not suppose, as twentieth-century "broker-state" political analysis does, that the push and pull of various factions would result in a compromise, which itself becomes the only practical definition of the public interest. In this modern view, factions are seen not only as inevitable, which Madison admitted, but also as positively useful because they bring to the attention of government the private needs of various segments of society, a point of view that Madison would have denied. To him a faction was a group whose interests were "adverse to the rights of other citizens, or to the permanent and aggregate interests of the community." Madison thus hoped that factions would so check one another that a truly "aggregate" view, an uncorrupted policy, a public interest could be asserted.

At Washington's right hand during the early years of government under the new Constitution, Madison sought to guard the president's dignity and powers as long as the executive department retained the nonpartisanship that *alone* could legitimize its authority. Madison soon came to believe, however, as Jefferson did, that Hamilton sought to make the presidential office into something quite different. The "cementing" of the public creditors to the national government, the corruption of members of Congress (meaning not so much bribes as the enlisting of the selfish interests of their constituents), the cultivation of party, the alignment with Britain's commercial policies, the enlargement of the public debt, and the chartering of financial institutions all pointed toward exactly the sort of partisan, corrupt, commercial, ministerial government the Augustan critics had scorned under Walpole. Madison asserted that "a government operating by corrupt influence; substituting the motive of private interest in place of public duty [was an] . . . impostor" under a republican constitution, while others accused Hamilton of being a Walpolean "prime minister" leading a "phalanx of stockholders."[36] With the executive thus tainted, Madison was forced toward the radical Whig "solution" of emphasis on legislative power and even on states' rights as *means* to resist a corrupted administration. He even joined Jefferson in founding an antiministerial, republican party, which each conceived as "a party to end all parties," that is, an instrument, a temporary *means* to overcome the power of party (inherently malignant) so skillfully mustered by Hamilton.

The aspirations Jefferson expressed in his first inaugural address, that the *partisan* electoral contest just over be the last such one in American history and that the time had come for all Federalists and all Republicans to "unite in common efforts for the common good," were also Madison's aspirations. Quaint or naive or forlorn as it may seem after nearly two centuries of unrelenting party battles and, more profoundly, after the enshrinement of the political party as the benign dynamic of democratic government, Madison thought it not only possible but also vital to the survival of good government that parties should disappear. The Jeffersonian Republican party of the 1790s and the following generation may in some senses be construed as part of the "great democratic party" that runs from Samuel Adams, Thomas Paine, and other "radicals" of 1776 through the Antifederalists of 1788 to the party of Jackson, Wilson, Franklin Roosevelt, and Hubert Humphrey. It was not, however, a *party* in the post-1829 sense, for its leaders did not seek its perpetuation (it would "succeed" in their eyes only if it became unnecessary) and did not see inherent virtue in its organizational strength or in its ability to sharpen partisan issues in the country.[37] Madison was, therefore, in the same paradoxical, perhaps inconsistent, position as Bolingbroke had been in the 1720s and 1730s when he assiduously cultivated an anti-Walpole "party" and sustained a brilliantly vituperative opposition newspaper—all in the name of putting an end to "government by party," that is, a government of special interests that failed to discern and rule in the public good.

During Madison's sixteen years as secretary of state and president, his objective, negatively, was to purge American government of opportunities for ministerial abuse of power and end the excessive influence of trading interests; positively, he aimed to restore a legitimate leadership that would be above party yet within the republican principle of consent. During Jefferson's first term, Madison took part earnestly in Republican efforts to dismantle and restrain the most high-toned and (in their view) partisan aspects of the federal government; that is, to make it "mild" rather than aggressively commercial. Jefferson's overwhelming reelection in 1804, evidence of wide public support for the "revolution of 1800," was especially pleasing to the administration leaders because "the party spirit" in the country seemed sharply reduced. But the intensification of the worldwide, life-and-death struggle between France and England, signaled by the guns of Austerlitz and Trafalgar in the fall of 1805, imposed a ten-year moratorium on Republican attention to domestic affairs and utterly preoccupied, indeed nearly overwhelmed, Madison's efforts in executive office until halfway through his second term as president.

As he passed through the trials and vicissitudes of the Embargo, the conquest of West Florida, the Macon Acts, and the War of 1812, he again and again discovered that the more Whiggish of republican principles— deference to Congress, protection of civil liberties, opposition to war preparations, support for international law, and so on—were not easily assimilated to the demands of war leadership. Combined with Madison's unimperious personality, these principles often led to vacillating, ineffective policies. One can easily imagine the different and at times more appropriate style of an Andrew Jackson or a Winston Churchill. Yet, Madison did make one surpassing contribution. He saw the nation through the trial in a way that caused French Minister Louis Sérurier to declare, as news of the Treaty of Ghent arrived in Washington, that "three years of warfare have been a trial of the capacity of [American republican] institutions to sustain a state of war, a question . . . now resolved to their advantage." By refusing himself to become a Caesar and by preventing any other leader from assuming that role, Madison had enabled the nation to survive the Napoleonic maelstrom and to "win" the War of 1812 in the most fundamental terms. By fending off partisans (near traitors, some accused) on all sides, by avoiding "perpetual taxation, military establishment, and other corrupting or anti-republican habits or institutions," and thus winning "the second war of independence," Madison offered important if imperfect lessons in how to join Whiggish principles and the demands of crisis leadership.[38]

With the return of peace, Jackson's victory at New Orleans, and the discrediting of the Federalist party in 1815, Madison had an opportunity to be the patriot leader on the model of Plutarch and Bolingbroke. He gave top appointments to able and proven colleagues—Monroe, Gallatin, John Quincy Adams, Admirals John Rodgers and David Porter, and Generals Jackson and Winfield Scott, for example—in whom the whole nation took pride. He provided leadership to Congress, especially in his annual message of December 1815 in which he recommended a broad national program. He proposed a rechartered Bank of the United States, an equitable commercial treaty with Great Britain, a mildly protective tariff, a small but high-quality defense establishment, a national university, and a program of internal improvements authorized by a constitutional amendment. This program was indeed "crypto-Federalist," as John Randolph of Roanoke charged, but not in the inconsistent and pejorative sense intended. Madison deliberately gathered the best ideas of all segments of national opinion and took it as his duty to outline and pursue policies for the "public good," regardless of previous party identification with them. Finally, Madison "passed on" the presidency to the republican variety of "heir apparent," that is, to a person of long public service, of unquestioned patriotism, of restrained partisanship, and of wide public support. Although intrigue and faction boiled below the surface of the Republican party and although the Federalists still managed a feeble opposition, nothing more pleased Madison and Monroe than the all-encompassing nature of their party, or, in other words, its aspiration to transcend the conventional, negative understanding of party.

In Madison's view (shared by Jefferson and Gallatin), the posture of the years 1815–1817 was a fulfillment of the good intentions and high hopes of 1801–1804. With the Hamiltonian engine restrained and in part dismantled, and the nation's republican institutions validated and revived, it was possible to use government for the public interest. And it was the particular responsibility of the president to articulate that interest. Although ultimate authority came from the people, and although it was the task of Congress to legislate, the need for both practical and symbolic leadership by the chief executive was, in the minds of men nourished on Cicero, Erasmus, and Addison, still crucial. In this tradition Madison furnished steady, principled guidance during two years of national euphoria. Viewed in this light, Henry Adams's often-repeated criticism, that Madison found himself forced to become a Federalist in order to govern properly, becomes a half-truth. Like Jefferson, Madison was a Federalist in that he believed in active, virtuous national leadership; he did not, however, abandon republican precepts or attempt to take over Federalism as a political party. Rather, he intended to eliminate party itself from public life. John Pendleton Kennedy, a Maryland writer and Whig politician who knew Madison well in his old age, wrote that it was the "glory" of the last years of Madison's administration "that it made peace between parties; that it established the true import of our fundamental law" by having tempered "the extremes of Federalism . . . with an infusion of democratic flavor; [and] the extremes of Democracy had been melted in an amalgam of Federalism." "The calm and philosophic temper of Mr. Madison, the purity of his character, the sincerity of his patriotism, and the sagacity of his intellect had inspired universal trust," Kennedy wrote in his own encapsulation of the qualities of the patriot leader. It had led to "a balmy peace . . . throughout [the] political world" and established a "Madisonian basis of . . . American government . . . by the almost universal consent of the country."[39] Although Kennedy penned these words for his own partisan political purposes, they nonetheless reveal the aura that surrounded Madison's last two years as chief executive and are the praise he would have most welcomed at the end of his public career.

Jefferson himself recorded his great pleasure at the political climate in the country in 1817 when he wrote to Lafayette that the best effect of the War of 1812 had been "the complete suppression of party" and that "the evanition of party dissensions has harmonized intercourse, and sweetened society beyond imagination." Observing the scene from retirement in Quincy, Henry Adams's great-grandfather, John Adams, also agreed with this view when he wrote Jefferson that "notwithstanding a thousand Faults and blunders, [Madison's] Administration has acquired more glory, and established more Union, than all his three Predecessors, Washington[,] Adams[,] and Jefferson, put together."[40] Thus, though Madison was in many ways a most unlikely patriot king figure, in forty years of public life he worked toward an executive office in accord with the ideal of the Augustan critics. His mind could no more make a virtue of partisanship than could the hero of *Cato* or the king of Brobdingnag.

In admiring this model, Madison agreed entirely, at least in principle, with his predecessor. They shared a sense that the ten years of preoccupation with the impositions of the Napoleonic Wars (1805–1815) were an unhappy, near-tragic interruption in the establishment in the United States of a more fully republican nationhood. In both the peaceful and war-dominated years of their administrations, furthermore, Jefferson and Madison struggled with problems from the same perspective and remained in close, congenial agreement on what was required of the president. That Madison was much less successful than Jefferson in guiding Congress, or even in resisting acts that undermined his performance in executive office, is to be explained not by the notion that the two men had different conceptions of leadership but by the very different circumstances surrounding their administrations and by their different personal qualities. The rise of a much more virulent factionalism among Republicans in Congress at the very moment of Madison's inauguration, and the revival of the Federalists as opponents of resistance to Great Britain, made it impossible for Madison to steer Congress in Jefferson's manner. Despite these serious political obstacles and his tendency to shun center stage, Madison took forthright and sometimes successful steps to lead the nation and guide the branches of government. When his secretary of state proved inept in writing dispatches and negotiating with foreign envoys, Madison wrote drafts himself, corrected impressions conveyed to ambassadors, and eventually fired the incompetent secretary despite the strong, some said irresistible, support for the secretary by a faction of the Senate. Also, in close collaboration with Monroe, who became his closest adviser as the War of 1812 approached, Madison appealed to the country through "editorials" planted in a Washington newspaper, sent a stream of proposals for war preparedness to Congress, and, at least as much as the so-called War Hawks themselves, led in carrying the nation toward the decision to declare hostilities in June 1812.[41]

In addition to these disparate circumstances, which account for much of the very different evaluations often made of their administrations (and even much of this fades if one compares the more peaceful and less divisive parts of their tenures, 1801–1805 and 1815–1817), two qualities of Jefferson's allowed him to have a style of leadership denied Madison. Most important, Jefferson's great personal magnetism gave him a matchless influence in private conversations and in small groups that was far more important than any formal or "party" mechanisms. The power he wielded as president, his biographer concludes, "was to an exceptional degree personal and little institutionalized." Jefferson was able to guide and lead because others so easily and so earnestly came under the spell of his character and personality, a sort of response Madison simply failed to evoke as readily or as pervasively. Furthermore, Jefferson's gift for the memorable phrase gave his words a range and indelibleness that Madison's writings (neither man was an eloquent orator), however cogent and carefully reasoned, did not attain. Thus, in gathering, retaining, and spreading the support vital to exceptional leadership, Jefferson had critical advantages that weigh heavily in assessing the effectiveness of his presidency, but the difference between him and Madison is almost entirely in those personal qualities rather than in their conception of the executive office. Indeed, when five months before he died Jefferson wrote Madison of "the harmony of our political principles and pursuits . . . [for] now half a century," and Madison replied extolling the "private friendship and political harmony" that had suffered not a single "interruption or diminution" over that period,[42] neither man would have had any thought of excepting their ideas of proper presidential leadership.

The Ebb of the
Republican Presidency

James Monroe

The harmonious circumstances of James Monroe's election to the presidency and his unique public career conspired to make him, excepting only George Washington, the most nonpartisan chief executive in American history. Winning the office with 183 of 217 electoral votes in 1816 and losing only one electoral vote four years later, Monroe held the presidency without a significant opposition party and with the nominal support, at least, of the various segments of what came to be called the National Republican party. In his first inaugural address he declared that "the American people . . . constitute one great family with a common interest." "Discord does not belong to our system," he affirmed, and he was pleased "to witness the increased harmony of opinion which pervades our Union." In his second inaugural address Monroe repeated his condemnation of party spirit, spoke again of the unique circumstances in the United States that made party struggles unnecessary, praised the workings of the "republican system," and went on to hope that with the demise of party it might "soon attain the highest degree of perfection of which human institutions are capable, and that the movement in all its branches will exhibit such a degree of order and harmony as to command the admiration and respect of the civilized world." Convinced therefore that the "existence of parties is not necessary to free government" and that "the Chief Magistrate of the Country ought not to be the head of a party, but of the nation itself," Monroe seemed, providentially, to have a chance to *achieve* the oft-espoused ideal of a party-free government resting on devotion to the general good.[1] This aspiration by Monroe was the high-water mark of the republican intention shared by the first six presidents to blend the public-spirited, harmony-loving Augustan world view with the self-governing ideals of the New World.

Monroe's fifty-year-long public career began in 1776 when his Virginia regiment reached New York in time to wage a tough delaying action against the British conquest of that city. In the rest of a distinguished military career Monroe played a key role in the Battle of Princeton (receiving a severe wound in the process), fought at Brandywine and Germantown, took part in thwarting the so-called Conway Cabal against Washington, endured the encampment at Valley Forge, and led a scouting party that helped Washington rally his army at the Battle of Monmouth.[2] After studying law with Thomas Jefferson, Monroe served in the Virginia legislature, the Continental Congress, and the Virginia Ratifying Convention before becoming a United States senator in 1790. During the next twenty-five years, he undertook diplomatic missions in France, Spain, and England, served twice as governor of Virginia, and acted as secretary of war and secretary of state under James Madison. In 1817 he was both the most widely experienced public servant ever to be inaugurated president and "the last of the cocked hats," that is, the last major political leader of the new nation to have been a hero of the Revolution.

Embodying the patriot leader in his career, Monroe was also ideally suited to republicanize the chief magistracy. He had been virtually reared by the leading republican theorists in Virginia, especially George Wythe and Jefferson. About 1780 he seems to have read at Jefferson's direction much of the same list of "a few only of the best books" on politics Jefferson had recommended to Robert Skipwith a few years earlier: especially Locke, Montesquieu, Algernon Sidney, and Bolingbroke, of the more modern writers. Monroe surely had a good grasp of the conventional, antiparty ideology, even if he did not have the intellectual power of his two predecessors as president.

During the 1790s, on the other hand, Monroe was a determined Jeffersonian partisan in opposing Alexander Hamilton's increasing domination of the federal government, and his experience as governor of Virginia, as a diplomat, and as a cabinet officer were often partisan in effect. He even took part in a major intraparty dispute that found him willing to oppose Madison for the "party presidential nomination" in 1808. Like Madison and Jefferson, however, he hoped the need for such a stance would pass away, and when he was inaugurated president in 1817, Monroe sensed deeply that he had to be both a faithful republican *and* a national leader.

As Washington had done nearly thirty years before and as patriot kings had done for centuries, Monroe determined to quicken and symbolize national identity by elaborate tours throughout the country. He began in the region of recent disaffection, New England, in the summer of 1817, planning to be in Boston on the Fourth of July. Monroe cherished the scene of thousands cheering as the Federalist and Republican leaders there joined in welcoming the old patriot—newly elected president on the national birthday. After a triumphal procession through Baltimore, Philadelphia, and New York, Monroe arrived in Boston, where 40,000 people lined his route. Both ex-President John Adams and old arch-Federalist Timothy

Pickering were among the welcoming dignitaries. In a week of celebrations Monroe visited Faneuil Hall and "Old Ironsides," Bunker Hill and the Boston Athenaeum, Harvard College and the Adams home in Quincy—all symbols of New England's devotion to Revolutionary ideals and to republican government. Although pomp, ceremony, and adulation were everywhere, Monroe sought as well to minimize the courtly aura that had surrounded Washington on his tours. In theory at least, Monroe traveled as a private citizen, paying his own expenses and doing without an official escort. He did not insist on formalities, as Washington had done, but mingled easily with everyone and made himself accessible to all parties. Even Abigail Adams, who during the 1790s had heaped scorn on Monroe and other Jeffersonians, was now pleased with Monroe's "agreeable affability . . . unassuming manners . . . [and] his polite attentions to all orders and ranks." A Boston newspaper reported gratefully that Monroe's visit made us "*one people*: for we have the sweet consolation . . . to rest assured that the president will be president, not of a party, but of a great and powerful nation." Monroe noted some years later that "both parties met me, embodied together," and that his purpose in making the tour was "to draw the people more closely together, and to leave the [still-factional] Federal leaders without support." Monroe, in sum, forty years after the Declaration of Independence, continued and in a way brought to a culmination the long, persistent effort to find a republican model for the patriot leader who would be above party and a symbol of national unity, yet unregal, unimperious, and unseparated from the people at large.[3]

Monroe knew, of course, as historians since have displayed in detail, that what a Boston newspaper during his visit had proclaimed as the "Era of Good Feelings" was in fact a time of bitter personal and factional dispute perhaps better characterized as an era of bad feelings. It is also true that Monroe, the assiduous party-builder of the 1790s, had in 1816 refused to welcome all Federalists into the Republican fold. He wrote Andrew Jackson that some Federalist leaders (happily a small minority, Monroe thought) still "entertained principles unfriendly to our system," so it was necessary in appointing officers for his administration to exclude such anti-republicans and instead rely on the "decided friends" of "free government." To do otherwise would by "too hasty an act of liberality to the [Federalist Party]" break "the generous spirit of the republican party" while keeping alive the factious minority of Federalists.[4] Beyond this initial need to protect the government from partisan excesses, however, Monroe generally followed the principle (as Jefferson had done in 1801) of rewarding merit and fidelity to public trust in federal officeholders. He opposed the 1820 Tenure of Office Act that limited federal appointments to four-year terms (thus potentially enlarging patronage opportunities), and after its passage he routinely reappointed officials not palpably corrupt or incompetent. He and John Quincy Adams both correctly saw the Tenure of Office Act as a device to reward party loyalty and increase congressional political power. In response, Monroe declared that "no person at the head of government has . . . any claim to the active, partisan exertions of those in office under him."[5]

Letters written by the three Virginia presidents in 1822, when personal partisanship reached new heights as the election of 1824 approached, reveal both rationalizations for their own party activity and their continuing rejection of a constructive, permanent party ideology. Jefferson bemoaned to Albert Gallatin that "the persons most looked to as successors [to Monroe] are of the President's Cabinet; and their partisans in Congress are making a handle of [public policy] to help or hurt those whom they are for or against." "Do not believe a word," Jefferson added, "that there are no longer parties among us; that they are all now amalgamated." Despite this furious politicking of which he was well aware, Monroe himself continued to consider "the existence [of parties] as the curse of the country" and to hope "the restless and disturbed state of the Commonwealth, like the rolling of the waves after a storm . . . will subside, and leave the ship in perfect security." The causes of party in other countries, and which perhaps even made parties beneficial to their public life (Monroe had Great Britain in mind), did not exist in the United States: "We have no distinct orders." "We are about to make the experiment," Monroe wrote his predecessor, "whether there is sufficient virtue in the people to support our free republican system of government"; that is, to see whether government without the corruption of party could work in the new society of the New World. Madison replied that he was not so "sanguine" that forces that at other times and places "have most engendered and embittered the spirit of party" would long be absent in the United States. "The most . . . that can be counted on," Madison thought, was "that the occasions for party contests in such a country and government as ours will be either so slight or so transient as not to threaten any permanent or dangerous consequences to the character and prosperity of the Republic."[6]

There were thus, by the end of Monroe's administrations, detectable, although not necessarily significant differences among the Virginia presidents on the place of political parties in American government. Jefferson thought, placing characteristic emphasis on ideology, that great divisions over principle, especially over the question of whether mankind was capable of self-government, would always exist, although he also, perhaps inconsistently, never ceased to hope for the suppression of party, "harmonized intercourse," and "sweetened society" he had rhapsodized about to Lafayette in 1817. Madison accepted much of this belief that enduring differences over principle were inescapable and was sure as well that American pluralism would result always in the existence of factions and parties in the nation. He even thought some good came from "making one party a check on the other," as he had put it as early as 1792, but he quickly added, again perhaps inconsistently, that this was valuable only "so far as the existence of parties cannot be prevented, nor their views accommodated."[7] Monroe's comments as president, on the other hand (thought not his vigorous partisanship of the preceding twenty-five years), seem to overlook more determinedly both the ideological and sociological foundations of party.[8] Despite these qualifications and variations, however, each of the three men continued to believe parties were unwelcome and dangerous, and each conducted his presidency, as far as possible, according to that conviction.

Fundamentally, each remained convinced that *republicanism*, to achieve its full, moral meaning, had to triumph over and exclude the spirit of faction and party. Indeed, some of the paradox of the Era of Good Feelings can be explained if we set aside modern connotations and instead recall Monroe's understanding of party. He had believed in the 1790s that he was forced into party activity by Federalist partisanship—and the Federalists had a parallel conception. Neither "party" supposed that the other was what British politics would later term (beginning, significantly, in the 1820s) "His Majesty's Loyal Opposition," a legitimate, permanently organized group, patriotic and honorable, expressing an honest difference of opinion and prepared to accept the responsibility of forming an alternative government. Although some politicians in the 1790s had begun to act in ways appropriate to a later era, and a few had even begun openly to accept the legitimacy of parties,[9] such was by no means the common view. Generally, each party still supposed the other to be a *faction* (whether a minority or a majority made no difference) and itself to be working for the public good. Hence the Federalists could pass the Alien and Sedition Acts as lawful means to prevent the spread of faction, Jefferson could after 1801 continue to proscribe unregenerate Federalists (monarchists), and Monroe in 1816 could still suppose himself to be acting above parties, to be working for their extinction, in refusing to bless those individuals he saw filled with "the spirit of party and faction." In each case the evil to be exorcised was a selfishness, a partialness, in a word, corruption—as Cicero and Alexander Pope had taught.

Yet, Monroe's presidency, like Madison's, differed sharply from Jefferson's both in its lack of general effectiveness and, more subtly, in its failure to attain a level of authority and power considered essential to positive, above-party leadership. Furthermore, there is some justice in the charge that the demise of the active republican "party" of Jefferson's presidency left the nation with a government "lacking the means either to check burgeoning forces of disintegration within itself or to resolve those conflicts which were bound, sooner or later, to irrupt into . . . Washington . . . from the outside." This decline, in Monroe's case as in Madison's, was due in part to differences in the personalities of each of these leaders and to special circumstances, but the sixteen years between 1809 and 1825 also revealed further the tensions between the Classical conceptions of party and leadership, clung to by Madison and Monroe, and the dynamics of a society where, as Jefferson put it in 1811, "men are at liberty to think, speak, and act freely, according to the diversities of their individual conformations."[10] The contrast between the rhetoric of the letters exchanged by the "Virginia dynasty" presidents in 1822 and the swirling, partisan disarray all too evident at the time in Washington can be described only as stark. One is forced to ask how Monroe could possibly have supposed that the president would be able to lead a "free republican system of government" without parties toward a condition where restlessness and disturbance would subside as the nation basked in "perfect security." The negative effects of this disjuncture have been brought out by critics of Monroe's presidency: first, that it caused Monroe not to "taste, through the use or misuse of patronage, the delicious fruits of power, [or to] create a machine or consolidate a party," and second, that it led to a "course of action [that] was perhaps politically wise, perhaps politically inevitable, but it abdicated leadership."[11]

Although these assessments do not share the Jeffersonian Republican assumptions about the essential qualities of presidential leadership that we have delineated here, it is nonetheless undeniable that by 1825 the tendency of Madison and Monroe to defer to Congress on legislative matters, to shun the use of patronage to gain political power, and to shrink from direct or even indirect appeals to the public had simply deprived the chief executive of the capacity to lead. Perhaps most important, these presidents' failure to control their cabinets and through their cabinets to influence Congress severely handicapped their exercise of power. In an irony as bitter to Monroe as it would have been to his predecessors, the very demise of open party opposition had surrounded him with a factionalism within his "amalgamated" party perhaps more intense and pathological than Jefferson or Madison ever faced from openly hostile Federalists. Most divisive of all was the contest for succession that found three cabinet officers and two members of Congress mustering supporters and subordinating all measures to that contest in ways reminiscent of the worst party strife ever seen in Rome, or London, or Philadelphia, or wherever free politics had given scope to human greed, chicanery, and ambition. Equally stark was the contrast between, on the one hand, Jefferson's cabinet meetings, where "there never arose . . . an unpleasant thought or word between the members," and "conversing and reasoning . . . scarcely ever failed . . . to produce an unanimous result," and, on the other hand, the grim, acrimonious confrontations in Monroe's cabinet described by John Quincy Adams. Animosity and obstruction became so severe that Monroe once drove his secretary of the Treasury from the White House with fire tongs and thereafter ceased to speak to the offending officer.[12]

What had happened, then, between the effective, almost idyllic leadership of Jefferson's first term and the factious disarray of Monroe's last term? Monroe's continued, earnest insistence on both the ancient antiparty ideology and the model of the patriot leader leave little doubt that his aspiration remained the same as Jefferson's—and, quite self-consciously for Monroe, the same as Washington's. Indeed, the factional warfare, so distasteful to Monroe, served only to heighten his sense of the harm it did to the nation and to reinforce his determination to refuse to indulge or validate it. Yet the disparity between political realities in the country and the president's ideal, and perhaps even the incompatibility between that ideal and the inevitable dynamics of public life in a free and open society, also contributed to the decline in the authority and power of the White House. Far from exalting the potential for leadership in a republic and supplying a needed source of national unity, the traditional model of the patriot king by the 1820s threatened to deny the country any means of leadership at all except that furnished by heads of factions and managers of coalitions inside and outside of the administration. The circumstances were not propitious for any antiparty chief executive who might emerge from the unprecedented campaign of 1824–1825—perhaps especially not for the son of John Adams.

John Quincy Adams: Public Servant

John Quincy Adams was the last president, before the triumph under Jackson of a conception of leadership tied to a positive idea of party, who aspired to embody all the dimensions of the patriot leader. In his boyhood he read, under the guidance of his parents, the ancient authors and the English Augustans. He inherited from his father an early edition of Bolingbroke's works, which still carries the marginal notations of both of them, as well, probably, as those of Charles Francis Adams, who as a nineteen-year-old in the White House in 1826 read *Idea of a Patriot King* under his father's guidance. John Quincy Adams's favorite author and guide, in rhetoric as well as in moral and public philosophy, was Cicero, whose complete works, in Latin, Adams read many times.[13] All his life he was devoted to these books and words—from Aristotle, Virgil, Plutarch, and Cicero to Erasmus, Locke, Pope, Bolingbroke, Lord Kames, and Jefferson—that upheld the belief that there is a moral order in the universe, that the community of man should live within that order, that government was instituted to that end, and that an "aristocracy of talent and virtue"—whether a patriot king, a senate, or an assembly of enlightened citizens—should rule.

In ways that both he and his parents at times regarded as providential, it seemed to John Quincy Adams that in his own life and career he might symbolize and sustain this world view in the public life of the new United States. As he often recalled with a poignant sense of destiny, he had, as a boy of eight holding tightly to his mother's hand, from a hill in Braintree watched the smoke and heard the cannon of the Battle of Bunker Hill. Three years later he accompanied his father to Europe, sharing further the danger of war, and, as an informal clerk and copyist, began his career as a public servant. He learned French so well that, returning home a year later, he taught English to the second French minister to the new nation and to his aide, who twenty-five years later would negotiate for France the sale of Louisiana to the United States. Again in Europe with his father, at age fourteen John Quincy undertook his first formal public employment: he went to St. Petersburg as secretary and French interpreter for Francis Dana to seek Russian support for the American Revolution. He returned to America in 1785 to enter Harvard (his mother and father did not want him exposed to the dissipations of European "higher" education). By then, at age eighteen, he knew three or four modern languages (plus Greek and Latin, of course), had lived in Paris, London, St. Petersburg, and The Hague, had traveled through all the great nations of northern and western Europe, and in the company of Benjamin Franklin, Jefferson, and his father had experienced the diplomacy of the American Revolution. Thus began a public career that ended in the House of Representatives after the Mexican War. In the intervening years John Quincy Adams served as American minister to the Netherlands and to Prussia (1794–1801), Massachusetts senator (1802), United States senator (1803–1808), American minister to Russia (1809–1813), negotiator of the Treaty of Ghent (1814), American minister to Great Britain (1815–1817), secretary of state (1817–1825), president (1825–1829), and member of Congress (1831–1848).

In each of these posts (save the presidency) he was praised exceedingly for his brilliance, independence, and patriotism. President Washington termed him, as a thirty-year-old diplomat, "the most valuable character we have abroad"; his service in the United States Senate earned him a place in John F. Kennedy's *Profiles in Courage*; historians generally regard him as the best secretary of state in American history; and there is not even a faint parallel to his postpresidential career as Old Man Eloquent, the intellectual and moral leader of the House of Representatives. He suffered a fatal stroke at his desk in the House chamber almost seventy years to the day after he had left Boston on his first diplomatic mission with his father. In the House on the day of Adams's stroke sat a new member from Illinois,

Abraham Lincoln, who called out "nay," as Adams had just done in his last vote, to repudiate the militarism and slavery expansion of the Mexican War.[14] No other public career in American history matches that of John Quincy Adams in either length or patriotic devotion, and no other mind felt more excruciatingly the dilemmas of republican leadership.

John Quincy Adams's long experience abroad, his eclectic education, and his attachment almost literally from birth to the *American* Revolution all served to make him one of the least sectional and least party-oriented politicians of his day. As the star-destined heir of the Colossus of Independence and the son of the fervently patriotic Abigail Adams, he wanted, as he later expressed in his diary, to "be the man of my whole country."[15] In his 1787 Harvard baccalaureate oration, "Upon the importance and necessity of public faith to the well being of the community," soon printed in Philadelphia, Boston, and elsewhere, he noted the tendency in Massachusetts and the other states to "an indolent carelessness, a supine inattention to the solemn engagements of the public." He called instead for an end to debt repudiation and paper currency and for the sound establishment of the public credit on principles of national honor. Although in the year after Shays's Rebellion, and during the summer of the Federal Convention of 1787, this call was in some respects politically divisive, Adams himself linked sound public credit to public virtue and believed that fidelity to financial obligations was the only honorable path to national greatness. Under such a policy the new nation would "soon rise superior to every temporary evil; gentle peace and smiling plenty would again appear, and scatter their invaluable blessings round the happy land: the hands of commerce would recover strength and spread the swelling sail: arts and manufacture will flourish, and soon vie with those of Europe, and science here would enrich the world with noble and useful discoveries." A Philadelphia magazine containing Adams's oration also offered a first printing of the new Constitution and a short extract from "Lord Bolingbroke's Idea of Eloquence" calling not only for skill in the techniques of oratory but also for more attention to "enlarging the stream from which it flowed," a view long encouraged in the substantial education of the young graduate.[16]

Four years later, entering the debate between Edmund Burke and Thomas Paine over the French Revolution, John Quincy Adams made explicit his approval of vigorous lawmaking in the public interest. Paine had endorsed the decree of the French National Assembly prohibiting monopolies or game laws in France, obviously responding to the abuse of such laws under the Old Regime and in England. Paine praised this restriction on the lawmaking power of the assembly as a bulwark for the liberty of the people. Adams argued in opposition that the solution to the passage of bad laws by a government ought not to be the removal of power to pass any laws at all. Rather, as "the preservation of game is an object of public concern, . . . the Legislature of every country ought to have the power of making game laws for the benefit of the public." At another time Adams noted that "where there are [no game laws,] there never is any game"—is the hunter more free in the absence of protective law as he searches in vain for his prey, or in the presence of a law that imposes some restraint but also prevents extinction? Two years later, in 1793 defending President Washington's right to dismiss French Minister Edmond Genet, Adams admitted that "the animated and vivifying spirit of party seems to be essential to the existence of genuine freedom" and even that "the general welfare is perhaps promoted, by placing the jealousy of one patriot as a guard over the ambition of another," but he also asserted that party spirit was "a prolifick source of misery" unless under "severe and continual . . . restraint and regulation." He further made clear his conviction that the paramount need was for the executive to transcend party spirit and to have wide powers to act in the interest of all the people.[17]

This conception of government as an agency for useful action stayed with Adams throughout his life. He frequently lamented the waste and abuse that masqueraded under the banners of individual freedom and commercial competition. In 1828, for example, he sponsored, in the interest of science and conservation, a United States law to protect a superb live-oak forest near Pensacola, Florida. The plan was aborted, he remembered scornfully, by "the stolid ignorance and stupid malignity" of Jackson's colleagues, who defended their action in the name of liberty, enterprise, and expanding settlement.[18] This enlarged and edifying view of the nation's affairs characterized all the landmarks of his prepresidential career: his support of Washington and his father during the 1790s, his votes for the Louisiana Purchase and the Embargo during Jefferson's presidency, his negotiations of the Treaty of Ghent and the transcontinental treaty with Spain of 1819, and his role in promulgating the Monroe Doctrine. In these actions Adams saw himself as living up to deeds of heroes and models he had read about in Plutarch, Joseph Addison, and Bolingbroke.

Yet, it seems paradoxical if not hypocritical that although Adams thus posed as the disinterested secretary of state, he was a participant in bitter political strife and as assiduously as the other leading aspirants gathered support for his own election to the presidency. His diary is, in fact, a remarkable record of the partisan battles of Monroe's presidency, full of sharp, often hostile, remarks about the character and intrigues of his principal opponents. In November 1819, for example, as Adams and Monroe discussed delicate relations with Spain over the impending American occupation of Florida, both men observed "with pain," as Adams put it, "that upon all subjects of eminent importance, [Secretary of the Treasury William H.] Crawford's opinion is becoming whatever is not mine." This tended "to weaken and distract the public councils," Adams thought, undermining "the happiest effects" produced by the "unanimity . . . throughout the country" that had previously surrounded the potentially explosive Florida situation.[19] The cause of this unwelcome divisiveness was Adams's rising fame, which made him a dangerous rival to Crawford for accession to the presidency on Monroe's retirement in 1825.

A further effect of this "continual and furious electioneering for the succession," Adams noticed, was that "in all important questions of public policy [where] it is difficult to choose the best and safest part, and where two [courses of action] present themselves with nearly an equal advantage, and nearly equal objectionable points, the mind in suspense upon their respective merits is easily determined by extraneous circumstances." Instead of careful, statesmanlike reflection deciding public policy, the quest for partisan political advantage infested the councils of government. Pondering the question further, Adams found that "the seeds of this discord are sown in the practice [of] the Virginia Presidents, . . . making it a principle that no President can be more than twice elected."[20] He probably remembered his own conclusion and that of his father in 1790–1791 that limited terms and regular turnovers in office vitiated executive power to act above party and that the Constitution ought to encourage long, perhaps even indefinite presidential tenure. Adams was willing to do almost anything to protect the presidency from partisanship—except let it go by his own inaction to its most zealously partisan aspirant.

In 1822 he wrote of the incessant exertions of congressmen and cabinet colleagues to "exclude me from the field of competition" in the 1824 presidential election. This intense partisan opposition, based, in Adams's opinion, on all the worst factional and selfish motives, served to rationalize his own "partisanship" in response, as had happened with Jefferson and Madison in the 1790s. Also, in acting to further his own candidacy (although never openly or publicly), Adams felt, as his father had, that the presidency was his due, considering the length and earnestness of his service to the public. Adams supposed that should he "perform to the satisfaction of the country" his duties as secretary of state, he would then, like his predecessors, be thought "a suitable candidate to succeed the President upon his retirement from office." As for personal motives, Adams pronounced it his duty "to serve the public to the best of my abilities . . . and not to intrigue for further advancement," although he knew as well that "the selfish and the social passions are intermingled in the conduct of every man acting in a public capacity. . . . It is no just cause of reproach to any man that in promoting to the utmost of his power the public good, he is desirous at the same time of promoting his own."[21] Thus, there can be no doubt that John Quincy Adams was aware of the mingling of personal ambition and public-spiritedness in his own breast and in the politics of the new nation. But he also believed that recognition of such mixed motives would help him maintain the dominance of the more honorable one and that recognition of the political realities in the nation at large would enable him also to resist the pathological aspects of public life. He never supposed, conversely, that because selfish ambitions existed, public officials had no choice but to ground their actions on self-interest, or that because parties and factions existed, the political arena had to be wholly at their mercy.

Although Adams acknowledged in his inaugural address (1825) that he was "less possessed of [public] confidence in advance than any of my predecessors," he nonetheless proclaimed triumphantly that since 1815 the "baneful weed of party strife" had been uprooted in the United States and that "ten years of peace, at home and abroad, have assuaged the animosities of political contention and blended into harmony the most discordant elements of public opinion."[22] Thus, he viewed the feuds of the Monroe presidency as merely personal or at most sectional and as evidencing none of the profound disagreements in political theory or foreign policy that from 1790 to 1815 had divided the Federalists and the Republicans. Adams, indeed, sensed no deep difference in principle from any of his rivals. All the leading politicians of the "Era of Good Feelings," whatever their personal rivalries, were, on the whole, "national republicans," that is, Jeffersonians who were willing to make wide use of the powers of the general government. Adams, for example, as secretary of state had been a defender of Jackson's conduct in Florida and hoped the general would be vice-president or secretary of war in his administration. He also refused to remove federal officials against whom no complaint of malfeasance could be made and declined in any way to use executive power to build a party. He intended, if he could, to banish partisanship—just as Washington had intended.

The new president expressed his broad, positive conception of national leadership in perhaps the most remarkable State of the Union Message ever made by an American chief executive, delivered to Congress in December 1825. Ignoring the objections of cabinet members that he was proposing much more than Congress would be willing to do, Adams went ahead, self-consciously blending the most far-reaching proposals of each of his predecessors. Liberty had been won and the Union assured, Adams thought, so now it was time to use them in the public interest. He proposed a series of activist measures: recognition of the South American republics, participation in an inter-American congress, a uniform bankruptcy law, the building and support of canals and other internal improve-

ments, surveys of natural resources, improvements in military preparedness (especially the navy), scientific explorations of the West, a better
system of weights and measures, and establishment of a national university
and a national observatory.

Adams forthrightly justified this bold program. "The great object of the
institution of civil government," he asserted, "is the improvement of the
condition of those who are parties to the social compact." "Moral, political, [and] intellectual improvement" are as legitimately an object of government support as are better communications and transportation. "In assuming her station among the civilized nations of the earth," the president
observed, "it would seem that our country had contracted the engagement
to contribute her share of mind, of labor, and of expense to the improvement of those parts of knowledge which lie beyond the reach of individual
acquisition." Adams hoped the United States would join Britain, France,
and other nations in "the common improvement of the species" by outfit-
ting voyages of discovery, by supporting scientific research, and by building a great national observatory—"a lighthouse of the skies." The powers
given to Congress by the Constitution, Adams insisted, were sufficient to
authorize laws to promote "the improvement of agriculture, commerce,
and manufactures, the cultivation and encouragement of the mechanic and
of the elegant arts, the advancement of literature, and the progress of the
sciences, ornamental and profound." Possessing these powers, "to refrain
from exercising them for the benefit of the people themselves would be to
hide in the earth the talent committed to our charge."

The president proclaimed that "liberty is power" and that "the tenure of
power by man is, in the moral purposes of his Creator, upon condition
that it shall be exercised to ends of beneficence, to improve the condition
of himself and his fellow-men." "While foreign nations less blessed with
that freedom which is power than ourselves are advancing with gigantic
strides in the career of public improvement," could the United States,
Adams asked, "fold up our arms and proclaim to the world that we are
palsied by the will of our constituents?" Americans must ask themselves,
Adams was saying in effect, What is liberty for? Noting that the state of
Virginia had just founded a new university and the state of New York had
just built a canal where "the waters of our Western lakes mingle with those
of the ocean," the president asked further whether "the whole Union
[could] fall behind our fellow-servants" and fail to accomplish the "works
important to the whole and to which neither the authority nor the resources of any one State can be adequate?" It "would be treachery to the
most sacred of trusts," Adams concluded, echoing John Winthrop, if the
representatives of the people failed "to give efficacy to the means committed to you for the common good."[23]

The Paradoxical President

It is one of the great ironies of American history that even before Adams delivered this message, in fact from before his minority election by the House of Representatives, his presidency was embroiled in partisan strife of unparalleled bitterness. Jackson and his friends charged after the election that there had been a "corrupt bargain" wherein Henry Clay threw his electoral influence to Adams in exchange for being appointed secretary of state in the new administration. Jackson wrote a friend that "the *Judas* of the West [i.e., Clay] has closed the contract and will receive the thirty pieces of silver. His end will be the same." Although Jackson had always considered Adams "a virtuous, able and honest man" and had thought him much less partisan than other leaders during Monroe's administration, when "the redemption of the pledge" occurred (Adams's appointment of Clay), Jackson "withdrew all intercourse with [Adams]." Furthermore, two days after the election a John C. Calhoun supporter (still protesting friendship for the president) informed Adams that Calhoun, the new vice-president, was determined to go into opposition unless his friends were given major cabinet posts.[24]

Even before Adams's inauguration, the supporters of three of his defeated opponents, Calhoun, W. H. Crawford, and Jackson, guided by Martin Van Buren and other regionally powerful politicians, were already forming a party, under Jackson's banner, to wreak vengeance on Adams and Clay. John Randolph of Roanoke charged venomously in the Senate that Adams and Clay were a "coalition of Blifil and Black George, . . . the combination . . . of the puritan with the black-leg" as infamous as the union between the "sanctimonious, puritanical Lord Mansfield . . . [and the] corrupt and profligate Lord Sandwich" that had disgraced British politics in the previous century. The images of Henry Fielding's Blifill, the pious, hypocritical parson, and Black George, the treacherous gamekeeper, were too much for Clay, who at once challenged Randolph to a duel, fought nine days after the offending speech. "There has never been a time," wrote Theodore Roosevelt in 1886, "when there was more rabid, objectless, and unscrupulous display of partisanship."[25]

Inescapably, the president himself was made to carry the onus of being the corrupt instrument of party. He probably did have an understanding with Clay before the election in the House of Representatives, although in Adams's mind the understanding was not corrupt, for he conceived of himself as the most able of the contenders for the presidency and believed that Clay was exceptionally well qualified to be secretary of state, as indeed he was. Yet, the circumstances made Randolph's allusions all too catching in the public mind and tarnished Adams's every word and deed as chief executive. Furthermore, Adams's political base was narrow, confined to New England and the seaboard Middle Atlantic states; he retained office-holders who in some cases were remnants from Washington's administration; he had close associations with unpopular commercial and financial interests; and rising industrialists eagerly supported his generally protectionist views. Altogether, these facts conspired to mark him as the leader of an aristocratic status quo, fighting off the democratic spirit of the burgeoning West, the prospering South, and the new politics of New York and Pennsylvania. When Clay and others organized meetings aimed at building support for the president's program and party, styled the "American Party," most people looked on the coalition as a revival of Federalism.[26] Despite the public-spiritedness of his own intentions, in short, the public perceived Adams as a minority president who led a sectional faction and was elected by means of a political bargain. Burdened with the ignominy of corruption and partisanship, his grand-sounding messages were dismissed as hypocrisy.

Furthermore, even though ex-Presidents Monroe and Madison sympathized with Adams and supported most of his program, the ailing Jefferson at Monticello resisted in principle the public philosophy of Adams's message of December 1825. Together with John Marshall's recent Supreme Court decisions and even some acts of Congress, Adams's address revealed, Jefferson charged, that the federal government intended "the consolidation in itself of all powers, foreign and domestic; . . . by constructions which, if legitimate, leave no limits to their power." If, under the interstate commerce clause, agriculture and manufactures could be regulated, and if "under the authority to establish post roads, they claim that of cutting down mountains, [and] of digging canals," Jefferson asked, "what is our resource for the preservation of the Constitution?" To him, such doctrine and such interpretation meant unlimited government, which was tyranny. There was, he felt, "a tendency to degeneracy," and among the self-styled nationalists who had "nothing in them of the feelings or principles of '76," a movement toward "a single and splendid government of an aristocracy, founded on banking institutions, and moneyed incorporations under the guise and cloak of their favored branches of manufactures, commerce and navigation, riding and ruling over the plundered ploughman and beggared yeomanry."[27] Jefferson regretfully heard in John Quincy Adams's proposals not the beneficent voice of the general welfare but the biased (and therefore corrupt) urging of special interests. Yet, Jefferson was opposing not the *intent* of Adams's view, the search for a national program above partisanship, but rather what the third president supposed was a flawed understanding of the specific role of the federal government. He as much regarded Jackson as unfit to be president and as much resisted the new partisan politics as did Adams, who in 1808 had resigned as senator from Massachusetts rather than obey instructions that he oppose the grand, national idealism of Jefferson's Embargo.

Indeed, Adams's ties both to the four ex-presidents who lived to see his inauguration as chief executive and to the rising politicians of the new Whig party of which he became a part reveal again the profound cultural changes surrounding his parodoxical effort at national leadership. Like his predecessors, his own values and public philosophy remained deeply Ciceronian (or what was to them much the same thing, Addisonian), but, as an active politician in the 1820s, 1830s, and 1840s, he lived in a world of political parties. Like the Whig party, he "took part" in order to win. Even that party itself, however, was rooted in the "Anglo-American 'country-party' tradition" of the preceding century. The Whigs sensed a widespread, enduring affinity to the precepts of that tradition and found also that the oppositionist part of the old radical rhetoric was peculiarly useful in resisting what it saw as corruption, demagoguery, and executive tyranny under Jackson—much as the Jeffersonians had done against their "Walpolean" foes in the 1790s.

Yet Adams, like his Whig allies, "had bade farewell to the distrust of wealth and commerce that had so long characterized the 'country party.'"[28] Although he never had anything like Daniel Webster's unalloyed enthusiasm for Massachusetts industrialists and financiers, Adams at least made his peace with them and amalgamated their economic interests with his conception of the public good. Furthermore, it was in part the intentions of his presidency, supported by Clay, Webster, and others who became Whig stalwarts, that attached the party to an active, positive idea of the purpose of government. Yet, the expansion and diversification of the economy and the spread of settlement across the Mississippi River (both of which Adams celebrated and had helped make possible as a congressman and diplomat) released energies and nourished political attitudes that moved the nation away from Adams's world view and led within a generation to the demise of the Whig party.

Perhaps the most revealing aspect of John Quincy Adams's presidency, then, is its subsequent perception as "unreal," or "lurid," or "futile," or "archaic." To students aware of the later history of American politics, the Adams presidency has seemed perverse at best: the president proclaiming the most high-minded ideas of public service amid the most outraged cries against his own corruption; the president repudiating party as an intensified party system took shape before his eyes; the president urging a strongly nationalistic program as sectional feelings burgeoned, and so on. If one believed the new directions were the irresistible wave of the future, the conscience-bound chief executive could seem only blind or antiquated.

He offered grand plans that bore no relationship to either the mood of the nation or the possibility of support in Congress. He kept ardently Jacksonian partisans in office, even at the cabinet level. He acted as though party organization did not exist, and he refused to use his high office to aid in his reelection. Meanwhile, Adams's opponents articulated programs attuned to popular sentiment, built party organization, electioneered assiduously, fused coalitions, and made clear their intent to use patronage to punish foes and reward friends, with the expected result: the Jacksonian movement acquired a force that swept the self-righteous president from office in 1829. Beginning in that year, "the rising spirit of democracy . . . simply took possession of the system through the instrumentality of the political party,"[29] thus virtually requiring a president to be a leader of party in order to be effective.

❦ 8 ❦

The Jacksonians and
Leadership through Party

Martin Van Buren and the New Political Party

More than anything else, a revised attitude toward party changed the nature and style of leadership when J. Q. Adams yielded the chief magistracy to Andrew Jackson. The man who most clearly perceived the significance of this difference and who most eagerly desired, cultivated, and used it was Martin Van Buren of New York.[1] He had begun his political career before the War of 1812 as a Jeffersonian, but opposed to the power of De Witt Clinton and the incongruous personal factions allied with him. New York politics at this time was akin to the eighteenth-century British model of rival politicians trading support and patronage in order to govern and remain in power. For a century "shifting alliances" within "a dense tangle of Livingstonians and DeLanceyites, of Lewisites, Burrites, and Clintonians" had shaped political groupings.[2] In confronting Clinton, Van Buren made good use of the centuries-old rhetoric of antipartyism that George Washington and Thomas Jefferson had accepted, directing it effectively at a political style so Machiavellian that Henry Adams would call Clinton's 1812 campaign for the presidency "the least creditable" in American history.[3]

But Van Buren and his cohorts also began to formulate a new, positive definition of party and of proper party behavior resting on one simple proposition: "Parties should be democratic associations, run by the majority of the membership."[4] Responding to the actual and impending enlargements of the franchise and the increasing spread of political information, Van Buren saw that a revised idea of party, based on *internal* majority rule, could be built into an attractive and doctrinally pure model of democratic government. As early as 1817, one of Van Buren's associates, William L. Marcy, declared himself proud to be regarded as one who had "more devotion to the cause [of his party] than to an Individual." Three years later Van Buren's party newspaper, the *Albany Argus*, scorned Clintonian politics as "characterized by personal attachments, . . . highly prejudicial to the interests of the people, and . . . [tending] to subvert our republican form of government."[5] Needed instead was acceptance of the new ideal of a literally democratic party and of a mode of leadership that embraced the new ideal.

In the course of the next ten years, as New York adopted a new constitution and played an increasingly pivotal role in national politics, Van Buren and his friends, known as the "Albany Regency," took infinite pains to organize, to propagandize, and to electioneer on behalf of their party. In so doing they laid aside the ancient distaste for competitiveness in politics (they intended to compete successfully) but at the same time took over for themselves the hallowed idea of "selfless" behavior in public life. To the Regency, the noble and disinterested citizen (qualities they extolled as much as did John Winthrop and Bolingbroke) was one who could sacrifice his own personal ambitions and advancement not to something as vague as "the public interest" but to the strength and well-being of a principled party. "Differences merely personal," said the *Argus*, "may be entertained to a reasonable extent . . . yet [must] by no means interrupt the harmony which ought always to prevail among those who feel and act from higher than personal considerations and attachments, for the common cause of the republican party." By putting the party itself, an organization inherently democratic and worthy of principled cultivation, at the center of the public life of the nation, Van Buren had both adjusted to what he viewed as the legitimate pressures of the people and transformed the connotations of the word *party*. Albany Republicans, having in mind Van Buren's services to the party, could thus take pride in him "because without the influence of fortune, or the factitious aid of a family name, he has by his entire devotion to the republican cause, raised himself to the first grade as a statesman and patriot."[6]

Before Andrew Jackson entered the White House, then, the New York State Republican (soon-to-be Democratic) party had, under Van Buren's guidance, repudiated nonpartisanship as an ideal and in its place fashioned a positive conception of party defended on five grounds.[7] First, it held that the antiparty rhetoric of even such an august figure as President Monroe was, whatever his good intentions, a mask for the continuance in power of the same aristocratic elite that had long managed the nation's affairs. Regency publicists noticed, as have a multitude of other opposers of the status quo, that an appeal to the public to close ranks, to abjure opposition, and so on, far from being nonpartisan was often actually a device to keep power in the hands of a ruling elite. Monroe's design "to destroy the old landmarks of party," the *Argus* declared, was both impossible and devious, because men could not be drawn "into a political union who were never united before, and who, from the utter dissimilarity of their views and notions, never could act cordially together."[8] The *Argus*'s position also scorned Monroe's style of leadership and forthrightly offered another model for politicians to emulate: the loyal pilot of the party.

Second, Van Buren and his friends came increasingly to view the political party as not only a device for achieving a principled goal but also an organization worthy in its own right and therefore to be nourished generation on generation. Party functionaries were to be valued as shepherds of the flock ensuring that parties would "TAKE DEEPER ROOT [and] outlive the causes of their commencement." "The alliance [of party] is cemented by time and strengthened by the strongest affections and antipathies," said the *Argus*, and parties should remain long unaltered as permanent parts of the body politic. Third, and following from this, the new party leaders took for themselves the mantle of principle, consistency, and morality that hitherto had been the garb of the nonpartisan. The "affected denial" of the existence of parties, the *Argus* intoned, "or an assumed independence of them springs rather from a propensity to trim, and a hankering after official rewards, than from any elevated or patriotic feeling." Furthermore, those who switched parties, or who paid little heed to party labels (like J. Q. Adams), were "inconsistent," even "apostates." "*Political consistency*," wrote one of Van Buren's close associates, meaning party loyalty, is "as indispensable as any other *moral qualification*."[9] (Van Buren's professed mentor, Jefferson, had expressed an opposite view: "I never submitted the whole system of my opinions to the creed of any party of men whatever in religion, in philosophy, in politics, or in any thing else where I was capable of thinking for myself. Such an addiction is the last degradation of a free and moral agent. If I could not go to heaven but with a party, I would not go there at all.")[10]

Fourth, the Regency politicians increasingly argued that the existence of parties, and of vigorous competition among them, was a vital characteristic of a free society. Parties were "necessary to the just exercise of the powers of free governments," and the absence of parties, or the lack of open competition among them, was seen as a sign of a dangerous oppressiveness in society. "When party distinctions are no longer known and recognized," a New York newspaper insisted, "our freedom will be in jeopardy, as the 'calm of despotism' will then be visible." With free government and party vigor thus linked, it was but a short step to the fifth justification for political parties: they were, in fact, the life blood of a democratic nation. In a series of articles, the Regency press asserted that "the spirit of party" was "the vigilant watchman over the conduct of those in power," "necessary to keep alive the vigilance of the people, and to compel their servants to act up to principle." "The solicitude and interest of political rivalship, will sufficiently expose the crimes, and even the failings, of competitors for the people's confidence." Van Buren himself stated that party differences "rouse the sluggish to exertion, give increased energy to the most active intellect, excite a salutary vigilance over our public functionaries, and prevent that apathy which has proved the ruin of Republics." If parties contended with "candor, fairness, and moderation," he argued in another place, "the very discord which is thus produced, may in a government like ours, be conducive to the public good."[11] In sum, apathy rather than self-interest became the poison of self-government and competition rather than harmony the measure of the healthy state. Such inversions would "have been unacceptable to Jefferson and Madison, incomprehensible to Monroe, and little short of satanic to Washington and the two Adamses," as Richard Hofstadter rightly observed.[12]

Although the validation of the new political system arose in large part from such new circumstances in Jacksonian America as an enlarged electorate, a diversified economy, a more pluralistic society, and the spread of literacy and political information in the new nation, it is also significant that Van Buren and his cohorts unapologetically and proudly celebrated the introduction of the competitive ethic into the councils of government. Although the passing generation, including the four ex-presidents still alive in 1826, had been well aware that, in Madison's famous dictum of *The Federalist*, Number 10, "the causes of faction are sown in the nature of man" and that difference of opinion would always characterize a free politics, they never ceased to regard this fact as a problem to be overcome or controlled rather than as a dynamic essential to good government. The new party leaders like Van Buren would have denied that their parties were equivalent to Madison's "factions," but from the older point of view, the similarities—divisiveness, self-justification, unashamed electioneering, coalition politics, and so on—were obvious and ominous, for the legitimization of the new party politics depended on the acceptance of a new ethic as well as on new circumstances. The Jacksonian political leaders and their followers were abandoning the world view of Alexander Pope, Jonathan Swift, and Joseph Addison that enthralled the early presidents and were moving to that of Jeremy Bentham, James Mill, and other philosophers of self-interest whose thought increasingly guided nineteenth-century Anglo-American politics and culture.

When Van Buren went to Washington as a United States senator in 1821, he was horrified at what he and his friends termed "the Monroe heresy . . . of amalgamation" of the parties, and he frankly avowed his intention to "revive the old contest between federals and anti-federals." He proclaimed his party the true successor to the Antifederalist-Jeffersonian tradition of resistance to aristocracy, commercial privilege, and centralization of power and branded his opponents as Federalists defensive of vested interests. Although there was some ideological continuity, Van Buren in fact understood little of the party attitudes of the era of Jefferson and

Hamilton—or perhaps he deliberately chose to misinterpret. During the 1820s Van Buren carefully measured the political scene in Washington and sought to establish ties with other state leaders whose party ideas and organizational skills were parallel to his own. At first he had little use for Jackson, who had often expressed the traditional contempt for "party spirit," but Van Buren soon came to see increasingly how valuable to the new notion of party competition the general's popularity might be. By 1827 the picture came into focus: under Jackson's banner, Van Buren and other "party professionals" perceived how they might weld a political instrument that could at once gain power, restore "Jeffersonian" principles, make the president the spokesman of the party, and enlarge the democratic spirit of the country.[13]

As Van Buren organized support to gain victory for Jackson in 1828, he explained his strategy to the influential Virginia editor-politician Thomas Ritchie. "The amalgamating policy of Mr. Monroe," Van Buren thought, had been a great mistake because it "weakened, if not destroyed," the nationwide sense of principled political difference that had existed between the Federalists and the Jeffersonian Republicans. These "party attachments . . . furnished a complete antidote for sectional prejudices by producing counteracting feelings" that transcended and subsumed divisive local sentiments. Van Buren proposed to Ritchie that a national nominating convention be held that would unite Jacksonians all over the country and sharpen the cleavage with what another Jacksonian organizer at the same time called "the purposes of the aristocracy." Van Buren hoped Ritchie could help him revive the coalition between "the planters of the South and the plain Republicans of the North," which, added to Jackson's personal popularity, would make an invincible political party. "We will always have party distinctions," the New Yorker averred, so the goal of the responsible and effective leader should be to organize "a combined and concerted . . . political party, holding in the main, to certain tenets and opposed to certain prevailing principles."[14]

President Adams saw Van Buren's party organizing less as innovation and more as the perpetuation of the old corruption, as is evident in his diary account of a visit from Van Buren in May 1827, after the latter had visited Ritchie in Richmond and seen other politicians on a tour of the South. Van Buren was "generally understood," Adams noted, to have become "the great electioneering manager for General Jackson." Van Buren "is now acting over the part in the affairs of the Union which Aaron Burr performed in 1799 and 1800," Adams mused, thinking of his father's defeat at the hands of an earlier New York politician thirty years before. The president noticed "much resemblance of character, manners, and even person, between the two men" and gloomily predicted that "Van Buren has now every prospect of success in his movements." He even foresaw that

Van Buren would "avoid the rock" that had ruined Burr, by adhering faithfully to Jackson and remaining content to succeed him as president, rather than succumbing, as Burr had done, to the ambition to displace his chief.[15]

Many years later, Congressman J. Q. Adams continued to see a profound division between his politics and that of the Jacksonians when he examined Van Buren's December 1837 State of the Union Message and compared it implicitly with his own. "[Van Buren's] message," the ex-president wrote, "gave me a fit of melancholy for the future fortunes of the country. Cunning and duplicity pervade every line of it. The sacrifice of the rights of Northern freedom to slavery and the South, and the purchase of the West by the plunder of the public lands, is the combined system which it discloses. It is the system of Jackson's message of December, 1832, covered with a new coat of varnish." The characters of the two presidents, Adams added, one "dashing and daring" and the other "insinuating and plausible . . . are comprised in the names of Shakespeare's two catch-polls—Fang and Snare."[16] Van Buren had been the clever politician balancing sectional interests and responding to them to gain political power, a skill in which he took pride and which would evoke praise subsequently from many students of political behavior. But to Adams, Van Buren's skill rested, as it would also have seemed to Washington and Jefferson, on an insidious misconception: a preoccupation with partial as opposed to common interests.

A similar disdain pervaded J. Q. Adams's observations of the new modes of campaigning of the 1830s and 1840s. He scorned the "fashion of peddling for popularity by travelling round the country gathering crowds together, hawking for public dinners, and spouting empty speeches." "This practice of itinerant speech-making," Adams noted with horror in 1840, had "spread its contagion to the President himself," as well as to ex-presidents, cabinet members, senators, representatives, and any aspirant to public office. The tendency, Adams said, "is to the corruption of the popular elections, both by violence and fraud," and the result was that "the Presidency has fallen into a joint-stock company."[17]

Indeed, as J. Q. Adams reflected on the political leaders he had known, he saw increasing declension from his own Plutarchian conceptions. His admiration for Washington was unqualified: the first president scorned partisanship and faction, and his political program included public-interest measures such as a national university, planned use of public lands, and a federal system of internal improvements. Adams had almost as exalted a view of Madison, but Jefferson he thought flawed by his excessive faith in "the people" and his sacrifice of principle to popularity. Adams admired the Calhoun of Monroe's cabinet as "a man of fair and candid mind, of honorable principles, of clear and quick understanding, of cool self-possession, of enlarged philosophical views, and of ardent patriotism," but for the ambitious politician, the defender of sectionalism, and the apologist for slavery, he had only contempt. De Witt Clinton also earned a mixed evaluation. Thinking of Clinton's advocacy of the Erie Canal, Adams praised his "great talents, . . . magnificent purposes of public service, . . . comprehensive views and great designs," but he was disgraced by "ambition . . . of a baser sort—the charlatanery of popular enticement." Consistently, Adams admired public men who "demonstrated intellect, patriotism, coolness, a talent for devising thoughtful programs, and a broad nationalism," while he scorned those who "appealed to the mass electorate via a party organization and personal demogogy."[18] It was not just that Adams was out of step with the new politics or that he belittled or envied the skills of the new politicians who replaced him; he took the most profound exception to their public philosophy, which placed competitive pluralism at the heart of the political system. The new ideology of party seemed to him to betray all he had learned from Cicero and Bolingbroke, and all he thought the new nation had stood for.

Adams could have had only contempt, then, for the articulation of the new theory of party by Enos Throop, who became governor of New York when Van Buren entered Jackson's cabinet as secretary of state in March 1829. In his first address to the state legislature, Throop raised the question he knew was perhaps most on the minds of those who had seen the Albany Regency leaders transform New York politics and who now seemed on the way to doing the same thing on a national scale: "whether political parties are or are not desirable or beneficial in a government like ours." He answered, as political theorists generally had done for a century or two, that "political parties . . . will prevail where there is the least degree of liberty of action on the part of public agents, or their constituents." Instead, however, of proceeding to deplore this result and to seek ways to ameliorate assumed harmful effects, as a David Hume or a Madison would have done, Throop predicted only public benefit from the existence of parties. "The spirit of emulation and proselytism," he noted, would tend always "to reduce many shades of opinion into two opposing parties." Then, within each party a "mutual concession of opinion" would soften "acerbity of spirit," while "ample discussion of public measures," persuading the people that "the prevailing measures are the results of enlightened reason, . . . would . . . restrain acts of violence" between parties. Far from being a source of tumult and disorder, strong political parties were essential to a conciliatory and reasoned public life.

Throop did not deny that "party spirit is but the passion with which opposing opinions are urged in the strife for possession of power," but he did insist, departing sharply from the argument of Washington's Farewell Address, that more than fifty years of republican experience had proven that this spirit had not in the least threatened "the integrity of the Union." Rather, the machinery of American government was "so nicely adjusted" that it had "tamed the spirit of party, and stationed it, as the vigilant watchman, over the conduct of those in power."

Throop proudly proclaimed his party, just beginning to be called the Democratic party, the legitimate successor to "the whiggism of the revolution" and the Jeffersonian triumph of 1801, and thus "vindicated . . . [in] its claims to supremacy." He also accepted, however, the idea of a loyal opposition in admitting that even when his party lost power the cause was "healthful fluctuations of the will of the people." "Our institutions have suffered but little, if anything," he concluded, "from the spirit of party, fiery and excited as at times it has been." For although "personal parties" might pursue vengeance or contemplate civil disorders, "a well regulated party spirit [that is, divided into two large organizations competing for public favor] . . . that employs the passions actively in a milder mood . . . shuts the door against faction." To Throop, such parties were a better antidote to the evils of Federalism than was the "amalgating" intention of Monroe and J. Q. Adams. After a long litany of the sufferings caused in many societies by various fanaticisms and persecutions, Throop congratulated his listeners that in the United States "knowledge abounds, to moderate the passions; just laws, enacted by the people themselves, and faithfully administered, afford protection against outrage; and opinion, exercising its moral power over the conduct of partizans, applies correctives, through regular party discipline."[19] Throop thus carefully distinguished harmful faction from benign party (in a way Madison would not have understood) and pictured a "disciplined party" not as a ruthless machine for making ciphers of its members, but rather as a highly useful, consensus-achieving device that could organize and gain power for good purposes.

Under this doctrine, Van Buren and others succeeded in forming, with Jackson at the head, the first modern political party. Organized openly and applauded as such, it was designed not to "amalgamate," or dissolve, or eventually extinguish partisanship, but to heighten and crystallize it in the pursuit of "certain tenets and . . . principles." With the vote-marshaling skill of party leaders such as James Buchanan of Pennsylvania, Caleb Atwater of Ohio, and Amos Kendall of Kentucky, as well as Van Buren, "the age of the professional politician had arrived. . . . To win those votes [of the newly enfranchised common people] and organize them into solid blocs became the special task of the trained politician."[20] Nominating conventions, rewards for party organizers, open electioneering, partisan platforms, and all the other now-familiar means of political party controversy became not signs of corruption and faction but the essence of the democratic political process. Jefferson and Hamilton and their allies had used some of these measures in the earlier party battles, especially the sharpening of issues and the gathering of support, but there were critically important differences. First, there was an indirect, stealthy, perhaps even hypocritical quality to the Hamiltonian and Jeffersonian parties; the leaders refused to proclaim themselves as party leaders (indeed, they vigorously denied such), they organized incompletely, and they electioneered largely through others. Second, at least to Jefferson, the political party was a temporary, unwelcome necessity, which explains why he, as well as Madison, Monroe, and the Adamses, so welcomed and applauded the dissolution of open party spirit under Monroe.[21] What Van Buren's party-building and Jackson's victory marked was the demise of this older view that there could ever be a triumph over party itself and the rise of a new conception to be championed by Robert Peel, Abraham Lincoln, William Gladstone, Benjamin Disraeli, Theodore Roosevelt, Franklin Roosevelt, and most of the political leaders of the great democracies in the nineteenth and twentieth centuries.

The development of the new idea of party in Great Britain paralleled the shift in American republican-democratic ideology. For example, the author of a history of Great Britain that was translated into English in 1818 could declare that "there is not less loyalty among the members of the opposition, . . . though they style themselves whigs, than among their opponents though they are called tories." Then, in 1826 John Hobhouse (later Lord Broughton) first used the revealing designation "His Majesty's Opposition" in Parliament, and a colleague at once observed that Hobhouse could not "have invented a better phrase, for we [the opposition] are certainly to all intents and purposes a branch of his Majesty's Government." Yet, older conceptions retained force; the duke of Wellington said in 1830 (as Washington might have forty years earlier) that he "could not bear the idea of being in opposition: he did not know how to set about it." In 1846, however, Disraeli advanced party ideology a crucial further step: "It is utterly impossible to carry on your Parliamentary Constitution except by political parties. . . . There must be distinct principles as lines of conduct adopted by public men. . . . It is only by maintaining the *independence of party* that you can maintain the integrity of public men, and the power and influence of Parliament itself" (emphasis added). Like Van Buren, the great English politician treated appeals to principle and to independence of judgment as values wholly consistent with party. Moreover, like their American counterparts, the British leaders knew full well that they were not inventing factional differences, electoral politics, or pursuit of office, but they were validating and celebrating these phenomena as the essence of a new and constructive political dynamic. Finally, in the twentieth century, after the great Liberal-Conservative party battles in and out of Parliament had been enshrined at the center of British public life, Lord Balfour could remark, in celebration rather than disdain, that the whole English constitution was arranged so that men might quarrel.[22] Yet no American president before Van Buren, or certainly Jackson, could have taken pride, or even found consolation, in such a statement. They had remained fearful of "the primal Augustan nightmare, discord—which is, institutionalized, faction."[23]

Jacksonian Partisanship

The underlying changes in the character of party and leadership that had begun during the preceding decade became more evident in Jackson's presidency. Although the president thought of himself as an "Old Republican" true to the tradition of Jefferson, and although "the Jacksonian persuasion" had its Classical aspects, the effect of Jackson's two administrations was to launch the nation on a new dynamic. Jackson's most notable battle, for example, waged to destroy the Bank of the United States, was a liberating effort, however mixed the consequences. The demise of the Bank did indeed remove a form of monopoly and privilege in the economy of the nation, and politically the veto of the Bank restrained an ominously powerful vested interest. The veto also "unshackled" the business and financial energies of the country, allowing an unimpeded decentralization and expansion of banks, credit, and commercial rivalry and facilitating the rapid movement of the frontier and the exploitation of the nation's resources. For a century (or at least until the creation of the Federal Reserve System in 1913), and in contrast to what had prevailed from 1791 to 1829, the United States had an exceptionally open, unregulated "system" of trade and finance.

Guided by a philosophy that advocated leaving "individuals and states as much as possible to themselves," Jackson proceeded to gather around him "a group of successful bankers, railroad builders, land speculators, and general promoters." One of them, Amos Kendall, explained that "things will take their course in the moral as well as in the natural world" and warned Congress to "be content to let currency and private business alone."[24] Instead of using the Bank of the United States to guide the national economy in "the aggregate interest," as John Quincy Adams and his predecessors had sought to do (not always successfully), Jackson and his colleagues simply abandoned that aspiration and instead assumed that the public good required of government no more than the removal of impediments to private enterprise—"combinations in restraint of trade," as the Sherman Anti-Trust Act would put it a half-century later. Men as varied as Jonathan Edwards, the Adamses, Washington, and Madison "were concerned to control the principles of possessive and competitive individualism by using the counterbalancing idea and ideal of the whole man obligated to other men within the framework of a true community. . . . Their rhetoric, their policies, and their actions converged in an effort to build an equitable and ethical community within the limits of capitalist economics."[25] Those men, that is, retained much of the "premodern" world view of Pope and Swift, whereas the Jacksonians candidly and enthusiastically accepted the ethic of self-interest and the politics of pluralism. The transition from old to new was not instantaneous. The spirit of commerce and competition was widespread before 1829, and the ideal of a harmonious public interest did not die when J. Q. Adams left the White House, but the Jacksonians did, as they often proclaimed, alter basic assumptions of American politics.

The Maysville veto, signaling the end of federal initiative in and direct support of internal improvements, further encouraged the era of laissez-faire and decentralization. Jackson's message that the Maysville Road bill was unconstitutional clearly argued as well that the country needed less, not more, national guidance of the economy. It should be left to individuals and corporations, or at best to state legislatures, to decide the paths of growth and development. In confronting the panic of 1837, President Van Buren reaffirmed the Jacksonian axioms. It was wrong, he said, to expect the government "to relieve embarrassments arising from losses by revulsions in commerce and credit. . . . [Government] was not intended to confer special favors on individuals or on any classes of them, [or] to create systems of agriculture, manufactures, or trade. . . . All communities are apt to look to government for too much." Any attempt by government to "interfere in the proper concerns of individuals," Van Buren warned, led "unavoidably . . . to neglect, partiality, injustice, and oppression." Instead, he asked the nation to have faith, despite the depression then underway, that "a system founded on private interest, enterprise, and competition, without the aid of legislative grants or regulations by law, would rapidly prosper."[26] The intention was always to diminish restraint and to shun plans and systems (and leadership) that might stifle individual energies or limit the opportunities of enterprising groups. Indeed, this repudiation of system seemed uniquely suited to an era when millions of immigrants would arrive and a continent was to be settled. Its combination of laissez-faire economics, democratic spirit, frontier individualism, immigrant opportunity, and business entrepreneurship became embedded in such phrases as "the American character," or "way of life," or "liberal tradition"—all of which received their essential, unashamed validation in the Age of Jackson.

Even the abandonment of the "first civil service system," wherein, generally, employees of the federal government had kept their jobs during good performance of their duties, had its liberating aspects. As Jackson expressed in famous, or infamous, sentences in his first annual message to

Congress, men who held office "for any great length of time . . . are apt to acquire a habit of looking with indifference upon the public interests. . . . Office is considered a species of property, and government . . . a means of promoting individual interests. . . . Corruption . . . and a perversion of correct feelings and principles divert government from its legitimate ends and make it the engine for the support of the few at the expense of the many." To overcome this elitist system, Jackson offered a startlingly new conception of government employment: "The duties of all public officers are, or at least admit of being made, so plain and simple that men of intelligence may readily qualify themselves for their performance; and I can not but believe that more is lost by the long continuance of men in office than is generally gained by their experience." As the experience of officeholding was deemed of little value, and as no one had an "intrinsic right" to be supported "at the public expense," the Jacksonians concluded that there was neither disadvantage to the public nor injustice to individuals in the removal of any civil servant from office. "To destroy the idea of property so generally connected with official station" by promoting a frequent rotation in office would vitalize, Jackson said, "a leading principle in the republican creed, [and] give healthful action to the system."[27]

Jackson's supporters in Congress soon justified the president's doctrine. Senator Ether Shepley of Maine asserted that "it is just, and proper, and useful . . . to change public officers. It is in accordance with our system of Government, which holds out equal rights and equal privileges to all." Senator William L. Marcy of New York stated, perhaps more candidly, the "principle" on which he expected officeholders and their aspiring successors to act: "When they are contending for victory [in elections], they avow their intention of enjoying the fruits of it. If they are defeated, they expect to retire from office. If they are successful, they claim, as a matter of right, the advantages of success. They see nothing wrong in the rule, that to the victor belong the spoils of the enemy."[28] Defenders of the principle of rotation thus saw it as part of the great democratic reforms that exalted the power of the common man and drew his government closer to him. And Marcy's idea of the usefulness of rewards was constructive if one accepted, as Van Buren argued, that the political party had a positive, indispensable role to play in democratic government. In any case, the Jacksonians had opened the political system, like the nation's economy, to a wider participation and to a competitive vitality (venality, Swift would have said). After a century, it seemed, Bernard Mandeville and Daniel Defoe had triumphed over Pope and Bolingbroke.

The Jacksonians had not, of course, invented patronage, but they reconceived it. The traditional use of political patronage, brought to a high art in eighteenth-century Britain, was to cement a personal following and thus to strengthen the power of a "parliamentary notable." Sir Lewis Namier offers the classic description of the English parties: "Whoever in the eighteenth century had the 'attractive power' of office, received an accession of followers, and whoever retained it for some time, was able to form a party." Although these parties, or factions, did not disappear at once on losing patronage and office, "every single group in opposition," Namier concluded, "was bound to melt, even if Opposition as a whole was on the increase: for the basis of the various groups ["parties"] was eminently personal." For Van Buren and the new American party leaders, however, patronage was not so much "centered on clients and family," the customary form in Anglo-American politics of the previous century, as on "interest-groups and constituents."[29] Although personal motives were by no means absent in the new system, Jackson's words in so candidly defending "rotation in office" are revealing. He had repudiated the old system in which a political office was considered "a species of property" or "a means of promoting individual interests" and recommended instead "healthful action to the system," that is, of bringing ordinary citizens into the process of government, both through direct officeholding and by cementing their loyalty to a permanent political party. Thus, although the word *party* was used in both cases, and although patronage was as important to the duke of Newcastle as to Van Buren, the structure and dynamic had been shifted fundamentally. Similarly, Jackson's phrase, "public interest*s*," meaning various projects of public usefulness, carried very little of the Classical connotation of disinterested understanding larger than any summation of parts.

The Jacksonian system, like Mandeville's, embodied its own conception of executive leadership and pursuit of the public good. Jackson once declared to the Senate that "the President is the direct representative of the American people" and therefore had to manage his branch of government in their interest without interference from Congress.[30] As the "direct representative of the American people," Jackson also insisted he had the authority to act as their guardian against any and all hostile interests. When, as under the Bank of the United States, "the rich and powerful . . . bend the acts of government to their selfish interests," Jackson proclaimed, "the humble members of society—the farmers, mechanics, and laborers—. . . have a right to complain of the injustice of their government." Because many of the rich men of America "have not been content with equal protection and equal benefits" of the laws but instead had sought and secured "monopolies and exclusive privileges," it was the duty of the "direct representative of the people" to strike down the injustices. There are, Jackson admonished, "no necessary evils in government. Its evils exist only in its abuses. If it would confine itself to equal protection, and, as Heaven does its rains, shower its favors alike on the high and the low, the rich and the poor, it would be an unqualified blessing." And this, to the president, meant for the federal government to leave "individuals and the States as much as possible to themselves."[31]

In striking down the Bank, in halting federal road building, and in rotating the offices of government, Jackson conceived of himself as the tribune of the people, freeing their energies from the limitations and inequities imposed by government itself. Executive leadership meant primarily restraining evil forces so that the people could be free—to do as they pleased. The Democratic party, furthermore, was the proper instrument of the president in exercising his power, and thus was the legitimate object of his nourishment and support. Although Jackson used the same rhetoric of "public interest" as his predecessors and fashioned his own highly effective means of executive power, the assumptions and means of leadership had in fact been transformed. As the Bank veto message stated so clearly, there were a multitude of forces at work in society, many of them selfish and evil, so it was necessary for "the humble members of society" to organize and to support the advocate of *their* interests, that is, to enlist in the Democratic party in order to achieve the power to strike down their enemies. And it was the president's role both to crystallize the sentiments of the common people and to guide and sustain a political party as the instrument of their protection against intrusion, monopoly, and oppression. The purpose of defeating oligarchic monopolies, and even of forming a political party to accomplish that, was not un-Jeffersonian (as Jackson himself perceived), but the differences in emphasis and connotation were profound: for Jefferson the party had to be temporary, not permanent; merely destroying the monopolies to let laissez-faire flourish would to him have been simplistic if not irresponsible, and setting aside the "humanizing" ideal in public life would to him have been a form of corruption. This polarizing conception of politics, which presents the central issue as that of either defeating or succumbing to the evil of special privilege, after 1829 became the reigning one in American public life and in many respects has been dominant ever since.

The Adamses and the "Degradation of the Democratic Dogma"

Against this essentially negative conception of the executive's role, the above-party, positive ideas of executive leadership so deeply embedded in Jackson's vanquished foe of 1828 (and in all of his predecessors) seem so quaint and unrealistic as to belong to another age—as indeed they did. In 1904 Henry Adams, recalling the venerable figure of his grandfather sitting in front of him in the church at Quincy, reflected on the "education" he had received at home and at Harvard. The industrial America of his adult life seemed to him more distant from the world of his statesmen fore-bears than they were from the age of Greece and Rome encased in the books of the family library. He had, he wrote, been reared to live in a world that had died.[32]

When asked nine years after his crushing defeat in 1828 for information about his presidency, John Quincy Adams wrote that "the great effort of my administration was to mature into a permanent and regular system the application of all the superfluous revenue of the Union." Such a system "would have afforded high wages and constant employment to hundreds of thousands of laborers" and would have caused "the surface of the whole Union [to be] checkered over with railroads and canals." "I fell and with me fell, I fear never to rise again," the old statesman complained, "the sys-tem of internal improvement by means of national energies." Instead of adopting this grand design, which Adams as the patriot leader had so boldly presented in 1825, national development had been consigned to "the limping gait of State legislature and private adventure, [and] the American Union . . . is to live from hand to mouth, and to cast away in-stead of using for the improvement of its own condition, the bounties of Providence."[33] Only five days after Jackson's inauguration, in fact, John Quincy Adams had predicted that "the day will be the day of small things. There will be neither lofty meditations nor comprehensive foresight, nor magnanimous purpose." The son to whom Adams made this prophecy would have understood the rich public philosophy from which it derived; during the early months of 1829 Charles Francis Adams had been reading Pope, Cicero, Adam Smith, Blackstone, Addison, Clarendon, and Burke. Theodore Roosevelt, just beginning in 1886 to develop his philosophy of positive government in the public interest, made the same point when he referred to the Jacksonian administrations as "the millennium of the minnows."[34]

Behind the halt of the orderly mobilization of the nation's energies and resources for the public good, for which Adams blamed the partisan, irre-sponsible, Jacksonian spoilsmen, the ex-president saw deeper causes than conventional political differences. "The Sable Genius of the South," he in-toned, in its fear and envy of the rising tide of northern prosperity, had "raised the standard of free trade, nullification, and state rights" as masks for a wicked, self-interested defense of slavery.[35] To him there could be no clearer example of the curse of faction and partisanship, no more un-mistakable corruption, than the virtual capture by the slavocracy of the government of the Union born in 1776. Adams's steadfast defense of the right to petition Congress for the abolition of slavery, a campaign that made him the first national champion of that cause, was not *just* a moral crusade. Adams's abolitionism derived not only from his conviction, held since the age of sixteen, that a people cannot "be happy who are subjected to personal slavery"[36] but also from his understanding of the ideals of the American Revolution. The slave power had to be destroyed in order to restore the very character of the nation, to rescue it from that worst of public crimes, the subordination of the general good to private greed.

The increasing insolence and self-assertion of the slave power was to Adams part and parcel of the Jacksonians' abandonment of the nation's public interest to the vicissitudes of party warfare. Under that banner, Adams foresaw, the slave interest was as legitimate as any other, as qualified to be voted up, to expand, and to resist being voted down as any other. In fact, the amoral doctrine of "popular sovereignty" defended by Stephen A. Douglas in the 1850s was one plausible fruit of the conception of party Martin Van Buren had devised in the 1820s to push John Quincy Adams from the presidency. Douglas's doctrine was also a repudiation of the long tradition that valued a polity attuned not to vox populi as such but rather to a higher law that might with good leadership enlist the support of the whole people.

As John Quincy Adams pondered the meaning of his public career, he sometimes interpreted his crushing defeat in 1828 and the consequent triumph of Jacksonian party politics as somber signs of the betrayal, or perhaps even the nonexistence, of Providence itself. He had always believed, he wrote in 1837, "that the ultimate extinguishment of slavery throughout the earth was the great transcendent earthly object of the mission of the Redeemer. . . . That the Declaration of Independence was a leading event in the progress of the gospel dispensation. . . . That its principles lead directly to the abolition of slavery and of war, and that it is the duty of every free American to contribute to the utmost extent of his power to the practical establishment of those principles." Under this belief, Brooks Adams noted, his grandfather had entered the presidency, supposing that "an honest executive . . . supported by an intelligent and educated civil service, who should hold their places permanently, . . . [might] devote their whole time, energy, and thought" to the providential task. John Quincy Adams had hoped for the "continual progressive improvement, physical, moral, political, in the condition of the whole people of this Union . . . by establishing the practical, self-evident truth of the natural equality and brotherhood of all mankind, . . . and by banishing slavery and war from the earth."[37] The biographer of John Quincy's son and Brooks's father, Charles Francis Adams, summarized the moral universe of the Puritan-Christian tradition accepted by the Adams family: "As true New Englanders, they believed firmly in a positive life, in the full exercise of their mental powers, and the full control of their 'appetites.' . . . Idleness was a sin and self-

satisfaction corruption. . . . Duty, determination, integrity, self-examina-
tion—these were their guides to conduct."[38]

Instead of this grand design working out in the United States, public
lands were, under Jackson, given away "to private land jobbers," spoilsmen
took over the public administration, and slaveowners came to dominate
the Union. Summarizing his grandfather's view, Brooks Adams concluded
that Jackson was "the materialization of the principle of evil . . . [because
he] embodied the principle of public plunder." Convinced that if "each
man [strove] to better himself at the cost of his neighbor," this striving
would coincide with the common good, Jackson and his followers sought
to enshrine "the instincts of greed and avarice which are the essence of
competition." Thus, instead of the continuing improvement of society under Providence and in accordance with a noble design John Quincy Adams
thought he had inherited from John Winthrop and George Washington
(as well as from Cicero and Saint Paul), the nation experienced what
Brooks and Henry Adams termed a "Degradation of the Democratic
Dogma" leading straight from Jackson and Van Buren to the presidency of
Ulysses S. Grant.[39]

Adams's deep disdain for sectional politics and individual aggrandizement also found expression during the Jacksonian era in a general "antipartyism" among an odd mixture of Whigs, anti-Masons, evangelical reformers, and latter-day Puritans who scorned the ethos and character of
the Democratic party as defined and defended by Van Buren and his allies.
Deriving in part from a Winthropian sense of an organic society knit together in brotherly affection for the good of the whole,[40] and imbued with
an Edwardsian vision of a worldwide "pious union" of Christian love, the
"antiparty" forces thought of government as beginning with society, not
with individuals, and believed that harmony, not conflict or competition,
should characterize human affairs. As late as 1848 a Whig orator could still
aver that a voter "does not exercise his franchise for himself, but for the
whole body politic . . . [in order to] place the administration habitually in
the hands of the most worthy." In this speaker's eyes, "Leaders, Lawgivers
and Instructors of the people" on the models of Moses and Joshua were
still needed. An evangelical spokesman, Horace Bushnell, called political
parties "the worst form of Papacy ever invented" because their demand for
total loyalty masked seething factional disputes. Another, Charles G. Finney, declared that "no man can be an honest man, that is committed to a
political party." Hostility to the Masons as a secret, divisive group, furthermore, had its roots in a similar suspicion of any force that set one part of
the community against another. "Party men" were viewed as grasping,
newly rich, unprincipled, alienated types who lacked a sense of community
responsibility, were devoid of Christian charity, and corrupted morals.[41] It

is not surprising that John Quincy Adams, a son of New England Puritanism, was deeply anti-Masonic and often, especially in his later career, found support from and made alliances with elements of this "general antipartyism" that remained an important force in American politics, at least rhetorically, through the first half of the nineteenth century. It would be a mistake to conclude, obviously, that everything changed abruptly in 1829 with Adams's defeat, or that the new Democratic party was totally unconcerned for "the whole body politic," or even that it was far more partisan than the groups that opposed it. Clay, Calhoun, and Webster, for example, conceded nothing to Jackson, Van Buren, and Thomas Hart Benton as inveterate partisans. But the second quarter of the nineteenth century did witness a growing party activity and validation of that activity on all sides even as party leaders continued to draw on a large reservoir of antiparty sentiment still strong in public opinion.

Defoe, Tocqueville, and J. S. Mill

The parallel of this antipartyism with the critique made by Pope and Bolingbroke of Robert Walpole's government is striking. Jackson and his followers, and the political system they espoused, accepted as benign the same enterprising, candidly partisan, openly competitive dynamic that Walpole had welcomed in England a century earlier. Although the Whig merchants and oligarchs who supported Walpole were vastly different from the mixture of farmers, workers, slaveowners, and entrepreneurs who sustained Jackson, nonetheless in each case the character of the nation was allowed to rest simply on the energies and enterprise of the individuals and groups within it. W. E. H. Lecky's praise of Walpole and his government, that under it Britain experienced a "long peace, . . . immense material development, . . . [and] the firm establishment of parliamentary government," has its American counterpart in Richard Hofstadter's characterization of Jacksonian democracy. It demanded "the classic bourgeois ideal, equality before the law [and] the restriction of government to equal protection of its citizens. . . . Its aim [was] not to throttle but to liberate business, to open every possible pathway for the creative enterprise of the people."[42] Each historian, that is, discerned a specific time in the history of the respective nations when key elements of "the liberal tradition"—freedom from restraint, enterprise, prosperity, and party government—experienced growth and validation.

   Classic accounts of each era, Daniel Defoe's *A Tour Thro' the Whole Island of Great Britain* (1724–1727) and Alexis de Tocqueville's *Democracy in America* (1835), also emphasize again and again the centrality of the commercial spirit and the transformation it was effecting on the land and its people. Defoe's work celebrated the growth of trade and the consequent rapid increase of wealth experienced by Great Britain during the rule of Walpole. Although the author on his tour noticed interesting "antiquities" and paid some attention to churches, country houses, farming, and other traditional aspects of English life, he became ecstatic over bustling marketplaces, improved transportation, new industries, ingenious inventions, and growing towns. Defoe saw England with a tradesman's eye, always aware of what was important to his prosperity, and utterly confident that the future greatness of the nation depended not only on its manufactures and commerce as such but also on its cherishing the habits and values of the tradesman: enterprise, diligence, autonomy, and pursuit of profit. Defoe found the West Riding of Yorkshire "a noble Scene of Industry and Application" where thronged marketplaces in "infinitely populous" towns made it clear that a welcome revolution was under way in English life. He was especially impressed with Hull, where there was "more business done . . . than in any other town of its bigness in Europe." Its greatest asset, moreover, was its merchants. There were none in Britain, Defoe asserted, with "a fairer Credit, or fairer Character . . . as well for the Justice of their Dealings as the Greatness of their Substance or Funds for Trade."[43] As Defoe was well aware of the misery and poverty still widespread in Britain, he also proposed countless "projects" showing how the expansive, energetic spirit permeating commerce could soon solve social problems—precisely the optimism and ingenuity that had so impressed the youthful Benjamin Franklin when he had read Defoe's *Essay upon Projects* (London, 1695). Quite simply, Defoe exulted at an ethic, an openness, a way of life, and a public philosophy attuned to the new world of commerce coming to England in the age of Walpole.

A century later Tocqueville found the same qualities in an America whose reigning folk hero was Franklin. Tocqueville was convinced that the commercial, enterprising style was the irresistible wave of the future and that this bourgeois culture was advancing in its most undiluted form in America. With a background different from Defoe's and with one hundred more years of bourgeois "progress" on record, however, Tocqueville saw the result as a mixed blessing. At the end of his travels in America he admitted, "I find my vision hazy and my judgment hesitant." That impressive, restless, vigorous, egalitarian nation, destined to fill a continent and dominate half the world, nonetheless "saddens and chills me," he wrote, because it also seemed "blunted," "less brilliant," "more average," and tinged with a "universal uniformity." He was therefore "tempted to regret that state of society which has ceased to be"—the same anxieties and forebodings Walpole's critics had felt. Yet, the French aristocrat accepted as in-

evitable what the Augustan writers had sought to hold back. "It would be
. . . unreasonable to expect of men nowadays," he wrote, "the particular
virtues which depended on the social conditions of their ancestors, since
that state of society has collapsed, bringing down in the confusion of its
ruin all that it had of good and bad."[44] It was John Quincy Adams's tor-
ment—and opportunity—as it had been Jefferson's, to lead the nation in
seeking to blend the virtues of the collapsing aristocratic world with the
coming age of autonomy, democracy, and equality heralded by Jackson
and his followers.

John Stuart Mill expressed a similar ambiguity when in 1840 he reviewed volume 2 of *Democracy in America*. He accepted most of Tocqueville's generalizations about American character and society, but he disagreed about their root cause. Tocqueville had mistakenly blamed the
leveling, grasping, ignoble aspects of life in the United States on the "ab-
stract ideas" of democracy and equality. These deficiencies, Mill insisted,
instead arose from "the tendencies of modern commercial society." He
thought the contrast between the equality of condition among the people
of lower (French) Canada, who had none of "that go-ahead spirit" of the
Americans, and the American-like enterprise of the English middle class,
in the midst of an aristocratic society, revealed Tocqueville's mistake. Mill
asked Englishmen whether "the American people, both in their good
qualities and in their defects, resemble anything so much as an exaggeration of our own middle class." He found "the spirit of commerce and industry is one of the greatest instruments . . . of improvement and culture
in the widest sense; to it, or to its consequences, we owe nearly all that
advantageously distinguishes the present period from the middle ages."
That spirit was dangerous, Mill thought, only when it "becomes prepon-
derant in a community, . . . [imposing itself] upon all the rest of society;
[and] . . . forcing all to either submit to it or to imitate it." The United
States in 1840, Mill implied, was not so much a unique land of democracy
and equality as a nation excessively dominated by a commercialization of
values long in development in England.

The need, therefore, was not to be "hazy" or "hesitant" about the spread
of democracy and equality, but rather to be sure that the "commercial
spirit" did not become utterly dominant—as seemed to be the case in the
United States. In this respect Mill thought Great Britain was fortunate because it still possessed a genuine "agricultural class" attached to the land
and devoted to farming as "itself an interesting occupation." American
farmers, on the other hand, who "range from place to place, [were] to all
intents and purposes a commercial class." Britain was also lucky that it had,
as America did not, "a leisured and a learned class" that were able to "control the excess of the commercial spirit by a contrary spirit." Although Mill
regarded "the ascendency of the commercial class in modern society as in-

evitable," it did not need "to be regarded as evil" as long as "counter-balancing" classes existed. Mill meant that society had to cultivate a higher morality "than either the calculations of self-interest, or the emotions of self-flattery" (all too prevalent in Jacksonian America, if Tocqueville was right). Furthermore, public life needed to be guided by "that order of virtues in which a commercial society is apt to be deficient: . . . with less benevolence but more patriotism; less sentiment, but more self-control; if a lower average of virtue, more striking individual examples of it; fewer small goodnesses, but more greatness, and appreciation of greatness." Without denigrating democracy, enterprise, or equality, Mill saw the need for other values in society—and for standards and modes of government akin to those lauded in the Roman Senate, especially "freedom from any class-interest" and the exercise of rational deliberation in pursuit of the public good. And he also agreed with John Quincy Adams that active, virtuous leadership was indispensable to the preservation of this counterbalancing element in a nation.[45]

Increasingly dominant in both Walpolean Britain and in Jacksonian America, however, was a world view congenial to a prospering, open society, requiring not so much guidance as free rein. One consequence of this dominance was observed years later by Herbert Croly: "When orators of the Jacksonian Democratic tradition begin to glorify the superlative individuals developed by the freedom of American life, what they mean by individuality is an unusual amount of individual energy successfully spent in popular and remunerative occupations. Of the individuality which may reside in the gallant and exclusive devotion to some disinterested, and perhaps unpopular moral, intellectual, or technical purpose, they have not the remotest conception."[46] This latter sort of "individuality" (before mid-nineteenth century, the term, if used at all, had generally negative connotations), however, is precisely what Washington and John Quincy Adams (to say nothing of Pericles, Plutarch, Swift's king of Brobdingnag, and a host of others) admired.

❦ III ❦

Republican Dilemmas: Virtue and Commerce, Leadership and Party

As we have seen, those responsible for molding ideas of what national leadership was supposed to be during the first half-century of government under the Constitution struggled with two serious theoretical dilemmas. The first, basically cultural and moral, concerned the problem of how, in the presence of a changing ethic and an enlarging democratic process, a government of virtue could nonetheless be sustained. If, on the model of Adam Smith's increasingly influential economic theories, the public interest consisted in the assiduous pursuit of infinite private interests, then perhaps in politics it was necessary to accept a pluralist dynamic of clashing groups (factions, in Madison's language) that leaders and political parties, working together, would resolve into public policy. In such a process, ancient aspirations for disinterestedness, for a standard based on a sense of the common good, for a patriot leader, and finally for a harmonious polity received, at the very least, radical redefinition.

The crucial questions were whether the "new-style" politics could be defended morally and whether there was any prospect that the people at large (the rulers in a self-governing polity) could possess the requisite qualities. Equally urgent and problematic was whether, with the changing moral climate and expansion of the franchise, the very idea of government aspiring to "higher law" and common purposes could be maintained. In both cases, the task of the national leader was important and perplexing.

The second dilemma concerned the purpose and role of political parties and the relation of the president to them. Parties and factions were ancient facts of political life and existed with increasing openness in modern nations, but throughout the eighteenth century they were seldom validated or celebrated. Rather, they were seen as resting on pathological tendencies that any country aspiring to virtue and nobility would have to curb, restrain, and control. The ambivalence and agony felt by each of the first six presidents as they faced the fact of burgeoning party activity on all sides while seeking earnestly to fulfill an ideal of leadership having no valid place for it is evidence of the changes underway. The idea of party, attuned as it was to the new commercial ethic and clearly requiring a new style of leadership, had particularly profound implications for the chief magistracy of a republic.

Something of these ideological issues and moral dilemmas can be grasped if we notice the parallels between the "mighty opposites" of Augustan Britain, Pope and Walpole, and the American presidents J. Q. Adams and Andrew Jackson. Pope and Adams assumed the existence of a moral order in the universe, in accordance with which a good leader would guide and rule. Walpole and Jackson, on the other hand, accepted more simply the benefits of limited government, enterprise, and the open society. With this emphasis, the eras of the first "modern" prime minister and of the first "modern" president are rightly regarded as epochal in the growth of Anglo-American liberty.

J. Q. Adams was still the tenacious embodiment of an antiparty model of active leadership as old as the heroes of Plutarch. Yet ambiguity and tension in conceptions of leadership at the time were inescapable, not only in traditional philosopher-statesmen like the Adamses but also in such avowed champions of the common man as

Franklin and Jefferson. The common man, too, as political participation gradually widened after 1776, had to respond to, and accept or reject, the models of leadership set before him. In the century between Franklin's first election to public office in Philadelphia (1748) and the end of J. Q. Adams's career in the House of Representatives, American politicians strove to accommodate time-honored ideas of national leadership to the new requirements of popular sovereignty.

Although the struggle of Jefferson to conceive and to be a patriot yet republican executive has already been touched on, it is necessary to return once more to the career of this crucial figure in order to deepen our understanding of the problem of leadership. Both Jefferson and Franklin found moral dignity in the lives of the common man, and both sought to nourish resources of virtue and responsible citizenship in the people, who were destined to rule in a self-governing nation. By looking at Franklin, too, whom we have so far ignored, we can shed important light on the difficult and dubious pathways of political leadership in the new republic.

Finally, in a different way, the thought of Alexander Hamilton, the American of his time perhaps most richly endowed with natural qualities of leadership, also illuminates the paradoxes of giving purpose and direction to a republican polity amid what J. S. Mill called "the tendencies of modern commercial society." Hamilton's unashamed intention of making the United States a prosperous commercial and industrial nation while at the same time guiding its political economy toward the common good propelled him into the center of the nation's leadership dilemmas even though he never became president. Indeed, one could argue that Hamilton's possession to such a preeminent degree of the traditional marks of leadership somehow incapacitated him for the presidency of a republic—so at least John Adams and Jefferson certainly thought. Hamilton's very zeal to guide the nation in the paths he thought best for it, then, caused him to confront with special urgency the significance both of the new commercial ethic, which he admired, and of the political party, which he as much shunned ideologically as did Jefferson—and as much nonetheless nourished into being.

❦ 9 ❦

Jefferson, Franklin,
and the Commonness
of Virtue

Jefferson and the Problem of Virtue in a Republic

Thomas Jefferson's most creative political thought, and his standing as *the* philosopher of American democracy, rest on his determination to implant in the new United States the benefits of what might appear to be incompatible values: the life of freedom espoused by Locke and the radical Whigs and the ideal of a moral human community responsive to nonpartisan leadership. At some point there is a contradiction or at least a tension between a "life of freedom" conceived of as basically a growing absence of restraint and any conception of society resting on a substantive ideal, whether phrased in Platonic, Christian providential, natural law, or any other terms. The difference is apparent if one contrasts "handbooks" of political action, goals, and leadership of what we may call a "guided society" with those of an "open society." Consider, for example, the differences in assumptions and dynamics implicit in Plato's *Republic*, Erasmus's *The Education of a Christian Prince*, and Bolingbroke's *Idea of a Patriot King*, on the one hand, and on the other, such more recent works as Harold Laski's *The Grammar of Politics*, John Dewey's *Liberalism and Social Action*, and Karl Popper's *The Open Society and Its Enemies*. In retrospect, and perhaps in logic, the two conceptions, one intent on ends and the other on process, seem incompatible, but it was precisely Jefferson's dilemma—burden or opportunity—that he lived when the dichotomy was incomplete, and political thinking thus sought creatively to realize the virtue in each ideal. New nationhood could have as its goal during such a transition both freedom and adherence to an objective "good."

In resisting British tyranny, in declaring independence, and even in helping to establish new governments, Jefferson bypassed the dilemma by focusing on restraint of excessive and arbitrary authority, drawing mostly on the radical Whig tradition of resistance to crown prerogatives. As attention shifted to the need for political leadership, however, the Bolingbrokean side of the search for liberty, which Jefferson also admired, became more relevant. Furthermore, like nearly all of his colleagues in nation-building, and following both conventional political thought and what the eighteenth century saw as "the lessons of history," Jefferson regarded "good government" as substantive, not procedural. That is, he accepted the Aristotelian argument that governments were good or corrupt according to the *quality* of life they sustained: was there peace and order, were the people virtuous, was the city prosperous, did the arts and sciences flourish, were creativity and good taste encouraged, and so on. If a polity nourished these characteristics, then it was "good," whether procedurally it was ruled by one, the few, or the many. If a polity lacked these virtues, it was corrupt. And Jefferson would have followed Aristotle, too, in designating these degradations "autocracy," "oligarchy," and "democracy," according to whether one, or a few, or "the people" was responsible for the corruption. A king could be good or bad, and rule by the people at large could also be good or bad. Hence, the critical question was not whether certain *processes* of government were present, such as universal suffrage, or legislative supremacy, or annual elections, but whether there was peace and community and justice, virtue, and prosperity.

Jefferson's reading of Locke and the other great Whig writers, and his experience of the American Revolution and of self-government in the New World, left him committed to the principle of government by consent because it restrained the sort of tyranny that had long oppressed mankind. But, in acknowledging the possibility (for many of his colleagues, including John Adams, it was a probability) that "democracy" could have Aristotle's meaning—mob rule and tyranny of the majority—Jefferson also acknowledged that simply letting the people have their way did not solve the problems of government. The crucial question was, How could "the people" be induced to rule well? What education, what economy, what livelihoods, what polity—eventually what *leadership*—would move toward that shining ideal?

Jefferson at first concentrated on social and political reforms that would adapt all laws "to our republican form of government." The laws he sponsored in Virginia, such as the abolition of entail and primogeniture, the establishment of liberal land policy, support of education, and the gradual elimination of slavery, would give rise to a society of yeoman farmers with the requisite virtue, he hoped, to be good citizens and to govern themselves well. These reforms reflected Jefferson's deep attachment to Physiocratic ideas and even to pastoral models going back to Aristotle and Virgil, but they also revealed his commitment to political participation by *all* people in a society. Full protection of liberty of conscience was both just in itself and useful in encouraging people to think for themselves, as good citizens would have to do. Similarly, laws "for a general education would [qualify citizens] to understand their rights, to maintain them, and to exercise with intelligence their parts in self-government."[1] These fundamental measures to "republicanize society" (some accepted and some rejected in Virginia) embodied a highly positive conception of government and initially emphasized new laws and institutions that would improve the people at large, the necessary basis of any good government resting on consent.

During the 1780s and 1790s, however, Jefferson came increasingly to realize that achieving good republican government was difficult not only in the elevated demands it made on the citizens but also in the arrangements required for leadership. Thus he proposed a pyramided educational system capped by a university where "the aristocracy of talent and virtue" could be trained Platonically, in the liberal and exacting arts of good government; but he also had, increasingly, to consider the actual mechanisms of leadership in a federal republic. The lessons he drew from the years between 1776 and 1800 were ambiguous and often troubling. On the one hand, his sense of the need for firm executive authority and leadership heightened as he experienced the ill effects of the hamstrung governorship in Virginia and the leaderless government under the Articles of Confederation. Hence, when he saw the new Constitution of 1787, he did not object to the *amount* of power given the executive but rather sought only to diminish the partisan (corrupt) influence on the president. Then, as a member of Washington's cabinet, he supported the firm and dignified administration of government. On the other hand, Alexander Hamilton's manipulation of Congress, the press, and eventually (so his enemies charged) even the president himself—that is, Hamilton's success at establishing a "Walpolean" system in the United States—thoroughly alarmed Jefferson.

The effort by Jefferson and his colleagues during the 1790s to justify and strengthen their opposition to Hamilton's policies also caused them to examine how the public might relate to political parties and how this dynamic might affect the quality of government. Jefferson probed for answers in 1795, for example, when he paraphrased Edmund Burke's justification[2] for forming a "party of virtue" to oppose "Rogues": "Were parties here divided merely by a greediness for office, as in England, to take a part with either would be unworthy of a reasonable or moral man, but where the principle of difference is as substantial and as strongly pronounced as between the republicans and the Monocrats of our country, I hold it as honorable to take a firm and decided part, and as immoral to pursue a middle line, as between the parties of Honest men, and Rogues, into which every country is divided." Jefferson also believed that "in every free and deliberating society there must, from the nature of man, be opposite parties and violent dissensions and discords." He even accepted that a profound, probably permanent cleavage existed between what Madison termed "a republican party" that believed "mankind are capable of governing themselves" and an "antirepublican party" that had "debauched themselves into the persuasion that mankind are incapable of governing themselves." In his closest approach to a modern view of party, Jefferson admitted to John Taylor of Caroline in 1798 that "perhaps this party division is necessary to induce each to watch and [r]elate to the people the proceedings of the other."[3] The apparent inconsistency between this more positive use of the word *party* by Jefferson and his expressed views in other places reveals the profound transition in political concepts with which he struggled.

Taylor sensed the large issues at stake when in reply he scolded Jefferson for conceding too much the inevitability of party spirit and for underestimating its baneful effects on both the public interest and the requirements of good leadership. Taylor hoped instead that the element of party spirit arising from the tendency toward evil in human nature "may yet admit of alleviations" and argued that the part arising from "political encouragement," itself a human contrivance, could be "counteracted" by other measures. He even saw the danger implicit in an already hallowed axiom of American government: "What are checks and balances, but party and faction? If a good form of government too often fails, in making bad men good, a bad form of government will too often succeed in making good men bad." The flaw in depending on checks and balances to preserve liberty was that to do so assumed and even encouraged a competition of self-interests (factions) that poisoned a virtuous pursuit of the public interest.

The need, Taylor concluded, instead of "balancing power against power . . . which artificially" produced parties, was to secure "to liberty an ascendant over power, whether simple or complex." Challenging Jefferson's view that a tendency toward party was inherent in human nature, Taylor asked whether "man's natural propensity for liberty," under a proper government, might not curb the "art and corruption" that spawned party. In a luminous remark, Taylor asserted that "monarchy will answer these questions." The "union in political principle . . . natural to man under a monarchy," he wrote, doubtless thinking of the great and good patriot leaders Plutarch and Bolingbroke had used as examples, could also be achieved in a republic that had annual elections, rotation in office, fair tax laws, and equal representation so that the people would have "a real influence over the government."

Taylor thought "the eminent example of Connecticut, which has [for] about two centuries enjoyed a compleat unanimity under a government the most democratic of any representative form which ever existed," showed that "parties . . . are not naturally the issue of every popular government." Although Taylor's opinion may reflect his ignorance of the realities of Connecticut politics, it nonetheless shows what was on his mind: that the evils of party were so great that he believed it impossible to suppose them rooted in human nature itself without at the same time impeaching the very idea of a virtuous republicanism. All history, Taylor thought, "violently opposes the idea, that party spirit is simply the child of nature." Therefore, to rest government on the inevitability of faction, and to suppose good decisions on public policy would arise from a clash of opinions, would make the nation "the vassal of a combination, cold pitiless and insatiable." Such a system, Taylor pointed out, in the 1790s had resulted in "avarice and ambition, entrenched behind perpetual taxation, in a disciplined corps, [having] become the lords paramount of the creation."[4]

What Taylor, and Jefferson, sought was a frame of government and a republicanizing of society that would allow the same "union in political principle," the same attention to the common good, that characterized monarchy at its best. That such a government would require mechanisms to encourage grass-roots virtue and influence they understood, but it is also clear from their reliance on patriot leader models that they were entirely open as well to the benefit that virtuous leadership might confer in a republic. Taylor's words and examples show how deeply he followed the ancient political axioms.

Although the Taylor-Jefferson exchange reveals that the two men had the same goal, a politics resting on harmony and universal principles, Taylor sought as well to keep Jefferson from viewing unwelcome realities (the bitter party strife of the 1790s) as so "indelible" as to make impossible any basic shift to a less demeaning polity. Only with such a faith, Taylor believed, could a period of public harmony resting on a common virtue and love of liberty follow the triumph over party each saw as the purpose of their vigorous partisanship in opposing Hamilton. Jefferson made clear his acceptance of Taylor's assumptions when he wrote four days after his inauguration as president: "I shall hope to be able to *obliterate*, or rather to *unite* the names of federalists and republicans" (emphasis added).[5] Neither the harsh nor the harmonizing word left room for party legitimacy, and each supposed it might be possible to find in the people, properly led and enlightened, a sufficient virtue and agreement to sustain good government.

Republican Leadership

In 1801, then, Jefferson was left with a problem at once difficult and challenging. He had both to lead an administration of national unity and to adhere faithfully to the principle of consent, all in the presence of the abuses of power and the remoteness from the people that the Jeffersonians thought had improperly characterized Federalist rule.[6] He accepted by then the insufficiency of Revolutionary nostrums such as Thomas Paine's about simple legislative government being all a republic required, but he also had had further lessons in the dangers of imperious administration. He had somehow to *lead* a government of the whole people, to *lead* in harmony with their interests, perhaps even in response to their express judgments. But how was that possible? To a man as practical as Jefferson, it was important to refine procedures and build institutions to that end. Was there any way that the time-honored, and to Jefferson still valid, conception of a government of talent and virtue could be accommodated to the dynamics of government by consent?

It is at this point that Jefferson's political thinking, and, in general, his political practice, accomplished the creative combination of the "English Cato" and the "patriot king" that establishes the basic article of faith underlying American government as it was understood by the first six presidents. The conception begins with the thought of "Cato" and Bolingbroke in profound opposition to Walpole's government of ministerial corruption. For a primary defense against such a system Jefferson followed Locke and "Cato" in championing legislative supremacy, bills of rights, limited government, and so on, but he also continued to pursue, with the utmost seriousness, even agony, modes of guiding the nation in the paths of virtue.

At times in this double pursuit he seemed incongruously to urge measures a "limited" government would shun. He suggested prosecution of libelous newspaper editors (to prevent the "pollution" of vital media of public enlightenment); he recommended a national university and national roads (to encourage public improvement); and he severely restricted trade with the Embargo (to substitute economic pressure for war). Two years after retiring as chief executive, when asked "whether circumstances do not sometimes occur, which make it a duty in officers of high trust, to assume authorities beyond the law," Jefferson replied that "a strict observance of the written laws is doubtless *one* of the high duties, . . . but it is not *the highest*. The laws . . . of saving our country when in danger, are of higher obligation." Then he cited his responses to opportunities to obtain Florida from Spain in 1805, to the *Chesapeake* incident, and to Aaron Burr's conspiracy in 1807 as examples of how an executive officer had "to risk [himself] on great occasions, when the safety of the nation, or some of its very highest interests are at stake," and then "throw himself on the justice of his country and the rectitude of his motives" for validation of his statesmanship.[7] As these cases show, there was indeed in Jefferson's mind a need to balance possibly incompatible goals, but he refused to relinquish either; he insisted on both a mild government mindful of the rights of the people and a positive government capable of acting to preserve the state and, in Aristotelian fashion, "for the sake of the good life."

The power of the executive, its definition and use, was at the crux of the problem. Unrestrained, manipulated, or encroaching, it was a sure source of first tyranny and then chaos: no proposition was more firmly fixed in Jefferson's mind. Yet, without firm, virtuous, patriotic guidance, without some direction by superior intelligence and good intent, mediocrity, discord, dullness, factional greed, and the other horrors of eighteenth-century political sensibility were bound to ensue. Jefferson sought instead to bring together in the office of the presidency, indeed, in the person of the president, a sense of nonpartisan devotion to virtue and the public interest akin to that espoused in *Idea of a Patriot King* and at the same time a sense of the aspirations and will of the people required by "Cato," Paine, and other radical Whig theorists. Ideally, the two would converge; that is, the people themselves would comprehend and seek the same public interest perceived by the nonpartisan leader. They would, in other words, resist corruption and achieve virtue.

This state of affairs was far off, as Jefferson often observed and complained, but it was always the goal to be sought. To give up on it was tantamount to admitting that republics could never take their place in the Aristotelian pantheon of good governments. Jefferson's most earnest efforts were on behalf of education, of yeoman farming, of vigorous local government, of religious freedom, of an enlightening press, and of peace: because progress in these areas would improve the quality of understanding in the people. Achievement of these ends would make possible broadly in the population the sense of civic virtue that Aristotle, Cicero, Erasmus, and Bolingbroke had supposed only a few (the *aristoi*) might achieve. The obvious difficulty of making the people themselves into a kind of universal aristocracy has stamped Jefferson, and democratic theorists ever since, as idealistic and naive. But if one accepts the requirements that society exists to achieve "the good life and not life alone" and that government exists to help realize that goal, then the wager on behalf of the people must be made—or the principle of consent abandoned. Because Jefferson refused to give up, he searched lifelong for the insights and the institutions that would make self-government good government. No other motif can make sense of his thought and career.

In old age Jefferson reviewed all the aspirations, tensions, and dilemmas of his time as he reread his favorite ancient authors and discussed the lessons of early American history with John Adams. He was struck, he wrote Adams, by Cicero's exalted patriotism revealed in his letters and by the "odious contrast" with "the parricide Caesar." He then wondered, "If Caesar had been as virtuous as he was daring and sagacious, what could he

. . . have done to lead his fellow citizens into good government?" Not much, Jefferson concluded, because "steeped in corruption[,] vice[,] and venality as the whole nation was, . . . what could even Cicero, Cato, Brutus have done, had it been referred to them to establish a good government for their country? They had no ideas of government themselves but of their degenerate Senate, nor the people of liberty, but of the factious opposition of their tribunes." For Roman government to succeed, the people would have to be totally reformed. Their minds would have to be "informed, by education, what is right and what wrong, to be encoraged in habits of virtue, and deterred from those of vice." They would have to be induced to "follow truth as the only safe guide, and to eschew error which bewilders us in one false consequence after another in endless succession. These are the inculcations necessary to render the people a sure basis for the structure of order and good government." But in this very same letter, still preoccupied with his reading of Roman history, he had noted not only Caesar's grave responsibility for having corrupted the people but also the probability that even if Cicero, Cato, and Brutus had established a virtuous government, the succession of "many Neros and Commoduses . . . would have quashed the whole process." Even Titus, Trajan, and Antoninus, "who had the will to make [the people] happy, and the power to mould their government into a good and permanent form," Jefferson observed, were frustrated in the long run because the essential control by the people, who "were so demoralised and depraved," could not be made "wholsome." The tensions are clear: although Jefferson's political thinking, and his hopes for the United States, rested on faith in the people and the possibility of forming government and other institutions to promote their virtue, and although his republicanism and his study of history had convinced him that a patriot king could not single-handedly create a good society, he continued to believe that the quality of leadership was inescapably important as he reflected on the "aenigma" of blending virtue and self-government. Indeed, the "aenigma" had been implicit in his own remark to Abigail Adams in 1804 that although the "honest portion" of both parties sought the public good, they differed as to the means: "One fears most the ignorance of the people: the other the selfishness of rulers independant of them."[8] Jefferson himself feared the ignorance of the people but thought it sufficiently eradicable to make good self-government possible, and he thought such improved understanding under such a government could expel selfish rulers. He did not, however, suppose that good and active leadership could be dispensed with.

The Jacksonians, however, crucially altered the ideas both of confidence in the people and of government itself. Their confidence was that the people could grow and prosper *on their own*, and they assigned government the largely negative task of destroying restrictive forces such as monopolistic banks and entrenched bureaucracies. They also moved steadily toward the propositions that political life was analogous to economic life (especially that the ethic of self-interest was as useful in one as in the other) and that therefore the public good could be defined only in the competition of political factions and parties. Ralph Waldo Emerson voiced the widespread moral distaste for such a view of politics in his *Journal*:

> When I . . . speak of the democratic element, I do not mean that ill thing, vain and loud, which writes lying newspapers, spouts at caucuses, and sells its lies for gold, but that spirit of love for the general good whose name this assumes. There is nothing of the true democratic element in what is called [the Democratic Party]; it must fall, being wholly commercial. . . . The spirit of our American [democratic radicalism] is destructive and aimless. . . . On the other side, the conservative party [Whigs], composed of the most moderate, able, and cultivated part of the population, is timid; and merely defensive of property; . . . it does not build, nor write, nor cherish the arts, nor foster religion, nor establish schools, nor encourage science, nor emancipate the slave, nor befriend the poor, or the Indian, or the immigrant. From neither party, when in power, has the world any benefit to expect . . . at all commensurate with the resources of the nation.[9]

Jefferson, who would have sympathized with this critique, stands as the preeminent philosopher of American democratic government because he sought most faithfully to accommodate the relatively new principle of government by consent to the ancient principle of respecting only governments that cultivated virtue, or, what is the same thing, resisted partial, self-interested views. His presidency, moreover, despite his own depreciation of it, can be accorded high honor not, as some of his "admirers" argue, because by becoming the master (manipulative) politician he managed to overcome his own principles and thus "accomplish things," but because he again and again perceived how to work toward the vital accommodation. He was approachable and modest without being common or demeaning himself. He created respect not by pomp and ceremony but by the way he fulfilled his responsibilities. He led Congress by appealing to its best, not its worst, motivations, and he led the people by asking them to share his aspirations, not by pandering to their special interests. He failed to achieve some of his goals, he proposed some unwise programs, and perhaps he even too often compromised his own principles, but the mark of his greatness as a president may be in his faith that he could both lead toward virtue and be in harmony with the people. Jefferson would not have put it as bluntly as Theodore Roosevelt, but the third president would have accepted his twentieth-century successor's assertion that he did not seek to "divine" what the people thought. Rather, Roosevelt said, "I simply made up my mind what they ought to think, and then did my best to get them to think it."[10] So did Jefferson.

Franklin, Commerce, and Virtue

In order to formulate democratic theory for a nation so rapidly becoming more than a land of farmers, however, Jefferson and many others were compelled to accept a wider definition of the virtuous person than the narrow one permitted by pastoral biases. In fact, Jefferson's own gentry ideal of a virtuous life on the land increasingly was broadened to include validation of the trading and enterprising habits of artisans and merchants as well as of farmers. He recognized further, as Albert Gallatin put it in 1799, that in America "the different professions and trades are blended together in the same persons; the same man being frequently a farmer and a merchant, and perhaps a manufacturer."[11] In the world of Daniel Defoe and Adam Smith, that is, the conception of good citizenship had to be expanded to include virtues found beyond the field and the farm, especially if it was expected that the people generally were to take part in government.

The pastoral idyll of the farmer and the shepherd, hallowed in Western thought since Aristotle, Virgil, and Horace, revived by the Physiocrats, and espoused by the Augustan critics, needed somehow to project its moral ideals into the era of trade and industry rapidly engulfing the Western world. Propitiously, Jefferson's friend Benjamin Franklin had, in *Poor Richard's Almanac* and in his autobiography, begun to discern and instruct an enlarged pool of potentially good citizens—a task of particular importance for a new nation in a new world. Franklin demonstrated that the rational, industrious, self-reliant, public-spirited qualities basic to good citizenship, which Jefferson and others associated primarily with farmers, could be cultivated in new occupations and in new social classes. Franklin had lived all of his life in cities and in a way epitomized the earnest Puritan turned diligent tradesman. He was neither a farmer nor a man of piety— could he then understand or achieve virtue? or be a good citizen? Could his values, his business, his way of life, rather than poisoning the body politic, be harnessed for the public good?

Franklin's vigorously eclectic life exposed him to all the cultural and ethical currents of his day. He valued Bunyan, quoted Milton and Pope, imitated Addison, met Mandeville, whom he found "a most facetious, entertaining companion," taught two sons of Bolingbroke's friend Sir William Wyndham to swim, enjoyed the friendship of Hume and Kames, and as much admired Defoe as Swift. He respected the character of Boston Puritans like his father, admired the business skills of Philadelphia merchants, moved congenially as a tradesman largely among Anglicans, and felt Quaker politicians provided Pennsylvania with good and honest government. He enjoyed living in London and Paris at least as much as in Boston and Philadelphia. He found in the arguments of Christian apologists better reasons to doubt than to believe in the God of John Calvin or even that of his friend George Whitefield, but he cheerfully contributed to the building funds of nearly all the churches of Philadelphia. He was never a farmer, but he insisted as much as Jefferson that the virtues traditionally associated with independent life in the country were essential to the good person and would, therefore, in a society resting on the consent of the governed, be essential to the health of the body politic. Franklin came to have the same disgust for the corruption of English society and politics as did Robert Walpole's "Country" party critics, but he shared neither their gentry bias nor their class consciousness. He lived apart from the style, privileges, and environment of the country gentleman that from Cicero to Bolingbroke and Jefferson had undergirded the emphasis on virtue and nonpartisanship in public life. Could such a person, with such an ethic and outlook, be of any use in improving the politics of the new nation?

By bringing the pastoral ethic into the shop and countinghouse, Franklin made possible a substantial expansion of the range of virtue-sustaining livelihoods. He patterned his virtuous tradesman not only to Defoe's model but also to the instruction of such moral philosophers as Aristotle, Plutarch, Bunyan, Cotton Mather, Pope, Addison, and Kames. He quite self-consciously sought to distill from the great writers, Classical, Christian, and Augustan, a pure solution that would nourish the "Art of Virtue," public and private. With equal self-consciousness he intended to make this "art" useful in the "modern world" he so enthusiastically heralded. As "Poor Richard" and in his autobiography, he set aside hoary theological debates, aristocratic conceits, pastoral preoccupations, and every relic of the past and instead spoke to the common man in the real world with its new needs and new tasks. In this attention to practical human behavior, Franklin also aligned himself with those who insisted conduct could be improved by training in good habits rather than requiring special knowledge or piety, as other moral traditions assumed.[12]

The hopes and the dilemmas facing thoughtful Britons in the eighteenth century who both embraced the commercial world view and cherished a more traditional morality are evident in Franklin's 1751 pamphlet, *Observations Concerning the Increase of Mankind*. In celebrating unfettered commerce, colonial enterprise, the growth of population, and material progress, this pamphlet exuded the spirit and ethic of Defoe. Reprinted many times between 1755 and 1775, it became part of the commercial and liberal ideology of the American Revolution. Yet, both Franklin and some of his friends who approved the pamphlet also retained a certain ambiguity and even uneasiness in assessing its full meaning. Richard Jackson, a member of Parliament for more than twenty years, colonial agent, scientist, and energetic Whig, praised Franklin's pamphlet but also observed that the "industry and frugality" it extolled "tended to destroy, as well as support, the government it flourishes under." "Commerce perfects the arts," Jackson noted, "but more the mechanical than the liberal, and this for an obvious reason; it softens and enervates the manners. Steady virtue, and unbending integrity, are seldom to be found where a spirit of commerce pervades every thing; yet the perfection of commerce is, that every thing should have its price. We every day see its progress, both to our benefit and detriment." Jackson deplored especially the decline of "rugged disposition," patriotism, and other traditional virtues under the influence of the "Luxury and Corruption" that seemed the "inseparable companions" of commerce, prosperity, and sophistication, but he offered no solution to the dilemma. Franklin in reply alluded only to the hope that the spread of virtue and good habits among the common people of such model colonies as Connecticut and Pennsylvania might mitigate the moral disadvantages of the commercial spirit.[13] Whatever their enthusiasm for trade and wealth, that is, Franklin and Jackson also felt the central eighteenth-century tension between virtue thought of as deliberate concern for the public good and its newer conception as simply enlightened self-interest.

As Jefferson realized in his deep affection for Franklin, the older man had made a career of seeking to introduce *everyman* not only to "the way to wealth" but also to a life of civic virtue analogous, at least, to that prescribed by Aristotle, Cicero, and the Renaissance humanists. In this way Franklin stands in much the same transitional position as a public philosopher as Max Weber found him as a moralist in the evolution of *The Protestant Ethic and the Spirit of Capitalism*. Following Weber's analysis, some critics have dismissed Franklin as merely bourgeois and would thus view his tradesman's Junto in Philadelphia and his own career as a printer as triumphs of the secularized Protestant ethic. Such an interpretation, however, grasps only part of what Franklin and his friends were doing. They did, of course, club together in their own self-interest, each Junto member intending to improve himself and make his business more profitable. But from the beginning they also linked their personal lives and livelihoods with the welfare of Philadelphia. All their civic projects—the library, the fire company, the insurance scheme, the night watch, the academy, the hospital, and so on—were useful personally, but at least as important, they were also ways to improve the life of the city, perhaps not on a Periclean scale, but with the same civic intent. The Juntoists, that is, bypassed the class and elitist bias of the Classical ideals of citizenship and patriotism and transformed them instead into attitudes and habits achievable by anyone, as republican theory came increasingly to require.

Had Franklin been no more than a successful businessman, purveyor of homely wisdom, and prototype Rotarian, however, he would not have furnished the essential ingredient needed to complete Jefferson's recipe for a society that could combine good government and self-government. Franklin accommodated many models of the enlarged, nonparochial view of life—Greek citizenship, Christian "general calling," Renaissance humanism, or Enlightened universal man—and he did it without grandeur or exclusiveness or hauteur, but simply as *le bonhomme Richard*. He progressively extended his personal values to local needs when he founded a hospital in Philadelphia, to provincial politics when he opposed arbitrary rule by the Pennsylvania proprietors, to the colonies as a whole when he signed the Declaration of Independence, and to international affairs when he declared that "there never was a good war or a bad peace." He thus linked the ethic and life-style of his father's humble home in Boston and his own printer's shop in Philadelphia to the great affairs of state long assumed to be the province of few. It follows that *Poor Richard's Almanac*, "The Art of Virtue," and the lessons of Franklin's public life were as much guides for statecraft as Erasmus's *The Education of a Christian Prince*, if in the new age the rulers were to be not a prince and perhaps a few advisers, but the people, and eventually *all* the people if the principle of government by consent was to reach its logical conclusion.

In showing how a tradesman could acquire the qualities of good citizenship, how the very habits conducive to rising in business—thrift, industry, prudence, self-reliance, independence, and civic concern—were the same attributes often thought to reside uniquely in those who lived on the land, Franklin offered an appealing solution to Jefferson's dilemma: the character needed to make republican government work could be cultivated not only in the countryside but also in the shops, stores, and counting-houses of the towns and cities spawned by the commercial and industrial revolutions. Franklin offered exactly the plebeian perspective, the grasp of the habits and attitudes of "the man in the street," needed to draw Jefferson's aristocratic and Physiocratic ideals into the common life of the new nation. Without "Poor Richard" to nourish virtue in the shops and cities, there could be no good self-government and no "empire of liberty" in a world of trade and industry; it was as simple as that.

Franklin summarized his view of the qualities necessary for the "good citizen" of the new United States when in 1782, from his post as minister to France, he furnished "Information to Those Who Would Remove to America." It was wrong, he began, to suppose that in the New World "Strangers of Birth must be greatly respected, and of course easily obtain the best of . . . [the] abundance of profitable Offices to be disposed of, which the Natives are not qualified to fill." In America, Franklin wrote, "people do not inquire concerning a Stranger, *What is he?* but, *What can he do?*" Furthermore, there was little in America of the monopolies and guild privileges that in Europe gave some people security and even wealth but at the same time prevented others of talent and ingenuity from making a living. The United States, Franklin pointed out, did not have a highly centralized government and could offer for "Encouragements" to new-comers "only what are derived from good Laws and Liberty." Who should come to America, then? "Hearty young Labouring Men, who understand the Husbandry of Corn and Cattle" might obtain land and in a few years become prosperous farmers. "Tolerably good Workmen in any of those mechanic Arts are sure to find Employ," Franklin added, beginning as ser-vants or journeymen, and "if they are sober, industrious, and frugal, they soon become Masters, establish themselves in Business, marry, raise Fam-ilies, and become respectable Citizens." "Persons of moderate Fortunes and Capitals" would also find scope for enterprise and investment in the opening of the frontier and the growth of trade and industry. The qualities of virtue, self-reliance, hard work, and prudence, that is, would in Amer-ica, whether on the farm, in the workshop, or in the countinghouse, make a person prosper *and* be a good citizen.[14]

Living among tradesmen and merchants whose livelihood depended on international commerce, Franklin had long assumed, a recent historian has noted, that "the simple republics of classical antiquity, particularly the primitive Sparta celebrated by [many American] Revolutionaries, could not provide a realistic long-range model for a rapidly expanding, indus-trious, prosperous republican America." He was a transitional figure who "somehow had to adapt the anticommercial spirit of classical republi-canism to [an] extensive and necessary involvement in commerce." To ac-complish this adaptation, he "embraced an ideology of free trade that tied . . . republican hopes to the prospects for a burgeoning, invigorating in-tercourse with the rest of the world." Franklin projected "Poor Richard'"s understanding of honest labor in pursuit of prosperity, which nourished the virtues necessary in the independent citizen, into an expansive political economy of growth through world trade. Thus, he showed how, "contrary to many traditional republican assumptions, the republican character of America was . . . tied" not to a self-sufficient pastoralism, but to "a vig-orous foreign commerce."[15] By this means America could accommodate to the modern world of Bacon, Mandeville, Richard Arkwright, and Adam Smith, without relinquishing the values of Plutarch, "Cato," and Pope.

Franklin had effected the essential moral enlargement when he noted that "the Husbandman is in Honor in America *and even the Mechanic*, be-cause their Employments are useful." Furthermore, "having in view the Formation of a future useful Citizen," apprentice contracts in America required not only that the master provide food and lodging but also that the apprentice "be taught to read, write, and cast accounts" while he learned his trade. Following Defoe, the English defender of trade, city life, and bourgeois values, Franklin saw in the enterprises of the new realm of commerce and industry, no less than in the traditional one of agriculture, opportunity for moral nobility. He envisioned human beings capable of fulfilling the exacting demands of republican citizenship emerging from all the tasks of a modern economy. He looked forward eagerly and hopefully to every liberalization in society and politics that would make it easier for moral virtue to be rewarded with material prosperity. Only by such changes would it be possible to derive good government from the consent of the people. In advising diligent, prudent workmen of all kinds, not just farmers, that in America they might find many honest tasks at once profitable and morally uplifting, Franklin tapped a vital supporting stream of potential good citizens for a Jeffersonian republic. Efforts akin to his would be crucial, too, in abolishing the old linkages exemplified in the argument of an Antifederalist of 1787: "The progress of a commercial society begets luxury, the parent of inequality, the foe to virtue, and the enemy to restraint"; the removal of explicit limits on executive power in the new Constitution will lead to "great power connected with ambition, luxury and flattery, . . . [and] as readily produce a Caesar, Caligula, Nero, and Domitain in America, as . . . in the Roman Empire."[16]

Antiliberalism among the Common People of America

However much Jefferson, Franklin, and others managed to find new foundations for morality and good government in the new era of commerce and self-determination, the old esteem for political harmony, virtuous leaders, and ancient privilege remained strong. The very nature of the American Revolution, for example, with its release of legislative power, commercial growth, and a rising individualism, left a distaste and even hostility among many observers who otherwise valued the opportunities opened up in America for ordinary people. The French aristocrat Hector St. John Crèvecoeur wrote poetically of "a new man in a new world," based on his experience in the farmlands of New York and Pennsylvania immediately before the Revolution. He had no use, however, for the agitation and distraction of the movement for independence, and he left the colonies when the war broke out. Although his aristocratic background might in part explain this attitude and departure, more profound ambiguities are also evident. His panegyrics about life in the New World rested on its moral and social as well as its material opportunities. The prospect of a simple man making a living for his family by sober hard work, and of then seeing his children become good, decent people as well as useful citizens because they had grown up in a society that encouraged virtue and fulfillment, was for Crèvecoeur an astonishing step forward for the human race. He thus sensed poignantly both the promise and the moral jeopardy of the American Revolution.

Crèvecoeur's letters on America contain no explicit public philosophy, but he did endorse two concepts: the great benefit to the common people of the absence of war, tumult, heavy taxes, and conscription, and the benefits to America derived from the benign protection (and neglect) of the British monarchy. To the farmer or the artisan, threats came not only from the immemorial oppressions with which the ancien régime and other tyrannies had always afflicted most of mankind but also from the sort of trade wars and imperial ambitions that had so burdened ordinary Britons in the age of Walpole and Pitt. To Crèvecoeur the impelling forces behind the American Revolution seemed committed to the same commercial aggressiveness, albeit under a different flag. "It is for the sake of the great leaders on both sides," he wrote in 1782, "that so much blood must be spilt: that of the people is counted as nothing. . . . What can an insignificant man do in the midst of these jarring contradictory parties?" "Whatever virtue, whatever merit and disinterestedness" a simple man displayed, Crèvecoeur lamented, was of no avail.[17] Crèvecoeur as firmly rejected the market ethic and the greed and corruption attendant on its infiltration into all aspects of life as did Pope and Swift. In an effort to protect deeply held moral values, Crèvecoeur, like Jefferson, accepted the Physiocrats' idealization of rural life and their contempt for a narrowly commercial civilization.

Crèvecoeur's goal was not simply the preservation of "high culture," but more fundamentally the development of a virtuous community of ordinary people in the New World. Hence, he more admired a benevolent monarch (as he perhaps misguidedly regarded George III) than crass, disputatious, democratic legislatures. The call to arms, the embitterment of political disputes, the setting of neighbor against neighbor, the destruction of life and property, the corrupt enrichment of military contractors, and all the other tragedies and demoralizations of revolution and war were to Crèvecoeur far worse than the relatively mild oppressions of George Grenville and Lord North.[18] Similar attitudes were pervasive among the plain people who had come to America from many parts of northwestern Europe, though perhaps temporarily submerged by the rhetoric and excitement of the revolt against the mother country. When, after Independence had been won, good government had to be established, this point of view took on prime importance. Many people who shared Crèvecoeur's perspective and values, if not his political loyalism, would find a public philosophy and a patriot leadership attuned to traditional ideals of virtue, selflessness, and the common welfare more attractive than a morally compromised politics, however wealth producing or democratic it might also claim to be. In an era when political philosophers still attended more to the *quality* of government than to its *process*, and when people in general were more inclined to worry about whether a governor was good or bad rather than whether he was elected or hereditary, it is clear that self-government alone was not enough. In fact, if Independence meant the celebration of self-interest and the factionalization of politics, many people would have found it not a gain but a loss.

Crèvecoeur's outlook as well as the opposed "liberal individualist" values were widespread among farmers and other common people in eighteenth-century America and produced tensions similar to those experienced in more literate and sophisticated circles. "Many of the settlers who elected to leave their European communities" during the eighteenth century, one scholar notes, had a "'liberal' middle-class orientation"; that is, they placed "individual freedom and material gain over that of public interest." Persisting in these values, and finding opportunities for them enlarged in the open spaces of the New World, the settlers "planned for themselves much more than they did for their communities," which, like governments, they viewed as "necessary evils to support individual fulfillment." The result was a liberal, entrepreneurial culture where western European settlers, whatever their differences in nationality, religion, or wealth, united in "goals of freedom from institutional constraints and of individual and family autonomy and success."[19] An analysis of an eighteenth-century Connecticut town found that its inhabitants also were characterized not so much by "the contented subsistence way of life as [by] the drive for profits." The population had been "raised on an economic tradition of land speculation and individualistic venturing."[20] All levels of society, it seems, experienced in some degree the spreading commercialization of values and the emphasis on individualism celebrated by Defoe.

Yet, one can find different emphases in examining "the *consciousness*, . . . the mental or emotional or ideological aspects," of the lives of colonial Americans. A careful review of the experience of several generations of American farmers during the eighteenth century, largely in New England, New York, and Pennsylvania, for example, shows that "these men and women were enmeshed . . . in a web of social relationships and cultural expectations that inhibited the free play of market forces." That is, in their effort to preserve kinship ties, and particularly the welfare of successive generations of the linear family, colonial farmers often subordinated their own individual advancement and persistently valued a wide variety of communal relationships above maximized profits. The "emphasis . . . upon the welfare of the entire family . . . inhibited the emergence of individualism,

. . . shaped the character—and often confined the scope—of entrepreneurial activity and capitalist enterprise."²¹ In a similar way, a study of attitudes toward work and commerce in eighteenth-century America reveals that "a desire to retain a sense of their social wholeness—and to avoid thinking of themselves as depersonalized economic beings—underlay the colonists' attitudes toward work." Ancient values had held that "exchange within a particular community was a social matter involving reciprocity and redistribution; competition, in the sense of one man's gaining at the expense of another, was a violation of this traditional ethic."²² Perhaps because they sensed the enormous social and moral changes implicit in the new economics, large portions of the population of British America seem to have retained a substantial residue of anticommercial sentiment.

A number of other studies of colonial and Revolutionary America have emphasized this central tension between communal and commercial values, between traditional and liberal conceptions of self and society. In Boston from 1765 to 1776 there was a struggle between common people attached to a radical ideology resting on Protestant-Puritan and common law communal values and a merchant elite espousing Whig commercialism.²³ Throughout the eighteenth century, in New York and Philadelphia as well as in Boston, as impersonal market forces unsettled traditional relationships, the new economic argument that individual profit seeking would foster the common good gained credence, but older ideas of regulation to promote social justice and an indivisible public good did not disappear, especially among "the lower orders."²⁴ Although a common revulsion at the corruption and oppression of British rule at home and in the colonies drew these views together in the republican ideology of the American Revolution, the underlying tensions remained to be reckoned with as the new nation turned its attention to frames of government and modes of leadership.

Other studies emphasize more explicitly the ambiguous or transitional quality of Revolutionary thought and society. Present in the Philadelphia that responded so fervently to Paine's *Common Sense*, for example, were both a liberal, commercial ideology and a traditional outlook that assumed the existence of a unified public interest. In consequence, Paine was able to espouse, plausibly, an eclectic republican ideology that extolled both competitive ideas of economic progress and contraction of government leadership, and harmonizing sentiments of egalitarianism and social accord.²⁵ Similar tensions as well as convergences can be found in a recent analysis of the varieties of republicanism in different sections of the colonies: a New England emphasis on a moral, organic society that still echoed Winthropian conceptions of strong government; a somewhat similar Middle Atlantic Presbyterian orientation receptive not only to appeals for social justice but also, increasingly, to open quest of individual aggrandizement; a cosmopolitan mercantile outlook also found in the Middle Colonies, inclining them toward both an active, centralized government and a provincial sense of social deference; and a libertarian emphasis in the South that shunned communalism and had little feeling of a shared public purpose.[26] Again, the joint Revolutionary struggle temporarily made possible an alignment of these various perspectives behind a common Revolutionary ideology, but legacies of deep cleavage remained for the public life of the new nation to deal with. Finally, the search for a republican political economy, especially by Jefferson and his closest colleagues, produced a tension between an economic "liberalism" resting on the thought of Adam Smith and a continuing concern for the Classical republican ideals of political and social harmony.[27] In eighteenth-century America, in sum, among the people at large as well as among educated classes aware of the moral debates and literary currents of Western society, a sense of cultural divergence, of transition, and of opportunity for creative combination was widespread.

It seems clear that the same social values that caused many colonial farmers to be less than enthusiastic entrepreneurs and individualists, that made artisans insist on a moral evaluation of work in order to maintain a sense of "social wholeness," that led evangelicals throughout the colonies to yearn for a union of spirit and piety rather than a mere union of convenience, and that drove "the lower orders" to place social justice above profit seeking also caused ambivalence on basic political questions. Americans understood that in many ways the dominant forces behind the Revolution reflected the commercial England of Defoe and Walpole, of "acquisitive capitalism, individual liberty, provincial autonomy and . . . oligarchy,"[28] and that thus more was at stake than independence from Great Britain. Although in some degree the common people in the colonies shared the new values with the oligarchic leadership and in many ways accepted the "liberal philosophy" of the Revolutionary era, the conversion was incomplete. As their familial, community, and religious behavior reveals, colonial farmers (90 percent of the population, including large numbers of non-British immigrants in many of the colonies) were deeply wedded to "pre-industrial" or "preliberal" values.

Thus, when the time came, after 1789, to set a permanent government in motion, substantial segments of the population were ready to respond to Washington's nonpartisan conception of leadership, which emphasized the public interest and a unified, morally oriented government purpose rather than party loyalty and special-interest politics. Americans would not have welcomed an Elizabeth or a Frederick the Great as their ruler, nor did they repudiate the ideals of the Revolution, but there can be little doubt that the climate of opinion in British America during the era when the office of the presidency took shape was deeply divided. We cannot understand the character of that office, therefore, unless we add to the restraints on it embedded in radical Whig thought the more positive, still-powerful world view that hearkened to appeals for social wholeness, for the public good, and for patriot leadership. Few farmers and townspeople probably had ever read the *Dunciad* or *Idea of a Patriot King*, but the political philosophy implicit in those works was remarkably in accord with "preliberal" family, religious, and community values. Recognition of this substantial public opinion, which pervaded all social classes and was likely to be responsive to a traditional sort of above-party leadership, explains a great deal about the wide popularity of Washington and Monroe and even helps us see why such determined "antipoliticians" as the Adamses could have led distinguished public careers. Neither Adams had or courted what a later age called "popularity" (in fact, each would have accepted the implications of Cotton Mather's phrase, "the crime of popularity"),[29] yet they had sufficient public support to be *elected* to high office in a self-governing republic. The Adamses' success may be a particularly revealing measure of the ambivalent public philosophy of the early national period, which only with the triumph of Jacksonian politics during and after the 1820s became more thoroughly and completely "liberal." A fully party oriented style of leadership was thereafter possible.

Nevertheless, throughout the Western world millions of people, well-born and lowly, continued to believe that the most deadly poison in liberal commercial culture was its annunciation, its acclamation as the incarnation of God, of "Acquisitive Man."[30] To so put the matter clarifies the full moral and cultural force of the hostility to the commercialization of values that began at least as early as the reaction of Milton and Bunyan against the selfish materialism of many of their co-religionists. The particular expression of this theme as articulated by Pope, Swift, and Bolingbroke and listened to by the early American presidents is properly understood, then, as much more than the rage of a threatened aristocracy. What John Adams and Jefferson responded to in the piercing words of *Gulliver's Travels* and the *Dunciad* was their sharp attack on a self-centered view of humankind regarded by many people, great and humble, as betraying the spirit of man. Furthermore, when the early presidents espoused an ideal of patriotic leadership closely bound, as they saw it, to the more traditional ethic and world view, it is not surprising that hundreds of thousands of ordinary Americans turned a sympathetic ear. Such political leadership was to these people attuned to their earnest efforts to preserve family and community from the alienations of "individual freedom and material gain." They were, so they sensed deep in their bones, struggling to preserve much that they believed was precious in human life.

It is worth remembering, furthermore, that in the eighteenth century, when voting was not yet regarded as the only meaningful participation in government, it was thought possible for people to "consent" willingly to a social order by embracing its purposes and moral cohesions rather than by explicit acts of suffrage. In this context, the administrations of the first six presidents of the United States can "be thought of primarily as a transitional phase of political culture in which the passage from a traditional, notable-oriented and deferential politics on the one hand to a party, electorate-oriented and egalitarian style of politics on the other, did not come about abruptly."[31] Hence, to understand the full force of early American antiparty sentiment and the deep popular appeal a morally defined patriotic leadership could have, we must see their relationship to the central, centuries-long tension spawned by the effort of the Western world to contend with the social and moral impact of the commercial and industrial revolutions. Although Franklin, for example, was an enthusiastic "new man of the new world" in the full meaning Crèvecoeur intended in using that phrase and delighted in the openness and opportunity of Philadelphia, he also retained an ancient sense of social cohesion and public obligation that gives him standing as an Aristotelian *civic* leader as well as a rising tradesman in the manner of Defoe. In thus embodying the cultural and moral tensions of his age, but most particularly in insisting on a sense of social wholeness and on the possibility of ordinary people in commercial as well as agricultural walks of life being good citizens, Franklin illuminates the assumptions, dilemmas, and creative opportunities of those entrusted with leadership in such an open, transitional polity. Both eclecticism like Franklin's and the communitarian, deferential values still strong among ordinary people, moreover, formed important parts of the problematic, indistinct collection of political ideas from which Jefferson and the other early presidents had to fashion a republican form of national leadership.

Alexander Hamilton and the Ideas of Leadership and Party

Commerce and National Greatness

I f Benjamin Franklin was of special relevance in showing how merchants and artisans might possess the virtues of republican citizenship, the other leading founder of the new nation who did not become president, Alexander Hamilton, showed in his thought and career how the habits and values of the commercial and manufacturing classes could be made to undergird the political economy of the republic. In evolving and working to fulfill this design during crucial years of almost continuous officeholding between 1782 and 1795, Hamilton grappled particularly with style and modes of leadership because he was so intent on guiding the nation toward an ideal and because his own instincts and talents were so much in that direction. Furthermore, as he lacked the more complete enthusiasm for self-government of Jefferson and other ardent republicans, Hamilton was especially alert to the contributions traditional kinds of leadership might make to the nation's well-being, as is illustrated by his proposal at the Federal Convention that the chief executive serve during good behavior and by his self-conscious effort as secretary of the Treasury to play the part that Jean Colbert, Robert Walpole, and the elder William Pitt had in guiding the public policy of their nations. Hamilton's reluctant, though in the end earnest, acceptance of the republican institutions of the new nation also brought him face to face with the restraints imposed on active leadership by the diversity and openness of a free and self-governing society, and especially with the role political parties might play both in furthering and in obstructing such leadership. Having declared his faith, as he did in the first paragraph of *The Federalist*, that good government could be established "from reflection and choice" rather than always by "accident and force," Hamilton confronted the considerable challenge of somehow organizing politics and public life to move deliberately according to that rational ideal; that is, to fashion a mode of leadership both purposeful and republican. In this effort, he shared the intentions in some degree of the early presidents and gave them and the nation at large dramatic and influential lessons, for good or for ill, in how executive power might be exercised in a new republic.

Like both the political thinkers and the common people of the late eighteenth century, Hamilton was caught in a turmoil of contradictory, or at least irreconcilable, moral systems. He was ardently Classical in his faith that some men possessed the wisdom, honor, and patriotism to make good (nonpartisan) government possible and that the character of a nation depended on the deliberate (intended, planned) quality of its public life. He also accepted the Christian world view enough to assume that mundane affairs should measure up to a higher law. He subscribed as well, however, to the ethic of Hobbes, Locke, and Mandeville in assuming that men were motivated primarily by individual self-interest and that therefore society and government had somehow to ground the public good in this motivation. Two or three generations earlier, English moralists had generally declared this linkage an impossibility. Hamilton's supposition, in the last quarter of the eighteenth century, that he could blend these moral traditions coincides with the general evolution in Western thought on the meaning of civic virtue. Hamilton revealed his dual devotion, and ambivalence, in statements he made at the New York Ratifying Convention. "Men will pursue their interests. It is as easy to change human nature," he declared, "as to oppose the strong current of the selfish passions." Yet he also remarked in the next sentence that "a wise legislator will gently divert the channel, and direct it, if possible, to the public good."[1]

Like many of his contemporaries active in politics, Hamilton was more intent on retaining what were to him the valid elements in various outlooks than on agonizing over tensions and inconsistencies. In his public career he drew, in not always compatible ways, first from one tradition and then from another. In 1775, as an ardent revolutionist, he accepted Lord Coke's axiom, that there was a higher law "written with the finger of God in the heart of man" containing "the first principles of civil society." Violation of these principles obliged men to "betake themselves to the law of nature" by disregarding unjust municipal law and disavowing allegiance to an unjust Parliament and even king. But the morally defined state of nature, in Hamilton's mind, did not rest on a primeval gathering of farmers and shepherds or on a "Spartan community of goods and wives," with "iron coin," simple dress, and austere manners. It was ridiculous, Hamilton insisted in 1782, in the age of Isaac Newton, and Joseph Priestley, and James Watt, "to seek for models in the simple ages of Greece and Rome."[2] Hamilton urged that the constitution of the new nation find its model of what is natural in the modern world, with its sophisticated, commercial economy, and thus link trade, growth, and opportunity with virtue and patriotism.

Although Hamilton continued to voice the conventional pieties about the yeoman farmer, he revealed his own predispositions when he asked the New York Ratifying Convention in 1788 to "look through the rich and poor of the community; the learned and the ignorant [to see] where does virtue predominate?" He concluded that all classes had their own peculiar vices but that those of the rich "are probably more favorable to the prosperity of the state, than those of the indigent; and partake less of moral depravity."[3] If this moral judgment could be sustained, and in Aristotelian fashion be encouraged by the institutions of government, then Hamilton saw for the new United States a truly revolutionary future: one where a great and powerful nation, with a free and republican government, might grasp all the benefits of trade and industry while retaining the moral emphasis of Plutarch and Erasmus and achieving the patriotic pride and cultural brilliance of the Athens of Pericles or the England of Elizabeth. Hamilton's thought, career, and statecraft make sense only within such an expansive, revolutionary conception of the possibilities of new nationhood.

In 1790 Hamilton had a propitious opportunity to implant this conception in public policy when President Washington and the Congress asked him to devise plans to support the public credit. The great reports Hamilton thus submitted were proposals in political economy, that is, recommendations for government-guided economic development that would sustain the social and moral principles of the nation. He urged that the public debt, foreign and domestic, be funded at full value both to encourage capital development *and* to make integrity and good faith national hallmarks. Similarly, the state debts would be assumed not only to impose order and equity on the chaotic residue of Revolutionary finance but also to heighten national as opposed to state loyalties. Hamilton's proposal for a national bank also combined strictly economic needs with social purposes. It was a means for rationalizing government fiscal operations and for further "cementing" the interests of wealthy merchants and bankers to the national government—a neat embodiment of Mandevillian "private vice, public benefit." Finally, the *Report on Manufactures* proposed an orderly stimulation of agriculture, trade, and industry that would give the United States a vigorous, diversified economy able to bring prosperity to all, encourage a laudable enterprise in its citizens, and soon make the nation impregnable in a warring world.

In these plans Hamilton quite candidly wedded Franklin's enlarged conception of virtue-sustaining occupations to a powerful and prosperous nationhood. He argued, for example, that a farmer, "from the peculiar fertility of his land, or some other favorable circumstance, may frequently obtain a livelihood, even with a considerable degree of carelessness in the mode of cultivation," whereas an artisan or manufacturer had to engage in "constant and regular" labor in order to match his competitors. There were probably "more examples of remissness . . . among cultivators of land . . . than among artificers," Hamilton concluded. The morally bracing discipline of manufacturing activities, combined with the diversified opportunities of a modern economy, was the sure path to a powerful and prosperous nationhood. "To cherish and stimulate the activity of the human mind by multiplying the objects of enterprise, is not among the least considerable of the expedients by which the wealth of a nation may be promoted." Echoing Daniel Defoe, Hamilton concluded that the "spirit of enterprise . . . must be less in a nation of mere cultivators, than in a nation of cultivators and merchants; less in a nation of cultivators and merchants, than in a nation of cultivators, artificers, and merchants."[4]

Hamilton and Franklin went beyond Defoe's simple defense of the commercial spirit, however, in making hard work, enterprise, technological progress, and the wealth they produced more explicitly the foundation of virtuous nationhood. For this program they derived particular support, probably, from the widely influential *Political Essays* of David Hume. Franklin and Hume were personal friends, and Hamilton concluded *The Federalist* with a long quote from Hume's *Essays*. Hume had argued that science and the arts could flourish only amid a people who "enjoy the blessing of a free government"—hence England's eighteenth-century preeminence in those fields, as Voltaire, Montesquieu, and others agreed. "Industry, knowledge, and humanity [meaning benevolent policy] . . . were linked together by an dissoluable chain," Hume maintained. This linkage, moreover, also worked in the reverse direction, causing liberty to grow in the presence of improvement in the arts and science. "Rude, unpolished nations," Hume asserted, invariably were composed of "vassals or tenants . . . fitted for slavery and subjection" and "petty tyrants" who either imposed a stagnant oppression or wasted resources in endless, bloody quarrels. "But where luxury nourishes commerce and industry," Hume argued, "the peasants, by a proper cultivation of the land, become rich and independent," and the tradesmen and merchants acquire both property and a "share of authority" that become a firm basis for both public liberty and national greatness. So vital was this connection between hard work, disciplined habits, wealth, and the progress of science and the arts that Hume regarded England, where "the land is rich but coarse, [and] must be cultivated at a great expense," as more blessed than nations in a "more southern region [where] agriculture is an easy art; and one man with a couple of sorry horses" could without diligence or forethought earn a tolerable living.[5] From such precepts and generalizations Hamilton readily concluded, as did Franklin, that the United States might take advantage of its bracing climate, its industrious farmers and tradesmen, and its free institutions to embark on a modern, commercial, and virtuous national destiny.

The Americans were also accepting, as Hume had, a profound reversal in the connection between luxury and virtue. At least since the legendary Spartan constitution of Lycurgus, Western moralists and political philosophers had generally supposed the relationship inverse: the more luxury the less virtue. Plutarch records Lycurgus as stating that "luxury . . . turns men into greedy brutes." But as luxury became more widespread as a result of advances in trade and science and took on positive value in the new commercial ethic, it assumed a more respectable place in public philosophy. In fact, Hamilton came at the end of a considerable evolution in Anglo-American thinking about morality, commerce, and national purpose. He accepted much of Bernard Mandeville's emphasis on self-interest as the basis of human motivation and also Mandeville's belief that these passions could be controlled in the public interest. He agreed with Mandeville that "*private vices by the dextrous management of a skillful politician may be turned into public benefits*" (Mandeville's emphasis).[6] Then, when Hume and other British thinkers began to find in commerce and wealth not only the basis of national greatness but also moral value, Hamilton understood how to put it all together: an enterprising, prosperous nation could be celebrated on moral and cultural as well as geopolitical grounds, and a skillful political leader could take pride in managing the whole effort.

Hamilton argued particularly that the entrepreneur would enhance the political and moral well-being of the nation by bringing to its councils the vigor, the optimism, the diligence, and the cosmopolitanism that characterized high-level business. Bankers, too, given an important influence on (but not control over) the nation's economy in the charter of the Bank of the United States, would impose a unique steadiness and integrity on public policy. It would be "little less than a miracle," Hamilton observed, if government officials (perhaps especially ones responsive to popular influence) put entirely in charge of the public credit did not, for political purposes, make "a calamitous abuse of it." It was safer, more morally sound, therefore, to give private financiers an influence on Bank policy by selling them a large share of its stock: "The keen, steady, and, as it were, magnetic sense of their own interest as proprietors [as directors of the Bank], pointing invariably to its true pole—the prosperity of the institution—is the only security that can always be relied upon for a careful and prudent administration."[7] Here, as always, Hamilton's main concern was not the promotion of any particular branch of trade or industry (in fact, his plans often were opposed by many American manufacturing interests), but rather the fiscal health of the government and the encouragement of stable credit and securities markets, which he believed were essential to both the prosperity and the integrity of the nation.[8]

Other Federalist spokesmen, especially from New England, supported the Franklin-Hamilton argument that virtue could be nourished by commercial and industrial occupations and that the government could legitimately encourage those aspects of the economy. On the first Fourth of July under the new Constitution Samuel Whitwell told a Massachusetts audience, "Industry and frugality must be adopted as the means of our political salvation. Extravagance of all kind abolished—the distaff and the spindle must be assiduously employed. The barren wilds of America cultivated and made fertile and economy in every branch rigidly attended to." Another orator on the same day in the same state saw that "a new, extensive and animating scene opens to the view of the great body of American merchants; who, as to a spirit of enterprize are exceeded by no men on earth. . . . By the revival and extension of commerce, shipbuilding will be encouraged, . . . the various classes of mechanics find employment, . . . [and] the ingenious and industrious tradesmen . . . support themselves and families." Two years later the Boston Fourth of July orator found "our country raised from contempt, . . . our national faith . . . redeemed . . . [and] the value of every species of property . . . appreciated. *Commerce* also begins to rear her drooping head; . . . *Manufactures* thrive, our publick *Seminaries of Learning* flourish; and the voice of gladness is heard throughout the land"—all, the orator proclaimed, because Hamilton had set in motion a strong, energetic government.[9] The virtuous republic in the United States, if these spokesmen were right, could indeed find the moral qualities of the yeoman farmer in the merchant and artisan, and then enjoy the material benefits of the expanded economy, all under the firm leadership of a proconsular secretary of the Treasury, or of a president who must have a nonparty vision at least as broad and positive if he were to fulfill the potential of his office and earn the admiration of the nation at large.

Classical Ideas of Leadership

If Hamilton had not gone beyond linking self-interest and the public good, however, he would have been simply a spokesman for the new ethic of Defoe and Mandeville, which had its fulfillment in the economics of Adam Smith. But Hamilton's thought and his career as a public official are at odds with that doctrine because, in part at least, he also accepted the theories of Malachy Postlethwayt and other British mercantilists, and he admired as they did the career of the preeminent state economic planner of the modern world, Louis XIV's finance minister, "the great COL-BERT."[10] More profoundly, Hamilton retained as the foundation of his political thinking Classical, and therefore moral and positive, assumptions about government. He believed that "the aggregate well-being of society," to use an oft-repeated eighteenth-century phrase, was more than the sum of the well-being of the parts. To him, as to Aristotle, man's "political nature" meant that the body politic must make a conscious effort to create "not . . . life only, but . . . the good life, . . . a perfect and self-sufficing life" in a state capable of "noble actions."[11] Hamilton's sense of political obligation was not far removed in spirit from the oath of the Athenian citizen: "We will ever strive for the ideals and sacred things of the city, both alone and with many; we will unceasingly seek to quicken the sense of public duty; and we will revere and obey the city's laws; we will transmit this city, not only not less but greater, better and more beautiful than it was transmitted to us."

It was this view that allowed Hamilton to state simply to George Washington in defense of the national bank that the Constitution "ought to be construed liberally, in advancement of the public good." In 1801, looking back on twelve years of Federalist rule largely dominated by his political philosophy, Hamilton insisted that although the "industry" of the people and "the blessings of Providence" were doubtless important to the nation's prosperity, a cursory comparison with the disarray of 1788 revealed an additional source of the nation's well-being. The peace, stability, good credit, and "enterprise" of the nation depended equally on "the vivifying influences of an efficient and well-conducted government."[12] Hamilton would, after his experience of the 1790s, have found his prediction in *The Federalist*, Number 26 (1787), confirmed: "I am much mistaken if experience has not wrought a deep and solemn conviction in the public mind, that greater energy of government is essential to the welfare and prosperity of the community." "Energy of government" and "vivifying influence" were nearly synonymous. Both implied positive action to create what Aristotle meant by the "good life."

Hamilton's problem, and creative opportunity, arose from his being rooted in this Classical conception while living in a world experiencing a commercial-industrial revolution that seemed to imply a radically new morality—a dilemma in one form or another thrust on all his colleagues in nation-building. Was it possible, in a world of individual competitive striving, of diversifying special interests, of international trade, and of industrial revolution, to retain a Classical sense of obligation, community, moral purpose, and national leadership? Jonathan Swift, Alexander Pope, and the other Augustan critics had generally answered no and had thus resisted the whole thrust and ethic of the world of Walpole and Defoe. Hamilton, both nearly a century later and aware of the arguments of Hume and others, could not fall back on a simple answer but sought instead to stand in both worlds. He attempted nothing less than to guide and organize a modern economy and its attendant ethic into a state that retained a classical purpose and unity. This tackling of a fundamental question facing the new nation in a revolutionary world, as Jefferson also did, is what gives each stature, in his own day and ever since, as a nation-builder of epic proportions.

Hamilton's Aristotelianism was so strong that all his life he held grave reservations about whether any form of self-government could resist degenerating into the turbulence and demagoguery the Greek philosopher taught attended any "mere democracy." But Hamilton nonetheless sincerely accepted the ideals of the American Revolution and sought to breathe enough vigor, efficiency, and purpose into the new Constitution for it to avoid becoming "the frail and worthless fabric" he feared in his more gloomy moods it was. He tried to work within republican forms, and to accept the new commercial ethic, and still mold a nationhood bearing some resemblance to the Athens of Pericles, or the Rome of Augustus, or, in a way, the Britain ruled and envisioned by the elder Pitt in 1760.

Hamilton's essential moral addition to the Classical model was his supposition, as Franklin and Hume had taught, that an artisan, a tradesman, a merchant, or a financier could be made virtuous by the rhythms of his calling, just as Jefferson had argued that yeoman farming was inherently conducive to virtue. Furthermore, Hamilton forthrightly moved beyond the radical Whig bias of the American Revolution to insist on the necessity for positive and energetic leadership in government. As he told his Whiggish critics in New York in 1787–1788, "Powers must be granted, or civil Society cannot exist; the possibility of abuse is no argument against the *thing*. . . . When you have divided and nicely balanced the departments of government; . . . when, in short, you have rendered your system as perfect as human forms can be; you must place confidence; you must give power."[13] By welcoming and sanctifying the occupations and interests of the new age, and by supposing that these energies could be guided and mobilized for good public purposes without subverting constitutional government, Hamilton opened up beckoning (his foes said dangerous) vistas for the new nation.

Given this emphasis on positive government and on building "the good society," it is not surprising to find Hamilton preoccupied with the role of the executive. Wide powers for that department not only suited his personal style but also were vital to the fulfillment of his vision of the national future. As a young man, when he read Plutarch's *Lives*, that vast compendium of history, morality, and political wisdom widely known among his colleagues, Hamilton took note that in the origins of the great states of antiquity there appeared first powerful founders, *conditiores imperiorum* in a phrase that Sir Francis Bacon used in his *Essays* (also read by the American nation-builders), and then the great lawgivers, or *perpetui principes* in Bacon's version. Thus, in Plutarch the pair of founders Theseus and Romulus came first and had distinctive qualities of force and vigor and even imperiousness, and next came the pair of lawgivers Lycurgus and Numa

Pompilius, whose distinctive qualities were wisdom and the capacity to adhere to enduring principles. Hamilton's copied extracts, taken especially from Plutarch's comparisons of the two pairs of leaders, accented the responsibility of the leader for avoiding the extremes of tyranny, on the one hand, and being "a slave to the people," on the other. "A Prince's first concern," Hamilton copied from Plutarch, "ought to be the preservation of the government itself." The way to do that, though, was not for a prince merely to be severe and thus become "odious or contemptible to his subjects," which would in fact diminish his power. Rather, wrote Hamilton, interpolating his own view, "it would often be praise worthy in a prince to relinquish a part of an excessive prerogative to establish a more moderate government, better adapted to the happiness or temper of his people!"

Hamilton also copied long extracts from Plutarch's commentary on Lycurgus, noting especially the intimate connection of equality and frugality to virtue, and then of virtue to the survival and good management of the state. Hamilton admired Plutarch's conclusion: "The Government established by [Lycurgus] remained in vigor about five hundred years 'till a thirst of empire tempted the Spartans to entertain foreign troops and introduce Persian gold to maintain them; then the institutions of Lycurgus fell at once and avarice and luxury were introduced." Although these extracts and commentary by a twenty-two-year-old army officer fighting foreign mercenaries do not reflect the revised relationship between virtue and luxury Hamilton expressed when he was a "chief minister" of government, he never relinquished his Plutarchian insistence on the importance of strong founders, wise lawgivers, and virtuous people. In a comment he copied into his notebook just before the extracts from Plutarch, furthermore, Hamilton had borrowed from Demosthenes a revealing metaphor of leadership: "As a general marches at the head of his troops, so ought wise politicians, if I dare to use the expression, to march at the head of affairs; insomuch that they ought not to wait the *event*, to know what measures to take; but the measures which they have taken, ought to produce the *event*."[14] Perhaps the young army officer, already preparing himself for civilian leadership, and reading not only Demosthenes' speeches but also Plutarch's vivid account of the orator's life, fancied himself playing Demosthenes' role, although in 1777 the tyrant was not Philip of Macedon but George of England.

The next year Hamilton applied his study of Plutarch to members of Congress, the nation-builders of 1778, who had "the most illustrious and important" work to do. Each member was "to be regarded not only as a legislator, but as the founder of an empire." He had not only to consider basic principles and deliberate on the public good but also to found an empire, that is, to act as a sovereign or leader in bringing into being a great nation that like Greece and Rome would last for centuries, full of power and glory and able to set standards of civilized accomplishment for all time. Such standards, Hamilton noted in a withering attack on a profiteering member of Congress, required that a virtuous legislator–nation-builder look down from that "commanding eminence . . . with contempt upon every mean or interested pursuit."[15] Hamilton thus had a high sense of the grand task of nation-building and, like many of his colleagues, was fully conscious of the good fortune that he might himself be such a builder. Significantly, he adopted as his models men acting on an epic scale who not merely promulgated laws but were required antecedently to act energetically to bring a state into being.

Given Hamilton's interest in executive initiative, it is not surprising to find him in 1780 complaining that Congress, "properly a deliberative corps," "kept [executive] power too much into their own hands," resulting in a serious defect: a "want of method and energy in the administration." Some of his most eloquent contributions to *The Federalist Papers* advocate both the general need for "energy" in the national government and the full grant of executive power to the president in Article II. He defended every aspect of the president's power and dignity: his reeligibility, his unitary responsibility, his veto and treaty-making powers, his independence of the legislature, and so on. "A feeble executive," he argued, "implies a feeble execution of government. A feeble execution is but another phrase for a bad execution; and a government ill executed . . . must be, in practice, a bad government."[16]

Hamilton insisted on a strong executive not only on these general principles but also because, harking back to the admired monarchs of all time, he envisioned the executive as a force representing the nation as a whole and much more capable than a legislative body of resisting the influence of faction and special interests. Indeed, in a legislature, Hamilton conceded in *The Federalist*, Number 70, "promptitude of decision is oftener an evil than a benefit. The differences of opinion and the jarrings of parties in that department of the government . . . often promote deliberation and circumspection; and serve to check excesses in the majority." No such "favorable circumstances . . . palliate or atone for the disadvantages of dissention in the executive department," where, Hamilton insisted repeatedly, "vigour, expedition, . . . energy, . . . and responsibility" were of the essence. At the Federal Convention of 1787, listening to Madison's key speech outlining the argument soon made famous in *The Federalist*, Number 10, that a large republic would control the harmful effects of faction, Hamilton noted that the counteracting force would be less than Madison supposed. A steadier resistance to faction would come from the establishment of a strong national government, Hamilton suggested, where "[great] objects" would command the attention of men who were more able than those ordinarily serving in state legislatures. The state legislatures were usually the

"worse composed," Hamilton thought, because "proper men" were not inclined to participate in their petty quarreling.

Five days later he noted that "vigour [in government] is the result of
several principles—Activity[,] wisdom—confidence" and that therefore "a
free government [was] to be preferred to an absolute monarchy . . . because of the tendency of the Free Government to interest the passions of
the community in its favour [and] beget public spirit and public confidence."[17] Perhaps influenced by James Wilson and other delegates who believed that public participation would strengthen government, Hamilton
was quite as willing to draw vigor in government from the "popular principle" as from the more conventional monarchical basis. "The success of
every government," he wrote in October 1792, "its capacity to combine
the exertion of public strength with the preservation of personal right and
private security, qualities which define the perfection of a government,
must always naturally depend on the energy of the executive department."
This "exertion of public strength" by the executive included, in Hamilton's
opinion as it would have in John Winthrop's, the duty of vetoing bills the
object of which is "either *unconstitutional* or *pernicious.*" Should the executive fail to so act, Hamilton insisted, his approbation of the legislation
would be implied and would make "him responsible to the community for
this opinion." "The measure becomes his by adoption," Hamilton concluded, and he would not be able to "escape a portion of the blame"
should it prove to be a "bad measure." Eighteen months later, when it
seemed possible the House and Senate would foolishly and precipitately
pass resolutions sure to lead the nation into a war with Great Britain,
Hamilton urged President Washington to use his veto power to thwart the
factious resolves. He had "an indispensable obligation," Hamilton wrote, to
use the weight of his office even against measures "adopted by both Houses
of Congress" when they were "contrary to the public interest."[18] There can
be no doubt that Hamilton worked toward a government at once genuinely
republican, explicitly national, and vigorously administered.

Executive Transcendence of Faction

Hamilton's opponents in the party rivalry of the 1790s, however, often
charged that his preoccupation with executive power was a cover for "Walpolean" manipulations of the government, and thus that he was himself
the supreme factionalist. In fact, he as much condemned party and faction
as any of the first six presidents and did not consider party any less pernicious than faction. Although some eighteenth-century writers had gone

beyond the common assumption that party and faction were inseparable from free government to argue that they could be *useful* to such a government, the pejorative view remained dominant, and Hamilton accepted it.[19] Like Madison, Hamilton considered the frequent squabbles and (in their view) the unwise and selfish actions of the state legislatures during the Revolution abundant proof of the factious tendency of free governments. The discords and ineffectiveness of the Confederation Congress were further evidence of this problem even beyond the level of state government. But rather than arguing, as Madison did, that in some clever, mechanical way factions could be made to control one another, Hamilton emphasized the need to *transcend* them.

In laying his own plan of government before the Convention of 1787, Hamilton had remarked as he began to discuss the executive department that "it seemed to be admitted that no good [executive] could be established on Republican principles." It would be necessary, therefore, he told the Convention, "to go as far in order to attain stability and permanency, as republican principles will admit." It was in this context that he made his controversial proposal that a senator hold office "at least during good-behaviour," and an executive "for life." Such "permanency" was needed, Hamilton argued, not only to ensure order and disinterested guidance in domestic affairs but especially to resist the sort of "foreign influence and corruption" that had perverted government in Sweden and had disgraced even the American Revolution when "the French and English had each their parties."[20] The executive, in all of Hamilton's admired models, had to rise above faction and party (including the possibility of foreign intrigue) so that virtue and the public good might characterize national policy.

In *The Federalist*, Number 9, Hamilton again, following Montesquieu, took the danger of faction seriously, especially in a small republic, and argued that in a large country it could be controlled directly, that is, suppressed in the interest of seeking the greater objects of the nation as a whole. In 1788 he insisted that Congress under the Articles of Confederation had been faction ridden because "state prejudices" prevailed. Under the new Constitution, he proclaimed boldly, "we are attempting . . . to abolish factions, and to unite all parties for the general welfare."[21]

Hamilton also followed conventional eighteenth-century political thinking in finding legislative bodies peculiarly prone to factious proceedings. He conceded that local and selfish inclinations in a legislature that is part of a "mixed government" may have positive value, for parochial and diverse views would be able to find legitimate representation. If the monarchical or aristocratic parts of the government became overbearing, the "democratic branch," as in the British House of Commons, would provide a salutary restraint. But in a republic, the problem was opposite: the legislature and the factions in it would be so dominant that the "aggregate and general interest" could be easily ignored, a conviction that the other "Publius," Madison, shared. Thus, although Hamilton always accepted, however regretfully, the inevitability of factions and party in a free society, he was unwilling to let them "decide policy" and hoped soberly that a proper energy and leadership might overcome them. Indeed, he argued at the New York Ratifying Convention that the bicameral character of the Federal Constitution would have the effect of supporting the two basic "objects in forming systems of government—Safety for the people, and energy in the administration." The House of Representatives, "the immediate agents of the people," would furnish protection and safety for their rights, and the Senate would incline toward the opposite principle, energy and permanence in policy. With both "objects" thus sustained, Hamilton concluded, "the certain tendency of the system will be to the public welfare."[22]

Yet the most important source of energy and leadership in government was not the Senate but the strong executive department Hamilton labored to construct from 1789 to 1794. Every part of Hamilton's thought, experience, and predilection pointed in that direction. To have good government in the United States required a strong executive capable both of overcoming factions (or, what was the same to him, rising above party) and of leading the nation toward greatness on a Classical scale. In a general way, at least, Washington shared this conception (because he derived his political axioms, though perhaps secondhand, from the same sources), and so did the other members of the talented cabinet gathered by the first president in 1789–1790, including Jefferson. Vice-President John Adams, too, as we have seen, despite his later quarrel with Hamilton, agreed with the conception of an administration above party.

Nevertheless, the public life of the new nation quickly fell into the bitter partisanship generally typical of politics in a free society. For all their rhetoric about being nonpartisan, the leaders, Washington, Hamilton, and the Adamses on one side and Jefferson, Madison, and Monroe on the other, engaged in intensely partisan acts, accused each other of near-treasonable betrayal of the public interest, and encouraged party "newspaper wars" as savage as any in American history. So important and consuming was this party strife that historians and political scientists have generally regarded the Federalists and Jeffersonian Republicans as composing "the first American party system," implying, at least, that they were an early version of the two parties characteristic of American politics. Much of this analysis is appropriate when attention is focused on behavior: the enlistment of support for favorite policies, the building of party machinery, polemical campaigns in pamphlets and newspapers, maneuvering in Congress, management of elections, and even intrigue with foreign powers. Full-scale, open party strife was indeed going on, and each side accused the other of being exactly the sort of "party" that had been condemned from the time of

Thucydides: a self-interested faction hostile to the general welfare; that is, a corrupt manifestation deserving of the contempt heaped on Walpole and his minions by Pope, Swift, and Bolingbroke.

Yet, the very bitterness, the sense of the other side being not His Majesty's Loyal Opposition but a parochial, selfish group of near traitors, reveals the *uncharacteristic* nature of the early party battles. It was precisely because the idea of party was so abhorrent to politicians in the 1790s that the emergence of party was greeted with epithets, the participants masked their partisan activity, the demise of party received such acclaim, and the early presidents so valued both the image and reality of nonpartisanship. Although there was a certain deviousness and even hypocrisy in such acts as Hamilton's writing under the cover of vituperatively partisan pseudonyms and Jefferson's virtual hiring of a "poison pen" journalist to espouse his cause, in fact the protestations against party and the efforts first to avoid and then to discard partisan activity consistently attest to a sincerely held nonpartisan ideal.[23]

Washington's response to the increasingly severe quarrel between Hamilton and Jefferson, and their replies to him, reveal poignantly the tension between the nonpartisan aspirations of all three men and the irreconcilable differences separating the two secretaries. As Hamilton wrote more openly against Jefferson in the newspapers (although still in the formal guise of a pseudonym), and as Jefferson more explicitly encouraged partisan response, the president's pain at the spectacle became unbearable. "Differences in political opinions . . . to a certain point," he wrote to each secretary, were unavoidable and perhaps even necessary, but he regretted charges impeaching the motives of officers of government and saw particular danger when "men of abilities, zealous patriots, having the same *general* objects in view . . . will not exercise more charity in deciding on the opinions and actions of one another." "Instead of wounding suspicions, and irritable charges," he begged that "there may be liberal allowances, mutual forbearances, and temporising yieldings on *all sides*." "How unfortunate," Washington wrote, "would it be if a fabric so goodly, erected under so many Providential circumstances . . . should from diversity of sentiments or internal obstructions . . . have brought us to the verge of dissolution." Although this is in part a conventional plea for compromise and conciliation, Washington's interpolated remark that he could not prevail on himself to believe that Hamilton and Jefferson were yet engaged in "the deliberate acts of a determined party" makes it clear that he did not accept as normal or helpful that permanent, fundamental divisions would exist among able and patriotic public servants. Without a willingness to subordinate differences to the general good, Washington warned, "every thing must rub; the Wheels of Government will clog; our enemies will triumph." "Melancholy thought!" the president exclaimed, fearing that under such circumstances "the Reins of government [could not] be managed, or . . . the Union of the States . . . much longer preserved."

In reply both secretaries expressed respect for the president's desire for national unity and agreed with his judgment that partisan quarrels were harmful to the body politic, but each also justified his own conduct and stated uncompromisable principles from which he would not retreat. Hamilton insisted that he could not sit by idly when "a formed party deliberately bent upon . . . [rendering] the funding system . . . odious to the body of the people" used every exertion to propagate its cause. He admitted therefore that he had yielded to the "strong impulse . . . to draw aside the veil from the principal Actors" in this party who were subverting the measures of government. History, he was sure, "will prove that I have judged rightly." Jefferson, for his part, proclaimed that his disagreement with Hamilton's program "was not merely a speculative difference," because "the system of the Secretary of the treasury . . . flowed from principles adverse to liberty, and was calculated to undermine and demolish the republic, by creating an influence of his department over the members of the legislature." "Those who wished for virtuous government," Jefferson declared, could not sit idly by in the presence of measures that "taken together . . . draw all the powers of government into the hands of the [federal Congress], . . . establish means for corrupting a sufficient corps in that legislature to divide the honest votes and preponderate, by their own, . . . and to have that corps under the command of the Secretary of the Treasury for the purpose of subverting step by step the principles of the constitution." (Jefferson's words sounded like Bolingbroke's assaults on Walpole in the *Craftsman*.) The three men, in using the phrases "determined" or "formed" party and "system" to characterize what they abhorred in government, revealed their noncomprehension of the idea of a well-organized, disciplined political party as an instrument of policy to which Martin Van Buren and Sir Robert Peel gave a central and positive role in democratic government.

In a later letter to Jefferson, Washington made clear his dismay and frustration at these unwelcome replies and his deep attachment to a nonpartisan, patriotic view of national leadership. Accommodation of principles, he explained, "would produce harmony and consequent good in our councils; and the contrary will inevitably produce confusion and serious mischiefs—and for what? because mankind cannot think alike, but would adopt different means to attain the same end." Washington acknowledged that "some of the best citizens of the United States—men of discernment—uniform and tried patriots—who have no sinister views to promote" disagreed on some of the particular measures of government, but he also believed that these men, as well as the two contending secretaries, shared much more than they disputed. He hoped, therefore, that "the cup which has been presented to us may not be snatched from our lips by a discordance of action, when I am persuaded there is no discordance in your views."[24] It was simply impossible for this patriot leader, that is, to conceive that sustained disagreement on public measures, however principled, to say nothing of contending parties, could somehow nourish the vitality of the body politic. Washington, furthermore, less attuned than his secretaries to the rising notion of nations committed to ideological purposes, held to a more traditional conception of harmony in the process of government as itself intrinsic to national well-being.

Anglo-American Conceptions of Party, 1770–1801

In rationalizing their increasing partisanship in 1792 and 1793, Hamilton and Jefferson were moving toward Edmund Burke's by-then-well-known redefinition of party: "a body of men united, for promoting by their joint endeavors the national interest, upon some particular principle in which they are all agreed." Each supposed, however, as Burke had taught and Bolingbroke before him had envisioned, that such a *party of principle* (this phrase for the first time was beginning to appear as something other than a contradiction in terms) would gather only in order to resist the usual factional party and that once the faction had been routed and the public interest revived, the party of principle would become a national administration.

Indeed, Burke's tract formulating the more positive conception of party arose out of the "Discontents" of 1770 when mobs roamed the streets of London and the ministry pursued policies toward the colonies that in Burke's opinion lurched at different times from futile, weak, and timid to rash and contradictory. He blamed the travail on an alliance, as had happened before in Walpole's day, between a faction and the power of the crown, newly sealed in the ascendancy of Lord North in January 1770. Under such circumstances, Burke wrote, where "the court party resolve the whole into faction, . . . a sullen gloom and furious disorder prevails by fits; the nation loses its relish for peace and prosperity." As anarchy grows, those in power lurch from incitement of the mob for their own purposes to stern repression. To quell resistance, the ruling faction propagates the doctrine that "all political connections are in their nature factious, and as such ought to be dissipated and destroyed."[25]

What Burke and the Rockingham Whigs saw happening during the 1760s, very much to their political frustration, was the cynical abuse of the idea of an inclusive, patriot party by George III, Lord Bute, and their friends. Their claim to encompass all virtue and public good in their administration may have had some substance in the climate of Britain's great victories and George III's coronation in 1760–1761. In 1770, however, after a decade of cynical, office-seeking politics, the "Court" party, in Burke's view, had become indelibly tainted. It was as factional and corrupt as any "connections" put together by Walpole, the duke of Newcastle, or any other political manipulator or court intriguer. "The Bedfords, the Grenvilles, and other knots," Burke wrote Lord Rockingham, "are combined for no public purpose, but only as a means of furthering with joint strength their private and individual advantage." Party meant organization to seek office for personal gain. The Court party's claim to be the only party of patriotism was so patently absurd as to give scores of London cartoonists and polemicists a field day and compelled Burke and others to reassess the idea of party and its relation to the public good.[26]

Amid such a scene, Burke asked, must a good man do nothing, or at best stand alone merely "voting according to his conscience and . . . haranguing against every [evil] design?" Such an "innocuous and ineffectual character," Burke responded, "falls miserably short of the mark of public duty. That duty demands and requires that what is right should not only be made known, but made prevalent; that what is evil should not only be detected, but defeated." "Public life," Burke said, "is a situation of power and energy; he trespasses against his duty who sleeps upon his watch, as well as he that goes over to the enemy." It was therefore the business of the virtuous politician "to find out the proper means towards the [proper ends of government,] . . . to pursue every just method to put the men who hold [these] opinions into such a condition as may enable them to carry their common plans into execution, with all the power and authority of the state." The need was to form a party of righteousness to defeat the power of evil and faction and return to the sovereign "the weight of the country [and] the force of the executory power," which can come only from adhering to principles of the aggregate and public welfare.[27]

Although some spokesmen on both sides of the Atlantic went beyond Burke's conception of a party of principle gathered to resist evil, moving toward the argument that parties by fomenting disagreement and criticism could be permanent and healthy contributors to an endless political dynamic of alternating governments,[28] in general until well into the nineteenth century a political party was not thought of as either permanent or an *organization*. Hamilton himself certainly conceived of his policies as embodying the national interest, and therefore he thought of his foes as factionalists, as Bolingbroke had done in the 1730s and Burke in the 1770s. And the intent of the Jeffersonians after 1801 to absorb into their party all virtue in the nation and thus end "legitimate" partisanship (for only factions would remain outside) also testified to a persisting idealization of the realm without party. Indeed, every political philosopher from

Plato to Montesquieu and Rousseau, every moralist from Plutarch to Bacon, and every historian from Polybius to Clarendon and Voltaire had so taught. Conversely, no conception would have been more alien, more abhorrent, than that of a party perpetual in its organization, managed by clever brokers, intent unashamedly on gaining power by satisfying "interest groups," about which it was supposed that its sharpening of ideological divisions improved the nation's political health.

Burke again made the distinction most forcefully: Parliament, he told his Bristol constituents in 1774 while defending American rights, "is not a *Congress* of ambassadors from different and hostile interests, which interests each [member] must maintain, as an agent and advocate, against other agents and advocates; but Parliament is a deliberative assembly of *one* nation, with *one* interest, that of the whole—where not local purposes, not local prejudices, ought to guide, but the general good, resulting from the general reason of the whole."[29] Thus even this early defender of party held firmly in a certain sense to the traditional insistence on a common, national good, and would have been understood by the early presidents as supporting their intention to lead nonpartisanly toward that ideal. Again, it was not that politics in free nations had not always been faction generating, or even that defenses of party had not been articulated. Since the polemics surrounding the English Civil War, politicians, especially those out of power, had defended their right to be partisan, and throughout the eighteenth century some pamphleteers and parliamentary orators had increasingly seen benefit and public virtue in party loyalty and party organization.[30] But the weight of sentiment was still overwhelmingly in favor of the nonpartisan, patriot ideal over the party leader model of the nineteenth century.

Hamilton's program, together with his zealous promotion of it as the "first secretary," then, rather than marking the beginning of a "modern" party system actually more resembled that of Walpole's England—just as the polemics hearkened to that era because the rhetoric of the age of Defoe and Swift still so resonated in the ears of Hamilton and his opponents. Burke's new concept of "a party of principle," on the other hand, only beginning to surface, had by no means replaced the ancient connotations of the words used in political discourse. Hamilton was in many ways uncannily suited for the role of the American Walpole: he encouraged the mercantile establishment, he was the master of the Treasury bureaucracy, he was the "prime minister" for a chief of state over whom he was thought to exercise undue sway, he influenced the legislature through "deals" with its members, he unashamedly championed an expansive commercial ethic, and he practiced "the politics of management" with great skill. One of his own admirers noted in 1792 that Hamilton's "well-earned Fame and general popularity [had] . . . traversed the ocean [where he] . . . was mentioned among the great ministers of the age," an unmistakable comparison of him with Walpole.[31] Hamilton was thus of the "Court" party, vulnerable to the thunder Pope, Swift, and their friends had hurled against Walpole and his government. Predictably, John Randolph of Roanoke, John Taylor of Caroline, George Logan, Benjamin Rush, and other Jeffersonian polemicists found Bolingbroke's "Country" party rhetoric almost precisely suited to their purposes, and in their writings they deliberately evoked its overtones.[32]

In fact, the rhetoric, the issues, and even the institutional growth that had followed the English revolution of the seventeenth century had parallels one hundred years later to the post-Revolutionary period in the United States.

> Each revolution bequeathed intense, brutal party conflict to the next generation [1689–1715 in Great Britain; 1790–1815 in America], a struggle that mobilized unprecedented numbers of voters, only to yield to a period of one-party rule—the Whig oligarchy in Britain, the Era of Good Feelings in America. In both cases, nobody really believed in parties; the contenders sought to destroy or at least absorb one another, not to perpetuate some kind of party system. The division between Whig and Tory in Britain closely parallels the split between Federalists and Republicans in the United States, with Hamilton assuming the role of Junto Whigs or Walpole, and Jefferson serving as . . . the Patriot opposition to Walpole that had united Tories with Real Whigs in the 1730s. . . . In 1791 Hamilton chartered the Bank of the United States, America's direct copy of the Bank of England. In place of England's great recoinage of the 1690s, the United States government established its own coinage and persuaded the American Newton, David Rittenhouse, to take charge of the mint, as Sir Isaac had accepted a century before. Not surprisingly, the New York Stock Exchange also dates from the 1790s, doubtless contributing to a projecting spirit that far exceeded anything Defoe's generation had known. . . . The number of federal patents nearly doubled in every five-year period from 1790 through 1814 [and] . . . the number of American banks exploded from four in 1791 to 29 by 1800.[33]

In leading the United States as he did, then, Hamilton copied eagerly from an era and an ideology he admired in English history. In doing so he simply continued the "Court-mindedness" of many of the nationalist-federalist leaders of the 1780s who, inspired by Hamilton's mentor, Robert Morris, sought to strengthen American government and enhance American prosperity by a candid promotion of the nation's commercial and financial interests.[34] Although it was unstrategic in republican America openly to describe oneself as allied with any "Court" inclination, at times Hamilton and his supporters even used the "Court" party arguments of Walpole's defenders. A Philadelphia newspaper supporting Hamilton's policies noted in 1790, for example, that "a national debt attaches many citizens to the government who, by their numbers, wealth, and influence, contribute more perhaps to its preservation than a body of soldiers"—exactly the nexus celebrated by Walpole's friends in the 1720s.[35] Hamilton's opponents, no less deliberately and earnestly, responded with the "Country," "Real Whig," and "Patriot" (each of the terms used in Bolingbrokean polemics of the 1730s conveys something important about Jeffersonian Republicanism of the 1790s) rhetoric of Walpole's foes.

In Britain, however, the original Court ideology associated with the Tories under the Stuart monarchs had become that of the Walpolean Whigs after their rise to power (allied with the Hanoverian kings) in 1721, and the Country ideology of the earl of Shaftesbury's Whigs in the 1680s was taken over by opposition forces (both Bolingbrokean and radical Whigs) during the 1720s and 1730s. This "inversion" had paradoxical and complicating echoes in the United States. Although Hamilton mustered a powerful interest on behalf of his Walpolean programs and was himself quite comfortable with their ethic, oppositionist ideas remained strong, even among Federalists. Most important in determining the shape of the early presidency, the moral and public philosophy articulated by Pope, Swift, Bolingbroke, and their allies in opposition to Walpole became standard opinion among those in power in the new United States and loomed large in American consciousness until well into the nineteenth century, as we have noted.

In fact, John Adams, despite his approval of many specific parts of Hamilton's program, was in many ways the staunchest and most profound "Country ideologue" among the early presidents. It was apropos that the bitterest quarrel in 1800 was between the Walpolean Hamilton and John Adams, whereas the differences between Adams and Jefferson were easily overcome as political circumstances changed, leaving the two men free to resume a deep personal and intellectual kinship. Nor was it inconsistent that after 1801 Jefferson undertook to *lead* the nation. All he had to do was move from the Country arguments that had been so useful in opposition during the 1790s to include the propositions on behalf of moral, patriot leadership that in the 1730s Bolingbroke had amalgamated into the Country ideology. The same eclectic dependence on Augustan and Georgian themes was evident in a public letter by the Virginia elder statesman and mentor of all the Virginia presidents, Edmund Pendleton. Alarmed in October 1801 that his young friends (Jefferson and Madison) might not pursue sufficiently pure republican objectives, he wrote a public letter entitled "The Danger Not Over," recalling, doubtless, a tract of that title by

James Burgh written in 1746 (and often reprinted in America) to warn
that the recent defeat of the Jacobite rebellion did not ensure the virtue
and justice of British government unless the victors adhered to their professed principles. Pendleton called on the administration to eliminate the
national debt, shun standing armies, renounce undeclared wars, restrain
the Senate and the federal judiciary, and otherwise root out Federalist
abuses. Yet, he ended his radical Whiggish appeal by affirming that "it is
only when great and good men are at the head of a nation, that the people
can expect to succeed, in forming new barriers to counteract recent en-
croachments on their rights."[36]

During the first nineteenth-century presidency, the "opposition" as well
as the administration responded to the mingled moral-political arguments
of the age of Walpole. "Federalists in dissent" after 1801, echoing the
words of the Adamses of Braintree more than those of "ex-Prime Minister" Hamilton, again and again called the nation back to a sense of its
organic, public wholeness as they saw Jeffersonian expansive individualism
undermining ancient verities. Federalists refurbished Augustan satire to
hurl at their opponents, and science-oriented Republicans such as Jefferson and Benjamin Rush were portrayed as being no less foolishly visionary
than the members of Swift's Grand Academy at Lagado. In charges that
recalled the battle between "Ancients" and "Moderns," out-of-office Federalists warned against dangerous experiments and the "wild theories of
crazy projectors" as they saw Jefferson and his colleagues plan for an age of
enterprise and progress.[37] Many Federalists yearned for the same revival
of Classical wisdom that had driven Pope and Swift back to the timeless
values and eloquent words of Cicero and Horace, Virgil and Plutarch.
Once again, it seemed urgent to challenge the power and egomania of
those who held high office. This switch in rhetoric by the Federalists toward oppositionist Country propositions reveals, as does the unabashed
celebration by many Jeffersonians of the *commercial* benefits of American
farming,[38] the eclectic uses of the brilliant Augustan arguments. The point
is not that either Federalists or Republicans were consistent in their evocation of the British cleavage or of the ancient sages, but rather that the assumptions and terms of Augustan discourse were able to dominate American political controversies well into the nineteenth century because the
momentous moral and social questions of the earlier period remained unsettled and were therefore still live issues in public life.

However much regional interests, the people's enterprise, and Hamiltonian rhetoric hearkened to the call of a commercial culture, deep, pervasive instincts still pulled the other way. The rural sentimentality, the anti-
statism, the conscious provincialism, and the animosity toward corrupt
"special interests" that coursed through American politics in the nineteenth century are all traceable in some degree to the ancient Country ide-

ology. And although the economy of the nation, both in its laissez-faire doctrine and in its growing sophistication, had strong Walpolean proclivities, what we might term the Jefferson–Tocqueville–Frederick Jackson Turner view of American character continued to be molded by an effort to keep an Old World Country ideology alive on the New World frontier. This effort was not merely nostalgic, or quaint, or backwardlooking, or quixotic; rather, like any attempt to sustain time-honored values amid flux, it represented a serious and profound intention to retain a sense of moral purpose and social cohesion in the face of hostile and corrosive tendencies.

Thus, a style of leadership linked to Country ideology and emphasizing uprightness and an attention to proper national character has had a continuing appeal in America from John Winthrop through Jefferson to Woodrow Wilson and Jimmy Carter. In any event, the party strife in the early national period is much better understood as the perpetuation of the long-lingering issues and cleavages of Court and Country world views than in the context of a backward projection of "modern party systems."

Hamiltonian Leadership: Intention and Party

Even Hamilton's outlook, although in some ways divergent from that of the early presidents and receptive to the Walpolean style, neither accepted the contention-of-interests notion of politics nor incorporated the positive understanding of political parties that became dominant in Britain and the United States from the 1820s onward. His enthusiasm for trade, enterprise, and political management, furthermore, "modern" as it was, did not carry him entirely away from the Classical maxims of political obligation that he absorbed from reading Plutarch or diminish the visions of national leadership he shared with Colbert and the elder Pitt. Hamilton exhibited a special version of the tension visible in his presidential colleagues: he was at once both the least conventional of the founders in his ambivalence toward "Country ideology" and the most Classical in accepting positive ideas of patriot leadership.

Hamilton showed his "modernity" when he aimed at his foes some of the most effective words used by Walpole's polemicists to celebrate commerce, its ethic, and its usefulness to the nation as a whole. Defoe's argument that England's greatness depended on its wealth, that its wealth depended on its trade, that its trade depended on the enterprising, industrious habits of its people, that these habits were morally and politically beneficial, and that therefore encouragement (or perhaps more precisely, *release*) of them was a responsibility of government suited Hamilton's vision of a nation skilled in "the arts of industry, and the science of finance, which," he insisted, "is the offspring of modern times."[39] In making this argument Hamilton could also find support in the policies and widely acclaimed achievements of such commerce-oriented leaders as the elder Pitt, Jacques Necker, and closest to home, Robert Morris.

Hamilton, that is, along with his Periclean conception of the public interest, was also enthusiastically and unreservedly on the side of "modernity," ready to accept both its political economy and its ethic—and ready, in a way, to celebrate freedom defined as openness and absence of restraint. It is no anomaly, therefore, that, more forthrightly than Jefferson, Hamilton condemned slavery and defended freedom of the press. Slavery inhibited enterprise and mobility, whereas restraint on the press imposed blinders and distracted energies in ways that at best added nothing to the growth and prosperity of a nation. Idealization of any premodern society, whether ancient Sparta, the medieval Anglo-Saxon kingdoms, or even Elizabethan England, was to Hamilton certainly futile and perhaps unpatriotic. Any political grouping that pursued such an ideal, or that insisted yeoman farming alone among occupations led to virtue, or that was reluctant to embrace a world of international trade was in Hamilton's eyes a party in the old corrupt sense: such views represented a partial interest in opposition to an enlightened view embracing the "aggregate interest." A figure like John Taylor of Caroline was worse than quaint; in his preoccupation with what to Hamilton was merely one narrow interest in the nation, he was manifestly irresponsible. The "nostalgic" Jeffersonians were to Hamilton as outmoded, as wrongheaded, and as dangerous to the public welfare as such "Ancients" as Pope and Swift had seemed to Walpole's defenders. "Not only wealth but the independence and security of a country appear to be materially connected with the prosperity of manufactures," Hamilton argued in the *Report on Manufactures*. "The possession of these is necessary to the perfection of the body politic; to the safety as well as to the welfare of the society. The want of either is the want of an important organ of political life and motion; and in the various crises which await a state, it must severely feel the effects of any such deficiency."[40] Any party, then, that impeded a strong, modern economy was a faction working for a special interest, not the public welfare.

Yet Hamilton's programs, including the Neutrality Proclamation and Jay's Treaty as well as the debt and bank policies, conceived a future for the United States so deeply at odds with Jeffersonian conceptions and so inherently needful of strong executive leadership that intense resistance was all but inevitable. Hamilton wanted the United States to become a strong nation with a diversified agricultural, commercial, and manufacturing economy, able to exert its power anywhere in the world. In envisioning this future, he in one sense merely adapted to America the Defoe–Walpole–elder Pitt model for British greatness in the eighteenth century: exalt the new commerce and its ethic, align national policy with this potential, and let the wealth and power thus generated ensure prosperity at home and influence abroad. In this conception Hamilton both transferred an English model to the New World and foreshadowed the growth of the American economy in the nineteenth and twentieth centuries, as both his admirers who share the substance of his vision and his critics who reject it have pointed out.

But Hamilton did not in the least accept, as Jacksonians and, later, Social Darwinists generally would argue, that this growth would best occur without public guidance. Both his Aristotelian public philosophy and his mercantilist political economy repudiated laissez-faire; every aspect of his thought and career underscores that rejection. Hamilton consistently believed that prosperity came not "from the *absence* of government, . . . but from the *presence* of government."[41] In 1781–1782 he labeled the idea "that there is no need of a common directing power" in a nation's economy a "wild speculative paradox" and affirmed instead that "J E A L O U S Y of P O W E R . . . has rendered our particular constitutions in many respects feeble and imperfect." It was necessary, he insisted, to give "the magistrate a proper degree of authority, to make and execute the laws with vigour."[42] Then, as "Publius" in 1788, as "Pacificus" in 1793, and as "Camillus" in 1795 he defended the broadest possible interpretation of national executive power to resist regional prejudices, to combat legislative factionalism, and to maintain American independence in a perilous world. Later spokesmen with these same intentions have admired Hamilton's thought and career. In 1909, for example, Herbert Croly, searching to justify positive action and planned pursuit of national objectives after nearly a century of laissez-faire politics, was delighted with Hamilton's "high conception of the duties of leadership." He realized, Croly noted, that "genuine liberty . . . could be protected only by an energetic and clear-sighted central government, and it could be fertilized only by the efficient national organization of American activities. . . . Hamilton's policy was one of energetic and intelligent assertion of the national good. He knew that the only method whereby the good could prevail . . . was by persistently willing that it should prevail and by the adoption of intelligent means to that end."[43]

The words and phrases suit Hamilton perfectly—energy, efficiency, intelligence, will, national good, and leadership—and in fact define the qualities of the only sort of republican executive he thought could vitalize the Constitution enough to make it work. His thought and career furnished a brilliant articulation and model of how even a Whiggish constitution, conceived in the power-suspicious, legislative-oriented aftermath of a revolution against a corrupt king and his governor-servants, could be interpreted so as to retain the exalting benefits every society could derive from firm leadership. In this sense, his public philosophy, more forthrightly than that of any of the other early leaders (possibly excepting John Quincy Adams), undertook to show how Classical conceptions of political obligation, positive government, and farsighted leadership could be reconciled with both republican government and an expansive economy. His opponents, charging that he went too far, that is, that some of these conceptions undermined rather than fulfilled the Revolutionary ideals of self-rule, may in part have hit the mark, but they did not wipe out the profound appeal of what he attempted: nothing less than the blending, in a modern, commercial nation, of Aristotelian standards of public pursuit of the good life with Lockean insistence on government by consent. Hamilton shared with Jefferson the basic tension imposed by this perhaps contradictory, perhaps creative, combination, which made their attitudes toward party and leadership in some sense the same, however much they differed in personal style and aspirations for the nation's future.

Hence, if one begins with Jefferson's insistence that an informed, virtuous citizenry is the only viable foundation for good self-government, and then adds Franklin's formula for including artisans and merchants to the ranks of those naturally encouraged in virtue and Hamilton's design for providing energetic leadership for the general welfare, a major part of the public philosophy of the first six presidents emerges. Although the facts of politics in a free society more or less drew them into party activity, and their sober view of human nature made this seem inevitable, they never (one is tempted to add "even for a moment") welcomed it. This gap between what they knew to be reality and what their ideal of leadership required imposed a conflict that impinged on them, one suspects, every day. At times, perhaps, the early presidents were so much compelled to cope with the realities of factional politics that their above-party ideals seemed irrelevant. Washington's politically motivated release of his Farewell Address in 1796, Jefferson's removal of some Federalist officeholders in 1801, the sectional inequities of "Mr. Madison's War," and J. Q. Adams's "bargain" with Henry Clay in 1825, for example, do not fit easily within nonpartisan conceptions of the presidency. Yet in each of these cases, and numerous others that might be cited, the presidents suffered bafflement, regret, and even grief at their inability to act as their conception of patriotic leadership required. Later presidents have no doubt felt something of this tension, but, given the glorification of party since the 1820s, one suspects a different order of regret: sorrow at not finding solutions to suit everybody, and so on, but not agony over the fact of partisanship itself.

Leadership, furthermore, was to be not only nonpartisan but also positive and active. The proconsular (or, to suggest a modern comparison, "Gaullist") way of Hamilton and even the broadly programmatic way of J. Q. Adams were not widely accepted, but it was expected that the president would be a standard setter. Washington's entire career and his private as well as his public personality were "active and positive" in that he meant to give tone, to offer guidelines that would elevate the public life of the new nation. He also was perfectly willing to decide and to act, to do things that impinged deeply on the life of the nation. Behind Jefferson's deliberate modesty and elaborate deference to Congress were a clear sense of what he wanted the nation to become and an equally clear sense of how his own style as a philosopher-statesman would set a moral standard for public and private life of immense, substantial importance. His dispute with Hamilton was not over *whether* to lead, as some of his critics (including Herbert Croly and Hamilton himself) have charged, but *how* and *where* to lead.

Even the less dynamic Jeffersonian presidents, Madison and Monroe, differed with their esteemed elder colleague only in habit, temperament, and personal magnetism, not in goals or conceptions of executive leadership. As Madison proved in his national program of December 1815 and Monroe demonstrated in the Missouri controversy and in the diplomatic triumphs of his administration, they were fully capable of taking the lead, and each did so in ways that baffled their more partisan (and usually younger) colleagues. And John Adams's defiance of his party (of which he refused, hardly, even to be cognizant) in sending the peace commission to France in 1799 is one of the classic acts of patriot leadership in United States history. Adams himself, in fact, saw the dispatch of the commissioners, along with his advocacy of the Declaration of Independence and his defense of American rights in the Treaty of Paris of 1783, as the three landmarks of his public career, one as decisive, as disinterested, and as fateful as the other, and all embodying the public philosophy of *Idea of a Patriot King*.

Although there was a wide difference between the affirmations and predispositions of Hamilton's career and public philosophy and the reticence of Washington or the lackluster inaction of Madison and Monroe at their most self-effacing, all four men understood the constructive aspect of Hamilton's insistence on a "proper degree of authority" in the chief magistrate. And all four agreed that the nation had a vital need for substantial guidance toward the public good. The paradox and agony of the careers of each of the pre-1829 presidents was that they shared much of Hamilton's idea of leadership but felt more strongly than he did the restraints imposed on a *republican* chief executive and the ambiguity of retaining a Classical model of leadership in a society characterized, as J. S. Mill put it, by a "spirit of commerce and industry" and by free, increasingly democratic politics. Hamilton's own career did not always achieve a consistent fusion of a Walpolean political economy and a Brobdingnagian moral concern, but his presidential colleagues nonetheless had in him a dramatic embodiment of the dilemmas, for better and for worse, of leadership in a new republic.

❦ 11 ❦

Executive Power and
the Nonpartisan Ideal

Executive Opportunities, 1789

In June 1783, as Abigail Adams waited anxiously for news of the final
ratification of the peace treaty with Great Britain that her husband
had just helped negotiate, she wrote him about her hopes and fears
for the future of the now-independent nation. "Domestick Jars and
confusions" loomed everywhere. The defeat of "near all the able and Skill-
full Members" of the Massachusetts legislature, quarrels among the states,
and "ignorance of our real Interest," she wrote, threatened to "crush our
rising greatness." She feared a "Theseus" who might take advantage of
popularity or military reputation to "subjugate our infant republick to
Monarchical domination," but she also hoped for "a Soloman in wisdom,
to guide and conduct this great people . . . at this critical aere [era]."[1] The
histories of Greece, Rome, and England had all taught her that in the aftermath of revolutionary war, disorder, ignorance, and factionalism often led
first to anarchy and then to tyranny. Yet it still seemed possible to her that a
good leader might, especially in the founding of a nation, fulfill expectations and launch an era of "Light and Glory," which she and her husband
had dared dream of in 1776. Either "a Theseus" or "a Soloman" would
confirm the maxim Benjamin Franklin had recalled twenty years earlier
when many Britons in North America had had high hopes for the reign of
George III: "The whole community is regulated by the example of the
King."[2]

In this "critical era," and under a new Constitution that evoked repeatedly from journalists and orators images of Lycurgus, Solon, and Publius,
as well as Solomon, George Washington was inaugurated as the first president of the United States. He soon had in office with him his five successors. The Constitution offered only a few short paragraphs defining the
powers of the executive department, powers clearly intended to be under
"republican restraints" but also resting on a vague phrase that left room for
a patriot leader, if such could be found, to "regulate the whole community

by his example": "The executive Power shall be invested in a President of the United States of America."

In the summer of 1789, then, Congress had to resume the debates of the Federal Convention on the meaning of "executive Power" as it struggled with statutes to establish the office of the presidency. The method of removals from office, for example, raised critical questions: By implication did the Senate have to consent to removals as it did to appointments? Or, was removal, again by implication, possible only through impeachment? Or, should Congress assume the power in each creation of office to define a removal procedure? Or, finally, was removal of inferior officers an inherent part of executive power, as the Constitution used that term, and therefore to be left to the discretion of the president?

Members of Congress who sought wide powers for the president were quick to point out that the language of Article II of the Constitution was more sweeping than that of Article I or III. Article I began by calling attention to "all legislative Powers *herein granted*," and Article III used the phrase "the judicial Power *shall extend to*" (emphasis added) before an enumeration of the cases to which it would apply. Article II, however, vested "executive Power" without stating or implying its limitation by any lists or enumerations to follow. This language suited, apparently, the preconceptions of the members of both the Federal Convention and the first federal Congress; at least formal objection to it is unrecorded. It seems that the idea of wide, discretionary power in the executive rested naturally in the minds of the men who fashioned the Constitution and set it in motion.

Although some members of Congress argued for the more restricted interpretations of the president's removal power, a substantial majority soon gathered behind the argument favoring the president's inherent, exclusive power to decide how long his appointees should remain in office. James Madison, in often-cited speeches, reasoned that in order to ensure the responsibility of the appointees of the executive department to its constitutionally defined head, they would have to serve only at his pleasure. Furthermore, in fundamental republican arguments echoing those of James Wilson at the Federal Convention, Madison went on to insist that with such dependence of inferior officers on the president, and then with his election as the Constitution provided, "the chain of dependence . . . terminates in the supreme body, namely in the people." Only thus, Madison concluded, could the people be sure of whom to blame for executive misconduct, and only with such responsibility for his appointees could a president be properly supported for the good conduct of his office. Fisher Ames backed Madison with characteristic lucidity: "The executive powers are delegated to the President, with a view to have a responsible officer to superintend, control, inspect, and check the officers necessarily employed in administering the laws. The only bond between him and those he employs, is the confidence he has in their integrity and talents; when that confidence ceases, the principal ought to have power to remove those whom he can no longer trust with safety."[3]

In addition to accepting this argument for executive responsibility, members of Congress made clear that their confidence in the president also rested on their distrust of *legislative* cabal and on an unwillingness to discard completely British, monarchical models. Speculating on the evils of having continuance in executive office contingent on Senate support, Madison drew an ominous picture: Is there not danger in such a case, he asked, that "an officer may choose rather to risk his establishment on the favor of that branch, than rest it on the discharge of his duties to the satisfaction of the executive?" Such a "connection" with the Senate, Madison insisted, "reduces the power of the President to a mere vapor, . . . his responsibility would be annihilated, . . . [and] high executive officers, joined in cabal with the Senate, would lay the foundation of discord" that might be resolved only "by a revolution in the government." Ames again clarified by pointing out that although under the Constitution the Senate "may check and regulate the appointment by the President, . . . they can do nothing more; they . . . do not secure any degree of responsibility. . . . The President . . . has expressly the power of nominating and appointing, though he must obtain the consent of the Senate. He is the agent; the Senate may prevent his acting, but cannot act themselves."[4]

When the bills to establish the executive departments, fashioned as Madison and Ames had urged, reached the Senate, that body accepted the explicit limitation on its power. Senator Oliver Ellsworth of Connecticut, who had also been a member of the Federal Convention, noted at once that the Constitution did not limit the president's powers to those "hereinafter enumerated and explained"; the Senate could only consent and advise, for it had "no executive power," he insisted. As if to reveal the origins of his sense of the proper understanding of executive power, he went on to "lament the want of power in the President" and even declared that the American Revolution had arisen from a dispute over the power of Parliament. "No one," he noted with some exaggeration, "ever thought the power of the Crown too great."[5] Although many members of Congress denied this view and were quick to repudiate analogies between the American executive and the British crown, it was also clear that a strong residue of sentiment remained in favor of an exalted, responsible executive power exercised independently of legislative contentions and thus protective of the welfare of the whole—exactly the role always assigned to the good ruler.

Even beyond this explicit and rather formal endorsement of a general executive authority, Washington and his colleague-successors found broad indications of the dimensions of their power all around them. In the English history closest to the framers, executive power meant the considerable powers of government left to the monarch after the reservations and parliamentary enlargements that had occurred especially since the reigns of Henry VIII and Elizabeth I. Although Parliament controlled the purse strings and influenced who would be the king's ministers, and although there were important restraints on the monarch's prerogatives, the residue of power, formal and informal, was still enormous. Every other model of executive power known to the framers was similarly characterized by ample prerogatives. Thus as Washington added flesh and blood to his skeletal office, keeping in mind both Whiggish restraints on his office and the intention of 1787 to revive executive leadership, he had room to maneuver and abundant precedent for accepting the Classical role later symbolized in Horatio Greenough's famous statue of him in a Roman toga.

Cultural Tensions and the Presidency

The crosscurrents, moreover, ran far deeper than the constitutional and political flows on the surface, because ideas of executive authority had mingled with economic and cultural transformations taking place in the Western world. The traditional idea of national leadership, in the blend of Classical and Christian conceptions articulated so compellingly by John Winthrop and the earl of Clarendon as well as by Alexander Pope, Jonathan Swift, and Lord Bolingbroke, was rooted in a pervasive folk spirit, a mystique of national character, and a monitory moral philosophy. All the strongest injunctions of the national past, of religion, of the mythology of the royal family, and of the land itself infused the role and standing of the reigning monarch. The title of the British ruler—"King by the Grace of God, of all Great Britain, Defender of the Faith" (to say nothing of the even grander titles of the king of France, the Holy Roman emperor, and other monarchs)—suggests some of the connotations that from time immemorial had attached themselves to the idea of leadership.

Thus when Swift scorned the England of his day as "Lilliputian" and Pope saw with horror around him a "reign of Dulness" and a cataclysmic chaos, the decline and corruption of the monarchy seemed both cause and effect. In their ideal world, divine will, moral rectitude, social order, and national dignity were symbolized and held together by the person and power of a virtuous monarch. In part and in less sophisticated form, moreover, it was a view accepted by the Tory throngs in London in 1710, by the English working class a century later, and by thousands of farmers who worked the lands of the New World. Breaches anywhere—in the standing

of the church, in the authority of the monarch or his ministers, in the virtue of the people, in family bonds, in the sense of community, in the root-
edness in the land, in the traditional values—were believed to weaken the
state, fatherland, nation, or whatever word carried the richest and deepest
connotations. Furthermore, in such an understanding of society, where
moral unity came from a clear sense of social rank and order that ensured
the proper distribution of deference and dignity, the broad mass of people
could give consent to government without having a direct share in it.[6]
With only occasional grumbles about republican inconsistency, Americans
expressed their sense of what was owed to a leader in *ca.* 1790 by celebrating Washington's birthday even while he was in office, as the peoples of
many lands did for their sovereigns. This coupling of the person of the
leader with the general welfare of the nation, still strong in Washington's
America, vaguely but significantly enlarged the leader's role. If there was a
focus of responsibility, a point where blame might be placed or from which
renewal might emanate, every tradition known to eighteenth-century Britons looked to the patriot leader—usually a king. But in a republic where
were the people to turn? Again and again the same unanswered question
arose: What could take the place in a republic of the enormously important symbol of the king, the mystical leader and ruler of the whole realm?

On the other side of the great cultural tension in eighteenth-century
Britain, the new world of Daniel Defoe, Robert Walpole, and Adam Smith
challenged not only the political economy and ethic of the past but also the
foundations and modes of leadership. Traditionally, ruling had ancient
links with land and family, faith and livelihood that legitimized and even
sanctified leadership in ways that left as little room for the power of new
wealth as for the consent of the governed. Furthermore, if the time-
honored system was thought of as part of a providential design or of a
primordial community and way of life, then the new world view threatened literally everything. As Pope put it in the famous last lines of the
Dunciad,

> Lo! thy dread Empire, CHAOS! is restored;
> Light dies before thy uncreating word:
> Thy hand, great Anarch! lets the curtain fall;
> And universal Darkness buries All.[7]

As new sources of power grew with the expansion of English trade, as
the Whig magnates fought wars to increase commerce and gain wealth, as
critical thought undermined orthodoxy, as "Moderns" challenged "Ancients" in the battle of the books, as Defoe, Bernard Mandeville, and others celebrated the ethic of self-interest, and as Walpole learned to govern by
manipulation, the whole idea of what government and leadership meant,

and what they derived from, lost a sure basis. "For the first time, eighteenth-century men were setting their conceptions of politics in a context of historical change, the transition from the agrarian world of the Middle Ages to the mercantile and specialized world of their own generations."[8]

Within the new commercial view, it was possible to conceive that the state had no foundation other than the need to impose order in a competitive, nasty state of nature, or, more benignly, its foundation might be regarded as a contract of convenience to protect property and other rights among those giving some form of consent. In either case an immense metaphysical baggage had been cast aside as material and secular considerations became more overt. In such a world, with divine right and an organic sense of community gone, together with their connecting, controlling, comforting foundations, the leadership questions were all reopened. How far did such guidelines as personal liberty, material well-being, social convenience, and what has been termed "possessive individualism," or "avaricious transactionism,"[9] answer the question of who, if anyone, should lead? Under what control would the leader be and selected by whom?

By 1789 even in Great Britain the sense of awe and sanctity surrounding the throne had vastly declined, while across the Atlantic the "forces of acquisitive capitalism, individual liberty, provincial autonomy and Anglo-American oligarchy" had won a revolutionary war and established a new nation.[10] Under such circumstances, to lead seemed to mean to be responsive to the (wealth-producing?) people governed, to promote national prosperity, to rule according to changing statute law, to be tolerant of creative diversities rather than protective of narrow orthodoxies, and to celebrate the values of enterprising men. All this was far removed from traditional ideas of leadership. The dictum "private vice, public benefit," for example, seemed to welcome to the public councils all the factions in the land, making the ruler one partisan among many, maneuvering among selfishly motivated groups and individuals. In such a model, although there would be need for political parties and political managers, there was little room for providential design, an objective public interest—or, a patriot leader.

As Washington and his successors pondered their role in the presidential office, then, they sensed convergences as well as tensions, some guidelines, but also much unsettledness. Each accepted the Revolutionary ideals of natural rights, formal executive limitation, and a legislative mechanism of consent. But they also shared a conviction of the inadequacy of these concepts alone as the basis of good government, and each was schooled in political ideas and habits that afforded a much wider scope to positive government and executive leadership than the circumstantially hallowed radical Whig axioms. Thus each of the first six presidents deliberately sought to dignify and enhance the executive branch, not for the most part with courtly pretensions or proconsular ambitions, but by steadily and often unobtrusively attempting to give the nation direction and unity. In so doing, each wrestled with the challenging theoretical and practical problems of republican executiveship—the peculiar need it imposed for limitation and control, but also the equally urgent need it created for vigorous, nonpartisan guidance amid the factiousness inherent in a free society, a factiousness only intensified in legislative bodies.

Beyond these more formal, political necessities, however, the early presidents sensed deeply (although with widely varying degrees of self-consciousness) the link between style and powers of leadership and the cultural and ethical convulsions of the Western world. It is precisely at this point that the most important convergence, the most basic shared values, of the six men takes on crucial importance: each was conventionally Augustan in his world view in that to each the urgent questions of noble nationhood, good government, and admirable leadership were those raised by the leading politicians and writers in the two generations following the Glorious Revolution. And on the whole they retained much of a traditional outlook—vivified for them in the brilliant literature of the Augustan Age but also implicit in their Classical and Christian backgrounds. A strong cultural nostalgia gave each of them, whatever differences they had in more immediate political outlook, an affinity for a nation still part of "Christendom" and for all the interwoven values and habits that word implied. The unities of the past were perhaps the more precious to them because they were so far from what, before 1776, they had reverently thought of as "home," the mother country, the England of Shakespeare, Milton, and Dr. Johnson. It was also true, of course, that a certain aristocratic class consciousness, best revealed in the characterization of the early presidents as "patrician," and even some common self-interest, united them and contributed a strong material basis to their cultural and ideological biases. But this fact neither contradicted their moral inclinations nor entirely explains their intentions and actions in office. A real part of the character of each feared and resisted "the commercialization of values," the moral revolution, and the social alienation that went with it, as was true for many people throughout the Western world.

Thus as each of the early presidents entered office he was bound to ask himself whether he could defend, or restore, or fulfill "the design of Providence" or "the good life" in the new nation. Although there were important differences in what these men took to be the substance of these goals, each one assumed that his presidency had a relationship to some such conception. To put it oppositely, none of them had surrendered very far to the new politics of competing self-interests that seemed to go with the new

economics and its ethic. Each saw his life and his country within the context of the unsettled controversy about the direction Western culture
would take as the commercial and industrial revolutions gained power and
sway. And given the influence leaders were assumed to have, they inevitably believed that how they acted as leaders would have a crucial bearing on
the character of the new United States. Each of these presidents could be a
Pericles or a Nero, an Elizabeth I or a James II, that is, a leader who ennobled or corrupted his country, a responsibility not altered fundamentally
in their minds because they were elected, republican leaders rather than
hereditary monarchs. Further, to fulfill such a role each man would certainly have to resist the corruption of party and be willing to act positively
for the public good. He would have to be a republican patriot king whose
role in government was to be neither Machiavellian nor "*luke-warm neuter-
passive*," but rather to sustain the basic moral and cultural values of the
nation.

For Jefferson, for example, there were many ways as executive he felt he
could not act, and there were critical restraints to which he felt bound, but
these did not include an unwillingness to lead, to set the tone, or to be at
the head of "an aristocracy of talent and virtue" that would give the nation
good government. He made the point implicitly during his first month as
president: "When we reflect how difficult it is to move or inflect the great
machine of society, how impossible to advance the notions of a whole
people suddenly to ideal right, we see the wisdom of Solon's remark, that
no more good must be attempted than the nation can bear, and that all will
be chiefly to reform the waste of public money, and thus drive away the
vultures who prey upon it, and improve some little on old routines."[11] He
intended, that is, to go slowly and to stay close to the public pulse, but he
also accepted the notion of a public "ideal right" and of the leader's responsibility to guide toward it. He was determined to be both a faithful
republican *and* a patriot leader.

Jefferson, moreover, was in tune with the deepest hopes and fears of
those who scorned the England of Walpole and Defoe. Culturally and
morally, Jefferson sided with Pope and Swift, despite a distaste for their
political Toryism, which he easily looked past because it seemed so incon-
sequential in the English New World. He learned from them his most
vivid lessons on the degradation of commercial values and of a manipulative, brokering politics, and he learned also the dangers inherent in dependence on merchants and bankers to guide national policy. To Jefferson,
there was no appeal in a stockjobbing, scrambling, greedy, exploiting,
"Lilliputian" nationhood, however democratic and "free" its political institutions might be. In fact, to him, raised on Classical and neoclassical
writers, to be free meant not to be merely unfettered but to be schooled to
know and do what was true and good and beautiful—as he incessantly tu-

tored his own daughters and any young people who asked his advice. They would have been taught, in Milton's words, that

> They bawl for freedom in their senseless mood,
> Yet still revolt when truth would set them free;
> License they mean, when they cry liberty,
> For who loves that must first be wise and good.[12]

And it was the obligation of the patriot leader (as well as the paterfamilias), above everything else, as Bolingbroke had explained, to sustain these moral foundations of society and, consequently, to resist any forces that would corrupt them.

Because Jefferson was so impressed by the Augustan writers, he was peculiarly open to their sense of the obligation of political leadership. The problem was that he took these ideas with him into an era of radical republicanism scarcely imaginable to the authors of *Gulliver's Travels* and the *Dunciad*. In the debates generated by the cultural and moral crisis of Western civilization, Jefferson was clear about his own preferences, but he was also a republican committed to human freedom and government by consent. Less dramatically and less clearly, and with different emphases in each case, all of the other early presidents were caught in the same crosscurrents.

Because Franklin and Hamilton so much more wholeheartedly embraced the new era of trade and industry, it might be assumed that they did not feel the same tension as Jefferson and his presidential colleagues, but in fact their response was complementary rather than contradictory to Jefferson's or Madison's. Franklin, an admirer of Defoe, showed how traditional moral qualities and a strong community spirit could be maintained and valued in a bustling world of trade, cities, and mobility. By finding grounds for virtue in the shop and forge as well as in the field and gentleman's library, Franklin held out the prospect that republican government might work in an expanding, commercial nation. He thus relaxed the constraints implicit in Jefferson's sociology and economics, not to promote a Walpolean merchant oligarchy, but rather to validate a political philosophy like Jefferson's of grass-roots virtue, local self-government, and the worldwide diffusion of republican principles.

Hamilton, on the other hand, was as thoroughly modern in his grasp of world trade and its geopolitics as the elder William Pitt, and he was eager for his new country to benefit from them as much as Britain itself had since the days of Marlborough and Walpole. He had as little fear, and as much trust, in the ethic of the banker and the merchant as did Defoe, and he was as willing as the Londoner to see the skills and enterprise of the counting-house introduced into the public councils. But Hamilton's political philosophy was as thoroughly Classical as Jefferson's and Bolingbroke's; that is, he believed in the primacy of the public interest, in the obligation of government to articulate and pursue that interest, and in the responsibility of the executive to stand above party in guiding the national destiny. Although he differed crucially with Jefferson on what the nation should seek to become, and on style of leadership, both men assumed that a necessary part of leadership was possession of a substantive conception of "the good life" toward which the nation was to be guided. Each sought to be a Pericles, though with different ideas of what Athens should become. Hamilton's innovation (in a way far more radical than anything proposed by Jefferson) was to suppose that the traditional responsibilities of executive leadership could be harnessed to a modern political economy. His efforts in this direction, moreover, were the grounds of *his* creative thought and career, and the source of his appeal to Herbert Croly, to Theodore Roosevelt, to Franklin Roosevelt, and to many contemporary scholars and politicians who see a need for an "intelligent and energetic assertion of the national good."

The first six presidents of the United States, then, because they held office at the confluence of these crosscurrents of political philosophy, of economic development, and of cultural change, had available to them a number of disparate models of both the mode and purpose of executive leadership. Perhaps the point can be illustrated if we try to imagine what sort of presidency might have emerged in America in the late seventeenth or early eighteenth century, the era of Sir Edmund Andros, of Robert Hunter, of Sir William Gooch, or even of Sir William Shirley, colonial governors who linked high conceptions of executive prerogative with grand visions of American empire. Would these loyal servants of the English crown have felt the same uncertainties and restraints as George Washington and Thomas Jefferson? Or imagine the presidency that might have been conceived and fashioned had American independence been delayed until the 1830s. Would party and laissez-faire public life have been subject to the same scorn and condemnation they received in 1789? It seems clear that the American presidency received its shape and posture at a historical moment that was as far from the party leadership conceptions of Robert Peel and William Gladstone as it was from the divine right insistences of James II.

In a closer American context, we can as little imagine Thomas Hutchinson suffering the creative doubts his bitter foe John Adams endured between 1787 and 1801 as we can imagine Martin Van Buren thinking about party as Jefferson and Madison did as they sought to define republican leadership. It might be difficult to find another era, in sum, when one could affirm, as unselfconsciously as Jefferson did in 1821, thinking back on a half-century in public life, that Thomas Paine and Bolingbroke were "both advocates for human liberty." And there can be little doubt that as the American nation-builders turned from the demands of revolution to the difficult task of fashioning executive power, the precepts of the author of *Idea of a Patriot King* echoed as loudly as those of the author of *Common Sense*.

Neither "Popular" nor "Partisan" Leadership

Perhaps the nonpartisan yet deeply principled conception of executive power held by the first six presidents can be further understood if it is contrasted not only with the party-oriented presidency on the Jacksonian model but also with what might be called "the popular presidency."[13] Many of the most notable American presidents fit the party-oriented conception. They articulated a highly partisan, widely attractive program, led a party committed to the program, and in office acted adroitly (and partisanly) to achieve its passage into law. Possibly the most successful of such presidents have been Jackson, Wilson, both Roosevelts, and Lyndon Johnson—each known for the accomplishments of his administration, aggressive leadership, and strong sense of party. The "partisan" presidency is close to the mode of leadership more explicitly built into systems of parliamentary democracy, where the chief of government, "the prime minister," is most importantly the leader of the party with a popular mandate, it having won the last election. Under such a system, opposition parties are regarded as benign, permanent, and loyal, there to clarify differences and to be as much as possible an alternate government should the one in power falter in any way.

It would be a mistake, of course, to assume that such partisan leaders, or their parties, in power or out, are indifferent to the general welfare; commonly they suppose, as Van Buren did, that *their* party embodies or at least pursues the common good most effectively. Furthermore, such leaders also seek broad support—what Lyndon Johnson called "consensus"—but they do so in order to strengthen their party (as an instrument of action) and to weaken the opposition party. At the same time, they also need, and in a way exalt, an opposition party as a kind of continuing evidence that difference of opinion on public policy is inevitable and that "correctness" is best clarified in debate. Franklin Roosevelt made the point when he asked the public to "judge me by the enemies I have made." Such a president's "hold upon his office, and his power to act," moreover, "arise from his being the leader of the stronger side in a divided country. He retains his leadership by satisfying his partisans, so long as his partisans, together with those who are merely loyal to the party, form a majority."[14] As John Kennedy put it, "No President, it seems to me, can escape politics. He has not only been chosen by the nation—he has been chosen by his Party. And if he insists that he is President of all the people and should, therefore, offend none of them—if he blurs the issues and differences between the parties—if he neglects the party machinery and avoids his party's leadership—then he has not only weakened the political party; . . . he has dealt a death blow to the democratic process itself."[15]

It may help to remember that this conception of leadership and party places Edmund Burke's "party of principle" at a midpoint in the movement away from the classical scorn of party. Burke would have approved the purposeful, active role of the Roosevelts, for example, and he would have applauded a clarification between the "good" and "bad" parties, but he would have been uneasy about the idea of an ongoing party "machinery," and he would have spurned the notion that a party was a coalition of self-interested, compromising groups bonded largely "to win an election." Burke would have been willing, that is, to use the idea of party to pursue an objective public good conceived in the traditional way—but at the center had to be "a particular principle . . . upon which all agreed." Mere coalition politics, only loosely tied to policy, violated not only the assumption that there was a "permanent and aggregate interest of the community" but also Burke's insistence that a holder of public office adhere to the "clearest conviction of his judgment and conscience."[16]

But John Kennedy had in mind, in alluding to presidents who blurred issues and neglected party machinery, not a Burkean type intent on principle but his predecessor, Dwight Eisenhower, who personified the "popular" president. Under this conception, the leader gains office not by fighting for his party and its platform, but by seeming not to have a partisan program at all. Then, once elected, he husbands and, ideally, enlarges his popularity by accommodating other parties, by sidestepping divisive issues, and by discerning common denominators however "least" or vague they might be. As Kennedy's pejorative comments make clear, to one with a positive view that government ought to lead and enact programs (as is expected after a party "becomes the government" in Great Britain, for example), the "popular presidency" model seems simply irresponsible. The leader basks in a public support (*acceptance* might be a better word) that either is wasted because of his unwillingness to use it or, if he does attempt to enlist it, disappears because it does not rest on a committed base. Thus, Eisenhower's popularity was of no significance on civil rights issues because he refused to take a stand (beyond "upholding the law"), and in 1956, when he did advocate federal aid to education, he failed because his "supporters" were vague and disunited on the issue.[17]

Against this kind of popular leader, the partisan model seems to have many virtues, especially if one supposes a need for active leadership. Indeed, it is virtually the only practical model of leadership left once party itself has been sanctified. If one conceives of politics as an arena of competing groups and programs, where agreement on "the aggregate public good" is held to be neither possible nor even desirable (how can ideas and programs be honed, except against opposition critiques?), one obvious dynamic is simply to let the forces and factions fight it out in accordance with democratic process. This approach was more or less that of the White House for more than a century (1829–1933), with the usually noted exceptions: Jackson, Lincoln, Theodore Roosevelt, and Wilson. Even with these more active leaders, however, their programs as president (Roosevelt's Bull Moose platform of 1912 is outside the pattern) had generally the bias of Jackson's signal vetoes: that of striking down privilege and entrenched interests in order to allow unfettered scope for enterprise and individual achievement—a motif clear, for example, in Wilson's "New Freedom." The objective in such cases appears to be more that of enlarging opportunities and purifying the system of aristocratic residues than of setting forth substantial programs in the public interest. Jackson destroyed the Bank of the United States so that other banks might do as they pleased, Lincoln opposed slavery so that free men might prosper, and Wilson attacked the trusts to give competition greater scope. In between these crusades against limitations on freedom, when the freewheeling "system" generally afforded opportunity to all, even the active presidents, according to their own principles, would have little to do beyond being watchful for the next appearance of privileged monopoly, "malefactors of great wealth," or "combinations in restraint of trade."

This model of politics, furthermore, generally accepts and makes use of the ethic of Defoe and Mandeville—or, in transatlantic versions, the spirit of the frontier and of industrial capitalism. Politics, like economics, is seen as a diverse, turbulent mixing of forces, factions, and energies where competition is normal and benign, virtue is linked to survival, and the public good is the sum or, more precisely, the resulting vector of conflicting private goals. Within such a conception, as Van Buren explained in forming the Jacksonian party in the 1820s, the political party has a critical role. At the very least it can draw interest groups into alliance (through compromise) so they can together win elections and thus be able, probably, to achieve something of their various goals. In such a party, vigorous interest-group spokesmen are valued and useful, political brokers indispensable, permanent organization a constructive framework, and platforms a device for giving something to everybody—how else, indeed, can elections be won in a large, pluralistic, democratic nation? At times of crisis, when even under this dynamic something must be done on a national scale (as was perhaps the case in 1829, 1861, and 1913), the need is generally for an active leadership to mobilize a majority against the pathological forces, as Wilson so self-consciously sought to do both before and after his triumph in 1912. Franklin Roosevelt's great victories in 1932 and 1936, and his style as president, are the supreme embodiments of this paradigm of partisan, democratic leadership.

Although there are certain parallels between these examples and Jefferson's presidency, just as one can in some ways fit Monroe into the "popular" role, in fact the conceptions of leadership of the pre-1829 presidents largely distinguish them from both of these latter-day models. Because the first six presidents, quite simply, had different valuations of partisan motivation and of the reality of the public interest, they had different standards of executive leadership. In contrast to John Kennedy, each sought to "escape politics," abhorred the idea of "party leadership," and hoped to end the "differences between the parties." Each man, moreover, would have seen a merely popular presidency as negligent and irresponsible and a politics founded on the competition between interests as fundamentally corrupt. If, as Washington believed as deeply as the Adamses, there was design and purpose in the world within which a nation should fashion its destiny, and if an executive had an obligation to lead in accordance with this design or purpose, as the presidents of the "Virginia dynasty" believed, then simply to accommodate or balance factions would be dereliction of duty. There was, furthermore, nothing "apolitical" about the early presidents (indeed, their Aristotelian orientation gave them a rich and comprehensive sense of "man as a political animal"), nor did they shy away from anything about public life except precisely the sort of electioneering and managing that went with the new party politics.

It is not that later presidents have not often had a deep sense of moral purpose and even providential design—one need only consider such diverse chief executives as Polk, Lincoln, McKinley, Wilson, Eisenhower, Kennedy, and Carter to see the point—but that they had different ideas of party, of a president's relation to it, and of its place in the body politic. Because Jefferson agreed with Bolingbroke and Madison that a party or faction arose from a "common impulse of passion, or of interest, adverse to the rights of other citizens, or to the permanent and aggregate interests of the community," he believed it was impossible for a president properly to be a party man. Rather, a patriotic leader had to be above party (a perfectly plausible and even obligatory idea, if one assumed a nation had "permanent and aggregate" interests), and he also had to furnish leadership that was fundamentally moral and in accord with a higher law. The goal was that of raising, even sanctifying, the quality of life in the nation. This was nothing more than what *great* and *good* leaders from time immemorial had done. In a new republic dedicated to "self-evident" truths, it was especially important that its leaders provide positive, inspired guidance, and that its people expect such of them.

It is true that this nonpartisan conception of executive power was deeply, perhaps inevitably and even fatally, at odds with the burgeoning life and politics of a free and expanding nation. It may be that the linkages between removal of restraints, the growth of trade, material well-being, and diversity, sometimes referred to collectively as "democractic liberalism," make that outlook the one best attuned to a modern, open society. It may even be true that an openly partisan politics, completely tolerant of opposition because it is committed to allowing diverse interests to bear on public policy, is the best, perhaps the only, way to make government truly responsive to the will and needs of the people. So avowed politicians and thoughtful analysts during the administrations of Andrew Jackson, Grover Cleveland, and Harry Truman have believed, as the commentaries of Alexis de Tocqueville, James Bryce, and Harold Laski attest. One may even suspect that a Washington or a Jefferson would have found much to admire in at least the programs and national aspirations of Theodore Roosevelt and Franklin Roosevelt. It is difficult, at any rate, to discern much congruity between the intentions and affinities of Alton Parker and Alfred M. Landon (the Roosevelt opponents of 1904 and 1936) and those of the pre-1829 presidents. But to make these points emphasizes again that the early presidents thought of the role of the executive in ways simply remote from, not readily amenable to, what soon became the dominant political style.

Instead of supposing that their nonpartisan conceptions are outmoded or irresponsible, however, we might look for an alternative view that could help to bring about better understanding of their intentions. The aspiration of the early presidents somehow to lead actively on behalf of "the permanent and aggregate interests of the community" (that is, to shun party) while also being faithful to the openness required under government by consent (Jefferson called it "mildness") may have placed before them an awesome and persistently useful challenge: nothing less than sustaining the virtues of a patriot king in the age of democracy. Such an intent, in fact, more nearly explains the words and deeds of the early presidents than does any other angle of vision on their administrations. Each was caught, often unselfconsciously, in perhaps the most profound shift in political thinking and practice in Western history. As liberal, utilitarian, pragmatic, and interest-group politics came to characterize public life in democratic nations in the nineteenth and twentieth centuries, with all their emphasis on openness, process, and pluralism, ideas of the body politic and of obligation to it altered radically; the world of Henry Adams overwhelmed that of his grandfather. More or less aware of this transition, and vacillating between awe and despair at its implications, the early presidents had somehow to furnish leadership. With political conceptions resting on Aristotle and Bolingbroke as much as on Locke and the English "Cato," the first

American chief executives had to lead amid a political dynamic rushing on toward the party modes of Jackson, Gladstone, and Franklin Roosevelt.

The tensions they felt, however, which make their administrations often seem unreal or incongruous, may in fact have produced creative accommodations. Was Washington naive to suppose he could retain both Jefferson and Hamilton in his cabinet—or was he wise in trying to keep in government the talent essential to its good conduct? Was Jefferson hypocritical in proclaiming, "We are all federalists, we are all republicans," or had he articulated a useful distaste for partisanship? Were John Quincy Adams's proposals that the United States cooperate with other nations in astronomical and oceanographic research and in suppression of the slave trade properly scorned, or had he farsightedly discerned important laws of moral and ecological interdependence?

The traditional conceptions of leadership were only half attuned, at best, to the relatively new axioms of government by consent. A republican leader should, one can imagine Adams or Jefferson conjecturing, aspire to the same standards of disinterestedness, of virtue, and of rational judgment as Plutarch's Lycurgus, Shakespeare's duke of Arden, Molière's idealization of Louis XIV, Addison's "Cato," or Swift's king of Brobdingnag. There was in these grand models, however, nothing about choice by the people or response to their particular interests—although everything about ruling in their aggregate interest. How, then, should an executive act when he accepts the new republican postulates but also believes in the time-honored models of good leadership? The early presidents are mainly distinguished from their successors in the hold this challenge had on them, and we still attend most to the thought of the one, Jefferson, who responded to its full dimensions by attempting most earnestly to bring talent and virtue to a government resting on consent. That this fruitful challenge was not present in the same way in the consciousness of later presidents is partly a consequence of the new conventional wisdom about the usefulness of party and conflict.

The early presidents were not superior in morality and patriotism to their successors, nor did they rationalize less their own self-interests or heed less the blandishments of faction. The many careful histories of early national politics reveal no such superiority, and presidents since 1829 have often demonstrated high standards of moral, patriotic leadership—but effected, in the mode of Gladstone and Wilson, by using party machinery, not by detaching themselves from it or seeking its demise. The challenge of bringing one's sense of virtue and righteousness to bear on public life is as great, perhaps greater, than ever, as Jimmy Carter, for example, was aware. It is rather the conception and the mode of leadership that has been transformed. For the post-Jacksonian president, the obligation to be a party leader has in general been accepted not only dutifully but also enthusiastically. That Eisenhower has been regarded as an exception only proves the rule. The nation has thus come largely to regard the president as a party leader as much as a national leader, and a chorus of historians and political scientists have evaluated our presidents favorably insofar as they have effectively combined the dual roles. "No matter how fondly or how often we may long for a President who is above the heat of party strife," Clinton Rossiter insisted in the midst of the Eisenhower presidency, "we must acknowledge resolutely his right *and duty* to be the leader of his party" (emphasis added). Ten years later, with Lyndon Johnson in the White House, Thomas Bailey proclaimed that "the successful President is a successful politician, at a high level. As the titular head—normally the actual head—of a powerful political party, he *should* know the tricks of the game and *delight* in playing them (emphasis added).[18] Curiously, modern students of the presidency assume as readily and completely, and almost as offhandedly, that a chief executive must and should be a party leader skilled at the intricacies of the "game" as the first six presidents rejected the notion. That the same "politicized" view of the qualities of good leadership prevails in modern Britain is evident in the opinion of both Sir Harold Macmillan and Sir Harold Wilson that the British prime minister they most admired was Robert Walpole because of his control of his party and skill at "wheeling and dealing" in Parliament (Walpole fascinated John F. Kennedy for the same reasons.)[19] There could be no clearer measure of the altered conception of the role of national leader.

Nonpartisanship and the Modern Presidency

Yet the longing, indeed the imperative, that the president be more than a party leader, that he retain something of the aura, posture, and power of the patriot king, has remained a recurrent theme among commentators on American public life. British observers have sometimes looked to the president to lift the United States above the hoopla and mediocrity they have often found so distastefully characteristic of American politics. John Bright rhapsodized in 1861 over the election every four years of "a President over [a] great nation." Echoing the sanctity traditionally associated with a good ruler but disdainful of "thrones based on prescription or on conquest [and] sceptres wielded over veteran legions ·and subject realms," Bright proclaimed instead that "there is nothing more worthy of reverence and obedience, and nothing more sacred, than the authority of the freely chosen magistrate of a great and free people; and if there be on earth and amongst men any right divine to govern, surely it rests with a ruler so chosen and so appointed."[20] A generation later James Bryce, visiting the United States during an era of weak presidents, wrote wistfully of the years before 1829, when "all the Presidents had been statesmen in the European sense of the word, men of education, of administrative experience, of a certain largeness of view and dignity of character." By contrast, he thought, the presidents of the next sixty years were generally "mere politicians . . . or else successful soldiers . . . whom their party found useful as figureheads," and in any case "not, like the early Presidents, the first men of the country." The only exceptions were the truly noble Lincoln and Jackson, who though "something of both politician and soldier [and] a strong character, . . . [had] but a narrow and uncultivated intellect."[21]

One might be inclined to dismiss this rather self-righteous estimate as chauvinism or class bias did we not find socialist Harold Laski also longing for the great man in his 1940 study *The American Presidency*. "A weak president," he insisted, "is a gift to the forces of reaction. . . . It enables them to manipulate and maneuver between every difference that is provoked by the absence of a strong hand at the helm. It arrests the power to transcend the negativism which the scheme of American government so easily erects into a principle of action." "A constitution works well when men are in large agreement over the ends it should achieve," Laski instructed, "but their minds must be directed to the definition of those ends. And that there may be clarity in the direction, it is essential that there be leadership of a kind that no one but the president is in a position to supply." Laski concluded with a plea that the president possess "power commensurate to the function he has to perform," which was nothing less than "to make possible a genuine freedom for the many and not a privileged license for the few." He could then exercise the "great power [that] alone makes great leadership possible" and open up "the unique chance of restoring America to its people"[22]—exactly the task and the role to which two centuries earlier Bolingbroke had called the heir apparent to the British throne amid the "Dulness" of Walpole's England. At the very moment Laski wrote, furthermore, in his country Winston Churchill, admirer of Edward III and of Washington, was waiting to assume for Britain the role of Elizabeth and the elder Pitt.

American observers of the presidency have in many ways no less persistently sought in the office some of the benefits of a traditional leadership. Although Woodrow Wilson in 1885 dubbed the American president merely "the first official of a . . . civil service system . . . [whose] duties call rather for training than for constructive genius," he also lamented that the American people had "not made enough of leadership." Impressed with the flood of immigrants and the burgeoning diversity of the nation, Wilson thought legislation in the United States resulted from pulls "in a score of directions by a score of crossing influences and contending forces." Policy in the nation was thus "a vast conglomerate, . . . a heterogeneity," he warned, in danger of "*disintegration,* nothing less." "This vast and miscellaneous democracy," Wilson asserted, "must be led: its giant faculties must be schooled and directed." The necessary direction, however, could not come from the people at large, who could judge or give sanction but "cannot direct or suggest," nor could Congress, where "each man stands but for his part of the nation," achieve the requisite sense of "energy and organization." In fact, as many foreign observers all too familiar with forceful but arbitrary rulers enviously pointed out, the American system excelled in "the *restraints* . . . effected upon the action of government." Wilson granted the virtue in this but insisted as well that "government is action" and that even democracy itself was "useless" unless its power could be directed "to drive the wheels of policy and administration." He then asked, "What is the valuable element in *monarchy* which causes men constantly to turn to it as an ideal form of government, could it but be kept pure and wise?" The answer was "its *cohesion,* its readiness and power to act." Therefore, Wilson advised, the only way to make democracy good government was to put forth leaders "vested with abundant authority in the conception and execution of policy." Although Wilson had specifically in mind the legislative leadership model of parliamentary governments, it is also clear that he retained much of the ancient conception of the need for a leadership, above faction and section, in the national interest.

Twenty-three years later, after observing Theodore Roosevelt's presidency and perhaps imagining what he himself could do in the White House, Wilson called for a chief executive to be "the representative of no constituency, but of the whole people." When the president "speaks in his true character," Wilson added, "he speaks for no special interest. If he rightly interprets the national thought and boldly insists upon it, he is irresistible, and the country never feels the zest for action so much as when its President is of such insight and calibre. . . . His office is anything he has the sagacity and force to make it."[23] At about the same time Henry Jones Ford wrote that "in the presidential office . . . American democracy has revived the oldest political institution of the race, the elective kingship. It is all there; the precognition of the notables and the tumultuous choice of the freemen, only conformed to modern conditions."[24] Although Ford understandably linked this "tumultuous" democratic process to the post-Jackson presidency, he nonetheless revealed the enduring hold of the idea that somehow an elected executive faithful to the principle of consent might also possess the valid qualities of kingship—precisely the intention of Washington and even of Jefferson to a degree. In a book positively celebrating the presidential office as he saw it in 1955, Clinton Rossiter scorned those who sought to weaken it. "In a country over which industrialism has swept in great waves, in a world where active diplomacy is the minimum price of survival," Rossiter intoned, "it is not alone power but a vacuum of power that men must fear. . . . No government can exercise the supervision that ours does over the economy at home or honor the bargains that ours has made abroad unless it has a strong, unified, energetic executive to lead it." This kind of presidency, Rossiter concluded, "is one of our chief bulwarks against decline and chaos."[25]

Hamilton and John Quincy Adams would have agreed, but they would have also supposed that the achievement of such leadership required diminution or suppression, not the exaltation, of partisanship in the holder of the presidential office. Thus, the early presidents would have disagreed not with the perennial longing that the executive furnish strong guidance and direction, but with the supposition that such leadership is compatible with open, ceaseless partisanship, even in the Oval Office itself. The distinction arises from the revaluation of the uses of political parties largely accomplished in the Jacksonian era. The first six presidents would have emphasized the importance of a different perspective. Rather than continuing, openly and eagerly, to be the party leader in office (as all twentieth-century presidents with the partial exception of Eisenhower have done), a John Adams would expect the president, at least while acting under the seal of his office, as much as possible to seek to take advantage of the ancient potential to gather nationwide support behind a leadership above party. If it is clear, for example, that at least part of the skepticism, even cynicism, that now often greets presidential initiatives arises from the incessant emphasis on speech making, fund raising, organizing, and the president's function as leader of his party, then a Monroe would favor limiting that role to diminish its corrupting effect. Nonpartisanship cannot, perhaps should not, be complete, a Madison would readily concede, but he would also insist that it would make an important difference to try to deemphasize, to neutralize, partisanship, as he had put it in *The Federalist*, Number 10, rather than to celebrate it.

Thus, the first six presidents did not regard their antiparty, patriotic, positive conception of national leadership as elitist, arrogant, naive, or undemocratic, although their views have come to appear that way from a perspective that considers permanent, free, recognized opposition parties to be indispensable to the liberal democratic state. The early presidents' realism about "the causes of faction [being] sown in the nature of man" led them, in framing government, to restrain as much as possible the influence of faction and party spirit and to guard against any concentration of power that would make greed and ambition dangerous to liberty. At the same time, they believed that virtuous—that is, nonpartisan—leadership was vital to what Swift called the public good, and they were willing, indeed determined, to encourage such leadership even if it meant putting some restraint on direct self-government. In so acting, they did not think they were showing hostility to democracy; rather, they thought they were being wise and creative democrats. As Jefferson said so clearly and so often, the true test of self-government was whether it cultivated talent and virtue, and he had no doubt that good, active leadership, above party, would provide vital assistance in meeting that test. Such was the aspiration and the republican faith of the first six presidents of the United States.

Notes

Introduction

1. Jefferson to Francis Eppes, Jan. 19, 1821, in H. A. Washington, ed., *The Works of Thomas Jefferson* (New York, 1884 [orig. publ. Washington, D.C., 1853–1854]), VII, 197–198.
2. Jefferson to Adams, Dec. 28, 1796 (not sent), in Lester J. Cappon, ed., *The Adams-Jefferson Letters* (Chapel Hill, N.C., 1959), II, 262–263.
3. Jefferson to Henry Lee, May 8, 1825, in Washington, ed., *Works of Jefferson*, VII, 407.
4. "Charters," *National Gazette*, Jan. 19, 1792, in Gaillard Hunt, ed., *The Writings of James Madison* (New York, 1900–1910), VI, 83.
5. Bernard Bailyn, *The Origins of American Politics* (New York, 1968), 26–27.
6. John Locke, *Second Treatise on Civil Government* (1690), chap. 14, "Of Prerogative."
7. Edward S. Corwin, *The President, Office and Powers: History and Analysis of Practice and Opinion* (New York, 1940), 9–10.
8. Madison's notes, June 1, 1787, in Max Farrand, ed., *The Records of the Federal Convention of 1787*, rev. ed. (New Haven, Conn., 1937), I, 64–66.
9. Emmet John Hughes, *The Living Presidency: The Resources and Dilemmas of the American Presidential Office* (New York, 1973), 40.

10. Charles C. Thach, Jr., *The Creation of the Presidency, 1775–1789: A Study in Constitutional History* (Baltimore, 1969), 138–139.

Chapter 1

1. "The King's Reasons . . . ," Jan. 21, 1649, reprinted in Stuart E. Prall, ed., *The Puritan Revolution: A Documentary History* (Garden City, N.Y., 1968), 186–189.
2. Edward Hyde, earl of Clarendon, *The History of the Rebellion and Civil Wars in England* (1704), 6 vols. (Oxford, 1827), V, Bk. ix, 2404–2405, I, Bk. i, 51.
3. T. H. Breen, *The Character of the Good Ruler: A Study of Puritan Political Ideas in New England, 1630–1730* (New Haven, Conn., 1970), 8.
4. Speech in Parliament, 1609, quoted *ibid.*, 19.
5. L. C. Knights, *Public Voices: Literature and Politics with Special Reference to the Seventeenth Century* (London, 1972), 81.
6. William Perkins, "A Treatise of the Vocations or Callings of men, with sorts and kinds of them, and the right use thereof" (London, 1603), reprinted in Edmund S. Morgan, ed., *Puritan Political Ideas, 1558–1794* (Indianapolis, Ind., 1965), 36, 55–56.
7. I Cor. 12: 4–6, 12, 26–27; Rom. 13: 1–3.

8. "Epiekeia, or a Treatise of Christian Equity and Moderation" (London, 1604), reprinted in Morgan, ed., *Puritan Political Ideas*, 71.

9. Alexander Leighton, Richard Carpenter, Richard Sibbes, and Robert Bolton, all quoted in Breen, *Good Ruler*, 25, 23–24, 12, 9.

10. John Winthrop, letter of Aug. 14, 1642, in Robert Charles Winthrop, *Life and Letters of John Winthrop* . . . (Boston, 1867), II, 278–279.

11. "Christian Charitie. A Modell Hereof" (1630), reprinted in Morgan, ed., *Puritan Political Ideas*, 90.

12. Quoted in Sacvan Bercovitch, *The Puritan Origins of the American Self* (New Haven, Conn., 1975), 73.

13. Samuel Ward, 1620, and Richard Carpenter, 1623, quoted in Breen, *Good Ruler*, 24, 25.

14. Winthrop, "Speech" of May 1645, reprinted in Morgan, ed., *Puritan Political Ideas*, 137–140.

15. Leo F. Solt, "Puritanism, Capitalism, Democracy, and the New Science," *American Historical Review*, LXXIII (1967), 28.

16. "Nehemias Americanus, The Life of John Winthrop, Esq., Governor of the Massachusetts Colony," in *Magnalia Christi Americana* (1702), reprinted in Bercovitch, *Puritan Self*, 187–205.

17. Bercovitch, *Puritan Self*, 66.

18. Donald M. Scott, *From Office to Profession: The New England Ministry, 1750–1850* (Philadelphia, 1978), 148–150.

19. John Dryden, "The Medal" (1682), lines 86–87, in George R. Noyes, ed., *The Poetical Works of Dryden*, rev. ed. (Boston, 1950), 129.

20. L. I. Bredvold, *The Intellectual Milieu of John Dryden* (Ann Arbor, Mich., 1956), 145.

21. Dryden, *Absalom and Achitophel* (1681), lines 779–954 *passim*, in Noyes, ed., *Poetical Works*, 119–121.

22. Abigail Adams to John Adams, July 16, 1775, in L. H. Butterfield *et al.*, eds., *Adams Family Correspondence* (Cambridge, Mass., 1963), I, 246, quoting Dryden's *Don Sebastian*, Act II, sc. i, lines 387–390, speaking of Almeyda, a female character, so the pronouns are feminine in the original.

23. Dryden, "Prologue to the King and Queen at the Opening of Their Theater" (1683), lines 1–3, 13–15, in Noyes, ed., *Poetical Works*, 153.

24. J. H. Plumb, *The Growth of Political Stability in England, 1675–1725* (London, 1967).

25. [Daniel Defoe], *The True-Born Englishman: A Satyr* (London, 1701), Pt. I and Conclusion.

26. Joyce Appleby, "The Social Origins of American Revolutionary Ideology," *Journal of American History*, LXIV (1978), 939.

27. Quoted *ibid.*, 941.

28. Joseph Lee, 1656, quoted in J.A.W. Gunn, *Politics and the Public Interest in the Seventeenth Century* (London, 1969), 221.

29. All quoted in Appleby, "Social Origins," *JAH*, LXIV (1978), 943, 944, 942.

30. Quoted in J. E. Crowley, *This Sheba, Self: The Conceptualization of Economic Life in Eighteenth-Century America* (Baltimore, 1974), 46–47.

31. Aegrement Ratcliffe, 1578, quoted in Gunn, *Politics and the Public Interest*, 207.

32. Richard Baxter quoted in Bercovitch, *Puritan Self*, 17.
33. Dryden, "The Medal," lines 167–174, 191–198, in Noyes, ed., *Poetical Works*, 130.
34. Quoted in Lance Banning, *The Jeffersonian Persuasion: Evolution of a Party Ideology* (Ithaca, N.Y., 1978), 66, 65.
35. *Ibid.*, 66, summarizing Davenant.
36. Quoted in Crowley, *This Sheba, Self*, 45.
37. Thomas Paine, *The Rights of Man* (1792), Pt. II, reprinted in Moncure Daniel Conway, ed., *The Writings of Thomas Paine* (New York, 1967 [orig. publ. 1894–1896]), II, 406, 408.
38. Jacob Viner, *The Role of Providence in the Social Order: An Essay in Intellectual History* (Philadelphia, 1972), 60.
39. C. B. Macpherson, *The Political Theory of Possessive Individualism: Hobbes to Locke* (Oxford, 1962), 3.
40. Norman Fiering, *Jonathan Edwards's Moral Thought and Its British Context* (Chapel Hill, N.C., 1981), 167–168.
41. Alasdair MacIntyre, *After Virtue: A Study in Moral Theory* (Notre Dame, Ind., 1981), esp. 56–59, 128–129.

Chapter 2

1. Jeffrey Hart, *Viscount Bolingbroke: Tory Humanist* (London, 1965); Isaac Kramnick, *Bolingbroke and His Circle: The Politics of Nostalgia in the Age of Walpole* (Cambridge, Mass., 1968); H. T. Dickinson, *Bolingbroke* (London, 1970); Maynard Mack, *The Garden and the City: Retirement and Politics in the Later Poetry of Pope, 1731–1743* (Toronto, 1969); and F. P. Lock, *The Politics of Gulliver's Travels* (Oxford, 1980), all emphasize the political-cultural ideology of this literary circle.
2. Agnes Marie Sibley, *Alexander Pope's Prestige in America, 1725–1835* (New York, 1949), 138–143, lists the American imprints, and David Lundberg and Henry F. May, "The Enlightened Reader in America," *American Quarterly*, XXVIII (1976), 262–293, lists the library holdings in America of many European authors (although, unaccountably, not Swift).
3. *South Carolina Gazette*, June 17, 1745, and *Essay on Man*, quoted in Sibley, *Pope's Prestige*, 114, 25.
4. *New American Magazine*, Apr. 1759, and *Massachusetts Spy*, Apr. 11, 1771, quoted *ibid.*, 86–87.
5. Bertrand A. Goldgar, *Walpole and the Wits: The Relation of Politics to Literature, 1722–1742* (Lincoln, Nebr., 1976), 3.
6. J.G.A. Pocock, "Civic Humanism and Its Role in Anglo-American Thought," in Pocock, *Politics, Language and Time: Essays on Political Thought and History* (New York, 1971), 89, 93.
7. "Reflections on the State of the Nation" (1749), in *The Works of Lord Bolingbroke* (Philadelphia, 1841), II, 458–459, emphasis added.
8. James Wilson, "Lectures on Law," Philadelphia, 1790–1791, in Robert Green McCloskey, ed., *The Works of James Wilson* (Cambridge, Mass., 1967), II, 577, I, 238, 406–407; Geoffrey Seed, *James Wilson* (Millwood, N.Y., 1978), 19, 23.
9. Bernard Mandeville, *The Fable of*

the Bees: or, Private Vices, Publick
Benefits (1714, 6th ed. 1732), ed.
F. B. Kaye (Oxford, 1924), I, 24,
36.

10. Thomas A. Horne, *The Social
Thought of Bernard Mandeville:
Virtue and Commerce in Early
Eighteenth-Century England* (New
York, 1978), 19–31, Bayle quota-
tions on pp. 30–31; Petty quoted
in J. E. Crowley, *This Sheba, Self:
The Conceptualization of Economic
Life in Eighteenth-Century America*
(Baltimore, 1974), 36.

11. Mandeville, *Fable of the Bees*, II,
144, I, 184–185.

12. *British Journal*, May 31, 1729,
quoted in Goldgar, *Walpole and
the Wits*, 64; Louis Dumont, *From
Mandeville to Marx: The Genesis
and Triumph of Economic Ideology*
(Chicago, 1977), 54–55; J. H.
Plumb, *England in the Eighteenth
Century* (London, 1950), 9, quoting Walpole.

13. Defoe, *The Compleat English
Tradesman* (London, 1725–
1727), I, 368–369; other Defoe
quotations from Kramnick,
Bolingbroke and His Circle, 198,
194–195.

14. Quoted in John Robert Moore,
*Daniel Defoe: Citizen of the Modern
World* (Chicago, 1958), 312.

15. [Daniel Defoe], *A Plan of the English Commerce* (London, 1728),
68.

16. Bolingbroke, "Remarks on the
History of England," Letter V, in
Works of Bolingbroke, I, 321–324.

17. *London Review*, V (1709), 574,
IX (1713), 176, quoted in Moore,
Daniel Defoe, 306; Defoe, *English
Commerce*, 121.

18. Bolingbroke, "Remarks . . . ," Letter IX, in *Works of Bolingbroke*, I,

341–346; Defoe, *English Commerce*, 123–131.

19. James Spedding *et al.*, eds., *The
Works of Francis Bacon*, XI (Boston,
1860), esp. 43, 333–336, 354–
365; Bolingbroke, "Remarks
. . . ," Letter IX, in *Works of
Bolingbroke*, I, 345.

20. Richard Foster Jones, *Ancients and
Moderns: A Study of the Background
of the "Battle of the Books"* (St.
Louis, Mo., 1936); John Mid-
dleton Murry, *Jonathan Swift: A
Critical Biography* (New York,
1955), 72–76; Ricardo Quintana,
*Two Augustans: John Locke, Jona-
than Swift* (Madison, Wis., 1978),
12–18, 71–82, 124–132; and
especially Joseph M. Levine,
*Dr. Woodward's Shield: History, Sci-
ence, and Satire in Augustan England* (Berkeley, Calif., 1977),
19–21, 125–127, 208–209.

21. Joseph M. Levine, "Ancients and
Moderns Reconsidered," in *Studies
in Eighteenth-Century Culture*, X
(1981), 72–89.

22. Samuel P. Huntington, "Political
Modernization: America vs.
Europe," *World Politics*, XVIII
(1966), 383.

23. John Morley, *Walpole* (London,
1909 [orig. publ. 1877]), 183.

24. No. 9, "On the Government," and
No. 10, "On Commerce," in *Philosophical Letters* (1733), The Library of Liberal Arts edition
(Indianapolis, Ind., 1961), 37–
38, 39–40.

25. Mack, *Garden and the City*,
225–227; internal quote from
J. H. Plumb, *The First Four
Georges* (London, 1956), 75.

26. Pope, "The First Epistle of the
First Book of Horace" (1738),
lines 97–104, 107–109, in Wil-

liam K. Wimsatt, ed., *Alexander Pope: Selected Poetry and Prose*, 2d ed. (New York, 1972), 313.

27. A 1733 poem quoted in Mack, *Garden and the City*, 192.

28. William Thomas Laprade, *Public Opinion and Politics in Eighteenth Century England, to the Fall of Walpole* (New York, 1936), 100.

29. *Examiner*, Dec. 28, 1710, quoted in Moore, *Daniel Defoe*, 307; Pat Rogers, "Swift and Bolingbroke on Faction," *Journal of British Studies*, IX (May 1970), 99; Richard I. Cook, *Jonathan Swift as a Tory Pamphleteer* (Seattle, Wash., 1967), 126–131, explaining Swift's *History of the Four Last Years of the Queen* (first published in 1758).

30. "Epilogue to the Satires," Dialogue I, lines 145–172, in Wimsatt, ed., *Pope*, 364. James Osborn, "Pope, the Byzantine Empress, and Walpole's Whore," in Maynard Mack, ed., *Essential Articles for the Study of Alexander Pope* (Hamden, Conn., 1964), 539–552, establishes the connection with Molly Skerrett.

31. *Dunciad*, Bk. I, line 6, in Wimsatt, ed., *Pope*, 444; Aubrey L. Williams, *Pope's "Dunciad": A Study of Its Meaning* (London, 1955), 31, 11.

32. *Dunciad*, Bk. IV, lines 453–458, 477–486, in Wimsatt, ed., *Pope*, 507, 508.

33. *Gulliver's Travels* (1726), Washington Square Press edition (New York, 1960), Pt. II, chap. vi, 117–125.

34. Lock, *Politics of Gulliver's Travels*, 60, 62.

35. *Gulliver's Travels*, Pt. II, chap. vii, 128–129.

36. *Ibid.*, Pt. IV, chap. vi, chap. xii, 256, 295, 297.

37. Goldgar, *Walpole and the Wits*, 49–63.

38. Tobias Smollett, quoted in John Brewer, *Party Ideology and Popular Politics at the Accession of George III* (Cambridge, 1976), 3; John Sekora, *Luxury: The Concept in Western Thought, Eden to Smollett* (Baltimore, 1977), 207–211.

39. Gay, *The Beggar's Opera* (London, 1728), Act I, sc. iii, Act II, sc. x; William Eben Schultz, *Gay's Beggar's Opera: Its Content, History and Influence* (New Haven, Conn., 1923), 108–112, 362–363; Donald Jackson, ed., *The Diaries of George Washington*, II (Charlottesville, Va., 1976), 247–248; Bernard Mayo, *Jefferson Himself: The Personal Narrative of a Many-Sided American* (Charlottesville, Va., 1970), 3.

40. *Common Sense*, Oct. 8, 1737, quoted in Goldgar, *Walpole and the Wits*, 9.

41. *Daily Courant*, Mar. 23, 1731, and Swift, 1730, both quoted *ibid.*, 18, 68.

42. Charles Francis Adams, ed., *The Works of John Adams, Second President of the United States* (Boston, 1865), IV, 382–389; Rush to David Ramsay, Nov. 5, 1778, in L. H. Butterfield, ed., *Letters of Benjamin Rush* (Princeton, N.J., 1951), I, 219. Chaps. 4, 9, and 10, below, further explain Hume's influence among the early American leaders.

43. Franklin to William Strahan, Feb. 12, 1745, in Leonard W. Labaree *et al.*, eds., *The Papers of Benjamin Franklin* (New Haven, Conn., 1959–), III, 13.

44. John F. Ross, *Swift and Defoe: A Study in Relationship* (Berkeley, Calif., 1941), 132.

Chapter 3

1. Frederic M. Litto, "Addison's *Cato* in the Colonies," *William and Mary Quarterly*, 3d Ser., XXIII (1966), 431–449.
2. Joseph Addison, *Cato* (1713), Act I, sc. iv, lines 30–36.
3. Quoted in Edward A. Bloom and Lillian D. Bloom, *Joseph Addison's Sociable Animal: In the Market Place, on the Hustings, in the Pulpit* (Providence, R.I., 1971), 17.
4. *Ibid.*, 25.
5. Madison to Richard D. Cutts, Jan. 4, 1829, in Ralph Ketcham, *James Madison* (New York, 1971), 41.
6. Trenchard quotations from Isaac Kramnick, *Bolingbroke and His Circle: The Politics of Nostalgia in the Age of Walpole* (Cambridge, Mass., 1968), 244–245; Swift to Pope, Jan. 10, 1721, in George Sherburn, ed., *The Correspondence of Alexander Pope* (Oxford, 1956), II, 70.
7. "Cato's Letters," No. 20, *London Journal*, Mar. 11, 1720, in [John Trenchard], *Cato's Letters; or, Essays on Liberty, Civil and Religious, and Other Important Subjects*, 3d ed. (1733), reprint ed. (New York, 1969), I, 140–141.
8. *Craftsman*, Aug. 21, 1731, quoted in Kramnick, *Bolingbroke and His Circle*, 248; Quentin Skinner, "The Principles and Practice of Opposition: The Case of Bolingbroke versus Walpole," in Neil McKendrick, ed., *Historical Perspectives: Studies in English Thought and Society in Honour of J. H.*

Plumb (London, 1974), 96–101; Bernard Bailyn, *The Origins of American Politics* (New York, 1968), 38–39, 53.
9. *Cato's Letters*, Nos. 90 and 91, 3d ed., III, 199–213.
10. Bolingbroke, "A Dissertation upon Parties," Letter XIX, in *The Works of Lord Bolingbroke* (Philadelphia, 1841), II, 160–171; Lance Banning, *The Jeffersonian Persuasion: Evolution of a Party Ideology* (Ithaca, N.Y., 1978), 66–68.
11. E. Millicent Sowerby, comp., *Catalogue of the Library of Thomas Jefferson* (Washington, D.C., 1952–1959), III, 132–133.
12. Voltaire to Thieriot, Dec. 4, 1722, quoted in Sheila Biddle, *Bolingbroke and Harley* (New York, 1974), 81–82.
13. *Daily Courant*, Dec. 26, 1733, quoted in William Thomas Laprade, *Public Opinion and Politics in Eighteenth Century England, to the Fall of Walpole* (New York, 1936), 351–352; *Corncutter's Journal*, Dec. 31, 1734, quoted in Pope's *Essay on Man*, ed. Maynard Mack (London, 1950), xvii, n. 5; Jonathan Swift, *The Journal to Stella, A.D. 1710–1713*, ed. Frederick Ryland (London, 1908), II, 287 (Nov. 25, 1711).
14. Swift to Pope, June 1, 1728, Pope to Swift, June 28, 1728, and Bolingbroke and Pope to Swift, Feb. 1728, in Sherburn, ed., *Correspondence of Pope*, II, 497, 503, 472; Pope, "The First Satire of the Second Book of Horace" (1733), lines 127–128, in William K. Wimsatt, ed., *Alexander Pope: Selected Poetry and Prose*, 2d ed. (New York, 1972), 303.
15. Benjamin Rush to Arthur Lee, May 4, 1774, in L. H. Butterfield,

ed., *Letters of Benjamin Rush* (Princeton, N.J., 1951), I, 85.

16. Laprade, *Public Opinion*, 303–364; Archibald S. Foord, *His Majesty's Opposition, 1714–1830* (Oxford, 1964), 168.

17. H. Trevor Colbourn, *The Lamp of Experience: Whig History and the Intellectual Origins of the American Revolution* (Chapel Hill, N.C., 1965), library and booksellers' lists, 200–231; L. H. Butterfield et al., eds., *Diary and Autobiography of John Adams* (Cambridge, Mass., 1961), I, 253 (Jan. 24, 1765).

18. Letter IX, *Works of Bolingbroke*, I, 344; Isaac Kramnick, ed., *Lord Bolingbroke, Historical Writings* (Chicago, 1972), Introduction, xviii–xxviii.

19. *Works of Bolingbroke*, II, 165–166, 243–245.

20. *Idea of a Patriot King;* page citations hereafter are from its reprinting in Jeffrey Hart, ed., *Political Writers of Eighteenth-Century England* (New York, 1964), 195–257, quote on 228.

21. *Craftsman*, Feb. 24, 1728, quoted in Bertrand A. Goldgar, *Walpole and the Wits: The Relation of Politics to Literature, 1722–1742* (Lincoln, Nebr., 1976), 57.

22. *Idea of a Patriot King*, 216–217, 236.

23. *Ibid.*, 196–198.

24. Jeffrey Hart, *Viscount Bolingbroke: Tory Humanist* (London, 1965), 85–87.

25. *Idea of a Patriot King*, 213.

26. Hart, *Bolingbroke*, 2–11.

27. *Idea of a Patriot King*, 209.

28. *Ibid.*, 221–222.

29. *Ibid.*, 208–209.

30. *Ibid.*, 246–253.

31. *Ibid.*, 223–224, 227–228.

32. Antony Netboy, "Voltaire's English Years (1726–1728)," *Virginia Quarterly Review*, LIII (1977), 350.

33. Franklin to Ferdinand Grand, Oct. 22, 1787, in Albert Henry Smyth, ed., *The Writings of Benjamin Franklin* (New York, 1907), IX, 619; Molière, *Tartuffe* (1669), trans. Richard Wilbur (London, 1964), Act V, sc. vii. Molière's plays and characters, furthermore, were well known and exerted a strong influence in Restoration and Augustan literary circles. *Tartuffe*, for example, was offered for the London stage in three different English adaptations in the century following its performance in France: first in 1670 by Matthew Medbourne, using the subtitle "The French Puritan" and ridiculing English Puritans; then in 1717 by Colley Cibber under the title *The Non-juror* and implanting an anti-Catholic bias; and finally in 1768 by "Isaac Bickerstaffe" using Molière's own subtitle, *A Hypocrite*. John Wilcox, *The Relation of Molière to Restoration Comedy* (New York, 1938), 59–64; *Some Account of the English Stage from the Restoration in 1660 to 1830* (Bath, 1832), II, 615–616, V, 218–219.

34. *Idea of a Patriot King*, 237–240.

35. *Ibid.*, 257.

36. *Examiner*, No. 44, June 7, 1711, in Herbert Davis, ed., *The Prose Works of Jonathan Swift* (Oxford, 1939–), III, 168.

Chapter 4

1. Franklin to Joseph Galloway, Feb. 17, 1758, in Leonard W. Labaree

et al., eds., *The Papers of Benjamin Franklin* (New Haven, Conn., 1959–), VII, 375; Sheffield ms., Rockingham Papers, quoted in John Brewer, *Party Ideology and Popular Politics at the Accession of George III* (Cambridge, 1976), 97.

2. Alison Gilbert Olson, *Anglo-American Politics, 1660–1775: The Relationship between Parties in England and Colonial America* (New York, 1973), 174.

3. Horace Walpole to H. Mann, Oct. 10, 1761, in W. S. Lewis, ed., *Horace Walpole's Correspondence* (New Haven, Conn., 1937–), XXI, 541.

4. Franklin to John Whitehurst, June 27, 1763, and to William Strahan, Dec. 19, 1763, in Labaree et al., eds., *Franklin Papers*, X, 407, 302–303, 329, 407–408. *Regis ad exemplar totus componitur orbis* is the Latin proverb Franklin doubtless had in mind.

5. L. H. Butterfield et al., eds., *Diary and Autobiography of John Adams* (Cambridge, Mass., 1961), I, 200–201 (Feb. 9, 1761); documents of 1762 and 1763 quoted in Brewer, *Party Ideology*, 47.

6. Connecticut Sons of Liberty to Portsmouth, N. H., Sons, Mar. 3, 1766, in Pauline Maier, *From Resistance to Revolution: Colonial Radicals and the Development of American Opposition to Britain, 1765–1776* (New York, 1972), 104, 105; William D. Liddle, "'A Patriot King, or None': Lord Bolingbroke and the American Renunciation of George III," *Journal of American History*, LXV (1979), 959.

7. See chap. 10, below.

8. "Summary View of the Rights of British America" (1774), in Julian P. Boyd et al., eds., *The Papers of Thomas Jefferson* (Princeton, N.J., 1948–), I, 121, 134.

9. Wilson, speech, Philadelphia, Jan. 1775, in Robert Green McCloskey, ed., *The Works of James Wilson* (Cambridge, Mass., 1967), II, 753–757; Lord North, quoted in Gerald Stourzh, *Benjamin Franklin and American Foreign Policy* (Chicago, 1954), 28; Washington to George William Fairfax, May 31, 1775, and toast of Aug. 14, 1775, in the *Providence Gazette* (R.I.), Aug. 19, 1775, both quoted in Liddle, "American Renunciation of George III," *JAH*, LXV (1979), 965, 970.

10. Abigail Adams to John Adams, July 21, 1776, in L. H. Butterfield et al., eds., *Adams Family Correspondence* (Cambridge, Mass., 1963), II, 56–57.

11. Stephen Saunders Webb, "'Brave Men and Servants to His Royal Highness': The Household of James Stuart in the Evolution of English Imperialism," *Perspectives in American History*, VIII (1974), 55–80; and Webb, "Army and Empire: English Garrison Government in Britain and America, 1569 to 1763," *William and Mary Quarterly*, 3d Ser., XXXIV (1977), 30.

12. Stephen Saunders Webb, *The Governors-General: The English Army and the Definition of the Empire, 1569–1681* (Chapel Hill, N.C., 1979), 451.

13. Jack P. Greene, *The Quest for Power: The Lower Houses of Assembly in the Southern Royal Colonies, 1689–1776* (Chapel Hill, N.C., 1963), 4, 18.

14. Robert Douthat Meade, *Patrick Henry, Practical Revolutionary* (Philadelphia, 1969), 139.
15. Webb, *Governors-General*, 465.
16. Jefferson, "Autobiography," Jan. 6, 1821, in Paul Leicester Ford, ed., *The Writings of Thomas Jefferson* (New York, 1892–1899), I, 112; Ralph Ketcham, *From Colony to Country: The Revolution in American Thought, 1750–1820* (New York, 1974), 15–75, describes the "Revolution in Loyalty."
17. Gordon S. Wood, *The Creation of the American Republic, 1776–1787* (Chapel Hill, N.C., 1969).
18. Peter Karsten, *Patriot-Heroes in England and America: Political Symbolism and Changing Values over Three Centuries* (Madison, Wis., 1978), 57–63; Butterfield *et al.*, eds., *Diary of John Adams*, III, 330; Samuel West, quoted in Wood, *Creation of American Republic*, 120.
19. John Murrin, "The Great Inversion, or Court vs. Country: A Comparison of the Revolution Settlements in England (1688–1721) and America (1776–1816)," in J.G.A. Pocock, ed., *Three British Revolutions: 1641, 1688, 1776* (Princeton, N.J., 1980), 368–453.
20. Herbert J. Storing, *What the Anti-Federalists Were For* (Chicago, 1981), 16.
21. *The Objections of the Hon. George Mason, to the Proposed Federal Constitution* (Oct. 1787); "Letters from the Federal Farmer," No. II, Oct. 9, 1787; Melancton Smith, speech at the New York Ratifying Convention, June 1788; and "John De Witt," "To the Free Citizens of the Commonwealth of Massachusetts," Nov. 5, 1787, all reprinted in Cecelia M. Kenyon, ed., *The Antifederalists* (Indianapolis, Ind., 1966), 192, 214, 384, 104–105.
22. Charles Turner, quoted in Storing, *Anti-Federalists*, 23.
23. Ketcham, *Colony to Country*, 127–135.
24. Samuel Adams to Samuel Savage, Oct. 6, 1778, in Harry Alonzo Cushing, ed., *The Writings of Samuel Adams* (New York, 1904–1908), IV, 286; and Samuel Adams to John Adams, Oct. 4 and Nov. 20, 1790, in William V. Wells, ed., *The Life and Public Services of Samuel Adams*, 2d ed. (Boston, 1888), III, 297–314.
25. Massachusetts Constitution of 1780, in Francis Newton Thorpe, ed., *The Federal and State Constitutions . . .* (Washington, D.C., 1909), III, 1888–1911.
26. Adams to Elbridge Gerry, Nov. 4, 1779, quoted in Willi Paul Adams, *The First American Constitutions: Republican Ideology and the Making of the State Constitutions in the Revolutionary Era*, trans. Rita and Robert Kimber (Chapel Hill, N.C., 1980), 273.
27. Pennsylvania Constitution of 1776, in Thorpe, ed., *Federal and State Constitutions*, V, 3090–3091.
28. John Adams to Samuel Adams, Oct. 18, 1790, in Wells, ed., *Life of Samuel Adams*, III, 302; *The Federalist*, No. 51.
29. Quoted in John Zvesper, *Political Philosophy and Rhetoric: A Study of the Origins of American Party Politics* (Cambridge, 1977), 35.
30. Chap. 6, below, explains Madison's views, during and after the

Convention of 1787, on these points.

31. William Symmes, speech in the Massachusetts Ratifying Convention, Jan. 27, 1788, quoted in Storing, *Anti-Federalists*, 49.
32. Kenyon, ed., *Anti-Federalists*, lxxxi–lxxxii.
33. "Letters from The Federal Farmer," No. XIV, reprinted in Herbert J. Storing, ed., *The Complete Anti-Federalist* (Chicago, 1981), II, 310.
34. Douglass Adair, "'That Politics May Be Reduced to a Science': David Hume, James Madison, and the Tenth Federalist," in Trevor Colbourn, ed., *Fame and the Founding Fathers: Essays by Douglass Adair* (New York, 1974), 93–106.
35. David Hume, "That Politics May Be Reduced to a Science" (1742), reprinted in Hume, *Political Essays*, ed. Charles W. Hendel (Indianapolis, Ind., 1953), 12–13.
36. Wilson, speech, June 1, 1787 (King's notes), in Max Farrand, ed., *The Records of the Federal Convention of 1787*, rev. ed. (New Haven, Conn., 1937), I, 70–71.

Chapter 5

1. Samuel Eliot Morison, *The Young Man Washington* (Cambridge, Mass., 1932), 19–21, 41; Douglass Adair, "A Note on Certain of Hamilton's Pseudonyms," in Trevor Colbourn, ed., *Fame and the Founding Fathers: Essays by Douglass Adair* (New York, 1974), 284n.
2. Washington to William Gordon, July 8, 1783, Farewell Orders to the Army, Nov. 2, 1783, to John Jay, Aug. 1, 1786, and to James Madison, Mar. 31, 1787, in John C. Fitzpatrick, ed., *The Writings of George Washington from the Original Manuscript Sources, 1745–1799* (Washington, D.C., 1931–1944), XXVII, 49, 226, XXVIII, 503, XXIX, 190; Harold W. Bradley, "The Political Thinking of George Washington," *Journal of Southern History*, XI (1945), 469–486.
3. From a discarded draft of Washington's first inaugural address, 1788, in Fitzpatrick, ed., *Writings of Washington*, XXX, 299.
4. Henry Cabot Lodge, *George Washington* (Boston, 1889), I, 109; discarded address, 1788, in Fitzpatrick, ed., *Writings of Washington*, XXX, 307.
5. Message of Dec. 10, 1796, in James D. Richardson, ed., *A Compilation of the Messages and Papers of the Presidents 1789–1897* (Washington, D.C., 1897), I, 203.
6. Discarded address, in Fitzpatrick, ed., *Writings of Washington*, XXX, 306–307; Franklin to David Hartley, Dec. 4, 1789, in Albert Henry Smyth, ed., *The Writings of Benjamin Franklin* (New York, 1907), X, 72; Washington to Lafayette, Jan. 29, 1789, in Fitzpatrick, ed., *Writings of Washington*, XXX, 185–186.
7. Ralph Ketcham, *James Madison* (New York, 1971), 285.
8. Chap. 10, below, explains Washington's effort to mediate between his cabinet members.
9. "Farewell Address," Sept. 17, 1796, in Richardson, ed., *Messages of the Presidents*, I, 205–216.
10. Felix Gilbert, *The Beginnings of*

American Foreign Policy to the Farewell Address (New York, 1965), 135–136.

11. Inaugural address, Mar. 4, 1797, in Richardson, ed., *Messages of the Presidents*, I, 221; John Adams to Abigail Adams, Mar. 17, 1797, in James Bishop Peabody, ed., *John Adams: A Biography in His Own Words* (New York, 1973), 359.

12. L. H. Butterfield *et al.*, eds., *Diary and Autobiography of John Adams* (Cambridge, Mass., 1961), I, 210 (Apr. 3, 1761); Adams to Jefferson, Dec. 25, 1813, in Lester J. Cappon, ed., *The Adams-Jefferson Letters* (Chapel Hill, N.C., 1959), II, 410; quotations from Adams's marginalia on his own copy of Bolingbroke's *Political Works*, printed in Zoltán Haraszti, *John Adams and the Prophets of Progress* (Cambridge, Mass., 1952), 49–64.

13. Haraszti, *John Adams*, 49–64; "Governor Winthrop to Governor Bradford," *Boston Gazette*, Feb. 16, 1767, in Robert J. Taylor *et al.*, eds., *Papers of John Adams* (Cambridge, Mass., 1977–), I, 204; Haraszti, *John Adams*, 62.

14. Adams to William Tudor, June 28, 1789, in James H. Hutson, "John Adams' Title Campaign," *New England Quarterly*, XLI (1968), 36–37.

15. Joyce Appleby, "The New Republican Synthesis and the Changing Political Ideas of John Adams," *American Quarterly*, XXV (1973), 584–586; John R. Howe, Jr., *The Changing Political Thought of John Adams* (Princeton, N.J., 1966); and Edward Handler, *America and Europe in the Political Thought of John Adams* (Cambridge, Mass.,

1964), further analyze Adams's political thought.

16. Charles Francis Adams, ed., *The Works of John Adams, Second President of the United States* (Boston, 1865), V, 473.

17. "Address of the Minority of the Virginia Legislature . . . ," [Dec. 1798], reprinted in John P. Roche, ed., *John Marshall: Major Opinions and Other Writings* (Indianapolis, Ind., 1967), 43, although Marshall's authorship of the address is uncertain.

18. Adams to James McHenry, July 29, 1799, in C. Adams, ed., *Works of John Adams*, IX, 4–5.

19. Adams to William Tudor, Aug. 4, 1774, in Taylor *et al.*, eds., *Adams Papers*, II, 127; Peter Shaw, *The Character of John Adams* (Chapel Hill, N.C., 1976), 35.

20. Adams made the comment in 1808; Haraszti, *John Adams*, 64.

21. All terms used in Shaw, *Character of Adams*, 247.

22. Page Smith, *John Adams* (Garden City, N.Y., 1962), II, 952–1017; Stephen G. Kurtz, *The Presidency of John Adams: The Collapse of Federalism, 1795–1800* (Philadelphia, 1957), *passim*.

Chapter 6

1. Gilbert Chinard, ed., *The Literary Bible of Thomas Jefferson: His Commonplace Book of Philosophers and Poets* (Baltimore, 1928), 20, 34; E. Millicent Sowerby, comp., *Catalogue of the Library of Thomas Jefferson* (Washington, D.C., 1952–1959), III, 130–132, 139–140; Jefferson to Francis Eppes, Jan. 19, 1821, in H. A.

Washington, ed., *The Works of Thomas Jefferson* (New York, 1884 [orig. publ. Washington, D.C., 1853–1854]), VII, 198.

2. Jefferson to Peter Carr, Aug. 10, 1787, in Julian P. Boyd *et al.*, eds., *The Papers of Thomas Jefferson* (Princeton, N.J., 1948–), XII, 15; Merrill D. Peterson, *Thomas Jefferson and the New Nation* (New York, 1970), 55; Elizabeth Flower and Murray G. Murphey, *A History of Philosophy in America* (New York, 1977), I, 224–226; Thomas A. Horne, *The Social Thought of Bernard Mandeville: Virtue and Commerce in Early Eighteenth-Century England* (New York, 1978), 86–89.

3. To Robert Skipwith, Aug. 3, 1771, and to Peter Carr, Aug. 19, 1785, in Boyd *et al.*, eds., *Jefferson Papers*, I, 76–80, VIII, 407; Garry Wills, *Inventing America: Jefferson's Declaration of Independence* (Garden City, N.Y., 1978), 181–239.

4. Jefferson, *Notes on the State of Virginia* (1782), intro. by Thomas Perkins Abernethy (New York, 1964), 198; Jefferson to Adams, Nov. 13, 1787, and Adams to Jefferson, Dec. 6, 1787, in Lester J. Cappon, ed., *The Adams-Jefferson Letters* (Chapel Hill, N.C., 1959), I, 212–214; Adams's inaugural address, Mar. 4, 1797, in James D. Richardson, ed., *A Compilation of the Messages and Papers of the Presidents 1789–1897* (Washington, D.C., 1897), I, 219; Jefferson to David Humphrey, Mar. 18, 1789, in Boyd *et al.*, eds., *Jefferson Papers*, XIV, 678.

5. Hamilton to James A. Bayard, Jan. 16, 1801, in Harold C. Syrett *et al.*, eds., *The Papers of Alexander Hamilton* (New York, 1961–),

XXV, 319–324; Jefferson's "Anas," written Feb. 4, 1818, in Adrienne Koch and William Peden, eds., *The Life and Selected Writings of Thomas Jefferson* (New York, 1944), 121–122.

6. Jefferson, "Anas," 1818, and to Mazzei, Apr. 24, 1796, in Koch and Peden, eds., *Writings of Jefferson*, 126, 537.

7. Philadelphia, 1794; Evans, *Early American Imprints*, No. 27782 (microcard reproduction).

8. John Taylor, *A Definition on Parties . . .* (Philadelphia, 1794), *ibid.*, No. 26861.

9. *Ibid.*, p. 2. See below, chap. 10, for more on attitudes toward political parties in the 1790s.

10. Daniel Sisson, *The American Revolution of 1800* (New York, 1974), 68.

11. To Elbridge Gerry, Jan. 26, 1799, in Koch and Peden, eds., *Writings of Jefferson*, 545.

12. Jefferson to Spencer Roane, Sept. 6, 1819, in Washington, ed., *Works of Jefferson*, VII, 133.

13. Jefferson to Du Pont de Nemours, Jan. 18, 1802, in Dumas Malone, ed., *Correspondence between Thomas Jefferson and Pierre Samuel du Pont de Nemours, 1798–1817*, trans. Linwood Lehman (Boston, 1930), 38–41.

14. Jefferson to William B. Giles, Mar. 23, 1801, in Paul Leicester Ford, ed., *The Writings of Thomas Jefferson* (New York, 1892–1899), VIII, 26; inaugural address, Mar. 4, 1801, in Koch and Peden, eds., *Writings of Jefferson*, 325; Jefferson to Garland Jefferson, Jan. 25, 1810, in Ford, ed., *Writings of Jefferson*, IX, 270.

15. Robert M. Johnstone, *Jefferson and the Presidency: Leadership in the*

Young Republic (Ithaca, N.Y., 1978), 54; Berlin quoted on p. 41.

16. Forrest McDonald, *The Presidency of Thomas Jefferson* (Lawrence, Kans., 1976), and Rodger D. Parker, "The Gospel of Opposition: A Study in Eighteenth-Century Anglo-American Ideology" (Ph.D. diss., Wayne State University, 1975), emphasize the "oppositionist" quality of both Bolingbroke and what Jefferson used of his thought.

17. Jeffrey Hart, *Viscount Bolingbroke: Tory Humanist* (London, 1965), ix.

18. Hamilton writing as "Pericles," *New-York Evening Post*, Feb. 8, 1803, in Syrett *et al.*, eds., *Hamilton Papers*, XXVI, 83; Gallatin to Jefferson, July 29 and Aug. 9, 1808, and Gallatin to Madison, Sept. 9, 1808, in Henry Adams, ed., *The Writings of Albert Gallatin* (Philadelphia, 1879), I, 396–412; Raymond Walters, Jr., *Albert Gallatin: Jeffersonian Financier and Diplomat* (New York, 1957), 202–203.

19. Jefferson, message to Congress, Dec. 2, 1806, in Richardson, ed., *Messages of the Presidents*, I, 409; Benjamin Rush to Richard Price, May 25, 1786, in L. H. Butterfield, ed., *Letters of Benjamin Rush* (Princeton, N.J., 1951), I, 388–389.

20. Harvey C. Mansfield, Jr., *Statesmanship and Party Government: A Study of Burke and Bolingbroke* (Chicago, 1965), 75–80.

21. Jefferson to William Duane, Mar. 22, 1806, and to Barnabas Bidwell, July 5, 1806, quoted in Noble E. Cunningham, Jr., *The Process of Government under Jefferson* (Princeton, N.J., 1978), 193, 189.

22. Jefferson to John Breckinridge, Nov. 24, 1803, quoted *ibid.*, 190.

23. Cunningham, *Process of Government*, 30; Jefferson to Bidwell, July 5, 1806, quoted *ibid.*, 189; Johnstone, *Jefferson and the Presidency*, 60–61.

24. See below, chap. 11, for further discussion of the partisan presidency.

25. Peterson, *Jefferson and the New Nation*, 177–178, 283–284, 745–746, 771–773, 932, 937, and Julian P. Boyd, "Thomas Jefferson's 'Empire of Liberty,'" *Virginia Quarterly Review*, XXIV (1948), 550, quote the relevant letters.

26. Tacitus, *Agricola*, sec. 3; Bacon, *Advancement of Learning*, First Book, VII: 4; Bolingbroke, *Idea of a Patriot King*; W. F. Monypenny and G. E. Buckle, *The Life of Benjamin Disraeli*, new ed. rev. (London, 1929), II, 855.

27. Ralph Ketcham, *James Madison* (New York, 1971), 36–45.

28. Madison to Edmund Randolph, June 4, 1782, in William T. Hutchinson *et al.*, eds., *The Papers of James Madison* (Chicago, 1962–), IV, 313.

29. Madison, "Vices of the Political System of the U. States," Apr. 1787, *ibid.*, IX, 353–357.

30. Sherman, speech, June 1, 1787, in Max Farrand, ed., *The Records of the Federal Convention of 1787*, rev. ed. (New Haven, Conn., 1937), I, 65; Edward S. Corwin, *The President, Office and Powers: History and Analysis of Practice and Opinion* (New York, 1940), 15.

31. Madison, speech, June 4, 1787 (King's notes), and speech, June 6, 1787, in Hutchinson *et al.*, eds., *Madison Papers*, X, 25, 35.

32. Madison, speeches, July 17 and 21, 1787, *ibid.*, 103–104, 111.

33. Madison to Jefferson, Oct. 24, 1787, *ibid.*, 207–208.

34. G. Morris, speech, July 19, 1787, in Farrand, ed., *Records of Federal Convention*, II, 52–54.

35. Taken from Wilson's speeches at the Pennsylvania Constitutional Convention, where he extended the arguments he had begun in 1787. Speeches of Jan. 1790 quoted in Geoffrey Seed, *James Wilson* (Millwood, N.Y., 1978), 134–137.

36. Madison, "Spirit of Governments," *National Gazette*, Feb. 20, 1792, in Gaillard Hunt, ed., *The Writings of James Madison* (New York, 1900–1910), VI, 94; Lance Banning, "Republican Ideology and the Triumph of the Constitution, 1789 to 1793," *William and Mary Quarterly*, 3d Ser., XXXI (1974), 183.

37. See below, chap. 10, for Jeffersonian ideas of party during the 1790s, and chap. 8, for the triumph of the new conception of party.

38. Ralph Ketcham, "James Madison: The Unimperial President," *Va. Qtly. Rev.*, LIV (1978), esp. 129–135; Gallatin to Jefferson, Mar. 10, 1812, in Adams, ed., *Writings of Gallatin*, I, 517.

39. [John Pendleton Kennedy], *Defence of the Whigs, by a Member of the Twenty-Seventh Congress* (New York, 1844), 12–24, reprinted in Daniel Walker Howe, ed., *The American Whigs: An Anthology* (New York, 1973), 86–87.

40. Jefferson to Lafayette, May 14, 1817, in Washington, ed., *Works of Jefferson*, VII, 66–67; Adams to Jefferson, Feb. 2, 1817, in Cappon, ed., *Adams-Jefferson Letters*, II, 508.

41. Irving Brant, *James Madison*, V: *The President, 1809–1812* (Indianapolis, Ind., 1956), esp. 11–21, 141–156, 390–405, 437–451, details Madison's leadership efforts.

42. Dumas Malone, *Jefferson and His Time*, V: *Jefferson the President, Second Term, 1805–1809* (Boston, 1974), xxiii; Jefferson to Madison, Feb. 17, 1826, in Ford, ed., *Writings of Jefferson*, X, 377–378; Madison to Jefferson, Feb. 24, 1826, and to N. P. Trist, July 6, 1826, in Hunt, ed., *Writings of Madison*, IX, 245–248.

Chapter 7

1. Monroe, inaugural addresses, Mar. 4, 1817, and Mar. 4, 1821, in James D. Richardson, ed., *A Compilation of the Messages and Papers of the Presidents 1789–1897* (Washington, D.C., 1897), II, 579, 662; Monroe to Andrew Jackson, Dec. 14, 1816, in Stanislaus Murray Hamilton, ed., *The Writings of James Monroe* (New York, 1898–1903), V, 346, 342.

2. Harry Ammon, *James Monroe: The Quest for National Identity* (New York, 1971), 8–24.

3. *Ibid.*, 372–377, describes Monroe's tour, and quotes Abigail Adams's letter of July 14, 1817, to Richard Rush; *Columbian Centinel* (Boston), quoted in Richard Hofstadter, *The Idea of a Party System: The Rise of Legitimate Opposition in the United States, 1780–1840* (Berkeley, Calif., 1969), 199;

Monroe to Madison, May 10,
1822, in Hamilton, ed., *Writings
of Monroe*, VI, 290.

4. Monroe to Jackson, Dec. 14,
   1816, in Hamilton, ed., *Writings
   of Monroe*, V, 343, 345, 346.

5. Monroe to John McLean, Dec. 5,
   1827, *ibid.*, VII, 128–129.

6. Jefferson to Gallatin, Oct. 29,
   1822, in Henry Adams, ed., *The
   Writings of Albert Gallatin* (Philadelphia, 1879), II, 258–259;
   Monroe to Madison, May 10,
   1822, in Hamilton, ed., *Writings
   of Monroe*, VI, 289–291; Madison
   to Monroe, May 16, 1822, in
   W. C. Rives and Philip R. Fendall,
   eds., *The Letters and Other Writings of James Madison* (Philadelphia, 1865), III, 270–271.

7. Madison, "Parties," "British Gov-
   ernment," *National Gazette*, Jan.
   23 and 30, 1792, in Gaillard
   Hunt, ed., *The Writings of James
   Madison* (New York, 1900–1910),
   VI, 86–87.

8. Hofstadter, *Idea of a Party System*,
   198–208.

9. J. R. Sharp, "The Jeffersonians'
   Conception of Party: The Devel-
   opment of the Idea of a Loyal Op-
   position" (paper delivered at the
   University of California, Berkeley,
   June 8, 1977). See below, chap.
   10, for ideas of party in the
   United States, 1770–1800.

10. James Sterling Young, *The Wash-
    ington Community, 1800–1828*
    (New York, 1966), 252; Jefferson
    to Destutt de Tracy, Jan. 26, 1811,
    in Merrill D. Peterson, ed., *The
    Portable Thomas Jefferson* (New
    York, 1975), 525.

11. George Dangerfield, *The Era of
    Good Feelings* (New York, 1952),
    100; Leonard D. White, *The

*Jeffersonians: A Study in Admin-
istrative History, 1801–1829* (New
York, 1951), 39.

12. Jefferson to Destutt de Tracy, Jan.
    26, 1811, in Peterson, ed., *Porta-
    ble Jefferson*, 522; Charles Francis
    Adams, ed., *Memoirs of John
    Quincy Adams, Comprising Portions
    of His Diary from 1795 to 1848*
    (Philadelphia, 1875), VII, 80–81
    (Dec. 14, 1825).

13. Daniel Walker Howe, *The Political
    Culture of the American Whigs*
    (Chicago, 1979), 78n; Aïda Di-
    Pace Donald and David D. Don-
    ald, eds., *Diary of Charles Francis
    Adams*, II (Cambridge, Mass.,
    1964), 81–89; C. Adams, ed.,
    Memoirs of J. Q. Adams, VIII, 243
    (Oct. 24, 1830).

14. Washington to John Adams, Feb.
    20, 1797, in John C. Fitzpatrick,
    ed., *The Writings of George Wash-
    ington from the Original Manuscript
    Sources, 1745–1799* (Washington,
    D.C., 1931–1944), XXXV, 394;
    John F. Kennedy, *Profiles in Cour-
    age* (New York, 1955); Roy P.
    Basler, ed., *The Collected Works of
    Abraham Lincoln* (New Brunswick,
    N.J., 1953), I, 450.

15. C. Adams, ed., *Memoirs of J. Q.
    Adams*, I, 249 (Jan. 28, 1802).

16. *Columbian Magazine* (Phila-
    delphia), Sept. 1787, 626–628.

17. J. Q. Adams, "Letters of Pub-
    licola," No. IX, "Columbus," No.
    II, *Columbian Centinel*, July 13,
    1791, and Dec. 4, 1793, reprinted
    in Worthington Chauncey Ford,
    ed., *Writings of John Quincy Adams*
    (New York, 1913), I, 99, 158–
    159; Robert A. East, *John Quincy
    Adams, the Critical Years: 1785–
    1794* (New York, 1962), 145.

18. Brooks Adams, Introduction to

Henry Adams, *The Degradation of the Democratic Dogma* (New York, 1919), 53.

19. C. Adams, ed., *Memoirs of J. Q. Adams*, IV, 450–451 (Nov. 26–27, 1819).
20. *Ibid.*, 452, 451.
21. J. Q. Adams to J. D. Heath, Jan. 7, 1822, in Ford, ed., *Writings of J. Q. Adams*, VII, 193; C. Adams, ed., *Memoirs of J. Q. Adams*, IV, 64, V, 13 (Mar. 18, 1818, Mar. 4, 1820); Ernest R. May, *The Making of the Monroe Doctrine* (Cambridge, Mass., 1975), 31, 36.
22. Mar. 4, 1825, in Richardson, ed., *Messages of the Presidents*, II, 862–865.
23. Annual message, Dec. 6, 1825, *ibid.*, 877–882.
24. Jackson to William B. Lewis, Feb. 14, 1825, and to Henry Lee, Oct. 7, 1825, in John Spencer Bassett, ed., *Correspondence of Andrew Jackson* (Washington, D.C., 1926–1935), III, 276, 291–292; C. Adams, ed., *Memoirs of J. Q. Adams*, VI, 507–508 (Feb. 11, 1825).
25. John Randolph, speech, Mar. 30, 1826, quoted in Dangerfield, *Era of Good Feelings*, 357–358; Theodore Roosevelt, *Thomas Hart Benton* (Boston, 1886), 63.
26. Robert V. Remini, *Martin Van Buren and the Making of the Democratic Party* (New York, 1959), 148.
27. Jefferson to William B. Giles, Dec. 26, 1825, and "Proposed Declaration," in Andrew A. Lipscomb and Albert Ellery Bergh, eds., *The Writings of Thomas Jefferson* (Washington, D.C., 1903–1904), XVI, 146–150, XVII, 442–448.
28. Howe, *American Whigs*, 9, 87.
29. Leonard D. White, *The Jacksonians: A Study in Administrative History, 1829–1861* (New York, 1954), 552.

Chapter 8

1. Richard Hofstadter, *The Idea of a Party System: The Rise of Legitimate Opposition in the United States, 1780–1840* (Berkeley, Calif., 1969), 212–270, sees Van Buren as a central figure, but Hofstadter's assumptions about the uses of party organization were very different from those of J. Q. Adams.
2. Michael Wallace, "Changing Concepts of Party in the United States: New York, 1815–1828," *American Historical Review*, LXXIV (1968), 455.
3. Henry Adams, *History of the United States*, VI: *History of the United States of America during the First Administration of James Madison* (New York, 1890), I, 410.
4. Wallace, "Changing Concepts of Party," *AHR*, LXXIV (1968), 457.
5. Marcy to John Bailey, Aug. 30, 1817, and *Albany Argus* (N.Y.), Feb. 11, 1820, quoted *ibid.*, 458.
6. *Argus*, June 4, 1824, and Feb. 29, 1820, quoted *ibid.*, 464n, 459.
7. The following summary rests on Wallace, "Changing Concepts of Party," *AHR*, LXXIV (1968), 481–491.
8. *Argus*, May 14, 1824, quoted *ibid.*, 483.
9. *Argus*, Sept. 12, 1823, and May 14, 1824, and Benjamin F. Butler to Van Buren, May 6, 1829, all quoted *ibid.*, 484–485.
10. Jefferson to Francis Hopkinson, Mar. 13, 1789, in Julian P. Boyd et al., eds., *The Papers of Thomas*

Jefferson (Princeton, N.J., 1948–), XIV, 649–651.

11. All quoted in Wallace, "Changing Concepts of Party," *AHR*, LXXIV (1968), 487–489.

12. Hofstadter, *Idea of a Party System*, 247.

13. Robert V. Remini, *Martin Van Buren and the Making of the Democratic Party* (New York, 1959), 15–29.

14. Van Buren to Ritchie, Jan. 13, 1827, and Allan Campbell to Jackson, Feb. 4, 1827, in Robert V. Remini, ed., *The Age of Jackson* (Columbia, S.C., 1972), 3–8.

15. Charles Francis Adams, ed., *Memoirs of John Quincy Adams, Comprising Portions of His Diary from 1795 to 1848* (Philadelphia, 1875), VII, 272 (May 12, 1827).

16. *Ibid.*, IX, 440–441 (Dec. 5, 1837).

17. *Ibid.*, IX, 25, X, 352–353, IX, 311–312 (Oct. 22, 1833, Sept. 24, 1840, Nov. 11, 1836).

18. *Ibid.*, V, 361, IV, 359–360 (Oct. 15, 1821, May 6, 1819); Daniel Blaine Boylan, "Towards a Definition of the Adams Tradition" (Ph.D. diss., University of Hawaii, 1974), 129–135.

19. Enos T. Throop, "Message," Mar. 12, 1829, in Charles Zebina Lincoln, ed., *State of New York. Messages from the Governors* . . . (Albany, N.Y., 1909), III, 269–278.

20. Remini, *Van Buren and the Democratic Party*, 193.

21. See below, chap. 10, for further discussion of changing attitudes toward party.

22. Wellington and Disraeli quotations from Sir Lewis Namier, "Monarchy and the Party System," in Namier, *Personalities and Powers* (New York, [1955]), 30n, 18; all

other quotations from Caroline Robbins, "'Discordant Parties': A Study of the Acceptance of Party by Englishmen," *Political Science Quarterly*, LXXIII (1958), 505–529.

23. Pat Rogers, "Swift and Bolingbroke on Faction," *Journal of British Studies*, IX (May 1970), 101.

24. William Appleman Williams, *The Contours of American History* (Cleveland, Ohio, 1961), 239.

25. William Appleman Williams, *The Great Evasion: An Essay on the Contemporary Relevance of Karl Marx and on the Wisdom of Admitting the Heretic into the Dialogue about America's Future* (Chicago, 1964), 131ff.

26. Special session message of Sept. 4, 1837, in James D. Richardson, ed., *A Compilation of the Messages and Papers of the Presidents 1789–1897* (Washington, D.C., 1897), IV, 1547, 1561.

27. First annual message, Dec. 8, 1829, *ibid.*, III, 1011–1012.

28. Both quotations in Leonard D. White, *The Jacksonians: A Study in Administrative History, 1829–1861* (New York, 1954), 320.

29. Sir Lewis Namier, *England in the Age of the American Revolution* (London, 1930), 211; Ronald P. Formisano, "Deferential-Participant Politics: The Early Republic's Political Culture, 1789–1840," *American Political Science Review*, LXVIII (1974), 479.

30. "Protest" to the Senate, Apr. 15, 1834, in Remini, ed., *Age of Jackson*, 115.

31. "Veto Message," July 10, 1832, in Richardson, ed., *Messages of the Presidents*, III, 1153–1154.

32. [Henry Adams], *The Education of Henry Adams: An Autobiography*

(New York, 1931 [orig. publ. Boston, 1918]), 53.

33. J. Q. Adams to Charles W. Upham, Feb. 2, 1837, in Brooks Adams, Introduction to Henry Adams, *The Degradation of the Democratic Dogma* (New York, 1919), 24–25.

34. J. Q. Adams to C. F. Adams, Mar. 8, 1829, quoted in John M. McFaul, "Expediency vs. Morality: Jacksonian Politics and Slavery," *Journal of American History*, LXII (1975), 35n; Aïda DiPace Donald and David D. Donald, eds., *Diary of Charles Francis Adams*, II (Cambridge, Mass., 1964), 329–371; Theodore Roosevelt, *Thomas Hart Benton* (Boston, 1886), 86.

35. Quoted in B. Adams, Introduction to H. Adams, *Degradation of Democratic Dogma*, 25.

36. J. Q. Adams to Abigail Adams, Sept. 10, 1783, in Worthington Chauncey Ford, ed., *Writings of John Quincy Adams* (New York, 1913), I, 10–13.

37. J. Q. Adams to J. Edwards, July 13, 1837, and "Address to His Constituents," Sept. 17, 1842, in B. Adams, Introduction to H. Adams, *Degradation of Democratic Dogma*, 29–30, 81, 27–28.

38. Martin B. Duberman, *Charles Francis Adams, 1807–1886* (Boston, 1961), 2.

39. B. Adams, Introduction to H. Adams, *Degradation of Democratic Dogma*, 1–122 *passim*.

40. See chap. 1, above.

41. Daniel D. Barnard, *The Social System. An Address Pronounced before the House of Convocation of Trinity College* (Hartford, Conn., 1848), reprinted in Daniel Walker Howe, ed., *The American Whigs: An Anthology* (New York, 1973), 116–

117; Bushnell and Finney quotations from Ronald P. Formisano, "Political Character, Antipartyism and the Second Party System," *American Quarterly*, XXI (1969), 706–708, which describes anti-Masonry and other elements of Jacksonian era "antiparty" sentiment.

42. W.E.H. Lecky, *A History of England in the Eighteenth Century* (London, 1883), I, 361, 363; Richard Hofstadter, *The American Political Tradition and the Men Who Made It* (New York, 1948), 62.

43. Daniel Defoe, *A Tour Thro' the Whole Island of Great Britain* (3 vols., London, 1724–1727), reprinted in 2 vols. with intro. by G.D.H. Cole (London, 1968 [orig. publ. 1927]); quotations from II, 610–615, 651–652.

44. Alexis de Tocqueville, *Democracy in America* (1835), ed. J. P. Mayer (Garden City, N.Y., 1969), 702–705. Ralph Lerner, "Commerce and Character: The Anglo-American as New-Model Man," *William and Mary Quarterly*, 3d Ser., XXXVI (1979), 3–26, further explains how Tocqueville's analysis fits an interpretation of the United States as a "commercial republic."

45. John Stuart Mill, "M. deTocqueville on Democracy in America," *Edinburgh Review*, Oct. 1840, reprinted in Mill, *Dissertations and Discussions: Political, Philosophical and Historical* (Boston, 1865–1868), II, 79–161.

46. Herbert Croly, *The Promise of American Life*, ed. Arthur M. Schlesinger, Jr. (Cambridge, Mass., 1965 [orig. publ. Indianapolis, Ind., 1909]), 65.

Chapter 9

1. Jefferson, "Autobiography," dated Jan. 6, 1821, in Adrienne Koch and William Peden, eds., *The Life and Selected Writings of Thomas Jefferson* (New York, 1944), 44, 50–52.
2. See below, chap. 10, for Burke's place in Anglo-American ideas of party.
3. Jefferson to William B. Giles, Dec. 31, 1795; Jefferson to John Taylor of Caroline, June 4, 1798; and Madison, "A Candid State of Parties," *National Gazette*, Sept. 26, 1792; all reprinted in Noble E. Cunningham, Jr., ed., *The Making of the American Party System, 1789 to 1809* (Englewood Cliffs, N.J., 1965), 10–18.
4. Taylor to Jefferson, June 25, 1798, in "Letters of John Taylor, of Caroline County, Virginia," *John P. Branch Historical Papers of Randolph-Macon College*, II (1908), 271–276. Robert Shalhope, *John Taylor of Caroline: Pastoral Republican* (Columbia, S.C., 1980), fully explains Taylor's political thought.
5. Jefferson to Horatio Gates, Mar. 8, 1801, in Paul Leicester Ford, ed., *The Writings of Thomas Jefferson* (New York, 1892–1899), VIII, 11–12.
6. On this point, see p. 104, above.
7. Jefferson to John B. Colvin, Sept. 10, 1810, in Ford, ed., *Writings of Jefferson*, IX, 279–282.
8. Jefferson to Adams, Dec. 10, 1819, in Lester J. Cappon, ed., *The Adams-Jefferson Letters* (Chapel Hill, N.C., 1959), II, 549–550; Jefferson to Abigail Adams, Sept. 11, 1804, *ibid.*, I, 280.
9. Edward Waldo Emerson and Waldo Emerson Forbes, eds., *Journals of Ralph Waldo Emerson* (Boston, 1909–1914), IV, 95, VI, 275 (Sept. 23, 1836, Oct. 12, 1842); Emerson, "Politics" (1844), in *Essays*, 2d Ser. (Boston, 1876), 209–210.
10. Quoted in Emmet John Hughes, *The Living Presidency: The Resources and Dilemmas of the American Presidential Office* (New York, 1973), 166.
11. Gallatin, speech in Congress, Jan. 14, 1799, quoted in Joyce Appleby, "Commercial Farming and the 'Agrarian Myth' in the Early Republic," *Journal of American History*, LXVIII (1982), 849.
12. Norman S. Fiering, "Benjamin Franklin and the Way to Virtue," *American Quarterly*, XXX (1978), 201–207.
13. Franklin's pamphlet is in Leonard W. Labaree *et al.*, eds., *The Papers of Benjamin Franklin* (New Haven, Conn., 1959–), IV, 225–234; the exchange with Jackson, June 17, 1755, and Oct. 7, 1755, is *ibid.*, VI, 75–82, 216–217; for Jackson, see Carl Van Doren, ed., *Letters and Papers of Benjamin Franklin and Richard Jackson, 1753–1785* (Philadelphia, 1947), 1–31.
14. Franklin, "Information to Those Who Would Remove to America," probably written in Sept. 1782, in Albert Henry Smyth, ed., *The Writings of Benjamin Franklin* (New York, 1907), VIII, 603–614.
15. Drew R. McCoy, "Benjamin Franklin's Vision of a Republican Political Economy for America," *William and Mary Quarterly*, 3d Ser., XXXV (1978), 618–627.
16. George Clinton, using the

pseudonym "Cato," in *New York Journal*, Nov. 22, 1787, reprinted in Cecelia M. Kenyon, ed., *The Antifederalists* (Indianapolis, Ind., 1966), 308–309; Franklin, "Information," in Smyth, ed., *Writings of Franklin*, VIII, 603–614.

17. J. Hector St. John Crèvecoeur, *Letters from an American Farmer* (Garden City, N.Y., [1963] [orig. publ. London, 1782]), 208–209.

18. Myra Jehlen, "J. Hector St. John Crèvecoeur: A Monarcho-Anarchist in Revolutionary America," *Amer. Qtly.*, XXXI (1979), 204–222, develops this point.

19. James T. Lemon, *The Best Poor Man's Country: A Geographical Study of Early Southeastern Pennsylvania* (Baltimore, 1972), xv, 227.

20. Charles S. Grant, *Democracy in the Connecticut Frontier Town of Kent* (New York, 1961), 29, 53, 171.

21. James A. Henretta, "Families and Farms: *Mentalité* in Pre-Industrial America," *WMQ*, 3d Ser., XXXV (1978), 3, 19, 26, 32.

22. J. E. Crowley, *This Sheba, Self: The Conceptualization of Economic Life in Eighteenth-Century America* (Baltimore, 1974), 12, 6.

23. Dirk Hoerder, "Boston Leaders and Boston Crowds, 1765–1776," in Alfred F. Young, ed., *The American Revolution: Explorations in the History of American Radicalism* (De Kalb, Ill., 1976), 233–271, esp. 234.

24. Gary B. Nash, *The Urban Crucible: Social Change, Political Consciousness, and the Origins of the American Revolution* (Cambridge, Mass., 1979).

25. Eric Foner, "Tom Paine's Republic: Radical Ideology and Social Change," in Young, ed., *American Revolution*, 187–232;

Foner, *Tom Paine and Revolutionary America* (New York, 1976).

26. Robert Kelley, *The Cultural Pattern in American Politics: The First Century* (New York, 1979).

27. Drew R. McCoy, *The Elusive Republic: Political Economy in Jeffersonian America* (Chapel Hill, N.C., 1980). Most of the sources for this paragraph and the preceding one are conveniently summarized in Robert E. Shalhope, "Republicanism and Early American Historiography," *WMQ*, 3d Ser., XXXIX (1982), 338–346.

28. See above, chap. 4, n. 11, quoting Stephen Saunders Webb.

29. Mather, "Nehemias Americanus, The Life of John Winthrop, Esq., Governor of the Massachusetts Colony," in *Magnalia Christi Americana* (1702), reprinted in Sacvan Bercovitch, *The Puritan Origins of the American Self* (New Haven, Conn., 1975), 193.

30. E. P. Thompson, *The Making of the English Working Class* (New York, 1963), 831–832.

31. Ronald P. Formisano, "Deferential-Participant Politics: The Early Republic's Political Culture, 1789–1840," *American Political Science Review*, LXVIII (1974), 483, 473.

Chapter 10

1. Speech, June 25, 1788, in Harold C. Syrett *et al.*, eds., *The Papers of Alexander Hamilton* (New York, 1961–), V, 85.

2. Hamilton quotations in Gerald Stourzh, *Alexander Hamilton and the Idea of Republican Government* (Stanford, Calif., 1970), 18, 22, 70.

3. Speech, June 25, 1788, in Syrett *et*

al., eds., *Hamilton Papers*, V, 43.

4. "Report on Manufactures," Dec. 5, 1791, reprinted in Samuel McKee, Jr., ed., *Alexander Hamilton's Papers on Public Credit, Commerce and Finance* (New York, 1934), 183, 196.

5. David Hume, "Of the Rise and Progress of the Arts and Sciences," "Of Refinement in the Arts," and "Of Commerce," published in various editions in 1742 and after, reprinted in Hume, *Political Essays*, ed. Charles W. Hendel (Indianapolis, Ind., 1953), 111–141.

6. John Sekora, *Luxury: The Concept in Western Thought, Eden to Smollett* (Baltimore, 1977), 21, quotes Plutarch on Lycurgus; Mandeville, "Vindication of the Book," *London Journal*, Aug. 10, 1723, quoted in Thomas A. Horne, *The Social Thought of Bernard Mandeville: Virtue and Commerce in Early Eighteenth-Century England* (New York, 1978), 72.

7. "Report on a National Bank," Dec. 14, 1790, in McKee, ed., *Hamilton's Papers on Finance*, 83.

8. John R. Nelson, Jr., "Alexander Hamilton and American Manufacturing: A Reexamination," *Journal of American History*, LXV (1979), 971–995.

9. Orations by Samuel Whitwell, Samuel Stillman, and Thomas Crafts, all quoted in John Zvesper, *Political Philosophy and Rhetoric: A Study of the Origins of American Party Politics* (Cambridge, Mass., 1977), 46, 53–55.

10. "The Continentalist," Apr. 18, 1782, in Syrett *et al.*, eds., *Hamilton Papers*, III, 77.

11. Aristotle, *Politics*, Bk. III, chap. 9.

12. Hamilton, "Opinion on the Constitutionality of an Act to Establish a Bank," Feb. 23, 1791, and "An Address to the Electors of the State of New York," Mar. 21, 1801, in Syrett *et al.*, eds., *Hamilton Papers*, VIII, 98–105, XXV, 366.

13. Speeches to the New York legislature, 1787, and to the New York Ratifying Convention, 1788, quoted in Stourzh, *Hamilton and Republican Government*, 182–183.

14. All extracts from Hamilton's "Pay Book," probably written in 1777, in Syrett *et al.*, eds., *Hamilton Papers*, I, 390–407. Hamilton used the popular Dryden translation of Plutarch in an edition published in London in 1758.

15. "Publius Letter III," Nov. 16, 1778, *ibid.*, 580–582.

16. Hamilton to James Duane, Sept. 3, 1780, *ibid.*, II, 404; *The Federalist*, No. 70.

17. Hamilton, Convention notes, June 1 and 6, 1787, in Syrett *et al.*, eds., *Hamilton Papers*, IV, 163, 165–166.

18. Hamilton, writing as "Metellus," Oct. 24, 1792, *Gazette of the United States* (Philadelphia), and to Washington, Apr. 14, 1794, *ibid.*, XII, 615–616, XVI, 276–278.

19. Stourzh, *Hamilton and Republican Government*, 110–111.

20. Speech, June 18, 1787, in Max Farrand, ed., *The Records of the Federal Convention of 1787*, rev. ed. (New Haven, Conn., 1937), I, 289–291.

21. Speech, June 25, 1788 (Childs's version), in Syrett *et al.*, eds., *Hamilton Papers*, V, 85.

22. *Ibid.*, 81–82.

23. Throughout the 18th century, "opposition to government . . . was regarded as a political evil of

the greatest magnitude. There was only one government, one administration; and everyone was bound (at least in theory) to support it. . . . For the most part, political opposition was considered illegal, subversive, and always dangerous." Daniel Sisson, *The American Revolution of 1800* (New York, 1974), 207–208.

24. Washington to Jefferson, Aug. 23 and Oct. 18, 1792, and to Hamilton, Aug. 26, 1792, in John C. Fitzpatrick, ed., *The Writings of George Washington from the Original Manuscript Sources, 1745–1799* (Washington, D.C., 1931–1944), XXXII, 130–134, 185–186; Hamilton to Washington and Jefferson to Washington, Sept. 9, 1792, in Syrett *et al.*, eds., *Hamilton Papers*, XII, 347–349, and in Paul Leicester Ford, ed., *The Writings of Thomas Jefferson* (New York, 1892–1899), VI, 101–110.

25. Edmund Burke, *Thoughts on the Cause of the Present Discontents* (1770), in *The Writings and Speeches of Edmund Burke* (Boston, 1901), I, 530, 482–484.

26. Peter J. Stanlis, ed., *Edmund Burke: Selected Writings and Speeches* (Garden City, N.Y., 1963), 103; John Brewer, *Party Ideology and Popular Politics at the Accession of George III* (Cambridge, 1976), 70–74.

27. Burke, *Thoughts*, in *Writings of Burke*, I, 524–525, 534–535, 537.

28. Brewer, *Party Ideology*, 74–76; Richard Hofstadter, *The Idea of a Party System: The Rise of Legitimate Opposition in the United States, 1780–1840* (Berkeley, Calif., 1969), 34–39.

29. Burke, "Speech to the Electors of Bristol . . . ," Nov. 3, 1774, in *Writings of Burke*, II, 96.

30. J.A.W. Gunn, ed., *Factions No More: Attitudes to Party in Government and Opposition in Eighteenth-Century England* (London, 1971), reprints a revealing collection of defenses of party.

31. William L. Smith, in a 1792 pamphlet, quoted in Sisson, *Revolution of 1800*, 147n.

32. Lance Banning, *The Jeffersonian Persuasion: Evolution of a Party Ideology* (Ithaca, N.Y., 1978), 185–207. See chap. 4, above, for more on Jeffersonian attitudes toward party.

33. John Murrin, "The Great Inversion, or Court vs. Country: A Comparison of the Revolution Settlements in England (1688–1721) and America (1776–1816)," in J.G.A. Pocock, ed., *Three British Revolutions: 1641, 1688, 1776* (Princeton, N.J., 1980), 368–453.

34. James H. Hutson, "Country, Court, and Constitution: Antifederalism and the Historians," *William and Mary Quarterly*, 3d Ser., XXXVIII (1981), 357–363.

35. Banning, *Jeffersonian Persuasion*, 137, quoting *Gaz. U.S.*, Apr. 17, 1790.

36. David John Mays, ed., *The Letters and Papers of Edmund Pendleton, 1734–1803* (Charlottesville, Va., 1967), II, 695–699; Bernard Bailyn, *The Ideological Origins of the American Revolution* (Cambridge, Mass., 1967), 86–87.

37. Linda K. Kerber, *Federalists in Dissent: Imagery and Ideology in Jeffersonian America* (Ithaca, N.Y., 1970), 18–22, quoting Noah Webster, 1798.

38. Joyce Appleby, "Commercial Farming and the 'Agrarian Myth' in the Early Republic," *JAH*, LXVIII (1982), 838–849.
39. *The Federalist*, No. 8.
40. McKee, ed., *Hamilton's Papers on Finance*, 227–228.
41. Stuart G. Brown, *Alexander Hamilton* (New York, 1967), 173.
42. Hamilton, "The Continentalist," No. 5, Apr. 18, 1782, and No. 1, July 12, 1781, in Syrett *et al.*, eds., *Hamilton Papers*, III, 76, II, 650–652.
43. Herbert Croly, *The Promise of American Life*, ed. Arthur M. Schlesinger, Jr. (Cambridge, Mass., 1965 [orig. publ. Indianapolis, Ind., 1909]), 44–45.

Chapter 11

1. Abigail Adams to John Adams, June 20, 1783, in L. H. Butterfield *et al.*, eds., *The Book of Abigail and John* (Cambridge, Mass., 1975), 353.
2. See above, chap. 4.
3. *The Debates and Proceedings in the Congress of the United States, 1789–1824* (Washington, D.C., 1834–1856), I, 1 Cong., 1 Sess. (June 16, 1789), 492–493, 518.
4. *Ibid.* (June 16 and 18, 1789), 480, 561.
5. "Notes of John Adams," in Charles Francis Adams, ed., *The Works of John Adams, Second President of the United States* (Boston, 1865), III, 409; Edgar S. Maclay, ed., *The Journal of William Maclay* (New York, 1890), 108.
6. J. R. Pole, "Representation and Authority in Virginia from the Revolution to Reform," *Journal of Southern History*, XXIV (1958), 16–18, 28–29.
7. *Dunciad*, Bk. IV, lines 653–656, in William K. Wimsatt, ed., *Alexander Pope: Selected Poetry and Prose*, 2d ed. (New York, 1972), 514.
8. J.G.A. Pocock, "Virtue and Commerce in the Eighteenth Century," *Journal of Interdisciplinary History*, III (1972), 129.
9. C. B. Macpherson, *Democratic Theory: Essays in Retrieval* (Oxford, 1973), 192–194, 199–200; H. Mark Roelofs, *Ideology and Myth in American Politics: A Critique of a National Political Mind* (Boston, 1976), 69.
10. Stephen Saunders Webb; see chap. 4, n. 11, above, for quote and source citation.
11. Jefferson to Walter Jones, Mar. 31, 1801, in H. A. Washington, ed., *The Works of Thomas Jefferson* (New York, 1884 [orig. publ. Washington, D.C., 1853–1854]), IV, 392–393.
12. Quoted by Dr. Johnson, at the beginning of *The Patriot* (1774), reprinted in Jeffrey Hart, ed., *Political Writers of Eighteenth-Century England* (New York, 1964), 288.
13. Stuart Gerry Brown, *The American Presidency: Leadership, Partisanship, and Popularity* (New York, 1966).
14. *Ibid.*, 56.
15. *Ibid.*, ii.
16. Burke, "Speech to the Electors of Bristol," Nov. 3, 1774, in *The Writings and Speeches of Edmund Burke* (Boston, 1901), II, 96.
17. Brown, *American Presidency*, 99–111, 176–181.
18. Clinton Rossiter, *The American Presidency* (New York, 1956), 16;

Thomas A. Bailey, *Presidential Greatness: The Image and the Man from George Washington to the Present* (New York, 1966), 188.

19. Reported by J. H. Plumb, in "Nixon as Disraeli?" *New York Times Magazine*, Feb. 11, 1973, p. 12.

20. John Bright, speech in Rochdale, England, Dec. 4, 1861, in J. E. Thorold Rogers, ed., *Selected Speeches of the Rt. Honble John Bright, M.P., on Public Questions* (New York and London, [1907]), 60–61.

21. James Bryce, *The American Commonwealth*, 2d ed. (New York, 1889), I, 80, 80n.

22. Harold J. Laski, *The American Presidency, An Interpretation* (New York, 1940), 274–278, based on lectures delivered in Mar. 1939.

23. Woodrow Wilson, *Congressional Government* (Boston, 1885), and address in Hartford, Conn., May 10, 1889, "Nature of Democracy in the United States," reprinted in Arthur S. Link *et al.*, eds., *The Papers of Woodrow Wilson* (Princeton, N.J., 1966–), IV, 140, VI, 234–239; Wilson, *Constitutional Government in the United States* (New York, 1908), 67, 73.

24. Henry Jones Ford, *The Rise and Growth of American Politics: A Sketch of Constitution Development* (New York, 1898), 293.

25. Rossiter, *American Presidency*, 159–160.

Index